"Forty Years On"

Life and Work

at the

CENTRAL TECHNICAL SCHOOL

SHEFFIELD

A

Reminiscence

for

'The Old Boys' Association'

Terence M. Russell

B.Arch. (Hons. Class 1), Ph.D., F.R.I.A.S.

Forty years on, when afar and asunder
Parted are those who are singing today,
When you look back and forgetfully wonder
What you were like in your work and your play —
Then it may be there will often come o're you
Glimpses of notes, like the catch of a song:
Visions of boyhood shall float them before you,
Echoes of dreamland shall bear them along.

Published & Printed by Pickard Communication

10-11 Riverside Park • Sheaf Gardens • Sheffield S2 4BB

Telephone 0114 275 7222 or 275 7444

Facsimile 0114 275 8866

email info@picomm.co.uk

www.picomm.co.uk

Inquiries concerning this book should be directed, in the first instance, to the publisher.

The author can also be contacted as follows:
Dr. Terence M. Russell
Architecture
The University of Edinburgh
20 Chambers Street
EDINBURGH EH1 1JZ

T.Russell@ed.ac.uk

Dedication

This book is dedicated with affection
to

The Old Boys' Association

The Central Technical School
Sheffield

Terence M. Russell

The Author of this book was School Captain at the Central Technical School, Sheffield for the years 1958–59. He is a professionally qualified architect, a Fellow of the Royal Incorporation of Architects in Scotland and Reader in Architecture in the Department of Architecture at the University of Edinburgh.
He has published the following books on architecture and related subjects:

Bibliographical Index

The Built Environment: A Subject Index 1800–1960

Architecture in the *Encyclopédie* of Diderot and D'Alembert
The Letterpress Articles and selected Engravings

Gardens and Landscapes in the *Encyclopédie* of Diderot and D'Alembert
The Letterpress Articles and selected Engravings
With Ann-Marie Thornton

The Encyclopaedic Dictionary in the Eighteenth Century
Architecture, Arts and crafts

The Napoleonic Survey of Egypt
The Monuments and Customs of Egypt

Front Cover
An engraving of Firth College, later the Main Building of the Central Technical School, Sheffield, at it appeared when inaugurated on 17 October, 1789. The crest illustrated is that of Firth College. The motto 'Rerum Cognoscere Causas' is taken from the writings of the Roman poet and philosopher Titus Lucretius, and translates as 'To know the causes of things'. These words are now the motto of the University of Sheffield.

Rear Cover
The changing styles of the Badge of the Central Technical School, Sheffield over the following years:

Top left:	1933 – 1947	Two tones of blue with gold lettering and decoration
Top right	1947 – 1955	Dark blue, red letter 'T' and gold lettering and decoration
Bottom left	1955 – 1968	Blue-black with gold lettering and decoration
Centre	1955 – 1968	Improved design with 'CTS' against a pale-blue background
Bottom right	1947 – 1955	Cap badge — shown enlarged

Contents

Illustrations

Acknowledgements

In the first instance I have to thank Mr. Stuart Green who, in his previous capacity as President of the Old Boys' Association, suggested that I should write a personal history of the former Central Technical School, Sheffield. His continuing enthusiasm for the project — in his subsequent roles as Secretary and Social Secretary of the Association — has also been a source of continuing help and encouragement. In addition, Stuart contributed a number of suggestions that have had a direct bearing on the final form of the book. Concerning such matters, I owe a special word of thanks for the scholarly insights and intuition of Mr. Tony Mooney, former President of the Association. Tony consulted an early draft of my text and gave me sound advice about the contents and structure of the work — all worthy of a former distinguished headmaster! My book has benefited considerably from Tony's views. Mr. Roger Child, Social Secretary of the Association, read and edited Chapter 6, 'The School in Sheffield with a Playground on the Roof'. For this I am grateful since Roger corrected several errors and put right a number of omissions. For contributing the Foreword to my book, I am especially grateful to Mr. Ken Westnedge — *doyen* of the Association.

My understanding of the early history of the Central Schools and, in particular, the origins of the Central Technical School, Sheffield, owe much to the *Leopold Street Open Day* — instigated by the Education Department of the Sheffield City Council — and to the commemorative publication bearing this title. It is from this source that I have derived my Frontispiece showing the Main Building of the CTS. More generally, the assistance provided to me by the Open Day helped me to explore other information sources in the National Library of Scotland, near to where I now live and work. This prompts me to add that I am indebted to the members of staff of the NLS for their typical courtesy and help. Mention of libraries redirects my expression of thanks to the City of Sheffield and, in particular The Central Library. The staff of the Local Studies Library were most helpful to me in providing me with copies of *The Handbook of Information* of the City of Sheffield Education Committee from which I have derived the factual records given in Chapter 2. My cover illustration, showing the CTS Main Building as it was originally conceived as Firth College, is taken from the leaflet *The University Sheffield Made* which was published by The University of Sheffield to mark the celebration of the founding of Firth College in 1879 — see Chapter 1.

As I explain in Chapter 3, the main title of my book, 'Forty Years On', is derived from the song of The Harrow School. For permission to use these words in the title of this book, and also for giving consent to reproduce two verses of the school song in my text, I am most grateful to the Headmaster of The Harrow School, Mr. Barnaby Lenon M.A.

I feel a special debt of gratitude to my good friend and school contemporary Mr. Gordon Swann for his proof-reading of the text. Gordon found several typos, as we now describe typographical errors, and I thank him for his diligence. He also paid me the compliment of saying that he had not found the book easy to proof-read on account of it being so interesting! By his testimony, he became so absorbed in what I have to say that he forgot all about errors of style and syntax. I hope other readers will feel similarly inclined when they read the book!

In my expressions of appreciation, I must not overlook those members of the Old Boys' Association who devote so much of their personal time and energy in promoting the activities of the Association. In particular, I have in mind the present, and former office-bearers, namely, the President, Secretary, Social Secretary and Treasurer of the Association who have done, and continue to do, so much for the OBA. 'Well done lads! And 'Thank You'! On a more personal note, I would like to acknowledge the encouragement I have received in recent times from several members of the Association; various members have urged me to make progress with my book in eager anticipation of its publication. I can but hope that the final outcome is worthy of their trust and expectations.

Lastly, I have to thank Mr. Michael Liversidge, Production Director of Pickard Communication, for his skill in converting my text and illustrations into their final published form.

TMR

Foreword
The Central Technical School Sheffield
A Personal View

Ken Westnedge

May I open with a quotation from 15 December 1933 on the occasion of the official opening of the Sheffield Junior Technical School:

> The aim in brief is that the Sheffield Junior Technical School, the public and industrial interests will provide a future for the Sheffield Junior Technical School's work in the City of Sheffield.

It was in this year, along with another 119 boys, that I first entered the West Street building. Here, the seeds of a great institution were sown and nurtured by six stalwarts of the teaching profession. In the following three years the school had a full compliment of 360 boys. The qualification after these three years was the school Diploma, graded one, two and three. After their examinations, and receiving of Diplomas, the first intake of 120 boys left for fields afresh.

Some seventeen years later, I once again entered the hallowed portals of West Street — BY THE FRONT DOOR THIS TIME — to be interviewed by the larger than life Mr. H. W. Wadge. Whether my acceptance was somehow linked to the fact that I was the first 'Old Boy' to return to the fold, I shall never know. Here I may mention that in later stages of the school life, three more 'Old Boys' became members of staff; Mr. T. Wiggett, Mr. G. Taylor and Mr. S. Gibbons.

The machinery in the Machine Shop (overseen by Mr. C.F. Bains) had little changed since 1933–36, with line shafts, pulley belts and a blazing forge. My domain for the first two years was the Fitting Shop. I've heard it called the 'Den'! Sawing, filing, forging and last, but definitely not least, 'polishing with an emery cloth'. Not many Old Boys will have forgotten the later, as this was the criterion for a good finish to a piece of work, even though hard labour and sore thumbs were paramount. Rewards for these labours were clearly shown when a recipient got 9 $\frac{1}{2}$ out of ten — this even brought a smile to a face!

I digress for a moment just to relate that on many occasions when meeting some of the 'Old Boys' at the Annual Dinner, I have been told by many that, stacked away in their tool boxes, were all the tools that they had made during their school life with me.

The first two years were just bearable: safety and discipline were paramount, the later was found by some individuals to be intolerable! Progressing year by year, teaching became much more enjoyable. Such classes as 6A and 6B gave me an enormous feedback in the work they produced — little could be said for 6C!

With the advent of the 'O.L.' and later the 'A.L.' examinations, the work increased as they were a more demanding syllabus.

When the school vacated its premises in the City to go to Gleadless Road, it was the turning point in its life. Mr. H. W. Wadge resigned as did Mr. W. Davies. Under a new headmaster, Mr. P. Dixon, the school still continued as the C.T.S. until the 'Axe Fell'. The C.T.S. was amalgamated with Hurlfield Girls to become Ashleigh Comprehensive.

Here my memories of the C.T.S. are now laid to rest. May I leave you with another quotation. This was told me by a lady teacher Miss Footitt at Carfield Junior School (this was years before the school time of our Author):

> Small beginnings make great endings

How apt to relate the above to the Sheffield Junior Technical School and the Central Technical School, Old Boys' Association!

Long may you flourish.

Introduction

The City of Sheffield has every reason to feel proud of the Central Technical School — the 'CTS'. From its inception in the early 1930s it nurtured technical education for many generations of boys. The school had two distinct curricula for pupils who were intending to be either Engineers or Builders. Boys were able to follow three-year courses in these subjects leading to a CTS Diploma. Over the years this qualification gradually acquired considerable standing and was recognised for employment purposes by, for example, the Building Trades Employers' Association and the Sheffield and District Branch of the Federation of Master Builders.

In the post-war era, with the advent of the General Certificate of Education, it became possible for boys who had studied for their Diploma to stay on at school and study for additional GCE qualifications. The two streams of boys — Engineers and Builders — merged, as it were, into more homogenous groups and took classes in, for example, mathematics, physics, English and French typical of those given in the grammar schools. But throughout its spirited, energetic and successful existence the 'Central Tech', as it was affectionately known to those who attended the school, remained true to its original ideals of providing a foundation of skills for boys intending careers allied to the engineering or building trades.

In many ways the Central Technical School filled another important role. It is not exaggerating to say that it provided an academic life-line to those boys who had failed the eleven-plus examination and who would otherwise have proceeded, through Lord Butler's system of post-war secondary education, to leave school at the age of fifteen. In saying this I realise that I have entered the somewhat specialised realm of the history of secondary-school education. Let me therefore say at the outset that this is not a book about technical education *per se*. That service has already been rendered by Adrian Bristow in his splendid little book *Pride and Some Prejudice — The Story of the Junior Technical School*. This brings me on then to say a few words about the aims of my own book.

My primary purpose in writing this book is to help to evoke what I know are, for many former CTS lads, very fond memories of life and work at the Central Technical School, Sheffield. In effect, my book is, as I have implied in its title, a *reminiscence* — more properly a whole sequence of reminiscences — which I have written for the Old Boys' Association of the Central Technical School — the 'OBA'. But my book is not intended to be exclusively for the members of the Old Boys' Association — by no means. I hope that what I have to say will have meaning, albeit of a more general

kind, for other readers about their own life and work at school. In this respect I should add that in my narrative I have quite a bit to say about the other schools that I attended before proceeding to the CTS, namely, Carfield Primary and Junior Schools and Anns Road Secondary Modern School. I trust these sections of my text will stir memories — I hope *fond* memories — for those readers of my book who attended these particular schools. More widely, I trust that what I have to say about the school curriculum, relating to technical education in the post-war era, will also be of interest to the more general reader.

At this point I should briefly introduce myself by way of explaining how I came to write this book. I attended the CTS from January 1954 to July 1959; I was School Captain for my last year at school. I then proceeded to the University of Sheffield where I studied architecture for the next five years, 1959–64. In fact I stayed on to do research for three more years — I was almost the 'eternal student'! After graduating from the University of Sheffield I left my home town in 1967 to live and work in Edinburgh — where I have resided ever since. From that time the CTS more or less receded from my consciousness as other events in my life took precedence. Moreover, living so distant from Sheffield made it difficult for me to take an active part in the affairs of the OBA. But, as in the case of so many other OBA members, I was eventually reached by the long arm of our dedicated OBA Secretary Stuart Green. To be more accurate he propositioned me, in the course of a long telephone conversation, into joining the Association.

On becoming a member I rapidly came to enjoy, as do the more active members of the OBA, the annual get-together in the form of the *President's Dinner*. Above all else this is a time for renewing friendships and, of course, for having a good chinwag about 'the good old days' at the CTS.

It was whilst swapping stories over our meal at the President's Dinner, in the Autumn of 2000, that someone suggested that I should put my recollections down on paper. Now, most sensible people would decline such a proposition; it is only the rash and foolish who would take up such a challenge — which is precisely what I did! In other words, the idea of my book was conceived. But, as we all know, it is one thing to conceive a project and it is quite another to bring it to completion. So let me now add a few remarks about the scope of my book and my working method.

What I have attempted is not an autobiography; my

book is more in the nature of a personal view of a time in my life which, although marred by occasional sadness — in particular the death of my mother — was one of much happiness and considerable formative influence for which I am deeply grateful. In recalling the events that make up my narrative, I have tried to call to mind moments in the life and work of others as they touched and influenced my own. In doing so I have been guided by the principles of honesty and candour. I say this because I am mindful that it is tempting to contemplate the past through a rose-tinted haze, further idealised by nostalgia, which efface pain and hardship — the 'good old days' syndrome. What you have here is a candid record of events at the CTS as I recall them. These were, as I have already implied, for the greater part constructive and beneficial to me and my contemporaries and, I believe, to the many hundreds of other boys who also experienced life and work at the Central Technical School, Sheffield.

I have remarked that during my time at the CTS I was the School Captain. This was not an idle boast; this circumstance has an important bearing upon my narrative. As School Captain I occupied a position of some responsibility and consequently I was entrusted with a range of duties that fell outside the normal sphere of daily life and work for the typical CTS boy. These duties brought me into contact with various members of staff, notably the Headmaster, and gave me valuable insights into the workings of my school. I will not elaborate on these circumstance here since they are themes of my book. Suffice it to say that my position as an 'office bearer', and the experiences I derived from this, have served me well when it came to writing this book.

In creating my narrative I have, for the most part, relied upon my memory of the events as I recall them — with some assistance from my surviving exercise books. The latter have served me particularly when it came to looking for visual material with which to illustrate specific topics. This brings me to the layout and structure of the work.

The reader will see from the Contents of the book that in Chapter 1 I discuss the origins and early history of the CTS and its important site in the centre of Sheffield. In Chapter 2, I list the names of the members of staff who worked at the CTS from the period of the appointment of its principal Headmaster, Herbert W. Wadge, until just before he retired in the early 1960s. Few would deny that this was the 'golden age' of the CTS. The principal part of the book is Chapter 3. In this chapter I discuss 'Life and Work at the CTS'. I do so in the form of a series of narratives The first two-dozen or so of these are subject-based and are therefore concerned with various aspects of the school curriculum. I then turn to themes of a more general nature. My narratives are not all of equal length and a few subjects that were taught at the school are not mentioned at all. There are two points to make here. Concerning the first: some subjects lend themselves more naturally to reflection than others; I also enjoyed some subjects more than others and they have therefore left a more vivid impression in my mind and so accordingly are given more coverage. The second point is that I have written my account from the point of view of my having been a pupil of Building at the CTS. Consequently, the specifically Engineering side of the CTS curriculum is not something which I experienced directly and therefore subjects such as Pattern Making and Moulding and Engineering Workshop Practice are not discussed. But, on the whole, I believe the reader will find that my sins of omission are not too great and that I do give a reasonably full and balanced account of life and work at the CTS.

Another general point worthy of mention here, concerning the subject matter of my book, is that it relates specifically to the period of my time at the Central Technical School. This was, as I have previously remarked, from January 1954 to July 1959. I have not therefore attempted to write a comprehensive history of the school curriculum. The reader interested in this aspect of technical education should consult Adrian Bristow's book to which I have also previously referred. Notwithstanding my time constraints, I trust that what I have to say will have meaning for those former CTS pupils who attended the school at other periods than myself. Additionally I hope my text will interest the more general reader. This prompts me to add another general point. Throughout the text I have frequently adopted a style of address as though I am referring directly to former pupils of the CTS — in such remarks as "You will remember …" and "You will recall …". I make no apology for this since I have assumed that my principal audience, perhaps I should say readership, will be composed of former members of the CTS — and in particular members of the Old Boys' Association. But at the same time I do not intend any exclusivity. On the contrary; I sincerely hope that the reader with little or no familiarity with the CTS will derive just as much pleasure from what I have written as former pupils.

It is a truism that distance lends enchantment to the view. In my case my viewpoint is now forty years remote from its subject matter. I am consequently well aware of the danger of misrepresenting a particular circumstance or of giving an unduly biased perception of events. I have tried hard to guard against these tendencies; inevitably however my account must to some extent be subjective. In this respect I can say that I have endeavoured to be fair, honest and candid. I have described events as I have been able to recall them with as much objectivity and impartiality as possible. Let me add that I have not tried to settle old scores — for the simple reason that I have no old scores to settle. Neither have I sought to unduly elevate the virtues of a particular teacher or former pupil; by the same tokens I have not attempted to put anybody down — for the simple reason that I have no cause to harbour ill feelings about any of my school contemporaries. I hope they feel the same way about me! Very occasionally I have felt the need to draw a veil over this or that youthful indiscretion and likewise I have thought it wise to steer clear from making any reference to affairs of the heart — the prospect of being pursued by the angry wives of members of the OBA remonstrating: "He never told me about her!" tempered any inclination I might have had in that respect !

I have said that in creating my account I have relied largely upon my memory and powers of recall. I am only too mindful how these can occasionally let you down or, like those curvy mirrors you sometimes see at fairgrounds, give you a distorted view. Moreover I have written this work with no recourse to archives, other than my own small collection of CTS memorabilia. I have also had to squeeze my enterprise into the busy schedule of academic life. These circumstances prompt me to say; if errors of fact and interpretation occasionally creep into my narrative, then may I commend to the reader the eloquent words of the writer Theodore Besterman:

May the noble minded scholars instead of cherishing ill feeling kindly correct whatever errors have been committed … in the way of wrong interpretations and misstatements.

I like to believe that the spirit of the CTS endures. I know it does in the Old Boys' Association. But there is more to it than that — much more. The formative influence of the CTS runs through the life of so many former CTS lads like a rich golden strand and continues to work its beneficial effects. Some Old Boys are now captains of industry with responsibility for many millions of pounds of trade and commerce — not forgetting the livelihood of their employees; some have distinguished themselves in sport at the national and international level; others have succeeded in the sphere of popular entertainment; a few, may I be allowed to add, have enriched academic life; and still others, the great majority, have lived perfectly ordinary but good and decent lives.

It is a curious fact that in a way the spirit of the CTS has been resurrected in recent years in the form of the new City Colleges. The CTS and her sister institutions up and down the country were, in many ways, the precursors of these modern-day pedagogical creations.

Earlier I made reference to the Headmaster of the Central Technical School Herbert W. Wadge. The CTS did of course have more than one Headmaster. But as far as the majority of CTS lads are concerned there was one, and only one Headmaster, namely Herbert W. Wadge. It is no exaggeration to say that Herbert W. Wadge dominated the Central Technical School during his term of headship. To us boys he seemed larger than life; a man of Herculean stature with a Stentorian voice to go with it. He presided over his school like a god — and it was a case of God protect anyone who got on the wrong side of him! But Herbert, as we 'Old Boys' now affectionately like to refer to him, was no bullying tyrant. He loved his school and in his way he loved his boys — each and everyone of us. He would have done literally anything — legal, moral and decent — to further the aims of his school. Such was Herbert's pervasive influence over the CTS that this work could easily have become a book about the man himself. The reader will indeed find references to Herbert W. Wadge abound in the pages of my book and I do in fact devote a whole section to him. But this is not a book about Herbert W. Wadge, nor should it be. A school is more than one individual, however powerful and all-commanding. A school is a community, and a vital part of the CTS community was the staff of the school. Herbert W. Wadge may have been at the helm but it was his colleagues who transacted the daily round of teaching and administration which kept the CTS on course. So my book makes reference, justly so, to the former staff of the CTS who did so much for us boys.

A few years ago the CTS was the subject of a radio programme that was broadcast on BBC *Radio Sheffield*. In effect a number of former CTS pupils undertook a walkabout of the premises and shared fond memories of their old school for the benefit of the listener. For the benefit of the reader of this book I have attempted to re-create the effect of this broadcast by creating a transcript of the radio recording which I reproduce in Chapter 5. The personal views and reminiscences of the various former CTS lads who took part in the original broadcast, make a fitting termination to my book.

I have remarked that I have written this book from a personal point of view and I have also said that it is not intended to be an autobiography. I have however allowed myself a departure from this plan in Chapter 4. This is a more personal account of my early upbringing in Sheffield including my schooling and admission to the Central Technical School. In this chapter I make reference to Carfield Primary and Junior School and to Anns Road Secondary Modern School. I hope that what I have to say here will help to stir fond memories for those readers who, like myself, attended these particular schools.

I am most grateful to have been able to secure the collaboration of Mr. Ken Westnedge. Ken, as we now know him, has the distinction of being not only one of the first pupil members of the CTS but was also a former member of the school staff. He now currently holds a special place in our affections as an active member of the Old Boys' Association. Some of Ken's more cherished memories are preserved here for all to enjoy as the Foreword to my book. By way of interest let me add here a note concerning a remarkable set of coincidences concerning Ken and myself. It so happens that Ken and I attended *all* the same schools before proceeding to the CTS. These were the ones to which I have just referred, namely, Carfield Primary and Junior School and Anns Road Secondary Modern School. Moreover, to complete the coincidence I can also reveal that Ken lived at Upper Valley Road whereas I lived at the other end in Valley Terrace just off Valley Road.

The reader will correctly infer that the effort I have expended upon creating this book is a measure of the regard I have for my former school and, indeed, the affection I feel for the Old Boys' Association — to whom I have pleasure in dedicating the work. My enterprise has indeed been a labour of love.

This latter remark leads me to say, by way of conclusion, that above all else my book is intended to give pleasure. Throughout my text I have consciously sought to enliven my reminiscences with a light touch — though not, I hope, ever descending to levity.

Finally, in commending my book to the reader, I can do no better than paraphrase the evocative words I quote in full elsewhere:

Let visions of boyhood float now before you.
Let echoes of dreamland bear them along.

Terence M. Russell
Edinburgh 2003

The Central Technical School, Sheffield: Main Building

The view is of the elevation of the former Firth College, as seen from West Street, complete with the additional storey that was added in 1892 — compare this with the illustration reproduced on the front cover showing Firth College as it originally appeared when it opened on 17 October, 1879. The figures over the main entrance celebrate the virtues of Science and Art and were carved by the sculptor Onslow Ford. The bust of the founder of Firth College, Mark Firth, originally stood in the vestibule leading from the main entrance. Today, two bronze plaques adorn the entrance; one commemorates the memory of former 'CTS' boys who lost their lives in the Second World War and the other acknowledges the occupation of the premises by the Central Technical School for the years 1933 – 1964. See Chapter 3, 'Homage to the CTS'.

1

The Origins and Early History of the Central Technical School Sheffield

The Central Area Site
The Central Schools

The origins of the Central Technical School at Sheffield are interwoven with the development of the central area site which took place in the latter part of the nineteenth century. The site in question is the extensive plot of land now bounded by Leopold Street, Orchard Lane, Bow Street and Holly Street. In the mid-nineteenth century this land was a patchwork quilt of lanes, shops, houses and small workshops in the middle of which was situated a large gasometer! Leopold Street then had the more lowly appellation of Smith Street and Holly Street was known as Sands Paviour. In 1874, in a bold and visionary gesture, the Sheffield School Board purchased the entire site with a view to developing it for educational purposes. The intention was to build offices for the School Board together with a new school — to be known as the Central Schools because of their central geographical location in the middle of the town. The action of the Sheffield School Board — what we would now call the Sheffield Education Committee — was quite remarkable. It is a shining example of what might be called enlightened Victorian philanthropy. The School Board envisaged that, in effect, several schools would be contained in one building catering for a range of educational needs — hence the plural designation 'Central Schools'. Indeed, with the inclusion of Firth College within the new buildings — to be discussed in a moment — the central area site would provide for the whole spectrum of learning, from the most elementary to the most advanced. Here is how the scheme was described in *The Builder* of 10 July 1880.

> *The Central Schools are intended to solve the problem of connecting the very earliest education with higher knowledge, in such a manner as to open the whole field, even up to university itself, to the poorest child in town. The schools comprise ... an infants' school, a general mixed school for boys and girls, to be taught together, and an upper school for boys and girls taught separately. The upper school [senior school], which is really the most novel portion of the undertaking, is intended by the School Board to be chiefly for the reception of clever boys and girls drafted from any of the elementary schools in the borough, on the recommendation of managers and teachers after due examination.*

It should be noted here that the title 'Central Schools' should not be confused with the name Central Technical School. The 'CTS' evolved some years later from Firth College — as will be explained shortly. The Central Schools, to which I have so far referred, occupied the premises along Orchard Lane — what boys of my generation knew as the City Grammar School — and part of the new buildings on Leopold Street. For completeness it will be useful to make a few concluding remarks about this school. By 1906 the Central Schools were so crowded that the girls were moved into the adjacent premises of Firth College — the future CTS main building. Four years later the Central Schools became two separate schools for boys and girls. In the early 1940s, following national educational reforms, what was by then the City Secondary School became City Grammar School. This school remained on the Orchard Lane-Leopold Street site until it was eventually transferred in 1964 to new premises at Stradbroke Road.

With these details established we can now turn our attention to the central area site as it impinged on the development of the Central Technical School.

Firth College
and
The Central Technical School

The action of the Sheffield School Board in 1874 inspired a wealthy Victorian philanthropist, by the name of Mark Firth, to respond with a parallel gesture of his own. This is how his action came about.

In 1875, a series of lectures commenced in Sheffield in response to what was known as the Cambridge University Extension Movement. In effect, a number of Cambridge scholars and Victorian-style philanthropists wanted as many people as possible to benefit from higher education. Lectures were instigated by Mark Firth who was at that time Lord Mayor of Sheffield — and a wealthy steel manufacturer with a deeply held conviction as to the benefits of higher education. The lectures given at this time included English Literature, Political Economy and Mechanics. They were so successful that Mark Firth was inspired to found a college where such educational activity could be pursued on a more secure basis.

In 1875 he announced that he had made an agreement with the Sheffield School Board to purchase a part of the central area site on which he planned to build a college for further and higher education; the college would bear his name and would, as previously remarked, be known as Firth College — what would one day be the home of the main building of the Central Technical School. A year later, on 3 April 1876, the Sheffield School Board instructed the Sheffield architect T.R. Flockton to prepare plans for a new school — the Central Schools as previously mentioned — in collaboration with the London architect E. R. Robson. At the same time Mark Firth requested the same team of architects to prepare plans and designs for his new college. On 22 September of the same year, *The Building News* announced, as was the custom at this period, details of the building contract. This is of interest since it provides the first architectural description of the new premises. The following is an extract from the text in question:

The tender is announced] for the erection of the new Central Schools of the Sheffield School Board. The design is English Renaissance in character treated freely. Both the offices of the School Board and the Central Schools front the new street [Leopold Street], which is intended to run from the foot of Bow Street across Fargate to Surrey Street. [Note: Some years later, Bow Street gave its name to the Central Technical School Bow Buildings and was subsequently renamed West Street.]

The article goes on to describe the premises of the new Central Schools in the following terms:

The school is arranged on the class system. Each class-room is really a little schoolroom in itself, with a cloak-room opening out into the general corridor, and there is in addition a small private room for the teacher. Further there are special rooms for physical science teaching and for lessons in practical cookery; whilst on the second floor … is a large hall, which will serve as an assembly-room, or for singing lessons, drawing lessons, lectures, examinations, and for similar purposes.

On 17 October 1879 *The Building News* gave the following more extended description of the new Firth College which is of interest insofar as it describes the building as it was originally conceived:

The Firth College, Sheffield, which we illustrate this week, is to be opened on Monday next by Prince Leopold. Internally, the building contains on the principal floor a hall for lectures on literature and other popular subjects, measuring 60 feet by 40 feet, extending through two storeys, surrounded on three sides by galleries, and lighted from the ceiling. Also a large room especially adapted for lectures on physics and chemistry, which, being fitted in the most approved lecture-room fashion, extends downwards to the basement, and is provided with revolving shutters so as to obtain darkness during experiments, etc. On the first floor the portion not occupied by the upper part of the hall is devoted to lecture rooms and classrooms. In the basement are the necessary services, the heating apparatus, kitchen etc. In the entrance hall, and opposite the outer door, stands the bust of Mr. Firth, from the chisel of Mr. Bruce Joy, which forms a portion of a testimonial presented to the donor of the college, Mr. Mark Firth, and was exhibited at the Royal Academy during the present year. This hall is fitted with swing doors, and has a groined ceiling.
Externally it forms one of a large group consisting the College, the School Board Offices, and the great Central Schools, all designed by the same architects, Mr. T. J. Flockton, of Sheffield, and Mr. E. R. Robson, F.S.A., of Parliament Street, Camden. The keynote of the style is said to have been given by Claire College, Cambridge, but the whole is treated with great freedom, and without any subsequent imitation of the prototype. It has been found exceedingly difficult to group three such wholly different buildings into one harmonious whole, and a close observer will notice that the detail of the Firth College is slightly enlarged throughout, in consequence of the greater height of its storeys over that followed on the other buildings.
The foliage sculpture on the other buildings has been executed by Mr. J. McCullock, of London, while the tympana [semi-circular decorative panel] over the arched head doorway forming the principal entrance to the College and

respectively representing 'Science' and 'Art', are from the chisel of Mr. Onslow Ford, of Blackheath. The clerk of the works employed by Mr. Firth was Mr. Laidles. The whole of the work has been executed by Mr. William Bissett, builder, Sheffield.

Four years later, in 1879, the new college building was erected on the corner of West Street and Leopold Street. The opening ceremony was presided over by Prince Leopold, the youngest son of Queen Victoria. Initially the building was known as Firth College, in honour of its founder, but Mark Firth did not live long enough to enjoy his creation — he died the following year.

The new buildings were described in the 10 July issue of *The Builder* to which I have already made mention:

A very important block of buildings, comprising the Firth College, Central Schools, and the School Board Offices, has been erected in Sheffield, to the great satisfaction of the townspeople. The style adopted may be called English Renaissance; the principal material employed is Huddersfield stone. There are two chief entrances, both handsome, that in Bow Street [later West Street], giving access to Firth College, and one to the new offices of the School Board, which form the central portion of the block fronting the new street [Leopold Street].
The buildings form three sides of a quadrangle, the forth side of which will be walled, so that the open space in the centre of the square may be used as a playground by the children. The Firth College occupies the Bow Street side, and fronts to a portion of the new street.

Firth College originally had just two main storeys above street level — see the engraving (cover design). A third storey was added to the imposing edifice in 1892 to give the building its appearance we recognise today. Students of Firth College took classes to degree level, and some received an external degree of the University of London.

Technical education so flourished at Firth College that the department was named the Sheffield Technical School — not to be confused with the similar nomenclature of the 'CTS'. Firth College eventually took the name University College and, with the Sheffield Technical School, was subsumed within the University of Sheffield when the latter received its Royal Charter in 1905 — eventually moving to Western Bank where the Faculties of Arts, Pure Science, Medicine and Applied Science were established.

For the interest of former CTS pupils, I can insert a personal observation here concerning certain technical aspects of the heating and ventilation system of the Central Schools and Firth Building. These were narrated to a class of boys by Mr. William Gregory — of whom more later — during a class sometime in 1955. The subject was 'building science' and I recall how Mr. Gregory told the class that the Firth Building was originally provided with a system of mechanical ventilation with air being ducted to all the principal rooms throughout the building. A system of jets, in the air ducts, sprayed a mist of water into the moving air so as to clean it of particles of grime. The clean air entered the classrooms through a system of grilles — some of you may recall these since they were, for the most part, bunged up with pieces of blotting paper — which we used in those days. The real point of interest, again according to Mr. Gregory, was that the only other building in the country, at the time, to have a similarly advanced system of mechanical ventilation was the Houses of Parliament!

Mr. Gregory's remarks were both scientifically and historically accurate. A brief version of his account appeared in *The Builder* article to which I have already made reference. This is how the heating system originally functioned:

The heating apparatus, supplied by Mr. D. O. Boyd, of London, is effective. It is fixed in a large chamber, 84 feet long, 5 feet wide, and 5 feet high in the basement of the Central Schools. It heats the whole building by twenty tiers of pipes, and not only warms but purifies the atmosphere. The air is brought into the building through an iron grating, but before it passes into the pipe chamber it is conveyed through a canvas, upon which a spray of water plays, the effect being that the atmosphere is cleansed from all impurities, such as dust and smoke, after which the clarified air passes through a series of cavities into the various rooms, the supply being regulated by easily-worked valves.

To complete this survey of the origins of the buildings of the Central Technical School, I will now make brief reference to the Holly Building and the Bow Building. For this part of my account I should add that I am indebted to information provided in the text of the brochure *Leopold Street Open Day* (October 5/6th 2001) which was published by the Education Department of the Sheffield City Council.

By the 1890s, such was the success of the Central Schools that they required additional facilities. Moreover, there were parallel developments taking place in the field of teacher training. The Education Act of 1870 required more school teachers to be trained, for which facilities were also required. Remarkably, by the standards of today, a 'pupil teacher' commenced training at the age of fourteen. Such an individual spent fours years in the classroom acquiring practical skills under the watchful eye of a qualified teacher — frequently the Head Teacher. Two years were then spent at a teacher training college to complete the pupil teacher's training. By 1884, the Sheffield School Board had five active centres of instruction for pupil teachers and, in 1887, decided to concentrate these into a single centre — for which new premises were required. The School Board held a competition for the required designs, the results of which were announced in *The Building News* of 24 July 1891. This article provides the first account of the new premises in Holly Street — *The Holly Building* — and Bow Street — *The Bow Building*:

The Sheffield School Board recently instituted a competition for plans for the additions to the Central Higher Grade School, and a new elementary school to be erected in Holly Street. The Central School was the first of its kind erected in England; but since then improvements have been made on that experimental effort, and it was desired that Sheffield should not fall into the rear, but that the high grade school appointments and fittings should be brought up to date. The designs marked "Labore et Perseverantia" [!] were selected, and on opening the sealed envelope it appeared that these were designed by Mr. J. B. Mitchell-Withers, of Sheffield … . The additional buildings will include the following departments:
[The Holly Building] In the basement — cookery classes, dining rooms, joiners' shop and metal working shop, and laundry; on the ground floor — machine drawing and lecture rooms to accommodate 120 students, physical laboratory, and lecture room for 50 students; first floor — chemical laboratories for 140 students, and lecture room, balance room, and other necessary stores. The present school will be modified to suit the new arrangements. The Peripatetic Demonstrators' Department at the corner of Orchard Lane and Holly Street contains preparation room,

joiners' shop, offices, with the caretaker's house adjoining. [The Bow Building] The elementary school building is placed at the corner of Holly Street and Bow Street. The accommodation provided is for 292 infants on the ground floor, and with a mixed school for 250 on the first floor. A playground is provided on the top of the building, and the basement is devoted to workshops and playsheds. The style adopted for the buildings is that of the English Renaissance, to harmonise with the present schools and offices, which were designed by Mr. E. R. Robson, F.S.A.

By 1896, work was under way in constructing the new premises which were duly opened in 1899. They functioned as such until 1933 when the Pupil Teacher Centre was transferred to the Central Secondary Schools and in 1936 its name was changed to City Secondary School. Former CTS pupils will have reason to recall some of these circumstances from the inscription placed high on the wall in the main entrance to the Holly Street Building which states:

This Building was opened as a Pupil Teacher Centre by his Grace the Duke of Devonshire KG, President of the Board of Education, on October 9th 1899 and was used as such until July 31st 1933.

A few years later the Holly Building, The Bow Building and Firth College were all united to form The Junior Technical School — precursor of The Central Technical School — under circumstances to which I will now make brief reference.

The Junior Technical School and The Central Technical School

The origins of the Junior Technical Schools — or Junior Day Technical Schools as they were sometimes called — has been handsomely told by Adrian Bristow in his book *Pride and Some Prejudice: The Story of the Junior Technical School*. In this book, Mr. Bristow has shown that the Great War exposed the country's need for many skilled men — and women — to service the technical trades and allied professions. Accordingly, in the 1920s and 1930s the government set about strengthening the provision of technical education for boys and girls. Junior Technical Schools were created which took pupils at the age of 13+ from the elementary schools and provided a form of apprenticeship-education of two years duration — extended later to three years. From the outset there was a strong focus of training on the engineering and building trades. Adrian Bristow comments: 'The aim of such schools was to provide a broad technical education to enable their pupils to adapt to whatever conditions they might meet, and a base from which they could specialise in due course according to the branch of industry and type of occupation they chose'. These words perfectly capture the spirit of the Central Technical School, Sheffield — what today we would call the *mission statement*.

The objects of a typical Junior Technical School of the 1930s are well described in the following extract from Adrian Bristow's researches:

The aim is to take boys about 13 to 14 years of age, who are completing their general education in the Elementary Schools, and to give them in the Junior Day Technical School, a sound preparatory training which will be of service to them on entering the works; to teach them the practical drawing, measurements and calculations needed in the workshops; the uses of the various tools in the working of wood and metal; together with the elementary principles of Mechanics, Physics and Chemistry. At the same time other elements of a general education will continue to receive serious attention.

In order to ensure that good workshop methods are employed the staff includes men who have had actual workshop experience as well as experience in teaching.

Boys who have completed the full course can generally be placed in suitable positions. Local industrial firms, with whom the School is in close touch, have shown readiness to take such boys into their service.

The reader who attended the Central Technical School, Sheffield will immediately recognise in the above quotation the broad principles upon which the CTS was founded. Boys were indeed recruited into the school at about the age of thirteen years, or, by the 1950s, a little younger. This was because by then the school had started to fulfil another educational and social purpose, namely, to give boys who had failed the 11+ examination a second chance of receiving a more extended education than that provided by the secondary schools. The second paragraph of Adrian Bristow's text is a salutary reminder that the members of the academic staff of the Junior Technical Schools were highly qualified in their particular trade and profession. This is a point to which I will make particular reference throughout the account which follows shortly concerning life and work at the CTS. This remark brings me now to the particular circumstances of the formation of the Junior (Central) Technical School at Sheffield — the information for which I am once more indebted to the text of the Sheffield Education Committee brochure *Leopold Street Open Day* to which I have already made reference.

On the 5 April 1933 a special sub-committee of the Sheffield Education Committee reported on the need to make provision for a Junior Technical School, presumably in response to the national educational trends in this direction to which I have made mention. Doubtless also this decision was given added impetus by a desire to sustain the spirit of the earlier pioneering developments that had taken place on the central area site in Sheffield almost fifty years previously. Be this as it may, the sub-committee gave encouragement to the creation of a Junior Technical School that would prepare boys for careers in the professions of Engineering and Building — more specifically, mechanical engineering and electrical engineering and the trades of carpentry and joinery. Thus, from its inception, the school was conceived as having two complimentary streams, one for Engineers and one for Builders.

The age of admission was set at thirteen years and the buildings designated for the new Junior Technical School were Firth College and the Holly Building. Boys occupied the Bow Building some years later when this facility ceased to be a school for young children under the original Central Schools system. Incidentally, this explains why, to this day, the designation 'Infants' can still be seen over the main entrance to the Bow Building. The original intake to the Junior Technical School was planned to be 360 boys.

According to the official records of the City of Sheffield Education Committee, the Junior Technical School duly opened on Tuesday 12 September 1933 with 117 boys enrolled. (The reader will note that the date and precise number of boys enrolled, stated here, are somewhat at variance with the recollections given in the Foreword by Mr. Ken Westnedge.) These circumstances

existed until the immediate post-war era, by which time the premises at Cathedral School and Arundel Street had also been added to increase the accommodation, doubtless to make provision for the increased number of pupils attending — which was of the order of 600 - 650 boys. Interestingly, in December 1945 the name of the school was changed to The Central Technical School. I have the impression that the designation 'Junior Technical School' must have persisted for a number of years afterwards in the minds of many Sheffielders. I say this for the following reason. As I will discuss in more detail later, I entered the CTS in January 1954 and I recall how, at this period, the Headmaster Herbert Wadge became quite heated in morning assembly on the subject of the correct use of the name of his school. From my recollection it appears that he used to receive letters from parents — writing to him about their son's abscence due to illness and such matters — and styling their letter 'The Junior Technical School'. This precipitated Herbert into something of a lather — as such departures from protocol were inclined to do! So we were sent on our way with the instruction to remind our parents that the correct name of our school was *The Central Technical School!*

I have just referred to the increase in the number of boys from an original intake of 360 to almost twice that number. Boys of my generation attending the CTS in the 1950s will remember how very crowded the school could feel at times, especially during morning assembly! It is still a cause of some wonderment to me as to how so many boys could be squeezed into the main hall of the Firth Building — our Headmaster was not the only one to become heated during morning assembly! Crowding became so bad that in 1956, a report of Her Majesty's Inspectors of schools actually pronounced the CTS as being unsuitable as a secondary school. I can recall this particular visit of several dark-suited HMIs to the school — indeed, I was introduced to one of them and had to show him a selection of my school exercise books — I will make passing reference to this occasion later in my section concerned with *Physics*. For the present, I will confine myself to remarking that the HMIs did not consider it appropriate for a school to be spread over five different buildings, the journey between two of them — Cathedral School and Arundel Street — necessitating a brisk walk of about ten minutes; actually I seem to recall we ran, especially at lunch time, to secure a good place in the dinner queue!

The Inspectors deplored the fact that the school's playing fields were a bus journey away at Ringinglow. Concerning the Firth Building, they observed how 'the ventilation was unable to cope and the atmosphere was often heavy'. Now there's an understatement! At the end of a typical morning assembly — especially when Herbert Wadge had been going at full strength — the atmosphere in the school hall was such that I recall a number of occasions when one or two boys actually fainted! However, at the time we boys took all this in our stride. Now, forty years on, the typical former CTS lad, looking back, will proudly assert that it is not the physical deficiencies of the school that he remembers but the wonderful education that prevailed. At the time of the inspection of the school (1956) this fact was not lost on the HMIs who observed how: 'Despite all the difficulties it was judged that the school made a considerable and increasing contribution to the life of the city'.

Change was however inevitable, not least with the advent of the comprehensive system in the early 1960s. And so it was that in October 1964 that the school left its location in the centre of Sheffield for the leafy environs of Gleadless. Here the CTS forsook its identity as a boys' school and amalgamated with Hurlfield Girls to become Ashleigh Comprehensive School. An era had passed and a new one was about to commence.

A number of general points can be made here in conclusion. In the late nineteenth century the City of Sheffield School Board — later the City of Sheffield Education Committee — may be considered to have led the way in education with its pioneering efforts to create a modern and well equipped complex of schools in the very heart of the city — all combined with administration offices of the highest standard for the Director of Education and his staff. Perhaps even more remarkable is the parallel philanthropic gesture of Mark Firth in founding the college of further and higher education that was to bear his name, and, significantly, would in due course become the principal building of the Central Technical School. As we have seen, the Holly and Bow buildings would follow at later periods. These circumstances lead me to the following observations.

It is interesting to reflect that fifty or so years before CTS boys commenced their education in the Firth Building, young men and women had assembled there daily to receive advanced instruction in Ancient History, Classics, Modern History, Theory of Music, Chemistry, Mathematics, Mechanics and Physics. And what a magnificent school hall they, and later CTS lads, had with its spacious roof-lit ceiling, cantilevered balcony and general air of a Methodist chapel. In effect, this hall was the forebear of the later Firth Hall sited at the University of Sheffield — in the splendid red brick buildings at Western Bank. It is here where I, and I know some of my readers, sat our university examinations.

Concerning the Holly and the Bow buildings, it is interesting to further reflect how several generations of young children had occupied these premises long before their CTS counterparts arrived on the scene. They had thronged the corridors, classrooms, drawing offices and workshops and, in the case of the Bow building, had chased one another about in the playground high up above street level on the roof. As we will see later in my narrative, it would be some years after this era before certain groups of intrepid CTS lads would discover how to gain access to this 'playground on the roof' — which was declared strictly out of bounds in the 1950s — for the purpose of their secret recreations!

Finally, we may reflect what a long gestation was required before the Central Technical School acquired its name. In the beginning, as we have seen, were the Sheffield Central Schools, later to become the Sheffield City Grammar School; in parallel was the Sheffield Technical School — part of Mark Firth's College with its connotations of further and higher education; then came the Junior Technical School — with its focus on secondary technical education for boys; and from this creation finally evolved the Sheffield Central Technical School. When we include the final phases in the history of the evolution of the CTS, these developments encompass almost a hundred years — from the 1870s to the 1960s

This concludes my brief survey of the history and origins of the Central Technical School. I will shortly invite the reader to step back in time with me to visit, through the medium of my various narratives, the classrooms, drawing offices, laboratories and workshops that composed the fabric of this once vibrant and dynamic institution. But before that I have some further preliminary — and most important — observations to make, namely, to introduce to the reader the members of staff who, at various periods, taught at the Central Technical School, Sheffield or contributed to its life and work in other capacities.

2
The Members of Staff
of the
Central Technical School
Sheffield

Even more important than the physical facilities of a school are its members of staff; without them there can be no school. This may be a statement of the obvious but it is nevertheless worth making. In my survey of the members of staff of the Central Technical School, Sheffield I have taken as my starting point the year 1947 — the year when Herbert W. Wadge was appointed as Head Teacher. I continue to the period 1962–63 just before he retired. Few would challenge the claim that this was the 'golden age' of the CTS. Herbert, as former CTS pupils well know, imposed his authority upon the school indelibly. But this section of my CTS narrative is not about Herbert Wadge; it concerns the CTS staff collectively — that dedicated group of teachers who did so much to uphold Herbert Wadge's ideals and, of course, there own standards and principles.

In researching this section of my text, I have consulted the *Handbook of Information* of the City of Sheffield Education Committee — for the various years under consideration. These list the names of the various members of staff, their date of appointment to the CTS, their title and — most intriguingly — their annual salary. I hesitated a moment before including the latter information but, since it is already in the public domain — and is now distant in time — I can see no harm in presenting it here. Indeed, the information is valuable insofar as it gives some idea of the relative positions of seniority of the different members of staff according to such considerations as their academic qualifications and years of teaching experience. However I have confined this information to the more distant years of the various staff appointments— I do not give this personal information for the more modern era.

The CTS Staff in 1947

Examination of the composition of the staff of the CTS shows the strong focus on technical, mathematical and scientific subjects, consistent with the ideals of the school as being a technical school. In 1947 there were three science teachers, four mathematics teachers, and no fewer than ten teachers for woodwork, metalwork, technical drawing, brickwork and plumbing. The humanities were not neglected; two teachers were appointed to teach French, one for English and another for scripture. Not surprisingly the majority of the staff were appointed in 1945 and 1946 with the cessation of the Second World War. Here are the details which include several names familiar to former CTS pupils:

Herbert W. Wadge B.Sc. (London) was appointed as Principal (Headmaster) in January 1947 with a handsome salary for the period of £1065.

Vincent W. McManus B.Sc. (London) was the oldest member of staff and was appointed as Assistant Primary Schools Teacher in August 1919; Intermediate Schools Teacher in October 1928; Physics Master to the CTS in September 1933; and was promoted to Second Master (Deputy Principal) in April 1937. In 1947 his salary was £580 — only about half that of the Headmaster. It is interesting to speculate if Mr. McManus, who, in 1947, had been Deputy Head for ten years, applied for the post of Headmaster but was passed over in favour of Mr. Wadge.

Fred Allen was appointed as Handicraft Instructor in Primary Schools in August 1936; he was appointed as Assistant Master to the CTS in July 1940.   (£460)

Charles F. Baines was appointed Handicraft Instructor in Primary Schools in December 1930; he was appointed as Assistant Metalwork Master to the CTS in March 1936.
          (£525)

Herbert Barton B.Sc. (Sheffield), M.I.Min.E. was appointed to the CTS as Mathematics Master in March 1936. He should not be confused with John E. Barton who was appointed later — but I wonder if they were related?   (£570)

William E. Davis was appointed Handicraft Instructor in Primary Schools in December 1930; he was appointed as Woodwork Master to the CTS in March 1935.   (£525)

Thomas H. Dove B.A. (London) was appointed as a teacher in 1922 and as English Master to the CTS in September 1940.   (£555)

Albert F. C. Foster M.I.M.E. was appointed as Mathematics Master to the CTS in September 1945.
          (£555)

William G. Gregory B.Sc. (Sheffield) was appointed as a teacher in August 1929 and Science Master to the CTS in August 1942.   (£585)

John H. Hunter was appointed Assistant Master for Carpentry and Joinery with Building Drawing in August 1942.   (£555)

Alban S. McCarthy B.A. (London) was appointed French Master in September 1934. (£555)

Harold Parkin was appointed to the post of Plumbing Instructor — note he did not have the formal title of 'Teacher' — in August 1944. (£365)

Charles Ridgeway was appointed Bricklaying Instructor — like Mr. Parkin not given the title of Teacher — in April 1945. He was more highly paid than Mr. Parkin which may reflect that he had additional classroom responsibilities. (£473)

Alfred Simpson A.M.I.M.E. was appointed Mechanics and Mathematics Master in April 1946. Mr. Simpson was one of the few non-graduate teachers at the CTS to hold what was known as a 'degree-equivalent' qualification, namely, Associate Membership of the Institute of Mechanical Engineers — a highly regarded qualification. (£473)

Cyril Walker B.Sc., A.I.C. was appointed Temporary Science Master in January 1945. (£393)

Frederick Whitham was the second oldest member of staff and was appointed as Handicraft Instructor in Primary Schools in October 1928 and Master in charge of the Machine Shop at the CTS in September 1933. (£525)

Donald Woolhouse was appointed as Handicraft Instructor in Primary Schools in April 1934 and to the same post at the CTS in June 1940. (£525)

John H. Housby B.A. (Liverpool) was appointed Assistant Master for Scripture and History in September 1946. (£585)

Stanley Pilling was appointed Assistant Master for Carpentry and Joinery in January 1946. Mr. Pilling was the most modestly remunerated of the CTS staff in 1947. (£300)

Peter Smeltzer B.Sc. (Durham) was appointed Assistant Mathematics Master in June 1946. (£400)

John E. Williams B.A. (Wales) was appointed Assistant Master for French and English in September 1946. (£476)

The technical support staff at the CTS were known as Maintenance Assistants'. In 1947 two members of staff held these posts:

Sydney Stacey was appointed in June 1934. (£210)

David Swallow was appointed in November 1946. (£210)

In 1947 the CTS had one secretarial member of staff with the title of 'Clark'. This was Marie Garnett who was appointed in January 1946 with a salary of £160. There were two 'Laboratory Attendants' both of whom were appointed in October 1946: William Turner had a salary of £171 and Martin Stewart had the princely salary of £46 — about 17 shillings per week!

Of some interest is that at this period (to be precise September 1946) a certain Mr. Ronald E. Bee B.Sc. (Sheffield) was appointed as Temporary Mathematics Master to the City Grammar School with a salary of £400. 'Buzz' did not join the staff of the CTS until 1951 — see later.

The CTS Staff in 1948

The following year added two more names to the staff of the CTS who will be familiar to most members of the OBA. But before I come to them, here are a few general items of information.

Herbert Wadge mysteriously received a *decrease* in salary of £50 — unless there is an error in the records. In contrast Mr. McManus received an increase of £45. To put these figures into context, I recall from conversations with my father — who was a factory worker — that a typical manual wage in the post-war period was £5 per week. This could be increased to about £7 by doing a lot of overtime. The records show that Mr. Dove received promotion to the post of Senior English Master — with an increase in salary of £45.

Here now are the names of the additional members of staff who joined the CTS at this period:

Felix M. Arscott B.Sc. (London) was appointed Mathematics Master in September 1947. (£393)

Frank W. Betts was appointed as P.T. Master in September 1947. (£508)

Kenneth C. King B.A. (Sheffield) was appointed as a teacher (Assistant Master) in Primary Schools in June 1947 and French and English Master at the CTS in September 1947. (£431)

Thomas L. Thornton was appointed Assistant Master for Mathematics in March 1947. Mr. Thornton is an example of men who at this time trained to be teachers under special 'fast-track' arrangements known as 'Emergency Training' — my father in law, John A. Tester B.Sc. (London) trained as a teacher himself by means of this method. (£376)

Two new Clerks were appointed, namely, Joan Deakin and Jean Taylor. The vacant position of Laboratory Attendant was filled by John M. Hardy who received about £2 per week.

The CTS Staff in 1955

We move forward in time now to the year after my entry to the CTS. The staff of the school had by then assumed its compliment with which many of us who attended the CTS, at this period, will be familiar. I reproduce below the full list of names which is of interest for identifying the new members of staff and the posts to which certain established members of staff were promoted. As before,

I gave the salaries for each member of staff.

Herbert W. Wadge B.Sc. (London) — details as previously given.(£1483)

Vincent V. McManus B.Sc. (London) — details as previously given. (£1085)

Charles F. Baines was promoted to Senior Engineering Workshops Master in April 1951. (£875)

John E. Barton was appointed Mathematics Master in November 1953. (£610)

James Bolton trained at the Bolton Technical College and was appointed Assistant Master for Brickwork in September 1955. His salary is not given in the records.

Ernest Clarke M.A., B.Sc. (Durham) was appointed as Senior Chemistry Master in September 1951. (On the basis of a conversation that I recall having with Mr. Alfred Simpson, Mr. Clarke's M.A. degree was conferred by the University of Oxford.) (£1101)

William E. Davis was promoted to Senior Workshops Master in April 1951. (£825)

Thomas H. Dove — details as previously given. (£935)

Stanley T. Farnsworth B.A. (London) was appointed as History Master in May 1954. (£810)

Geoffrey W. Firth M.A. (Cantab.) was appointed Geography Master in May 1949 and Senior Social Studies Master in September 1950. (£853)

Robert W. Freeman was appointed Assistant Master for Patternmaking and Moulding in January 1949. (£643)

Frederick A. Frow was appointed Mathematics Master in September 1952 and had his post made permanent in 1954. (£643)

Edgar A. Grantham trained at the Leeds College of Art and Crafts and was appointed Art and English Master in 1952. (£643)

William G. Gregory — details as previously given. (£821)

Samuel Hedley — details as previously given. (£975)

Robert J. Howell trained at the Bangor Normal College and St. John's College, York and was appointed Assistant master for Physical Education and Junior Mathematics Master in 1951. (£691)

Roger Hughes B.A., B.Mus. (Sheffield) was appointed English and Music master in September 1952. (£717)

John H. Hunter — details as previously given. (£875)

Kenneth C. King B.A. (Sheffield) — details as previously given. (£920)

John McCallum B.A. (Sheffield) was appointed as Assistant Master in Primary Schools in 1946 and English and French Master at the CTS in February 1948. (£951)

Harold Parkin — details as previously given. (£576)

Stanley Pilling — details as previously given. (£725)

Leonard Shipley trained at Padgate Emergency Training College under the post-war arrangements and was appointed Assistant Master in Primary Schools in December 1947 and Mathematics master at the CTS in September 1948. (£699)

Alfred Simpson A.I.M.E. — details as previously given. (£785)

Gilbert M. Thompson B.Sc. (Sheffield) trained as a teacher at Brincliffe Emergency Technical College under the post-war arrangements and was appointed as Assistant Master for Mathematics in July 1950 and Senior Mechanics master in November 1953. (£896)

Thomas L. Thornton was promoted to Engineering Science Master in January 1948. (£785)

Kenneth Westnedge was appointed Engineering Workshop Practice Master in September 1954. (£681)

Joseph B. Whitlow B.A. (Liverpool) was appointed Assistant Master for English and French in April 1952. (£655)

Donald Woolhouse — details as previously given. (£825)

Two Clerical Assistants were appointed in 1953, namely, Margaret Bryan and Mrs Ouida M. Robinson. Mr. Henry McClean joined Mr. Sidney Stacey as Workshop Technician. The Laboratory Technicians were William Parker, Robert J. Simpson and Anthony M. Gilbert.

The CTS Staff in 1958
New Appointments and Promotions

In this section I list only new appointments to the staff of the CTS or staff already in post, previously mentioned, who received promotions. All the promotions listed took place in October 1956.

Charles F. Baines was promoted to Head of Engineering Workshop.

Ronald E. Bee was promoted to Head of Mathematics.

Alfred E. Bunn B.A. (Sheffield) was appointed French and English Master in September 1956.

Thomas H. Dove was promoted to Head of English Department.

Albert B. Fairbrother studied at the Sheffield Training College and was appointed a teacher in 1951 and Master of Art at the CTS in September 1957.

Donald B. Charlesworth M.A. (Edinburgh) was appointed Head of Geography in April 1957.

William G. Gregory was promoted to Head of Chemistry.

Samuel Hedley was promoted to Head of Technical Drawing.

John H. Hunter was promoted to Head of Brickwork, Joinery and Plumbing Department.

Kenneth C. King was promoted to Head of French Department.

Francis A. Groarke studied at St. Mary's Training College, Twickenham and was appointed a teacher in 1951 and Temporary Mathematics and Physics Master in September 1956.

Edward J. I. Brennan B.A. (Sheffield) was appointed Assistant Master for English and French in September 1956.

Derek J. Pitman studied at the Sheffield Training College and Redlands Training College and was appointed Mathematics and Science Master in April 1957.

Arthur A. Hill M.A., B.Sc. (Oxford University) was appointed as Head of History Department in April 1957.

Ronald Underdown B.A. (Sheffield) was appointed teacher of English and French in September 1957.

Stanley Crisp was appointed Assistant Master for Brickwork and Building Drawing in September 1956.

John W. Winter B.A. (Durham) was appointed Assistant Master for English and French in September 1956.

Mrs Marion Hill (wife of Arthur Hill) B.Sc. (Exeter) was appointed Part-Time teacher in Physics in September 1958.

Two Clerical Assistants were appointed, namely, Enid M. Miller, in May 1958, and Thelma Crick in October 1956.

An additional Laboratory Technician was appointed, namely, Brian Lawrence.

The CTS Staff in the period 1959–63 New Appointments and Promotions

As in the previous section I here list only new appointments to the staff of the CTS or staff already in post, previously mentioned, who received promotions.

George R. Nicholls B.Sc. (Durham) was appointed in January 1958 as Deputy Headmaster and Head of Physics. He left the CTS shortly after.

Gilbert M. Thompson was appointed to the vacant post of Deputy Headmaster in September 1961.

William E. Davis was promoted to Head of Mechanical Science in September 1961.

Alan Davison B.Sc. (Sheffield) was appointed as Science Master in September 1962.

Terence Green B.A. (Sheffield) was appointed Head of English in September 1962.

Sydney A. Gibbons was appointed Mathematics and Mechanics Teacher in September 1959.

Eric Harrington was appointed as physics master in 1959 and was promoted to Head of Science Department in September 1961.

Dorothy Hilliard B.A. (Manchester) was one of the very few women to be appointed to a full-time post at the CTS, in her case as French Mistress in September 1962.

Peter Lee B.A. (Cambridge) was appointed English and French Master in March 1960.

Gordon Saul held the City and Guilds London Institute Full Technical Certificate and was appointed Assistant master for Patternmaking and Foundry Practice in May 1959.

Geoffrey Taylor B.A. (Sheffield) was appointed Science Master in September 1960.

Andrew Walker B.Sc. (Sheffield) was appointed Head of Mathematics in April 1962.

Terence Wigget B.Eng. (Sheffield) was appointed Mathematics and Science Master in September 1961.

Edward Williams was appointed as Handicraft Teacher in the early 1960s — the precise date is not given in the records.

Ronald Upton and *John Godbehere* were both appointed as Temporary Teachers in September 1962.

Two Clerical Assistants were appointed, namely, Miss M. Proctor and Carole A. Lynch, in December 1961 and September 1962 respectively.

Three Laboratory Technicians were appointed, namely: Michael Furness, John K. Prior and Phillip I. Bellamy.

Having introduced the members of staff of the CTS I will now direct my narrative to the principal theme of this book — *'Life and Work at the Central Technical School, Sheffield'*.

3
Life and Work
at the
Central Technical School Sheffield

Admission to the CTS

Life and work at the CTS commenced by first gaining admission to the school — which meant passing the entrance examination. To put this into its context it will be helpful to make a few remarks of a general nature concerning the post-war educational reforms which had such a profound bearing on the lives of the young people of that generation.

R. A. Butler — 'RAB' — is justly credited with pioneering the *Education Act* of 1944 which is generally regarded as being one of the major landmarks in the history of education in the UK. The Act dispensed with the pre-war system of 'elementary' education and made provision for a radically new scheme of primary and secondary education. It also raised the school leaving age from fourteen to fifteen years. In passing I will add that, under these arrangements, I came within one year and two terms of leaving school and would have done so had I not been admitted to the CTS. Under the Act secondary education embraced a tripartite division of grammar, modern and technical schools. As we of that generation are well aware, selection was by means of the eleven-plus examination failure in which meant attending a Secondary Modern School.

In effect technical schools such as the CTS gave boys a second chance to experience an education which combined vocational training with academic learning — but there still remained the small problem of passing the entrance examination!

In the 1950s there were two entrance examinations to the CTS; one was for entry to the Engineering Department and the other was for entry to the Building Department. It is a curious circumstance that the examinations were exactly similar; I know this for a fact since, as I will explain in a moment, I took them both! The Engineering Examination was held in the late summer and successful boys duly entered the CTS in the following September for the start of the Autumn Term. The Building Examination was held in the autumn and successful boys entered the CTS in the following January.

News of the forthcoming entrance examinations was circulated to the secondary schools who informed boys of the event. It is possible that some schools only informed their more able boys of the exam but at my school — Anns Road Secondary Modern — there was an announcement in class. I discuss these circumstances in some detail in the more autobiographical chapter of my text titled *Admission to the Central Technical School, Sheffield: A Personal Account* — for the benefit of the reader interested in such matters. I will outline these circumstances here briefly which may help others to recall their own impressions of sitting the entrance examination.

One day my teacher asked — of the boys in my class — "Who would like to go to the Central Technical School to learn how to become an engineer"? Three of us responded, myself and two lads by the names of David Dickson and David Collins — they may well be known to some of you. There were no formalities, no practice-sessions tests or anything like that — we were simply given time off from school to go and sit the exam. So a few weeks later I and my two companions set out for the CTS.

We were ushered into the main hall where rows of the ubiquitous examination-style desks were set out. I am speaking of 1953 — which should help to establish this event in the minds of those other CTS Old Boys who also sat this examination. There were papers on: English including comprehension, spelling, word usage and sentence structure; multiplication and division; an arithmetic paper which included questions concerned with the areas of irregularly-shaped objects; and there was a brain-teaser type paper to test our powers of logical reasoning — which was my undoing. A typical question went as follows: "Imagine a line of paving stones bear the letters of the alphabet. Commencing at 'A', proceed five steps, then return three, go forward eight, back five, now forward again ten, back two and finally forward three. What letter does the paving stone bear on which you are now standing?" Confused? So was I. I could see my chances of becoming an engineer receding. I failed!

Having failed the entrance exam I returned to Anns Road School. Almost a whole academic year passed. By now, in third year, the end of my secondary schooling was in sight; I was thirteen and a half — just eighteen months short of the then school-leaving age of fifteen. This time my teacher, Mr. Cartwright, said one day — again to the boys in the class — "Who would like to go to the Central Technical School to learn how to become a builder?". I resolved to sit the entrance examination once more.

Again I set forth for the CTS, one day in the autumn of 1953, in the company of my class mate John Butcher and, from the year below us, Gordon Swan and Gordon Wragg. The now familiar rows of examination desks awaited us in the school hall. I remember that I took a seat in the second row from the left at the back — from where I could contemplate all the candidates. Just for a moment the demon monsters of apprehension gripped me, but I banished them determined to do my best. The arithmetic and English papers both went well. Then came the 'IQ' reasoning tests; would the lettered paving-stone questions be set, I asked myself? No, in their place was an ingenious group of questions based upon a rather complex geometrical figure. This consisted of a circle, surmounted by a triangle, surmounted by a square — with letters of the alphabet scattered everywhere. For each of the letters — about twenty in all — you had to identify in which combination of the geometrical figures each letter lay — circle only?, circle and triangle?, or all three? This required some thought — but all went well. I left the CTS with my Anns Road School companions and we discussed the various tests — and conjectured the outcome. There was nothing else to do but wait.

News of achievement in the entrance exam was posted to candidates a few weeks after sitting the tests. In my case never has a postman been so eagerly awaited — I imagine that is true of many others also! A few days later, on 8 December 1953, a large envelope arrived bearing the postmark of the Education Committee! I snatched it with a mixture of jubilation and apprehension. I was alone, my father having gone off to work in his customary manner just after 6.00 a.m. and my mother an hour later. I could not wait. I opened the letter to read the following:

Examination for Entrance to the
Central Technical School
Building Department

I have pleasure in informing you that your son has qualified, on the results of the above examination, for admission to the Central Technical School (Building Department) as from January 1954.

The Central Technical School will re-open after the Christmas vacation on Tuesday, 5th January, 1954.

Yours faithfully
STANLEY MOFFAT MA

Director of Education

Those of you who attended the CTS during the 1950s and early 1960s will have received a similar letter to mine — perhaps a few other such letters as mine have also survived? Stanley Moffat was a well-respected Director of Education; he was a graduate of Cambridge University and earned the Military Cross during the Second World War for his bravery. In effect, he was the next-door neighbour of the CTS since his office was in the Education Offices in Leopold Street.

Together with our admission letter you may recall there was a list identifying all the new things that we were required to purchase. These included the school uniform, boiler suit, woodwork apron, drawing instruments and so on.

My preparations for starting at the CTS involved going into town with my mother to purchase what was required in the way of uniform etc. I recall trying on a boiler suit at the Army & Navy Stores. My mother beamed with satisfaction but I felt self-conscious — even rather silly. I still have this garment — perhaps I'll wear it one day at an Old Boys' Association dinner! I took more pride in purchasing a set of drawing instruments at a shop opposite the Town Hall. The instructions with which we had been provided informed us that we were required to have a bag or satchel in which to carry our books. In her enthusiasm, my mother — always one to

err on the side of the generous — persuaded me to buy a particularly large case! It turned out to be sufficiently spacious to be capable of containing *all* my school books and equipment. Consequently, as I left for the CTS on my first day, I had the feeling that the people observing me go down Valley Road, where I lived, must have presumed I was taking a holiday!

First Day at the CTS

Memories of my first day at the CTS are etched in my mind for a number of reasons. When attending Carfield Primary and Junior Schools and Anns Road School, I had been able to walk to school — usually leaving my departure to the last possible minute. Now I had to travel into town by tram. This made me feel more grown up but also required me to be more organised. I caught the tram at Chesterfield Road, at the junction with Valley Road, on the Woodseats and Millhouses route. This was to be the basis of my departure for school for the next five years. My subsidised fare was one penny which increased over my five years at the CTS to three and then six pence. The tram took me to Pinstone Street from where it was but a few minutes walk to the Firth Building.

By way of interest, one of the trams on which I regularly journeyed to school — tram No 535 — is now preserved at the Beamish Heritage Museum. So it is still possible to re-create some of the enchantment of childhood by going for a tram ride. At the time of my schooling we considered the trams to be rather rickety old conveyances but they could deal with inclement weather — with the noteworthy exception of frozen points in winter. Also on occasions the overhead trolley bearing the electrical current would slip from the wire requiring the driver to restore it with the help of a large wooden pole — a rather hazardous operation. On rare occasions I arrived at school having journeyed on a single-decker tram. Even in 1954 it was a veritable museum piece. The seats were in two long rows down each side of the 'saloon'. A message in gold lettering read: "No spitting"!

On arriving in town I used to check the time with a glance at the imposing clock of the Town Hall. You will recall that our morning bell was 8.45 a.m. — prompt! I made the return journey catching the tram at the covered tram stops outside the Peace Gardens. Sometimes I varied the journey home by walking down to Fitzalan Square with some CTS lads who also went that way, in which case I travelled home by Queen's Road or Shoreham Street. I believe the CTS served quite a large catchment area and I know some CTS lads travelled considerably further afield than myself.

On my first day I arrived at the Firth Building and went into the School Hall to join a tightly packed throng of boys of different ages and stages in their school careers. The new boys were easily distinguished by their brand new school uniform — some even wore caps. Our rather uncertain demeanour also betrayed us as being new boys but this also provided us with a way of recognising one another and so we gradually fell into conversation. Inevitably we discussed our previous schools and we chatted about the things we had been required to purchase — and I tried to conceal my oversize case! I found out that one boy had actually passed the eleven-plus exam but had decided on a change of school and so duly sat the CTS entrance exam as well. There can't have been many CTS lads who achieved that particular feat.

I remember looking up into the gallery at the older boys who almost seemed middle-aged to my youthful gaze! This produced a reaction. Having taken the entrance exam twice, I was almost a year older than most of the new entrants and, being already on the tall side, it seemed to me that I stood out from the crowd of new boys rather as did General Charles de Gaulle amidst his contemporaries — in fact there were a few other new boys taller than myself. As we new boys stood in the School Hall my stature caught the gaze of a boy looking down from the balcony — perhaps it was one of you reading this? He called down something onomatopoeic like: "Na den thee, 'ow old o tha?" I replied, dutifully, "Thirteen and a half". The lad turned to share this information with his companions who promptly all stared at me with curiosity. One of them pointed to my over-large case. He was about to pass a, doubtless pejorative, remark when — deciding that attack is the best form of defence — I resolved to get in first by pretending my case weighed a ton. It was in fact empty since we had not yet been given any school books. My show of humour worked; it disarmed my would-be-tormentors who all bust out laughing. I recall having two thoughts: one, "Mum why did you buy me such a large case?"; and two, "I think I'm going to get on OK here"!

A teacher, whom I later discovered was named Mr. Thomas Dove, arranged us into two neat rows. To achieve this he directed our attention to the underside of the balcony where small pieces of paper were pinned bearing the designations of our classes; 3X, 3Y, 3A and so on. Amazingly, on the occasion of the *Open Day* of the City of Sheffield Education Department (5/6th October 2001) those of us who visited the CTS buildings were able to see these markers still in their respective positions.

When we were assembled into an orderly line, Mr. Dove walked amongst us with the Class Register, calling out our names and requiring us to reply: "Yes Sir"! We were all present and correct. And how correct! Each boy had a new blazer, grey flannel trousers, school tie and a satchel or case — some larger then others! A bell then sounded and the assembled concourse of boys, with remarkable discipline, fell into a state of absolute silence. Something was clearly about to happen! And it did!

Herbert W. Wadge

Moments later the floor seemed almost to vibrate as in strode a black-gowned colossus — I contemplated, for the first time, the magnificent and intimidating form of our new headmaster Herbert W. Wadge.

"Be seated"! he thundered, with stentorian vigour — in Greek legend Stentor had a voice as loud as fifty men (see *Iliad* 5. 783–5). The shear volume of this admonition stirred in me the thought that, on a clear day, Herbert Wadge must have been audible in Rotherham! I surveyed the noble form before me. His six feet two inches was further enhanced by massive, shiny-black shoes with triple-thickness soles. "What a work is man", remarks Shakespeare. He could well have had Herbert W. Wadge in mind. Here, indeed, was an impressive mortal! A veritable god — an *Osymandias* (Shelly's name for the ancient Egyptian god *Rameses*). Once we boys were seated, cross-legged on the floor, an

address followed exhorting the virtues of punctuality, school uniform, not dropping litter, of moral wholesomeness and steadfast resolution — and a dozen more similar themes. School uniform, I recall, came in for Herbert's most earnest exhortations. We were not to be seen wearing, the then fashionable, 'donkey jackets'; drainpipe trousers were equally taboo — fit only for 'Teddy Boys'; 'beetle crusher' shoes were out, as were 'winkle-pickers'; finally, we were exhorted to carry our school books in bags or satchels — not 'pokes' which were a form of duffel-bag that made soft-backed books crumple. Then we received encouragement to eat wholesome food. This was my first introduction to one of Herbert Wadge's eccentricities of punctuation, namely, 'fud' for food. Another one was 'fo' for four. With the passing of time we accepted these little peculiarities of Herbert's style of delivery as being perfectly normal.

At the close of his 'sermon', Mr. Wadge introduced the new boys to the tradition of 'Formal departure from Assembly', conducted by the School Captain — a boy by the name of Rudd who, to my youthful gaze, looked so grown-up he could have been my uncle. "School — Aaatteeennnsssshhhuuunnn!", croaked Rudd, in vocal imitation of his intimidating mentor. At his command, we all stood rigidly to attention. It was then that I noticed how Rudd's legs were gently swaying in the manner of the simple harmonic motion that I was to eventually learn about in physics. Assembly, and its rituals over, we made our way to our form classroom to be introduced to our form master.

First Class Meeting

First Year Builders were admitted to either Class 3Y or Class 3X; First Year Engineers were admitted to the equivalent Classes 3A, 3B, 3C or 3D. All these classes had the same academic standing; there was no streaming according to ability — everything was fair and democratic.

I was in Class 3Y, the form room of which was located on the upper floor of Bow Building. I recall once trying to explain the CTS system of class nomenclature to a boy from another school. He had assumed that 'A' represented the top of academic excellence and 'Y' the 'pits'. Mr. Dove was our form master and he did his utmost to put us at our ease. He told a joke along the following lines; at break our liquid refreshment was to be a bottle of milk and we should resist all temptation to call next door to the Red Lion to get a quick pint — we laughed dutifully. We were then initiated into the formalities of a typical Monday morning the most important of which was the collection of dinner money and the issuing of dinner tickets. The latter were colour coded and had to be kept carefully because if you lost your ticket you had to go without your school dinner. All of this was a completely new experience for me since, until then, I had always gone home for my dinner — what we now call lunch. One boy in our class, by the name of Wright, was exempted from paying for his school meals because he had no father — what we now call having a single parent. The alternative to school dinner was to bring sandwiches and to eat them in the gallery in the School Hall — something I never did.

Having considered matters temporal, Mr. Dove then turned to matters spiritual and issued us with our timetable. We quickly noticed this included 'mechanics'. "But, sir, I thought we were going to be Builders?", queried one boy. Mr. Dove explained that mechanics was something to do with the laws of motion and pulleys and levers and other incomprehensible things. He reassured us that mechanics at the CTS was nothing to with old cars and vehicle maintenance. But we didn't really believe him, after all we had each of us been equipped with a boiler suit. "What are our boiler suits for then sir?", we chorused. "You will see", replied the ever-patient Mr. Dove.

I went home that evening feeling very proud. Here I was at a new school, attired in a new uniform, with an attaché case full of new books and equipment, and, moreover, going in and out of town, like a 'grown-up', on the tram. The collective effect of all of this was to confer upon me hitherto inexperienced feelings of status and well-being. We had been provided with a considerable number of textbooks and exercise books which were all required for our future studies. Mr. Dove's first-day instructions to us were for each of these to be covered with plain brown-paper. I dutifully spent the next few evenings covering every single book — it took some boys about a year to achieve this — and a few boys never bothered at all despite Mr. Dove's dark imprecations. Soon in my possession was a copy of that stand-by for CTS Builders, namely, the Collins *Architects & Builders Diary*. I have a surviving copy before me now and I see it provides such useful information as — 'the flushing capacity of a urinal' — fascinating!

My career at the CTS followed the class sequence, 3Y, 5X, 6X (one term only), A1Y (two terms only), A2Y and A3. By the way, do you remember your class register? I wonder how many times each week we recited our names by way of checking the class attendance? I suppose the answer is ten since completing the register was part of our twice-daily routine — morning and afternoon — so much so that we took it for granted. I still recall how one of my Class Registers (Form 5X) started; here it is: 'Akaster, Allen, Baker, Butcher, Caunt, Dearden' — that's enough. It was the responsibility for the Form Monitor to take the completed register to the Firth Building and to return it to its allotted place in the rack on the stair-landing outside Herbert Wadge's office. I did this for a whole term.

Have you ever considered how our class designations came about? I don't suppose you have lost much sleep over this, but here, for the record, is what I was once told by no less an authority than Herbert Wadge himself. Apparently it was decided to start the class numbering at '3' instead of '1' so that we boys at the CTS would be in step with our contemporaries at other schools — all very logical. 'A', 'B', 'C' and 'D' were reserved for Engineers as I have already explained and 'X' and 'Y' for Builders — but only for the first three years. Many boys left at that point with either the Engineering Diploma or the equivalent Building Diploma. However, by the time of my joining the CTS, boys were staying on to take their O.L. and A.L. General Certificate of Education, the 'GCE', for which three more classes were added, namely, A1Y, A2Y and A3 — in which Engineers dominated in terms of numbers. You all knew that but I thought I would just mention it by way of saying:

In the following narrative I do not conform to a strict chronological class sequence but recall events, and some of the personalities who shaped them, under broad subject headings.

English

Class 3Y

It is fitting that I should start this part of my reminiscence with English, since this subject was taught to Class 3Y by Mr. Dove, my form teacher as I have remarked, our class being located in Bow Building. Our inadequacies often provoked him into a lather of cosmetic fury when he was given to exclaiming: "You duck eggs!", often followed by a little smile to reveal that — this inherently kindly man — was not being too serious. On another occasion we had experience of Mr. Dove's gentle humour when he introduced us to 'Naughty Benny' as follows. One day we came to a passage in our class textbook which was marked 'NB'. "Ah", remarked Mr. Dove, "You have to be on the lookout for 'NB'! He appears in the most unexpected places". Then he became more serious, explaining that NB denoted *nota bene*, in Latin, or 'Note Well' — hence Mr. Dove's play on words 'Naughty Benny'.

On one occasion, when Mr. Dove did become rather cross, he said to the offending boy: "When I am about to take my last breath I will think of how I wasted it on you"! One of Mr. Dove's favourite sayings was: 'Manners Maketh Man', usually by way of gaining the attention of someone who was creating a distraction by talking. A frequent cause of such distractions was a boy called Phillpotts — excuse my making this accusation Mr. Phillpotts if you are reading this. Mr. Dove would glare and remark: "You will never be as good as your namesake if you fail to pay attention" — this was, of course, a reference to the novelist Eden Phillpotts. The name of another boy from Class 3Y comes to mind, namely, Jack Timms. Mr. Dove once disclosed to us, by way of achieving a friendly rapport, that he had taught Jack's father; this inclined me to conjecture that Mr. Dove must be quite old; he was, of course, relative to our youthful selves and lived, I believe, to well into his nineties. Jack, by the way, on leaving school became a bricklayer. I know this because I recall seeing him one day as we were walking (running) down to Cathedral School for dinner — he was working on a building site. I called out a friendly greeting, which he misinterpreted as irony or sarcasm, thereby inducing him to proffer me the victory sign — so much for 'Manners maketh man'. Now a brief digression from English lessons.

At this period I recall Mr. Dove occasionally came to school in a Jowett Javelin motor car which was so spotless Mr. Davis once remarked: "I think Mr. Dove just drives his car on a Sunday and brings it to school only when he has to"!

One of the pleasures of Mr. Dove's classes was to listen to him read extracts from short stories and books. He had us convulsed with laughter at the antics in Jerome K. Jerome's *Three Men in a Boat* and there was a little morality tale called *The Mixer*, all about a dog which had to go out and scrounge for a living urged on by his mother who barked (literally): "Life's not all bones and liver you know"! How very true.

Mr. Dove was good at imparting a touch of humour to learning about certain aspects of English which could otherwise be rather dry and intimidating. This was evident one day when he discussed the question of 'style' in writing. This is quite a difficult concept. We could recognise that Shakespeare had a different style from the way we talked, not least because to our ears his language sounded so elaborate and 'old fashioned'. But the more general question of style in the works of other authors we found rather perplexing. To help us along, Mr. Dove read various texts to us from the writings of various authors to illustrate how grand and eloquent words are appropriate for some circumstances and how more everyday words are acceptable for others. Then we had some fun by listening to him reading to us a selection of texts which were either deliberately too grand and pompous or which were too casual and informal. We had to suggest alternatives. To show how this went here are some examples: 'We ceased from our labours and partook of a frugal repast'. (We stopped work and had lunch.); 'We went for a quick spin on our grid irons'. (We went for a short cycle ride.); 'We undertook a peregrination of the surviving remnants of the venerable edifice'. (We had a walk round the old ruins.) and so on. Lessons like this started to make English language more accessible to us and a pleasure to learn.

More philosophical was Hilaire Belloc's *The Perfect Game*, concerning a man who, whilst playing croquet, discovers he can't do anything wrong — and the prospect of being so perfect terrifies him. More serious was George Orwell's *1984* which was shown at this same period in time on BBC TV, featuring a youthful Peter Cushing, before his *Hammer House of Horror* fame — or, should one say, notoriety. At the time the sombre 'predictions' of the broadcast caused something of a national sensation.

At this time at the CTS, a number of us had occasion to incur the wrath of Herbert Wadge. Our misdemeanour was to have been dilatory in returning from Cathedral School. This circumstance arose from the fact that we had lingered behind a few moments talking about a piece of instruction that had been left behind on the blackboard. We eventually arrived back at the main building and who should be on the lookout for such stragglers but Herbert himself. He roared at us, somewhat like a lion in the undergrowth announcing its presence to its prey, and duly appeared in our midst. He chastised us for being late — may I say within earshot and in full view of the passers-by in West Street. Our protests were to no avail. He took our names and said we would be reported to our Form Master — Mr. Dove. News of our supposed wrong doing eventually reached the ears of Mr. Dove who required an explanation; it was left to myself to supplicate on behalf of the small group of errant lads. I explained, with some indignation, that, far from being wayward, our only sin was that of being diligent — in staying behind after class to talk for a few minutes about some aspect of the work which had perplexed us. Mr. Dove was clearly impressed, either by my powers of advocacy or the reasonableness of our case — or both. The outcome was that we were spared the ordeal of having to do further penance before Herbert Wadge — which, needless to say, we had all been dreading. The matter passed without further incident — well, almost. Herbert was not a man to give in too easily! A few days later in morning assembly he did a rant on the need to be punctual for classes at all times, adding: "Did you speak to those boys whom I caught the other morning Mr. Dove?". "Yes", replied Mr. Dove — dutifully. Herbert then changed his subject and we errant lads could at last breath more easily.

It was also at about this same period that a small group of us attempted to prevail upon Mr. Dove to let us establish a School Magazine. At the very mention of this proposal his face assumed a look of reproach that was quite untypical of Mr. Dove who was the mildest and most good-natured of teachers. He listened to our arguments patiently. Our ambitions knew no bounds; we would have sections devoted to news, personal achievements, jokes! — and so on and so forth. Mr. Dove shook his head wearily remarking: "Boys. I've heard all this before — and what happens? A few individuals work hard to produce but a single issue and then all interest wanes and the enterprise fizzles out". We looked at one another rather sheepishly somewhat disappointed but also recognising the truth of what we had been told. So that was the last that I ever heard of a School Magazine.

Two years later, in preparation for our Building Diploma, Mr. Dove took us once more for English language and literature. The latter included reading *A Midsummer Night's Dream*, whose plot-within-a-plot I found difficult. More to my liking was *The Tempest* which has remained my favourite Shakespeare play. It was produced at one of Sheffield's lesser-known theatres called *The Lantern*. I went along to see it. What I most recall of the production was the back-lighting which rendered Miranda's dress diaphanous! This prompts me to recall how Mr. Dove explained that the line 'Admired Miranda!' was a pun, or a play on words. Another TV broadcast at this period was Henrik Ibsen's *Peer Gynt*. It was broadcast in two parts, part one on Tuesday evening and part two the following Thursday evening. Peer was performed by the youthful Peter Ustinov — a *bravura* performance. What still lingers in my memory, however, was the effect of Grieg's incidental music. Indeed, following the production I went to see Mr. Dove to ask: "What is that lovely song the woman sings"? "*Solveig's Song*", came the reply from a rather startled Mr. Dove — more used to boys going to see him to do a penitential grovel for late homework! Another broadcast stands out in my mind resulting from Mr. Dove's own enthusiasm for music. One day, at the end of a lesson, he sent us away exclaiming: "Boys! Tonight is an historic occasion"! This secured our attention at once. "Tonight", continued a clearly excited Mr. Dove, "the eighth symphony of Vaughan Williams will be performed for the first time"! The news was greeted in disappointed silence, punctuated with a few ironic remarks of the kind "Great", and "What's a symphony"? But, ever dutiful, I tuned in to the Third Programme that eventful evening, in 1956, to listen to this new work — to be honest, I found it hard going. By way of an aside, I will insert here that a teenage girl called Mary, played the violin in the first few performances of this very symphony at the Royal Academy of Music and the Festival Hall in the presence of the composer. This young woman later became Mrs. Mary Russell B.A., A.T.C.L. — but that is another story! Allow me to say I took leave of Class 3Y with the English Subjects Prize, Form Prize and First Year Prize.

Class 5X

In Class 5X, clause analysis was taught by Mr. Colin Brook, who had shiny 'Bryllcreamed' hair. With Mr. Brook we struggled with clause analysis, endeavouring to learn about sentence structure and syntax. Few of the class found any of this congenial. Notwithstanding the class got on with Mr. Brook rather well and when Christmas time came we had a whip-round for him and collected 15/6s — I think that's how we used to write fifteen shillings and six pence. I was given the responsibility of purchasing a present for him; I chose a book called *A Leopard in My Lap* by Armand and Micaëla Denise — two then popular presenters of a TV wild-life programme. I had to go to the front of the class to hand over the book and to make a short presentation speech — the first time I had ever done so. I tried so hard that I rather over did it. As I went back to my seat, my *gravitas* prompted a boy in the class called Cosgrove, who had a delightful wit to remark: "Where's he get all them bleedin' big words from"? This was the perfect antidote and made everyone laugh. Mr. Brook, in response to the gift, opened his bag and took out a bottle of whisky which, he explained, he could not share with us but he also produced a bag of sweets that he handed round the class — making us all feel very convivial.

I recall another time in class with Mr. Brook when he made us laugh by poking gentle fun at the Yorkshire idiom. He did not himself have the slightest trace of a Yorkshire accent and spoke very posh, so to hear him use our Yorkshire dialect and vernacular words had us in fits of laughter. Here is a selection of words and phrases he cited with 'interpretations' in brackets: 'Geronanit' (Get away); 'Shut thi' cake hole.' (Close you mouth.); 'Lug hole' (Ear); 'Obstrocolous' (Obstreperous); 'Mardy' (Churlish); 'Nesh' (Susceptible to cold) — and lots more. His intention was to encourage us to learn how to 'talk proper' and this humorous approach helped us by not being too moralistic or censorious.

English was also taught to 5X by Mr. Joseph Whitlow — who was also our Form Master for one term. Our other two Form Masters in 5X were Mr. Brook and Mr. Thomas Thornton. The most striking recollection I have of Mr. Whitlow was that he was completely ambidextrous. He never made any great show of this nor did he discuss it. In fact this ability of his only came to my notice one day when — attentive as always (!) — I observed him pass the chalk from one hand to the other. It came about like this; he was writing something on the blackboard (with his right hand) when, approaching the left-hand corner of the room, he resumed writing with his left hand to give himself more space. I have other reasons for recalling Mr. Whitlow. It was with him that we read, amongst other things, John Buchan's counter-espionage thriller *The Thirty-Nine Steps*. In this work we became acquainted with the hero Richard Hanney. Another text we studied with Mr. Whitlow, which formed the basis for a question on the Class 5X English exam paper, was Oliver Goldsmith's *She Stoops to Conquer* — or, *The Mistakes of a Night*. The play is all about deliberate confusion and mistaken identity. The exam question, by the way, was on this very aspect of the play, namely: "What were the mistakes of the night in *She Stoops to Conquer*"? Your answers to me please, in soft pencil, on the back of a £20 note.

Mr. Whitlow was good at making us laugh. This was most evident when he made references to word misuse — malapropisms. — or slips in pronunciation. In this spirit he once recalled a boy who endeavoured to make use of his rather limited French in an essay. The lad wrote: "Parlez vous français?", for which the reply should have been "Oui"! Instead the lad wrote: "Parlez vous français?" "Oy"!

A temporary teacher of English joined the school at this time by the name of Mr. Jones. He had a disfiguring scar down the right side of his face. He was essentially a classicist, being an authority on Greek and Latin — he did not have much scope for demonstrating those skills at the CTS. Chance conspired that I should fall into conversation with Mr. Jones one night as we went home on the tram — he lived near Meersbrook Park. On disembarking (if that is what getting off a tram is called) we continued our conversation for the best part of an hour on the pavement. We talked about 'everything'; our exchanges became a kind of contest — very much a David and Goliath affair. I remember we disputed whether the symphonies or the late quartets were Beethoven's greatest legacy to mankind — all very elevating. At the end of our conversation, Mr. Jones said he would place me, according to intelligence, in the upper ten percent of the population. On reflection, I am not sure whether to feel proud, of being so favoured, or offended, at being so lightly rated! Of wider interest are two other of his observations which I will relate. He said how he much admired Mr. Wadge for his passion and commitment and Mr. Hughes for his intelligence and musicianship. This was a rare instance of a member of staff expressing his views, about his colleagues, to a pupil.

In our English lessons, we were encouraged to read 'good books', "to widen our knowledge of elevating literature" — or something of the kind. I embarked upon Henry Rider Haggard, working my way, during the holidays, through *King Solomon's Mines, She, Allan Quatermain* and half a dozen other novels. Then I set about Charles Dickens and read *Oliver Twist, Nicholas Nickleby, The Old Curiosity Shop* and *Barnaby Rudge*.

The exhortation to read works of literary merit was also endorsed by Mr. Wadge. Some of you may recall how the entire school was required to learn by heart Rupert Brooke's *The Soldier.*

If I should die think only this of me:
That there's some corner of a foreign field
That is for ever England. There shall be
In that rich earth a richer dust concealed;
A dust whom England bore, shaped, made aware,
Gave once, her flowers to love, her ways to roam,
A body of England's, breathing English air.
Washed by the rivers, blest by suns of home.

There must be many of you of my 'generation' who still carry these famous and moving lines in your head.

Allow me to say I took leave of Class 5X with the English Subjects Prize, Form Prize and Second Year Prize.

Class 6X

I spent one term only in Class 6X and therefore participated in relatively few English lessons. These were taken once more by Mr. Dove. There were two broad themes to his classes. One aspect concentrated on grammar, syntax and correct word usage — learning to say '*our* books' and not '*us* books' and so on. The other aspect was, in effect, English Literature and had more of a focus on plays, passages from books and selected texts. Let me briefly call to mind the Building Diploma exam in English (1956). We were set questions on Shakespeare's *The Tempest*, which, if you have been paying attention (!), you will recall my saying was my favourite Shakespeare play. There was also a set of questions of a biographical kind. We were asked to write about Madame Curie — remember, Nobel Laureate in Physics *and* Chemistry and about Dame Emmeline Pankhurst — remember, the ardent campaigner for womans' suffrage. Some time after the exam I chanced to meet Mr. Dove who called out to me: "Russell! Your English paper was very good!". "Nice one", I thought, "Sounds like that's another Distinction in the bag"! Excuse the lack of modesty but that's the way it was.

O.L. English

In my time at the CTS, preparation for English O.L. was entrusted to Mr. Roger Hughes. We worked intensively on past papers — not to be confused with 'passed papers'! There was general agreement that English was a 'hard' subject to get through. It was indeed rumoured at my time that a boy had once achieved a mark of 70%, but most of us were more than willing to settle for a basic pass. Mr. Hughes drilled us in the skills of précis writing, parts of speech and writing short commentaries on extracts from books. I have an anecdote from this time as follows. Some of you may recall a film titled *The Man Who Never Was*. It purported to be based on the real-life circumstances of an episode in the Second World War — the details of which need not concern us. What is relevant is the manner of the film's opening which depicts a scene of waves washing upon a shore following which a voice is heard to say: 'Last night I dreamed a deadly dream where, beyond the Isle of Skye, I saw a dead man win a fight — and I think that man was I'. These are haunting words and I was captivated by them. I resolved to find out more and so, believing that teachers know everything, I recounted them to Mr. Hughes and asked: "Can you tell me who wrote these lines"? He paused for a moment, reflected and then said: "Samuel Taylor Coleridge — *The Rime of the Ancient Mariner*"? And then he added: "No that's not right, sorry I can't help"! Well, I am still waiting to learn the identity of the author of my 'haunting lines' but my exchange with Mr. Hughes had introduced me to Coleridge's epic poem concerning the hapless mariner who, in case you are unfamiliar with the work, incautiously slays an albatross, innocently attendant upon his ship, with unrelenting awesome consequences. By way of a footnote to this tale I can add that I once saw a memorial to the fallen in the Great War bearing the moving lines: 'And the many men so beautiful, they all dead did lie'! These come from Coleridge's poem. If you are not familiar with this work may I take the liberty of encouraging you to search it out — you will find it even more gripping than *Match of the day*!

With the advent of summer and the warmer weather, Mr. Hughes took to wearing a light beige-coloured linen jacket. We affectionately called this his 'ice-cream coat' because of its resemblance to the similar-looking jacket typically worn by an ice cream vendor. I recall how one afternoon a boy in class overstepped the mark and, on seeing Mr. Hughes in his linen jacket — which suited him (no pun intended) very well, called out "Ice cream"! Mr. Hughes simply responded with a dark withering gaze. When truly provoked, and there were times when we undoubtedly tried his patience, he would admonish the class in such a manner that his voice — normally set rather high in the tenor range — would lower to the baritone register. This was usually sufficient to restore order. Mr. Hughes's ultimate disciplinary sanction was to threaten with the words: "Look, do you want me to send you to Mr. Hedley"? That could only mean one thing! Perhaps some of you reading this actually experienced the 'ordeal' of paying a visit to Mr. Hedley! There was in fact very little class disruption in our year of O.L. English — for two reasons. The first is we were only too

mindful of the need to concentrate and to work hard. The second is more subtle. I do not wish to sound sycophantic but it was beginning to dawn on the class that Mr. Hughes's was a bright chap with good critical skills — and was prepared to work hard on our behalf!

Notwithstanding what I have just written, levity was never very far below the surface in some of our lessons, no more so than on 1st April — *All Fools' Day*. I imagine this is a day most teachers dread, or, at least, have to endure. Here's how things went one day when fate conspired that 1st April should coincide with one of Mr. Hughes's English lessons. Earlier in the morning in class with Mr. Alfred Simpson — of whom more later — we had tried staring at the ceiling with a fixed gaze but he didn't fall for that. Later in the day with Mr. Hughes, we realised we had to be more subtle. Someone had the idea of inserting a match into the folds of the board rubber — you may remember the eraser part consisted of layers of compacted felt. It worked like a treat. An unsuspecting Mr. Hughes vigorously dusted off the blackboard — and duly ignited the match! He dropped the rubber, with a mixture of fright and self-protection, picked it up and acknowledged our inventiveness with the observation: "That's a fair cop"! We had our little laugh and work then resumed in orderly fashion on clause analysis and similar wonderful things.

Let me return to being generous about Mr. Hughes — not least because there was an occasion in class when he was generous to me. One day, at about this period, reading through one of my compositional efforts, Mr. Hughes paid me the following compliment: "Russell, I think you are beginning to be able to say what you mean"! I think I was more perplexed than flattered — but I appreciated the remark. This leads me to something altogether more significant. We were certainly all perplexed one day by a comment which Mr. Hughes made that was clearly intended to provoke us. It came one afternoon just as we were packing up to go home — waiting for the 4.10 p.m. bell. Mr. Hughes, being in one of his more reflective moods, engaged our attention with the observation: "What is the most challenging thing that an individual can do"? This certainly had us guessing; what was he getting at? Was the answer to run a mile faster than Roger Bannister? — which had only just then been achieved. Was it to understand the Theory of Relativity? Was it to understand the meaning of life? The answer was none of these — and when it came it perplexed us even more. "One of the most difficult things for each of us", said Mr. Hughes, "is to think"! There was silence — then uproar — which made Mr. Hughes smile. Moments later he was, as it were, 'saved by the bell' and he left the room leaving us debating amongst ourselves what his proposition concealed. We failed to grasp his meaning and left it at that. Reflecting on this episode sometime later, I concluded that Mr. Hughes was in effect saying that it is for each of us, within our powers and limitations, to reason and to take a view about things based upon a rational assessment of the evidence. That's all rather grand but it has been a guiding principle for me ever since in my own life and work. So thank you Mr. Hughes for opening that particular window of my mind.

At the time in question the teaching of English was shared with another teacher by the name of Mr. Edward Brennan — who was at the CTS for only a few years. He stayed long enough to be our Form Master in A1Y jointly with Mr. Charlesworth. With Mr. Brennan we read

Joseph Conrad's somewhat melancholy tale *Heart of Darkness*. I believe it was from this short story that I became acquainted with the aphorism 'Death, the gateway to life'. Words were beginning to have a fascination for me, and, perhaps for that reason, one day I put up my hand and asked: "Sir, how do you say that in Latin"? Mr. Brennan looked rather startled but, quite unabashed replied: "*mors porta vitae est*". I suppose he considered being asked such a question as one of the occupational hazards of being a school teacher. At this period he acquainted us with some of the writings of Milton, one such text including the tag 'The life so short, the craft so long to learn'. I have since worked out my own Latin for this, namely, '*ars longa, vita brevis*' — that's close enough. I often use this saying with my First Year students to convey the idea that whilst the length of time required to qualify to be an architect is seven years, the real business of mastering the subject requires a lifetime.

We had a good rapport with Mr. Brennan and one afternoon the class discussion took an inclination towards the supernatural — i.e., he invited us to offer views about para-normal happenings. I should add this was prompted by the theme of a class text we had been considering. The drift of the discussion led Mr. Brennan to tell us a story — a good ploy to secure the attention of a class. It concerned a drinking glass that appeared to move under its own free will! In his student days, following a drinking session (!), Mr. Brennan and some companions resolved to put the theory of levitation to the test. Apparently, each member of the group placed a hand above the glass and issued it with the command to move. "And do you know", affirmed Mr. Brennan, "to our amazement the glass began to move"! All he failed to add was how many pints he and his pals had had to drink!

There is a corollary to the tale I have just recalled — a kind of psycho-analytic reflection. As teachers began to share with us little insights into their own lives — and Mr. Brennan was by no means the only one to do so — it increased what today we would call our 'feel good factor'. By this I mean our self-esteem was enhanced; we were made to feel less like little school boys and more like young men in whom a teacher could confide.

One particular afternoon in Mr. Brennan's classes will always stand out in my mind because, with hindsight, I see it as a moment of 'intellectual coming of age' — this is what I mean.

Mr. Brennan started his lesson with the question: "Which writer has the claim to being the 'father of science fiction' "? Before you read on, take a moment to think about that — and consider how you might have replied. I had no doubt and volunteered the answer: "Jules Verne"? A rather startled Mr. Brennan asked me why. Now, "Chance", said Dr. Johnson "favours the prepared mind". In a way my mind had long been prepared for this question. Let me explain; in 1948 my aunt had bought me a copy of Jules Verne's *A Journey to the Centre of the Earth* and, in 1952, whilst rummaging in the attic of my friend David Dickson — to whom I have already referred — I 'found', and set about reading, a copy of *Twenty-Thousand Leagues Under the Sea*. I went on to discover other works of Verne including; *Earth to the Moon* and, the better known, *Around the World in Eighty Days*. I offered these books as examples to Mr. Brennan of Jules Verne's claim to be the father of science fiction on the grounds of his anticipation of space flight and international travel by flight and submarine. "Very interesting", came Mr. Brennan's riposte, "Nevertheless, I think H. G. Wells has the stronger claim". It so happens that *Encyclopaedia Britannica* describes Jules Verne as: 'A French writer … a founder of modern science fiction'. Shall we leave it that our point-scoring exchange was about even!

Mr. Brennan clearly enjoyed teaching older boys. I think this was because it gave him the opportunity to engage our minds with more serious propositions than was the case with younger lads lower down the school. I can illustrate this point by making reference to one of Mr. Brennan's personal enthusiasms, namely the young romantic poet Keats. In so doing, allow me to be rather more serious here myself. One afternoon, during a lesson which we were having down at Cathedral School, Mr. Brennan paused in what he was saying. His subject was Shakespeare and, with some emotion, he exclaimed: "Do you know, if he had lived longer, I believe the reputation of Keats would have rivalled that of Shakespeare"! I remember being quite startled by this assertion. I am not sure if, at that age, I had even heard of Keats. So, to hear of him as being a possible challenger to Shakespeare, the *ne plus ultra* observer of, and commentator upon, the human condition was a somewhat remarkable proposition. Be this as it may, for a few minutes there was no stopping Mr. Brennan in his enthusiasm for the doomed poet — who died, of consumption, at the shockingly early age of twenty six. He intrigued us by making references to the imagery to be found in *The Eve of St. Agnes, To a Nightingale* and *On a Grecian Urn*. He elaborated his views with various lines from Keats' works including: 'A thing of beauty is a joy forever', 'Season of mists and mellow fruitfulness/Close bosom-friend of the maturing sun' and other equally evocative fragments. I have since made my own 'discovery' of Keats and can now understand why Mr. Brennan was so captivated by the man and his work. This prompts me to take leave of this episode with a challenge — I told you this bit was going to be serious. Consider that you have to select a single piece of literary text to deposit in a time capsule — to be opened in a thousand years time. The idea is to inspire our remote descendants as to the grandeur of the human condition as we have known it. What text would you choose? Here is my choice — and it comes from the works of Keats:

'Beauty is truth, truth beauty', — that is all
Ye know on earth, and all ye need to know.

Now let me get back to Mr. Brennan, but still in a rather serious vein.

One day I arrived early for a lesson — nothing unusual in that for one so punctilious and hardworking as myself (!). As a matter of fact, it was raining hard and I had simply gone inside to shelter. Be this as it may, I found myself alone for a moment with Mr. Brennan — who most certainly was punctilious and hardworking. At this stage in our lessons he was encouraging us to practice 'essay writing' — what, lower down the school, we called 'composition'. He confided his feelings in me with the following remark: "Russell, you don't know what a pleasure it is to work with this class"! I was somewhat taken aback — used as I was by then to believing we were generally thought to be little more than a bunch of idle slackers. He explained the reason for his high estimation of us. He had been reading through our latest essays and was suitably impressed. Looking through my own efforts to master this aspect of the curriculum, I unearthed the following youthful creation — it comes from my time in Class 6X. The theme is somewhat topical and I use it to conclude this part of my reflections. In the essay which follows I have corrected the spelling and revised the punctuation, otherwise the text is as I originally wrote it.

I was a Titanic survivor
An Essay for Mr. Brennan
Terry Russell
1956

Throughout the great shipyard of Southampton, initially during the cold winter months and through to early spring, the sounds of the world's greatest ship being born had been heard. At first her ribs had pierced the sky like stricken pines beneath the Mistral. Then her jacket, tooled and machined with infinite care, had enveloped her entrails to produce the most beautiful silhouette since that of the Cutty Sark's. All this was some weeks ago, and now the Titanic, for this was the ship that had been under construction, was carrying us ever closer to Cape Race — and disaster.

There were 1,800 passengers, amongst them members of every aristocratic circle in Europe. The elite mingled with the nobility whilst lesser folk were confined to the steerage. Little did anyone realise in what short space of time they would all be reduced to the same common level.

The Titanic, sister ship to the Olympic, was the very embodiment of twentieth-century comfort, equipped with lavish and luxurious fittings well worthy of some apartment at Versailles. On the night in question, I was dining in one of her sumptuous restaurants which was bedecked with splendid tapestries complete with a magnificent Greek entablature executed in rosewood.

There was a calm atmosphere that night but somehow it was impregnated with expectancy. A feeling of events to come was upon me, a presentiment hung in the air like a cloud charged with electricity — but, even so, it was difficult to believe that anything could befall that utopian vessel. By eleven o'clock, I had said my adieus to my friends and had retired to my cabin, reflecting on the very agreeable day I had spent.

Earlier in the evening a friend had told me that since it was spring, and we were in northern latitudes, it might be possible to see the Aurora Borealis. As I was interested in this phenomenon, I glanced out of my porthole to see if I could view this spectacle. Imagine my horror when I saw, not coloured lights, but an iceberg of monolithic proportions — an iceberg which would have towered many feet above the pyramid at Cheops! The light from our ship was reflected from the many facets of the ice and gave it the false appearance of making the iceberg look like some angry glowing monster.

In a moment, our hull had been opened as if with a scalpel and already the ship began to writhe like some great beast in its death throes. At first, nothing could be heard save the ship's telegraph which rang out messages in organised confusion. Silence, born of people at rest, pervaded the ship. In minutes, however, our stricken ship was alive with frightened crowds of anxious passengers. The ship's air was forced out from her by the incoming waters and rose to the surface where it joined the environment with an arpeggio of rumblings.

The events which then passed now appear to me as being misty and unreal. It was as if we were plunged into an abyss of despondency and despair. We all ran around in a helpless manner and did nothing, whilst the half muffled strains of Auld Lang Syne were intermingled with cries of "Women and children first"! And, all the while, the water-level continued to rise. I remember staring into the darkness watching two lifeboats drift away on the icy waters when — there was a tremendous explosion. The cold water had flooded into the boiler room and had submerged some pipes carrying super-heated steam. This

had caused rapid condensation which contributed to the violent outburst — but which saved my life!

I was overcome by a sensation of lightness, and found myself blasted into the air and thereby precipitated into the unwelcoming sea. In a few seconds I had regained my senses and was striking towards a piece of flotsam which served me as a raft. I was saved!

On turning my head, I perceived the leviathan — once as firm and unbending as a caryatid — now broken and distressed. With a final convulsion, she settled into the water, very slowly upended and sank down to the sombre depths of the watery world of my dead companions.

French

Class 3Y

By happy coincidence, concerning what I have said previously about English, my first lessons in French were given by Mr. Dove in the form room of Class 3Y in Bow Building. Our first text was called, predictably, *La Salle de Classe*. I remember thinking, equally predictably, what odd ideas the French have about word order. Mr. Dove made our introduction to French as gentle and as interesting as possible. He told us how the soldiers in the Great War used to pronounce *Ypres* as *Wipers* and remarked about their army songs such as *Mademoiselle from Armentières — Parley Vous, Parley Vous*. Inevitably, we became familiar with *Sur Le Pont D'Avignon* and learned to sing it in rounds to Mr. Dove's vigorous style of conducting. This was all good fun.

For French lessons when I was in Class 3Y I sat next to a lad called Michael Porter. His father was rather fond of taking the family to the theatre and liked to splash out on occasions by sitting in the front stalls. At this time the tradition still prevailed in the theatre of calling these seats by their rather posh French name of *fauteuil* — literally 'armchairs'. Fauteuil is a difficult word to pronounce, especially if, as in the case of Michael's father, you have never studied any French. It appears that Michael's father had been in the habit of asking for so many seats in the 'fotails'! So Michael, on hearing Mr. Dove pronounce *fauteuil* correctly, resolved to go home and give his dad a French lesson. I don't know what his old man's reaction was to all this.

After the initial novelty of learning a foreign language had worn off — that is by our second lesson — we realised learning French was all about the assimilation of vocabulary, grammar, prose and comprehension. We learned about the role of different words, such as nouns, adjectives and verbs — especially the latter. We were told there were verbs of different types which ended with 'er', 'ir' and 're'. And we discovered that these had to be conjugated and learned by wrote, often to the rhythm of Mr. Dove's cane tapping against the blackboard — and it would, but only very occasionally, tap against more sensitive objects! It was by similar methods that we learned the order of pronouns remember; *me, te, se, le, la, les, lui, leur, y* and *en*. My head is still packed with 'rules' like 'indirect before direct except when they are both first person' — whatever that's supposed to mean!

Our first textbook ventures into these realms of foreign words were enlivened, in the time-honoured tradition of educators, by means of pictures. On leafing through my rather dog-eared, tear-stained copy of our class text book, my gaze fell upon a line drawing of a very pretty Esmeralda, which accompanied a text, much simplified, extracted from Victor Hugo's *Notre-Dame de Paris* — more familiarly *The Hunchback of Notre Dame*. Now, some previous owner of the book had thought to 'improve' upon the illustration of Esmeralda with the addition of a representation of a large phallic object. I took a dim view of this since I dreaded Mr. Dove accusing me of the indiscretion, in one of those interrogatory dialogues: "Who Sir?" "Me Sir?" "No Sir"? To my relief, such an exchange never came about.

Mr. Dove had recourse to a number of rather endearing expressions which he used to inculcate an aspect of French grammar or word usage. Worthy of recall is his 'Johnny construction'. Allow me to explain. You will recall that the French pronoun *en* means *some* or *any* — it has several other meanings but they are not relevant here. "Now", said Mr. Dove, "If I say: '*J en ai six*' it means I have six — of them". "This", he added, "is what we can describe as the *Johnny* construction"! For those who require a little help, *J en ai*, in French, is phonetically close to the English *Johnny* — hence Mr. Dove's play on words to help us to remember. This however is not the point of the story. What Mr. Dove had overlooked — in his delightful innocence — was the contemporary colloquial meaning that 'Johnny' then had to denote a contraceptive. So, on hearing Mr. Dove make reference to the 'Johnny construction' the class erupted in titters of mirth. Mr. Dove's response was to beam with pleasure, doubtless gratified that he had for once been able to rouse us from our slumbers — though not quite for the reasons he imagined!

Classes 5X and 6X

I started to enjoy French, as, indeed, did several others as we progressed through Class 5X to Class 6X. Our powers of expression steadily improved, our French 'rs' sounded more authentic and less like gargling, our grammar become more secure, we learned how to ask the time and translated useful phrases like: "Innkeeper, my horse has been struck by lightning"!

As always, things took a more serious turn — in the case in question in the direction of preparing for the O.L. French examination. To see if we were ready for this, the boys in Class 6X, my form at the time, sat a mock exam — alas, more of a mockery for some. We were required to write out a passage, from dictation, which, I recall, included such words as *malheureusement*, *espagnolette* and *essentiellement*. Some of the class sought inspiration by looking up at the ceiling, others stared rather dazed as though struck behind the head with a large lump of wet cod. But clever clogs myself did rather well, and, a few days later, Mr. Kenneth King, who than took the O.L. French class, came into Class 6X and told me to take my books to join the Engineers. They were in Class A1Y. In effect I thereby took the course in one year — instead of the normal two. So, it is to Mr. King's O.L. French class that I will now direct my narrative.

O.L. French

Our O.L. French classroom was located on the ground floor of the Bow Building, at the far end of the corridor near to the staircase which led up to Mr. Hedley's drawing office. There was a fireplace in one corner which gave the room a feeling of domestic comfort. Invariably Mr. King wore his gown giving him, and his lessons, an air of 'no nonsense' authority. His class handout *Difficult Phrases & Constructions* helped us to find our way around the 'depuis' and 'après avoir'

constructions, the passive voice — 'On vendait les billets', how to use 'pour' — 'trop occupé pour se reposer' and a dozen similar linguistic devices. A companion sheet *Vocabulary Exercises* had to be committed to memory. With this in mind, regular tests were set and all failed words had to be written out three times — inducing Mr. King to remark sardonically: "It would be much easier to learn them once than to write them out three times"!

I recall that Mr. King taught German at night school. He was much given to making comparisons between French and German, especially in the remark: "What I want is more *sprachegefühl*' — 'feeling for language'. A particularly pathetic effort at translation, or pronunciation, would invariable prompt the condemnation: "Where's your *sprachegefühl* lad"?

Mr. King was so imbued with French culture that he could not resist for very long straying away from his set theme to make some digression or other about the development of the French language. In this context one of his favourite themes was *Les Immortels*. The name derives from the Latin *immortalis* and in classical antiquity denoted the ancient Greek and Roman gods. The French bestowed the title on selected academicians who had, and retain, the custodianship of the French language. In effect they are the guardians of the French language and are dedicated to retaining its purity. They have been gradually working their way through the alphabet at the rate of about one word every twenty years — or something like that! Mr. King used to narrate these details gleefully, wondering if *The Immortals* would ever complete their work in his own lifetime. It would be quite interesting in fact to find out just how they have been getting on these last forty years or so!

At a somewhat less exalted level than the French *Immortels*, I remember once landing a boy, by the name of Bagshaw, in a spot of bother over incorrect French pronunciation. I deceived Bagshaw — *Baggy* as we used to call him — into believing that the French name *Croisilles* was pronounced 'Crosilles' — the very sound of which induced Mr. King into a rage. I should add that Baggy, who sat next to me, had not been paying much attention to our lesson as a consequence of leafing through a magazine depicting the actress Diana Dors in her underclothes!

There was an occasion when Mr. King really did get cross. He once caught a boy in class with a German revolver! He sent the lad home on the spot — I think he was called Ryder — and then lectured us on the evils of the Second World War and reflected on the lives of those of his French friends that had been blighted by the German occupation of France — Mr. King was a true Francophile.

Mention of the revolver, prompts me to recall how Mr. King once became involved in a 'dual' — a linguistic one. Here's what happened. To his great credit, Mr. King placed emphasis on learning French by practicing spoken French. A part of each lesson was set aside for French conversation and verbal reflections upon the piece of prose upon which we had been working. The afternoon came when a 'student' teacher joined us — fresh from his 'honours year' in France. The prose passage for the lesson concerned a weather vane, in the form of a cockerel, mounted on a church steeple. Asked to comment, I attempted a reply stating how, from its vantage point, the cockerel surveyed (*surveiller*) all below, turned (*se tourner*) in the wind and appeared almost to fly (*voltiger*) — then I foundered upon a subjunctive. Mr. King came to my rescue, supplied the difficult construction and then cautioned: "Don't try to be clever. Keep it simple"! At this point the student intervened (not on my behalf I should add) and set up an extended exchange with Mr. King — in French. The verbal ripostes developed into a contest of linguistic prowess. Honesty requires me to say that I think the student teacher won — his aural French was somewhat fresher than Mr. King's.

Mr. King was a linguistic purist who did his best to improve our English as a prerequisite to helping us on our way with French. Here, by way of illustration, is what I mean. He insisted that we place the adverb 'only' in its correct place. His favourite illustration was to compare the following two statements: "I only drink water" and "I drink water only". Think about it. The former means: "Of the many *uses* to which water can be put, I avail myself of it for drinking"; the latter means: "Of the many *drinks* available, I partake exclusively of water". Here's another of his favourites, namely the distinction between 'will' and 'shall'. Mr. King explained the difference by contrasting the following: "I shall drown, no one will save me!", and: "I will drown, no one shall save me"! One is a cry for help, the other is the defiant affirmation of someone with suicidal tendencies — but which is which? Once again, your correct answers to me please written in soft pencil on the back of £20 note!

Mr. King was always one to take advantage of an opportunity to promote our understanding of French, even to exploiting a popular tune of the day. Who remembers the following?

> 'K' sera, sera, whatever will be, will be.
> The future's not ours to see,
> 'K' sera, sera.

I believe that is how the lyric went. Mr. King said his daughter used to go around singing this song and then he explained to us the origins of *sera* as being a derivation from the French verb 'to be' in the future tense. The 'K' bit of the lyric led us into a class discussion of the *Qu'est-ce qui* (*what* as subject) and *Qu'est-ce que* (*what* as object) constructions — which of course you will all still remember? This was a good example of a teacher capitalising on popular culture as a means of getting inside our minds — although, to be honest, it didn't exactly make French-language construction any easier or more interesting!

A few reminders about the O.L. French exam will serve to recall how we learned our French. We had a written paper — French to English and, much harder, a paper English to French. Mr. King had a brilliant tip as to how to succeed with the latter, or at least how to make a good stab at it. His advice was, when writing out the required passage in French, to look through the exam paper and then to use as many French words as you could that appeared on the paper. This way you stood a good chance of spelling the French words properly! It was a good tip and I followed it dutifully. There was also a French aural dictation and a short aural test conceived to assess our pronunciation — for the majority of the class it has to be confessed that our pronunciation was rather Churchillian! The aural test also assessed our skills in French conversation. The aural dictation took place in Cathedral School — what a grand name by the way for such depressing surroundings. Mr. King read the French text moving to a different location so as to be equally audible to everyone. The text in question for our O.L. French was about the agreeable effect of sunlight entering a room. By happy chance, that same morning Mr. King had rehearsed several of the constructions that occurred in the exam text. So that part of the exam went well for me. The aural test is no less clear in my mind. We were required to read a set piece from Georges Simenon's *The Choir Boy's Evidence*. It commenced: "On entering the room, one noticed that it was too bright with wallpaper decorated with flowers and bizarre furniture". After reading the text, we were required to comment, in French, on a picture of a boy climbing a tree in which a bird's nest could be seen. A short period of conversation followed in which we were asked to talk about the work we did at school. This aural test was conducted by an external examiner. I had my aural exam in one of the small rooms in the Holly Building. The examiner was a kindly, middle-aged woman who did her best to put us candidates at our ease by smiling a lot. Now, at the time that I was preparing for French O.L. a story was circulating that a lad by the name of Ron Saville, who was of course to go on and be such a distinguished School Captain, had totally bowled over the French examiner by the shear force of his personality — as a consequence of which he had been awarded an all-time high mark in aural French. I didn't think I could emulate Ron's achievement so I contented myself with talking about a few rather conventional topics. I remarked that I liked drawing but not mathematics — not very original, but it fulfilled Mr. King's exhortation: "Don't stay silent! For goodness sake say something — anything"!

During my year of O.L. French we were given a quite wonderful opportunity to improve our understanding of spoken French. Mr. King informed us that on a forthcoming Saturday morning there would be a special showing — for schoolchildren about to sit their O.L. French — of Jean Cocteau's visually stunning *La Belle et la Bête. Magnifique! Magnifique!* Make a pledge, here and now, that if you have not seen this film you will endeavour to do so before you die. It is an amalgamation of surrealism, enchantment, fantasy — and yes — it is enriched by the French language. It bowled me over. When the film ended I didn't want to leave the cinema for fear of breaking the spell it had created. Concerning improving our French, which is what the experience was supposed to be about, the first twenty minutes of the presentation included sub-titles; thereafter, the film was shown without them. But with *La Belle* to feast your eyes upon, it didn't really matter if some of the words passed you by uncomprehendingly! Back at school the following Monday — what a come-down to-earth — Mr. King asked who had seen the film. Just a few of us had done so. We had a chat about it and I recall asking Mr. King why *beast* in French, a rather masculine word, has a feminine pronoun. I received an elaborate scholarly answer — the details of which I have completely forgotten. But not so the visual imagery of *La Belle et la bête* which still haunts my imagination!

I will conclude my reflections about O.L. French with a little anecdote concerning the inadequacies in this subject of my good friend and CTS contemporary Charlie Prime — a former CTS Vice Captain. If this seems an unchivalrous thing to do let me hasten to add that I will make amends later by paying him a compensating compliment when I discuss mathematics — Charlie was a gifted lad. My point concerning French is that Charlie Prime must hold the CTS record for the number of times any candidate had to sit O.L. French — to be precise no fewer than *five* times. You may well ask — "Why bother"? The general answer to that question is interesting. At this period, a boy or girl planning to go on to university had to have a foreign language as part of what were designated as *The General Entrance Requirements*. It didn't matter what the language was — Chinese, double Dutch etc. — provided it was a language other than English. (Unfortunately, broad Yorkshire did not qualify!) Without a foreign language, no matter how able you were, your progress to university was blocked. It was even more challenging to gain admission to the University of Oxford and the University of Cambridge which required demonstration of a working knowledge of Latin. So, it was important for young Charlie Prime, and the rest of us, to pass our O.L. French. In the case of Master Prime there was an added complication which I shall now narrate because it led to an amusing incident one day in morning assembly. Herbert Wadge had been informed by the University of London — which was the examining body for our O.L. and A.L. examinations — that there had been an inadvertent clash in the published timetable. The consequence was that candidates taking both O.L. French and A.L. Chemistry were required to be in two places at once — a feat even beyond the very able Charles Prime Esq. Mr. Wadge drew the circumstances of the confused timetable to our attention adding: "Is any boy affected by this problem or knows of another boy who is"? Aware that this had a direct bearing on my friend — and ever dutiful — without taking time to think I put up my hand and blurted out: "Charlie!" … "Er … Charlie Prime, Sir"! This somewhat colloquial interjection of mine, into morning assembly, invoked universal titters of mirth. I should explain that Charlie Prime, by then a prefect, was carrying out his responsibilities as 'late monitor' at the door in the Holly Building — you may recall how prefects 'guarded' all the entrances to the CTS at 8.45 a.m. to intercept late-comers. I can conclude this little episode by informing you that Richard Charles Prime, to give him his full name, subsequently passed his O.L. French — by sitting the exam at the Mechanics' Institute in darkest Bradford — and in time became a proud B.Sc. Eng. of the University of Manchester.

French beyond O.L.

Let me now tell you how, whilst still at the CTS, I continued my study of French beyond O.L. and the reason why — the story has an almost tragic/comic outcome. I had set my sights on studying architecture at the University of Sheffield and had discovered, by reading the regulations (very diligent of me), that to get the B.A. degree in architecture you had to also study a modern language in the First Year of the course. I realised that to attempt this with only O.L. French would be too much of a challenge — more French study was clearly required. But how? A.L. French was not on the CTS curriculum. Night school was the only answer — even though this meant fitting in French alongside the study of my other A.L. subjects, namely, Maths (Pure and Applied — taken as two subjects) and Physics. I found out that classes were available on Friday evenings — located in the City Grammar School next door to the CTS — by the way do you remember being able to look down from the CTS playground into the girls' cookery room?

I duly enrolled for French classes (1957-58) and found myself in the company of about a dozen people old enough to be my parents — each one of them was a *Francophile*. Our 'set book' was *Complete French Course For First Examinations* by W. F. H. Whitmarsh. I still have my copy, much thumbed and its margins scribbled with my pencil annotations. There are forty prose passages listed — and I translated thirty-three of them into French! I can scarcely believe it but it's true — such a vast amount of work. I discarded the pile of texts just a few years ago. I used to set aside Sunday afternoons to work on the translations, whilst listening to Anthony Hopkins on the radio in his programme *Talking About Music* — I learned much of the musical repertoire through Hopkins' analysis of musical form. (By the way, the musical Anthony Hopkins should not be confused with the actor Anthony Hopkins.)

About half way through my first year of French evening classes I needed some help in the form of set books, so I confided details of my 'extra-curricular' studies in Mr. Dove — the only fellow pupil I recall ever similarly informing was Gordon Swann. Mr. Dove, after some words of encouragement, let me borrow his copy of Alexandre Dumas's *Le Comte de Monte Cristo* — set in the original French language. My request prompted Mr. Dove to entrust me with some details of his own study of French language. From what he said, I formed the impression he had, at some point in his university education, undertaken advanced study — with a focus on the French language. Be that as it may, I worked on (struggled with) Dumas's text — rendered difficult by reason of its florid, poly-syllabic language and complex sentence structure. Then a moment of revelation. I read the following passage — so clear in my mind, it could be but yesterday: 'There are the learned and the knowing, philosophy makes one and memory the other'. Dramatic as it may seem, my understanding of myself was from that moment permanently transformed. I realised that we each have the power within us to change and improve our circumstances — by application and hard work!

The next year (1958-59) I embarked on stage two of my evening classes armed with Whitmarsh's *Advanced French Course* — as the name implies, very demanding. I will leave out the detail and jump forward in time to October 1959 when I enrolled ('registered' — in Scotland we say 'matriculated') at the University of Sheffield to commence the study of architecture. On arriving at the university, I completed the admission paperwork and proudly informed the course secretary of my two-year long efforts to strengthen my French. Now we come to the tragic/comic aspect of the tale to which I earlier alluded. "Oh", said the secretary — Miss Crawford, "did no one tell you"? "What?", I asked — seized with apprehension. "We have just changed the regulations. You don't need a foreign language now!" At that moment, I really did not know, as they say, whether to laugh or to cry. My mind passed over those many Friday evenings and Sunday afternoons spent toiling with the intricacies of French grammar and syntax. I left the office in a daze.

In effect in those distant times at the University of Sheffield the study of architecture, under the old regulations *with* a language, led to the B. A. degree in architecture. The study of architecture under the revised regulations with a subject *other than* a language led to the B. Arch. degree. It so happens, as I will disclose in due course, that my hours of application to the French language were not wasted. But, as I will also later reveal, it would require additional study before the university authorities would allow me to register for the B. Arch. qualification in architecture.

I will close this section by briefly returning to my O.L. French studies. I want to do so in order to place on record my debt of gratitude to Mr. Ken King — for the following reason. In my subsequent professional life, as an academic that is rather than as an architect, I have worked extensively in the French language — mostly on translation work. I will say a few words about this later since it has a direct bearing on my overall narrative. What I want to say here is simply: "Thank you Mr. King for all your enthusiasm for the French language and for all your efforts in endeavouring to communicate it to us — and not forgetting, of course, your very own *sprachegfühl*'!

Technical Drawing

We all enjoyed technical drawing. I think the pleasure we derived was something to do with the appeal, and challenge, of learning how to represent three-dimensional forms in two-dimensional orthographic projection. For the Engineers, the subject was an introduction to the realms of blueprints, the machine shop and the fabrication of metal objects; for the Builders, the subject was an introduction to the realms of plans and elevations, to the conventions of the drawing office and to the technology of building construction. At the CTS these two approaches to the subject were quite distinctive. For the Engineers, technical drawing was closely allied to pattern-making, moulding and foundry work; for the Builders, technical drawing was closely allied to carpentry and joinery and, as stated, building construction. The two approaches came more closely together in the study of O.L. and A.L. Technical Drawing. I will now trace my experience of these subjects as I pursued them as a Builder.

Class 3Y

In their First Year, Builders at the CTS were introduced to technical drawing in the form of 'geometrical drawing', indeed we each labelled our large-format exercise book with the title *Geometry*. This part of the syllabus consisted of twenty-nine 'problems' of the kind: 'To bisect a given straight line', 'To bisect a given angle', 'To draw a perpendicular' ... and so on until we gradually embraced more complex propositions — *Gradus ad parnassum* (Fig.1). All these propositions are still vividly clear in my mind for a singular reason. I let someone borrow my book to copy from — and it was never returned! So, anxious to make good the deficit, I had no alternative but to re-draw the whole year's work!

Geometrical drawing was taught to Builders by Mr. John H. Hunter in Drawing Office 1 — 'DO1' — which was located in the Bow Building. At that time Mr. Hunter wore a pin-striped suit and, being a smoker, smelled of tobacco. DO1, as I remember it, was equipped with four long rows of drawing tables, large enough to take an imperial-size drawing board with space for drawing instruments. I have good reason to remember my first lesson in technical drawing. It was Tuesday afternoon on my second day at the CTS and teachers' names were still unfamiliar. Mr. Hunter asked me to take a message to a certain engineering workshop in the Firth Building. I duly set out on my way but, by the time I had made the journey from the Bow Building

to the Firth Building, I had forgotten the name of the teacher I was seeking. It so happens I saw another boy and explained to him my dilemma. He looked at me, I thought just a little disdainfully, and then said: "Tha wants old spanner 'ed — but 'e's all reyt"! I said thank you, resumed my way more confidently but then realised I still did not know the true identity of 'Spanner Head'. I subsequently learned his name was Mr. Charles Bains. Remarkably, this was the only time in my five years at the CTS that I ever had occasion to speak to Mr. Bains or, for that matter, to go into the machine shop — which I remember was meticulously clean and orderly. And I should that Mr. Bains was a highly skilled teacher of workshop practice.

In our first lesson with Mr. Hunter we had to hold out our hands, palms uppermost, so that he could inspect them to see if they complied with the standards of cleanliness he required for drawing-office practice. One boy, by the name of Wood, had particularly dirty hands which prompted Mr. Hunter to remark: "Are you in mourning son"? On occasions Mr. Hunter could be rather sardonic. I do however have another recollection concerning Mr. Hunter and this self-same boy which will reveal a very different side to Mr. Hunter's nature — more of that later. After the hand inspection, the class was told that henceforth we were all required to wash our hands before each drawing lesson, and, to this end, throughout First Year, we each carried a piece of towel and soap — and tried to remember to use them.

By lesson eleven, we had progressed to 'properties of triangles' which was the moment for us to be introduced to the axioms of Euclid — 'The angle in a semicircle is a right angle' and so on. Mr. Hunter was clearly in awe of Euclid and was given to stating — hand inserted in his waistcoat for added gravitas — "However hard you may try, you will never disprove the axioms of Euclid"! We were more than prepared to take his word for it. I am tempted to insert here that our passive acquiescence was in striking contrast to that of my illustrious namesake Bertrand Russell. This is what he has to say about Euclid in Volume One of his *Autobiography*:

> At the age of eleven, I began Euclid, with my brother as my tutor. This was one of the great events of my life, as dazzling as first love. I had not imagined that there was anything so delicious in the world ... . I had been told that Euclid proved things, and was much disappointed that he started with axioms ... . I reluctantly admitted them pro tem. The doubt as to the premises of mathematics which I felt at that moment remained with me, and determined the course of my subsequent work.

Now, back to Terry Russell and his contemporaries in DO1. I sat in the front row; on my left was a boy called Heathcote and on my right was a boy called Wright. One day Mr. Hunter — often given to 'moralising' — invited the class to consider the approach that we three boys exemplified in our work. "Wright", Mr. Hunter wryly observed, "dedicates himself to the belief that work should be finished as quickly as possible — with little regard for care and workmanship"! Turning to Heathcote he resumed: "Heathcote is a perfectionist, a born draftsman who works with little concern for time in pursuit of excellence"! Then it was my turn: "Russell combines the efficiency of Wright whilst striving for the high standards of Heathcote"! I recognised that I had received a compliment, but I considered it to be eclipsed by the praise lavished upon my 'rival'. Barry Heathcote, to give him his full name, was, indeed, a born draftsman and proceeded to qualify, like myself, to be an architect — achieving the coveted Diploma of the Architectural Association, London. A few years ago I met-up with Barry and he related to me the following anecdote. Barry once had occasion to tell his father how he had been awarded 80% in an exam. His father replied: "Never mind that, what mark did Terry Russell get"? (The answer was 90%.) Sorry about that Barry!

Mr. Stanley Pilling — of whom more later — occasionally took us for technical drawing. We would sometimes go to the front of the class to his desk to have our homework checked. This afforded me with an opportunity to witness his remarkable visual powers at close range. I am convinced that with one eye he could examine your work and simultaneously scrutinise your countenance with the other eye. Remarkable! By way of interest, it is from this precise moment that I took to wearing spectacles. Mr. Pilling pointed something out to me on the blackboard at the far end of the room which I had some difficulty in making out. This prompted Mr. Pilling to remark: "You ought to pay a visit to the optician", This almost prompted me to reply: "Hark who's talking!" — but of course I didn't. But I did soon afterwards get my eyes tested and was told I should start to wear glasses for distant work. I did so and I can say they did improve my outlook on life!

In parallel with our geometrical-drawing exercises, we undertook a series of drafting studies of a more practical nature based upon building elements — doors and windows and such like — gradually broadening into the study of composite constructions such as floors and roofs. This part of the syllabus was called, appropriately, 'Building Construction'. Looking back, I consider my course to be quite remarkable for its rigour and thoroughness — and all for we relatively young boys aged between twelve and thirteen. No less praiseworthy was the manner in which our drawing-office studies were integrated with practical work in carpentry and joinery, or 'woodwork' as it was termed — more of which later.

Mr. Hunter was a strict disciplinarian. This was nowhere more evident than in the care required of DO1's supply of 'T' squares — especially regarding the protection of their inlaid ebony edge. To drop a T square was to incur four 'de-merits'. The sound of a T square falling upon the hardwood floor of DO1 had a chilling resonance — rather as the turning of the key must sound to a prisoner when the door is shut. I remember the day came when an unfortunate lad had the misfortune to knock over the entire DO1 supply of T squares — in theory, a total of about 120 de-merits! I can't remember the outcome — perhaps the individual concerned is still serving time somewhere for his indiscretion!

If dropping a T square was guaranteed to work Mr. Hunter into a frenzy, close behind in his list of sins was failing to take care in following the strict stylistic conventions of upper- and lower-case lettering, especially with the block style of lettering we used for our drawing exercises. A lad by the name of Jack Timms, to whom I have made previous reference, was a cardinal offender. For a whole year I recall Mr. Hunter calling out, as he sat at his desk marking our work: "You're still putting lids on 'Js' Timms — and I'm still crossing them off"! Jack's response was to give Mr. Hunter the 'V' sign — safely concealed out of sight beneath his desk!

At this point I can set a brain teaser, for the former CTS Builders reading this, as follows. What are the following; — *Smalls, Doubles, Ladies, Countesses, Duchesses, Princesses* and *Empresses*? Here's a clue; Mr. Hunter explained these words in a lesson concerning pitched roof-coverings. To be honest, I had forgotten all about these terms until a few years ago when I saw them all on display at the Penrhyn slate mine — there's another clue. They are, of course, the names that the Welsh Victorian slate quarry-men gave to differently sized slates. We were taught that on May 7th, 1954 — I offer this reflection as a small illustration as to how thorough Mr. Hunter was in his teaching.

I recall Mr. Hunter was proud of being a 'certified carpenter' — more correctly, a Fellow of the Institute of Certified Carpenters. When he first disclosed this fact I was, for a moment, somewhat confused because, back in my days at Carfield Junior School, one of my teachers used to rail at the class: "You should all be certified" — and I don't think she meant we should all become carpenters!

Mr. Hunter was an External Examiner for the Institute of Certified Carpenters and made frequent reference to the exacting standards required for membership — by way of exhorting us to elevate our own standards of workmanship. Reflecting once upon his own first day at work, he recalled proudly presenting his certificates to the foreman, only to be rebuffed with the rejoinder: "Neer mind thi certificates lad, can tha work"? We all laughed, not so much at the foreman's pragmatism, but at the broad Yorkshire accent Mr. Hunter had adopted for his anecdote — a rare moment of relaxation in what were normally rather tense, highly disciplined lessons.

A stupendously magnificent technical drawing was displayed on the wall of DO1, immediately to the right of the door. This portrayed a cross-sectional view of the domestic building construction required at the ground and first floors, to meet the requirements of fire protection with timber floors. This *tour de force* was the work of Roy Tandy. Try as I did, I never was able to elevate my draughtsmanship to the standard as exemplified in Roy's drawing — he had attained exhibition quality. Nice one Roy!

Sitting at the front of DO1, beneath Mr. Hunter's searching gaze, was something of an occupational hazard, by which I mean he was prone to asking a boy to fetch something from his room — located in the basement of the Holly Building. This required sorting out the correct key from a perplexing confusion of about twenty similar-looking keys — of the 'Yale' type. The day came when I had to return from such an errand defeated and confused. I requested help in identifying the required key. Now, Mr. Hunter was a master of the 'slow burn', or excoriating gaze, following which, after an interval of time — that seemed interminable — he would ask: "How old are you"? On the occasion in question, I experienced the slow burn and interrogatory put down. I replied — before the full gaze of the class — "Twelve Sir", in fact, I had taken a year from my age in an attempt to seem more youthful and innocent. A short lecture followed on the intelligence necessary to sort out keys. As a matter of fact, I had never actually handled a Yale key before. My knowledge of keys at that time was limited to our front door key at home — a piece of cast iron forged somewhere in the Don Valley. I earned the slow burn on another occasion during my technical and geometrical drawing lessons with Mr. Hunter in DO1 — again concerning keys. I was entrusted to lock all the cupboards — including the one where the famous T squares were stored — and I forgot to secure the inside bolts. With lofty and measured actions, Mr. Hunter proceeded to demonstrate, once more before the full gaze of the class, how the doors, although locked, could be pulled open. The "How old are you?" routine followed — this time I gave my age as twelve and a half!

Notwithstanding my incompetence with keys, allow me to say I took leave of Class 3Y with the Drawings Subjects Prize and also took leave of Class 5X with the Drawings Subjects Prize which was the gift of the Sheffield Building Trades Employers' Association.

O.L. Technical Drawing

Instruction in technical drawing for O.L. was entrusted to Mr. Donald Woolhouse, the most kindly of teachers. He presented the appearance of one whose formative years had been spent upon the back of a horse, by which I mean he appeared to be somewhat bow-legged. Far from being an impediment, this physical characteristic lent to his demeanour a certain jaunty swagger. Together with his kindliness he manifested the virtues of simplicity, straightforwardness and a complete lack of guile. Let me tell a little story to illustrate the equable nature of Mr. Woolhouse's temperament — a tale rather to my own discredit. One day, at the time when I was School Captain, Mr. Woolhouse happened to pay the prefects a 'social' call. He entered our room, the one at the back overlooking the playground — I believe this was officially called the Senior Prefects' room. I was talking — probably denigrating a member of staff — when someone gave me a wink, by way of inclining me to caution. I turned to find Mr. Woolhouse standing behind me. I recall exclaiming: "Oh he won't mind, he's not important"! I immediately endeavoured to retract my words in favour of a more felicitous greeting. Mr. Woolhouse, smiling benignly, put his hand on my shoulder, gently silenced me with a rueful shake of the head and commented: "It's all right. I know what you mean. And you are right, I'm not important". Not many members of staff would have responded so graciously. Sorry about that Mr. Woolhouse! Now, back to O.L. technical drawing.

The G.C.E. syllabus for O.L. technical drawing consisted of three components: *Plane Geometry* — triangles, quadrilaterals and the loci of circles; *Solid Geometry* — cones, cylinders, spheres and oblique sections; and *Machine Drawing* — two or more views in orthographic projection of machine parts. We acquired some intriguing vocabulary from this syllabus such as 'inverted frustum'. Once, when I was a student working on a vacation project, I used this latter expression to impress my employer. He looked at me quizzically and exclaimed: "*Inverted frustum* perfectly describes my secretary"! I hasten to add, Mr. Woolhouse's lessons left a more durable legacy than that little anecdote.

I have to say I had limited enthusiasm for technical drawing — which should not in any way be taken as an indictment of the lessons we received. My inclinations were more to freehand drawing in '2B' soft pencil than to the carefully crafted studies we were required to undertake in '2H'. I did benefit however from the exercises we undertook of the inter-penetration of three-dimensional solids; these problems inculcated an understanding of thinking in three dimensions — good for an intending architect (Figs 1–3).

In common with so many CTS teachers, Mr. Woolhouse endeavoured to make his subject communicable by relating the topic of the lesson to some aspect of personal experience. One day, the study of machine parts set Mr. Woolhouse reminiscing. He described a time in industry when he, with two of his former colleagues, had constructed some huge moulding in wood. They were so proud of their achievement they had a photograph taken whilst standing before their creation. We listened to this anecdote attentively — stories always went down well in class. Mr. Woolhouse, having become somewhat impassioned, checked himself remarking: "You must think I'm silly" — but we didn't — we thought too kindly of him to entertain such thoughts.

In my narrative I have so far resisted trying to score points by comparing the relative virtues of Builders and Engineers at the CTS but I have to say something here in favour of the Builders. We had all of us — Builders and Engineers — just joined the O.L. technical drawing class and were settling in to get to know one another. As part of the process Mr. Woolhouse asked for a show of hands to sort out which boys were in fact from which particular side of the school. Then he said: "I've got to admit that Mr. Hunter can certainly get his Builders to draw! They're far better than the Engineers"! Quite right Mr. Woolhouse! As a Builder myself I couldn't agree more — even if your remark did produce a few jeers at the time from the Engineers in the class!

By way of further illustration of the friendly and approachable nature of Mr. Woolhouse I will recall a circumstance that arose during one of our first lessons with him in our O.L. technical drawing class. He entered the room, to be more precise we were located in the drawing office on the first floor of the Bow Building, only to discover a couple of lads having a friendly wrestling match on the floor — a kind of 'trial of strength' that erupts between young lads every now and then. He just smiled and took up his place at the front of the class by which time the all-in wrestling match was over and the class was paying attention. Instead of moralising about good behaviour Mr. Woolhouse started to reminisce about his days at school and how he was once having a friendly tussle with a school pal. Then he said there was suddenly a sharp crack which prompted him to say to his pal: "Now see what you've done! That's my drawing pencil broken"! Mr. Woolhouse then went on to explain to us that it was in fact one of his ribs that had cracked and he ended up in the casualty ward of the hospital. He concluded the incident by giving one of his big toothy smiles and shook his head ruefully as though to say: "Those were the days"!

Before moving on, I have another personal anecdote to tell of Mr. Woolhouse. He told me once how he had considered improving his technical qualifications. He had the City and Guilds Technical Certificate and he explained how it was possible to enhance this by taking a residential course followed by a series of examinations. This apparently led to the Full Technical Certificate conferring on the recipient the letters F. Tech. Cert. "You get a cap and gown and all that paraphernalia", mused Mr. Woolhouse, adding — "But I couldn't be bothered with it"! "Shame" I thought as I contemplated, in my mind, the sight of Mr. Woolhouse's shapely bow-legs emanating, on Speech Day, from beneath an academic robe!

The O.L. exam in technical drawing was something of a disaster for me for the following reason. The exam was in two parts; the first part consisted of a series of technical exercises — geometrical constructions and such like problems. This went OK for me, it was the second part of the exam which I messed up. This was the main part of the exam and required candidates to draw two cross-sectional elevations through a machine casting. I drew the sections well but located them on the wrong side of the casting — a major defect in engineering drawing practice. What I mean is that view 'A', which should have appeared to the left, I drew at the right, and view 'B' which should have appeared to the right, I drew at the left! That was my confusion. Got it? I lost marks for that. I was not the only one; there were several others in the class who made the same mistake. After the exam Mr. Woolhouse held a review to see how we had got on — it was more of a post-mortem for some of us! I could not help but think at the time how so much work and preparation — extending over a whole year — could be marred by such a simple slip in a three-hour exam. For this reason, speaking as an educationalist myself, I am now a keen believer in the 'continuous assessment principle' whereby a candidate's achievement is made up, at least in part, of the evaluation of the coursework that is undertaken throughout the year. As far as my O.L. technical drawing was concerned, my slip meant that I achieved only a bare pass — in what was my best subject. I resolved to do much better at A.L. — and I did! Read on!

A.L. Technical Drawing

Instruction in technical drawing was entrusted to Mr. Samuel (Sam) Hedley. I can set a brain teaser here for former CTS pupils; what had Mr. Hedley in common with Mr. Hunter? The answer — they had both lost a piece of finger from their left hand. Mr. William (Bill) Davis once told me how he had found Mr. Hunter collapsed in a faint on the workshop floor, following an accident. I have no information as to how Mr. Hedley came to lose his finger tip.

Our A.L. drawing classes were held in the big drawing office situated on the upper level of the Bow Building. It was in this large room that Telford House held its monthly meetings. The syllabus was, logically, a progression from the O.L. curriculum. We studied more complex propositions in Plane Geometry — true lengths, inclined planes the properties of circles and such like exercises; we enlarged our understanding of Solid Geometry — sections through, and developments of, cones and pyramids; and we made endless studies of machine parts such as — lathe steady, lever safety-valve and ram pump. The course was well taught, rigorous and, under Mr. Hedley's watchful eye, highly disciplined. Very occasionally we converted our tracing paper drawings into blueprints. To make these, we used an ancient printing machine which was installed in a small room situated outside the drawing office at the top of the stair. The machine looked so old it was probably designed by Count Rühmkorff. (In case you require a bit of help here, I will add that Rühmkorff invented the induction coil used in early incandescent discharge lamps.) Sensitive paper was exposed to a brilliant light achieved by passing a current between two carbon rods. This illuminant was drawn horizontally under the pull of a heavy weight which made the lamp gently oscillate, filling the room with wraith-like striations — and a gaseous discharge of ozone. The contraption stood on a thick rubber mat — clear evidence that it was potentially lethal!

I have fond memories of spending extra drawing periods in this back room with Jack Glossop, a very gifted boy — of whom more later. It was Jack who told me he had discovered that, by standing on a stool, you could get a direct view into the senior girls' playground at the City Grammar School next door — so as to enable you to feast your gaze on the talent as it were! The day inevitably came when in walked Mr. Hedley, to see what progress was being made with inclined planes — or something of the kind — only to find Jack at his vantage point standing on a stool by the window. I remarked, tactfully, on the need for ventilation, "It's the ozone Sir", and the incident passed — and with it our prurient gazing. I should add that I never did let on to Jack that I had made his 'discovery' several weeks before his worthy self!

The A.L. examination in technical drawing was in two parts. One paper was concerned with problems in geometrical drawing and the other was an elaborate exercise in machine drawing. A few days before the exam, Mr. Hedley convened a special revision class; I remember it well because it was after school which gave the event an added air of importance. Mr. Gilbert Thompson — of whom more later — was responsible for the official conduct of the A.L. exams that year (1959) and I remember with what *gravitas* he opened the brown-paper envelop containing the exam paper before handing it to Mr. Hedley for distribution to the candidates. To my amazement, three of the problems that we had revised came up in the geometrical drawing paper. One of these, by way of interest, was to draw the plan and elevation of three spheres, of different diameters, as they nestled in mutual contact — quite a tricky little problem. The machine drawing exam required us to assemble, in our imagination, several machine parts and to produce a plan, elevation and section of the unified assembly. I found I had about an hour to spare so I set about hatching and shading every nut and bolt in sight. Although I say it myself, my submission was a veritable *tour de force* of ornate pencil work. It paid off — I was subsequently awarded a distinction! Allow me to say I took leave of this class with the A.L. Engineering Drawing Prize with which I purchased Volume I of Simpson's *History of Architectural Development.*

Woodwork Carpentry and Joinery

Class 3Y

Mr. Stanley Pilling taught Builders woodwork in the large workshop on the ground floor of the Holly Building. I recall our very first class-meeting distinctly, for reasons of what I will describe as the ambiguity of Mr. Pilling's gaze. By this I mean, such was the acute nature of his squint that when he called out — "Come here boy!" — he would look in one direction and gaze in another so that *two* boys simultaneously responded to his summons! Indeed Mr. Pilling's affliction was so evident that to my generation he was known as *Isaiah* for the reason — yes you have guessed — one eye appeared to be higher than the other! Mr. Pilling had a dry sense of humour. He would say, if someone had made a loose fitting joint: "Well, now we know where the flies go in winter"! Better still was a remark he once made as part of a general caution to remember that the more you plane off a piece of wood, the smaller the dimension becomes. He observed: "There's only one exception to this universal law — and that's when you are planing the hole in a lavatory seat"! Ah, they don't make them like that any more.

As I have remarked, we Builders had our woodwork lessons in the long workshop situated on the ground floor of the Holly Building. Down below, accessed from the school playground, the Engineers had their similarly proportioned pattern-making and moulding workshop. In all my time at the CTS I made only one visit to the latter workshop to take a message to Mr. Freeman. On the occasion of my visit, the entire class was hell-bent on compacting sand into moulding boxes as though their young lives depended upon it — perhaps they did! Our woodwork workshop was magnificently equipped. There must have been something like twenty woodworkers' benches distributed around the centre of the room. At one end was an area set aside for teaching; here we would gather in a large semi-circle to either watch a demonstration or to listen to some piece of formal instruction. At the opposite end were powerful machines which included a planing machine, circular saw, band saw, spindle moulder, drilling machine and a sanding disk. We were generally not allowed into that part of the room unless it was to use the sander — and only then rarely. I did once use the circular saw to help Mr. Hunter draw a long length of wood through the machine.

In addition to Mr. Pilling, Mr. Hunter was responsible for instruction in woodwork — see below — and he was prone to testing our vigilance and powers of general observation. By way of illustration of this, one morning (we had woodwork on Tuesday morning) he called us to attention with his familiar exclamation — "Boys"! "Now", he proclaimed, "You have all been here several weeks and have had the opportunity to read the inscription by the front door. Who was it who opened this building in 1899"? Only one boy was able to give the correct reply — no, it was not yours truly but a lad called Michael Porter. He received a merit for his vigilance and I resolved then and there to sharpen my own awareness of the things around me — which has helped me in the writing of these remarks.

I will stay with the subject of Mr. Hunter a moment longer to recall an incident in the Holly Building which reveals what a stickler Mr. Hunter was for maintaining school traditions of courtesy and discipline. Early in Class 3Y, just a few weeks after joining the CTS, he admonished us in the following manner: "Boys! When you meet a teacher at the door, what do you do"? (Mr. Hunter was fond of introducing a morally improving proposition in the form of a question — for which he would then provide the answer. On this occasion it went as follows.) "You don't dash through the door before he gets there — you stand and open it for him don't you"? "Yes Sir", we chorused in unison. "Good", came the reply. "Try to remember that". Now, to return to my recollection; the day came when we all (i.e., Class 3Y) trouped off to the Holly Building for our woodwork lesson. I was near the end of the line and, arriving at the Holly Building entrance, I encountered Mr. Hunter standing holding the door open as the class marched passed him. Meanwhile he was gradually turning purple with rage! I remembered the pledge we had given, so I stepped aside, held open the door and allowed Mr.

Hunter to pass through. He raised his trilby hat rather ceremoniously to me and said in a very grandiloquent manner: "Thank you"! I had the presence of mind to reply: "Just what you expect from a boy from Telford House Sir" — the point being that Mr. Hunter was also a member of Telford House. He just stared icily at me and went impassively on his way.

In the workshop we worked two boys to a bench, one on each side with a duplicate set of tools in the well of the bench. Lesson one was concerned with Face, Edge, Breadth, Thickness and Length — inculcated as *For Every Boy To Learn*. Practical work included learning how to set out and make such basic joints as; housing, mortise and tenon, dovetail and — the ultimate challenge — secret-mitre dovetail. We were also introduced to more specialised joints like the tusk-tenon, in anticipation of our later assumed apprenticeship to the building trade. We were allowed to keep these youthful efforts and for years I had a suitcase crammed with miscellaneous timber artefacts until the day came when, I have to say, I consigned them to the fire!

Two activities were integrated to run in parallel with our practical work. One of these was homework. We were usually required to draw and describe hand tools (Figs 4 & 5). I felt a natural affinity for this aspect of our learning for a rather special reason. Let me explain. My father worked for C. & J. Hampton Ltd., better known as *Record Tools*. For the record (no pun intended) he actually worked for Hampton's for an unbroken period of 53 years — his *Long Service Certificate* now hangs on the wall in my study. I got to know several of my father's workmates rather well and I actually visited C. & J. Hampton Ltd. on a number of occasions. Indeed, I once met the son of the founder of the firm Mr. Anthony Hampton who was known to the 'workers' as 'Mr. Tony' — a rather nice mixture of respect combined with friendliness. I gradually acquired a good set of Hampton's tool catalogues and my father was able to purchase tools for me at the handsome discount of 33% off the normal retail price. So you see, drawing tools as part of woodwork homework came, as it were, second nature to me.

In the illustrated part of our homework, a form of friendly rivalry established itself to see who could achieve the most authentic pictorial representation of a particular woodwork tool. Three levels of effort were discernible; pencil sketches, line drawings in Indian ink and the latter with added shading and colour. The day came — to be precise 28th September 1954 — when Mr. Pilling held aloft my drawings of a jack plane to Class 3Y, remarking: "These are the best 'ave seen for a long time" (Figs 6 & 7). I experienced a pleasurable moment of pride, but, alas, it was inadvertently diminished. For the reasons I have already explained as Mr. Pilling paid me this compliment, he looked in my direction but fixed his gaze upon another boy!

I will insert here that I once asked Mr. Pilling if he was a certified carpenter. He looked at me — more-or-less looked at me — quizzically, half believing that I was trying to, as they say, 'extract the water'. But, realising by then that I was a good and virtuous lad (!) he perceived that my question was serious and replied: "Yes". I persisted, asking: "Are you a *Fellow*, like Mr. Hunter"? "No", came the abrupt response, "I am an *Associate*". He then drew from his pocket a whistle, of the kind policemen used to carry in their top pockets, gave it a blast — by way of indicating that break was over — and the matter was closed. Notwithstanding the finality of our conversation, chance provided me with a further occasion to pursue the matter of Mr. Pilling's woodwork qualifications. Here's how the circumstance came about.

The windows to the workshop had deep sills that were used to display miscellaneous items crafted in wood — turned handrails, complex mouldings, intricate joints and such like. They silently gathered dust and seldom attracted our attention until one day Mr. Pilling was motivated to remove one of these constructions from its resting place. I could tell, from the manner in which he held it, that the said article was an object of some veneration. It was a rooflight that had provision for double glazing, the lower section being hinged to give access for cleaning. "Who made that?", I asked inquisitively. "I did", replied Mr. Pilling — with manifest pride. Seeing that my curiosity was roused — and evidently wanting to talk about his creation — he added that it was his 'Certified Carpenter's Apprentice Test Piece' and that he had made the article in an examination in the remarkably short time of five hours! "Did you pass?", I asked disarmingly. "I did", came the emphatic but terse reply — Mr. Pilling seldom showed any inclination to oratory. Nevertheless, I, and by then several other boys who had congregated, quietly admired Mr. Pilling's handiwork — but not to the extent that any of us resolved to become Certified Carpenters!

I will stay with the theme of Mr. Pilling for a moment and recall how he said something one day which rather puzzled me at the time — in fact for a long time. A boy asked him a question of an opaque and obscure kind prompting him to exclaim: "Don't ask me a question like that, I'm not a genius"! This in its self is nothing remarkable being no more than a 'throw away' line. But then he added: "I'm glad I'm not a genius"! That's the bit that puzzled me. Surely, I thought to myself, it must be wonderful to be a genius — to have all those unique insights into things and to receive the adulation of your fellow men. Then gradually, as time passed, I realised what Mr. Pilling was probably getting at, namely, that to be endowed with very special gifts imposes the obligation to use them. Not that I can speak from any personal experience of this particular problem! But I do now agree with Mr. Pilling; life is indeed much easier by not being burdened by genius!

Our theoretical knowledge of woodwork was examined each year. This provides me with the opportunity for a rather disgraceful anecdote — but my narrative should, after all, be a 'warts and all' commentary on life at the CTS which was not always a seamless fabric of virtue. To come to the point, we had a rather degenerate boy in Class 3Y — who shall be nameless. In the exam to which I refer, we were required to draw and describe a mortise chisel. I remember casting a glance in the direction of the boy to whom I have alluded and noticed that he had clasped in his hand what I thought was the handle of a mortise chisel. I felt somewhat resentful that he was cheating in this way. And then I noticed that it was not a chisel handle he was holding but — how shall I put it — his organ of gender! I will now draw a veil over that episode.

I remarked earlier that two activities ran in parallel with practical woodwork. The second of these was a series of technical-drawing studies allied to building construction — to which I have already made brief reference. These studies were, as also previously remarked, carried out under the direction of Mr. Hunter

in his class in D.O.1 (Figs 8–10). With hindsight, and speaking as an educationalist, I find it quite remarkable that so high a level of integration was achieved between different parts of the curriculum. This must have required much planning and collaboration between the different members of staff responsible for the various aspects of our studies. With that compliment, I will proceed to Class 5X.

Class 5X

In addition to taking us for technical drawing, Mr. Hunter was also responsible for a substantial part of our instruction in woodwork. I have good reason for recalling this since, at the very start of my woodwork classes with Mr. Hunter, an incident occurred which, as it turned out, worked to my advantage. Let me say first that Mr. Hunter was not averse to confronting a boy with a perplexing proposition — as a means of exposing some weakness or inadequacy — by way of then making a moral generalisation to the rest of the class. (I have already explained how his 'slow burn' featured in this particular form of intellectual confrontation.) I narrowly escaped this treatment on the occasion of our being introduced to the rule-of-thumb proposition that a tenon joint is one-third the thickness of the wood. "Let us assume", said Mr. Hunter, "that a carpenter has started with a piece of wood 2″ thick which he then reduces to 1 15/16″. What is the width of the tenon required"? No response — we just stared like goldfish. He then tossed a piece of chalk to me with the command: "How do we work it out"? Now, having by then already received the "How old are you?" treatment and the slow burn — over the incident of the keys — I resolved to keep my cool. I proceeded to the blackboard and, with a slightly faltering hand wrote; 1/3 of 1 15/16″ = 1/3 of 31/16″ = 31/48″. I turned to face Mr. Hunter with a sense of achievement, but, his expression suggested the "How old are you?" routine was about to be administered, so I took another look at the blackboard. I decided to be creative, in part impelled by Mr. Hunter's observation: "We don't usually measure in 48ths of an inch do we"? I continued my work at the blackboard: 31/48″ is about 30/48″ = 10/16″ = 5/8″. The problem solved, I resumed my place in the class. "Boys!", exclaimed Mr. Hunter — now what I thought? "For years I have been asking that question, and, at last, I have received a satisfactory answer"! I received a merit for my endeavours — about the only one I ever did receive from Mr. Hunter who was rather curmudgeonly over such things.

Following this little episode Mr. Hunter went on to have a little dig at the Engineers — this was one of his favourite pastimes. He would refer to them as the *Gingerbeers* and await our smile of approval — being a class of Builders this was usually forthcoming. But he reserved his sharpest irony for the precision to which Engineers worked and in particular their fine tolerances. He would always conclude his observation with the punch line: "They even use hundredths — and there's thousands of them in an inch"! We laughed dutifully.

There was a further occasion when the models on the window sill to the woodwork workshop yielded an interesting anecdote this time prompting Mr. Hunter to shed light on his personal skills in woodwork. It was morning break — drinking milk time — and a number of us were admiring a full-size replica of a curved stair, complete with two treads, risers and balustrade. It appears that a boy, who had left the CTS a few years earlier — I am speaking of 1954 — had gone to work for some high class joiners who were given the commission to equip Cole Brothers Store with a new 'geometrical' (elliptical) stair; I can still remember it as being located by the main entrance — on 'Cole's Corner'. Such a stair poses a supreme technical challenge of setting out — especially concerning the handrail and associated mouldings. Let me be more precise. Any continuous moulding which changes its inclination or its position, relative to the vertical plane, changes its section. In staircase work, mouldings change their position relative to both the horizontal and vertical planes, calling for different sections in order to produce a continuous section, either on the curve, or, intersecting in straight-line mitres at the angles. A little perplexed? So, it seems were the joiners on the Cole Brothers job. The CTS lad, in question, remembering the 'exemplar' stair joinery-construction in our workshop promptly paid Mr. Hunter a visit, explained the dilemma and enlisted his help in setting out the work. Mr. Hunter derived evident pleasure in outlining these events and even abandoned his normal somewhat taciturn reserve. I remember feeling sufficiently inspired to find out more about the technicalities involved and — conscientious as always (!) — I purchased *Geometry of Construction* by Nichols and Keep — it has been, in a manner of speaking, my companion ever since.

In Class 5X, we made a few objects of more lasting value than the joints (firewood) we had produced in Class 3Y. One of these was a bathroom stool, complete with a hinged top that was covered with cork. We were expected to purchase our productions, presumably to help to defray the expense of the materials. Mr. Pilling took us for this project and, upon its completion, I went to explain to him that I did not wish to buy mine. "And why not?", he asked with some irritation. "Well sir", I faltered, "you see, we don't have a bathroom"! The logic of my reply carried such unassailable force that it was accepted and I duly placed my bathroom stool on the window sill where it could be stored. I noticed how, over the next few weeks, my masterpiece was joined by several others, leading me to conclude that the homes of other CTS boys were also without bathrooms — vivid illustration of how representative we were of 'the unwashed masses'!

Another object of utility we made in Class 5X, again under the direction of Mr. Pilling, was a folding fisherman's stool. I did purchase my stool — I hadn't the courage to tell Mr. Pilling that I didn't go fishing! It had a sad ending; it collapsed under the weight of a friend of the family who thought he would try it out — the consequence was more firewood!

On one of the window sills was an electric plate which was used to heat a glue pot. The glue consisted of animal gelatine, derived from old bones, the smell of which was suggestive of certain school meals. For reasons of safety, only one boy at a time was allowed near to the glue pot. More generally, the discipline of safety, and secure workshop practice, was enforced by Mr. Hunter with a rod of iron — actually a cane. When he observed any boy transgressing his workshop precepts, concerning the safe use of tools, he would immediately exclaim: "Boys, stop work! Gather round"! It was the signal something was amiss. The poor lad caught doing something wrong was then required to re-enact his misdemeanour — under the full gaze of the class. It was a chastening experience which none of us wanted to undergo. In fact, in my time at the CTS, I remember only one accident in the woodwork shop. A

boy called rather appropriately by the name of Wood — the one with the dirty hands to whom I made earlier reference — cut his hand rather badly (between his thumb and forefinger). Mr. Hunter was the first on the scene and held Wood in his arms — the poor lad had fainted. For a moment, we witnessed the more kindly and compassionate Mr. Hunter that was normally concealed beneath the rather forbidding exterior of the pedagogue. He called for someone to fetch Mr. Pilling — who was a fully qualified First-Aid Officer. Wood had stitches put in his hand and survived to make many more botched woodwork joints.

Before my time at the CTS (1954–59) there was a very serious accident — perhaps some of you can recall the circumstances. Mr. Wadge drew the tragedy to our attention in morning assembly — he used to exhort us to take great care on the roads, especially if we cycled. To emphasise the point, he would read from published annual statistics of injuries to school children — he made several such statements over the years. On one occasion, to add reality to the rather dry statistics, he called to mind the misfortune of a CTS boy who lost a leg in a road accident — I think whilst cycling home from a sports day. I also recall a boy called Hardcastle falling from his bike and requiring minor plastic surgery to his right ear. But this is becoming too sombre — back to woodwork.

Although Mr. Hunter was essentially a somewhat forbidding teacher, it would be wrong to portray him as being intimidating; there were, indeed, occasions in his woodwork classes when he could be witty and jovial. Moreover, to our innocent susceptibilities, it seemed that Mr. Hunter knew 'everything' about woodwork — particularly tools and their uses. In this context, I remember well his advice as to how we should approach our first day at work. He first cautioned us to expect how some self-appointed wit would ask us to go and fetch the 'glass hammer', or the 'long stand', or the 'sky hook' etc. "Boys", said Mr. Hunter, "get it over with, let them have their little joke, we've all been through it"! The day came when we decided to exploit the more approachable side of Mr. Hunter's nature and, in addition, to put his credentials to the test. We decided to wait for a suitable opportunity. It duly came when Mr. Hunter set time aside to explain the different types of planes and their uses. For this purpose he made a splendid display of tools including: bench planes — smoothing, jack and trying planes; rebate and grooving planes; special planes like the shoulder and compass planes; grooving planes like the plough plane; culminating in the *tour de force* of all planes, namely the universal plane — which has no fewer than 55 cutters. Someone in the class then chose his moment, picked up his courage, raised his hand and said: "Sir, we think we know of a plane you may not have heard of — it's the cheese plane"! Mr. Hunter made an impressive display of looking perplexed — to what extent this was real or counterfeit I am not sure. Either way, he went along with our little subterfuge and we had a good laugh. But he rather got the better of us. He went off to his room and returned with a book, made a pretence of searching through it and confessed to not finding any reference to a cheese plane. This was of course a ruse, to enable him to reveal to us that it was a book about carpentry and joinery which he had proof-read prior to its publication — he proudly showed us his name in the 'Acknowledgements'. He then remarked that it was the only book in his life which he had read, literally, from cover to cover. So we finished where we had begun, with the realisation that Mr. Hunter did indeed know a great deal about his subject. Allow me to say I took leave of Class 5X with the Carpentry and Joinery Craft Prize.

Class 6X

I have remarked previously that I spent one term only in Class 6X and therefore my woodwork classes were somewhat curtailed. This was the year which, for Builders, culminated in the award of the *Building Diploma* that was accepted by the Sheffield Building Trades Employers' Association as a recognised qualification. An air of added seriousness therefore pervaded the workshop as we endeavoured to raise the level of our understanding of more complex constructions such as that required for a moulded mortise-and-tenon rebated window frame — which, some of you will recall, requires a tricky scribing joint to be performed with a gouge. The discipline of Mr. Hunter's pedagogic regime continued unrelenting — there was no escape because he was also our Form Master. We were required to draw tools of a more complex kind and to become familiar with their use (Figs 11 & 14). These tools had to be checked and counted at the end of every lesson and, if a special tool had been in use, such as the metal plough plane or the universal plane, all its parts had to be verified. There was an occasion when the depth stop of a plough plane was discovered to be missing. Mr. Hunter insisted that the cleaners' bags of floor sweepings — wood shavings — should all be searched. It paid off; the lost part was found amidst the detritus!

One of the window sills to the workshop was used to display a range of tropical hardwoods, others were contained in a large bookcase on a shelf marked 'colonial timbers' — a reminder of the days when we had a British Empire. From time-to-time Mr. Hunter used to add to the collection, informing us of the species, giving us its botanical name and urging us to commit the details to memory. Following such an event, I used to walk about dutifully repeating: 'Sapele' (*Entandrophragma clylindricum*), 'Lignum Vitae' (*Guaiacum officinale*), or such like, until I had them by heart — and, you see, it worked.

There were times when such fragments of coloured hardwoods were put to practical use. I can give one such illustration. In Class 6X my workbench was positioned adjacent to the lathe — I never recall seeing any boy use this lathe in my entire time at the CTS. But I do have good reason to recall Mr. Pilling working at the lathe. He made an ornate bowl consisting of numerous coloured hardwoods. Wedge-shaped pieces of these were first glued together to form a laminated matrix which, when set, was turned to create the required bowl. When smoothed and polished it looked superb. The artefact took several weeks to complete, we admired it and then it disappeared. It reappeared a month or so later on the evening of Speech Day as the centre-piece on the table mounted on the platform in the Victoria Hall. Mr. Wadge proudly presented it to the wife of the Guest Speaker remarking: "Made by some of the boys"!

Mr. Hunter was, without doubt, a pillar of moral rectitude, so what I now have to relate may cause a little stir of surprise. I once had to repair a defect in a piece of oak for which a compound made from beeswax and resin was required — it almost sounds like mediaeval alchemy! These materials were kept in a cupboard in Mr. Hunter's room which was situated just outside the workshop. In making my search for the aforementioned compound I discovered, amidst a pile of back issues of *The Woodworker*, a small bundle of the much more visually interesting *Men Only*! "Well I never", said I to myself, all thoughts of beeswax and resin now set aside! The mags were neatly tied with string so I could not explore their contents — I was thwarted you might say! But what were they doing there? Here is how I found out.

At the period of which I am writing Mr. Harold (Harry) Parkin, of whom more later, had been confined to hospital with a hernia — or something of the kind. Shortly after his return to school I chanced to meet him and respectfully enquired if he was feeling better. "Yes", he responded although I still thought he looked rather unwell but, to my youthful gaze, Mr. Parkin always did seem to be about 110 years old! He then said, somewhat confidingly: "I had a visit in hospital from Mr. Hunter, and guess what? He brought me some naughty magazines"! So I then realised that the *Men Only* of which I had caught sight were after all intended for Mr. Parkin. I did not have the presence of mind, even less the temerity, to say, as I might now: "Were they to help you to keep your pecker up Sir"?

In Class 6X we had a rather unique opportunity to observe Mr. Hunter demonstrate his skills of craftsmanship. This was the period when Mr. Gregory, of whom also more later, was developing his interest in clay-pigeon shooting. The sport requires the use of two perfectly matched guns so that when one gun has been discharged it can be quickly set aside and replaced by its companion — and so on in quick succession. I recall Mr. Hunter explaining how Mr. Gregory had told him that the key to a pair of well-balanced guns is the design and construction of the head stocks. These have to be of the best quality walnut and be so perfectly matched that both guns feel identical. Mr. Hunter was given the responsibility of making these for Mr. Gregory and how magnificent they looked when completed. They must also have performed well since Mr. Gregory went on to become the National Clay-Pigeon Champion.

The discipline maintained in Mr. Hunter's workshop was no more evident than at the end of term when a whole class period was set aside to polish and oil all the steel hand tools. We burnished those tools with emery paper until they looked better than new. Beech wood planes also had to be cared for with liberal applications of linseed oil. I remember also how utterly fastidious Mr. Hunter was to ensure that all cupboards were securely locked after each lesson. This was not only for reasons of common-sense security but was also due to the fact that the workshops were used regularly in the evening by trainee apprentices working for their City and Guilds Certificate in Handicraft. I recall how one day a boy called Shaw revealed that he had seen an evening class trainee striking a mortice chisel with a hammer instead of a mallet. This was a cardinal sin in Mr. Hunter's book and, on hearing of this, he raised his eyes heaven wards as though invoking the gods to turn the culprit into a pillar of salt.

When in Class 6X, I once had occasion to admire the craftsmanship of an older boy who was I believe preparing for his A.L. woodwork exam. If I remember correctly he was called John Mawkes. He was a prefect and undertook additional periods of woodwork by way of putting in the extra time which was necessary to complete his A.L. project — as I was destined similarly so to do (more details about that shortly). John was intending to be a teacher of handicraft which, at this epoch, could only be achieved — that is effectively to the highest standards — by attending Loughborough Training College (now The University of Loughborough). John was the only pupil I ever heard Mr. Hunter call by his forename — doubtless a measure of respect for his youthful protégé.

I will set a little test of memory at this point in my woodwork narrative. Who can remember the *Toppers* — more correctly *The Television Toppers*? If you had a television set in the mid 1950s the TV Toppers appeared at 8.00 p.m. each Saturday night. They were a group of young women famous for their long fish-net stocking legs and their high-stepping dance routines — somewhat in the style of those of the choreographer Busby Berkeley of Hollywood fame. For their day these girls were ever so slightly risqué — by today's standards they would be considered less erotic than a hot water bottle. What has this to do with woodwork do I hear you ask? The answer is as follows. One day Mr. Hunter was describing the *sequoia* or giant Californian redwood tree. He explained, reading from a magazine article, how the younger specimens were occasionally felled to yield very wide planks. "The upper parts of the tree are first removed by agile lumberjacks who ascend the trees with the assistance of specially spiked boots"! Then came a moment of unintended humour — he added: "These men are known as *Toppers*"! Mr. Hunter contrived to keep a serious face — but he knew that we knew what he was thinking!

Meanwhile in our companion lessons concerned with technical drawing, we continued to make progress with our understanding of more advanced building construction as exemplified by Figs 15–17.

The day of our Building Diploma examination in woodwork practice duly arrived. The test piece was a rebated frame. This required the setting out and making of four haunch mortise and tenon joints with the added complication of rebates on their inner edge. Two boys worked, in the usual way, at a bench. I was paired off with my friend, from Anns Road Secondary School days, John Butcher. Half way through the test John's wooden jack plane became clogged in the throat and he was allowed to complete his work with the much superior metal jack plane. This gave him an edge, no pun intended, and, whereas I made a good job of the required frame, John's was fantastic. Allow me to take leave of Class 6X therefore by saying that the prize for woodwork in the Building Diploma Year was awarded, deservedly so, to my good friend from junior-school days John Butcher.

A.L. Woodwork

Reference to woodwork at the CTS would be incomplete without mention of Mr. Henry Mclean. He was known, appropriately as 'Mac', by Messrs Hunter and Pilling, under whose direction he worked as a technician. Mr. McClean was constantly employed in sharpening tools and sawing and planing wood. He had hands the size of the proverbial dinner plates, the nature of his rough work imparting to his fingers calluses that seemed to render them impervious to hardship. I got to know Mr. Mclean rather well, by virtue of the fact that my woodwork bench, for my A.L. studies, was as at the back of the workshop close to where he undertook his seemingly endless operations of enabler and provider.

One day he overheard me whistling a passage from Mozart's *Eine Kleine Nachtmusik* — like you do when you are happily engaged in your work! Mr. Mclean confided in me that he had the Mozart on record — but that his wife did not like it and would not let him play it if she was in the house! Poor man. Mr. Mclean was a most kindly and amenable individual. On another occasion he let me know that it was his ambition to do some teaching but that Mr. Wadge did not regard him, at that time, to be adequately qualified — on paper that is. It is possible that this circumstance may have eventually changed since I recall, about a year later, Mr. Wadge announce at Speech Day that Mr. McLean had been awarded the City and Guild's Certificate in Handicraft — no small achievement for a man of little formal education who had, as they say where I now live in Scotland, 'come up through the tools'.

A.L. woodwork was the culmination of craft training for a Builder at the CTS — I suppose the equivalent for an Engineer would be A.L. Metalwork. Only a few of us took the course, in parallel with our more academic studies in maths (pure and applied) — or 'full' pure and 'full' applied maths and physics — and/or possibly chemistry. For our A.L. woodwork course we had to design and construct a 'special project'. I decided upon a record cabinet to house my collection of LPs — all six of them! The cabinet was made from oak framing with oak side panels and doors. It was a very ambitious undertaking and I had to put in extra time during the lunch break in order to have any chance of completing the work in the stipulated period. On one of these occasions I found myself in the company of Mr. Hunter who was hard at work on his own special project, namely, an elaborate conservatory, the timber parts of which he was pre-fabricating. Builders had been commissioned to erect the structure and the deadline was fast approaching. Mr. Hunter asked me if I would lend him a hand. What else could I say but, "Yes Sir"! So, setting aside my unfinished record cabinet, I found myself entrusted to construct the sill of Mr. Hunter's conservatory which was made from no less a material than teak — the prince of hardwoods. It was a considerable responsibility; I had to set out all the required profiles and the weathering and throating which I then shaped with a plough plane. It felt just like taking an examination! On completion of the sill, I eventually finished my record cabinet. I still have it as a reminder of those halcyon days when time seemed to be available in abundance and a task could, in pursuit of perfection, be allowed to fill all the hours available.

Another boy in the A.L. woodwork class at this time was Ken Taylor who was of mixed nationality. I remember that Ken wanted to become an architect but went instead into the Sheffield Town Hall to work for the Local Authority. For his A.L. test piece he made a coffee table, the top of which was made from jointed boards of a beautiful tropical hardwood which varied in colour from dark brown — almost black — to cream. This had to be French polished in the manner required by tradition, namely, using button shellac dissolved in methylated spirit. Poor Ken had to apply about a dozen coats before Mr. Hunter was satisfied that the resulting surface was, to quote: "as smooth as a baby's bottom"!

I will interrupt my woodwork narrative for a moment and insert a few remarks here of a more personal nature. These concern the death of my mother to which I will make fuller reference later. A few days after my mother's funeral I was working alone in the Holly

Building woodwork shop when in came Mr. Hunter. It was in fact morning break time and I had stayed behind for a few minutes to finish something off. Perhaps Mr. Hunter had tactfully chosen a quite moment so that he could say a few words to me unobserved from the gaze of the rest of the class. Be this as it may, he called me over to his desk — significantly in a subdued voice. He looked at me over the top of his glasses, which was one of his mannerisms, and said: "I'm sorry to hear about your mother — its a bad business"? And that was it. Short, to the point, compassionate and effective. I thanked him and got on with my work.

The A.L. woodwork examination was a real challenge. It consisted of three parts; a written paper, a practical exercise and a design study — in all about ten hours of application. The written paper went well for me. It contained a question on modern chemical adhesives — which were then starting to supplant the traditional animal-based gelatine glue. I had revised this so I was OK on that part of the paper. I could add here, by way of more general interest, that I distinctly recall Mr. Hunter using, for the very first time, a new adhesive called *Evo Stick* — now a household commodity. We were all astonished how effectively it was possible to bond two surfaces together without the use of 'G' cramps. Also on the exam paper was a question concerning the influence of historical styles on the design of period furniture — Chippendale, Hepplewhite and Sheraton. With these also revised I was, as we now would say, 'on a roll'. The practical examination was a very different matter. It gave me cause for much anguish as I will now explain.

The tribulations of that afternoon, one day way back in 1958, are as fresh in my memory as if it were but yesterday. We had to make a lapped dovetail joint surmounting a mortise and tenon — a complex joint used in high quality carcass work. The enthusiastic will find this joint illustrated at p.108 in *The Woodworker's Pocket Book* — which was required reading for A.L. woodwork candidates. To my lasting regret I made a major error in the setting out of the various parts of the joint such that my lapped dovetail — above — would not unite with the mortise and tenon — below. How I anguished over this. There was nothing I could do to redeem the situation. Five years of workshop practice, characterised until then by — although I say it myself — good and careful work, now culminated in a monumental botch. Some days later, whilst working on my then unfinished record cabinet, Mr. Hunter came over to me saying: "Russell, that was a bad mistake you made the other day"! "Thanks a bundle Mr. Hunter", I thought to myself. But, he added: "Remember, there's still the design paper to come. You may do well on that". Thus consoled, I awaited the day of the design paper — which followed about two weeks after the disastrous practical. Here's how it went — a quite different story.

It was not possible to revise for the examination in woodwork design; you could but put your trust in the experience gained in making projects and looking through previous papers. We assembled in Mr. Hedley's drawing office for the exam which was supervised by Mr. Thompson. The papers were issued and I looked at mine with that sense of apprehension which is an integral part of such occasions. Then, with some incredulity, I read: "You are required to design — a record cabinet"! I could not believe my good fortune; this was the very article upon which, as I have intimated,

I had worked throughout the year as my special project. I knew my design by heart. Never, may I venture to suggest in the history of A.L. woodwork, has a candidate embarked upon the design paper so well prepared and with such a sense of confidence — by reason of shear good fortune. I embellished my design with every artifice and ornament known to draughtsmanship — determined to expunge my ignominious efforts in the practical of two weeks previously. Several weeks later, in the summer holidays, a slip of paper arrived from the School Examinations Council of the University of London informing me of my success in A.L. woodwork. My good performance in the design paper had, it would seem, offset my poor achievement in the practical. There is a little more to tell. When we returned to school in the autumn, I paid a visit to see Mr. Hunter by way of expressing a word of appreciation for his efforts. I was by then School Captain — in point of fact it was my *first* day of being School Captain — and I consequently thought that I should behave in the courteous and gracious manner expected of me (pass the sick bag). After receiving my little encomium, Mr. Hunter, somewhat pleasantly surprised, remarked: "Russell, you were just three marks short of a distinction"!

Absurd as it may seem — after all these years — I can still not forgive myself for my lamentable performance in the woodwork practical. No matter, Mr. Hunter's rigorous pedagogical legacy is such that I cannot, to this day, pick up a woodwork tool — I have several and a good workshop — without bearing in mind his strictures and precepts, half expecting to hear his admonition, if I do something wrong: "How old are you Russell"? To which I would now have to reply: "Knocking on Sir. Knocking on"!

Allow me to say I took leave of my studies in woodwork with the A.L. Handicraft Prize. With the prize money I purchased a copy of Sacheverell Sitwell's *British Architect's and Craftsmen*.

Plumbing

Classes 3Y and 5X

Builders received their practical training under the direction of Mr. Harold (Harry) Parkin R.P. — the 'R.P.' stands for 'Registered Plumber' — of which he was justly proud. Now, sadly, the citation reads Harry Parkin R.I.P. The workshop, known affectionately as Harry's Tin Shop, was situated close to the Lyceum Theatre. We used to walk down to the workshop from Leopold Street, along Chapel Walk to the workshop entrance which I believe was accessed from Arundel Street. This, seemingly innocent journey, was not without its hazards. For example I was told how one day a class of First-Year Engineers were making their way down the street, Mr. Parkin in charge — in a manner of speaking — when one lad, larking about, contrived to put his foot into a window cleaner's bucket, sending himself, and the contents, all over the pavement. We Builders were much better behaved!

I have a little story that in its way sums up Mr. Parkin rather well — at least in a manner of speaking, by which I mean it captures the manner in which things could go sadly wrong for dear old Harry. The story is as follows. At some period during one of the terrible conflicts in the Great War, Harry's Commanding Officer ordered him, and a small number of soldiers, to venture into 'no-man's land'. It appears that a large tree still remained standing and was being used as a landmark by the enemy to judge the range of their fire. The task was to set charges around the base of the tree, and, when at a safe distance, to detonate these and thereby bring the tree to the ground. At first all went according to plan; the brave lads laid the charges, retreated and then detonated them. It was then that things did not go according to plan. Harry Parkin himself relates: 'The charges placed around the tree blew it right out of the ground and sent it up in the air — like an umbrella. However, since its branches were still intact, it descended back to earth, like a parachute, whereupon the trunk impaled itself in the mud — leaving the tree just as it was before, standing bolt upright'! I don't suppose he got a medal for that! But now back to Harry and the CTS.

On the 18th January 1954, I recorded in my notebook: 'Overalls should be worn; lead is poisonous; a piece of rag should be carried to wipe the hands, damage to any tool must be reported and wrist watches should not be worn lest they be thrown out of order'. Such was Class 3Y's introduction to the mysteries of plumbing.

"Lead", Mr. Parkin explained, "is a ductile material which, because of its malleable nature, is capable of being shaped into a variety of forms"! We certainly put this proposition to the test and contrived to bash sheet lead into shapes not ordinarily found in any plumber's manual. Mr. Parkin was very sanguine about this, remarking, dolefully, that our efforts were destined to be molten back into fresh lead sheet — doubtless to be mutilated by yet another generation of apprentice plumbers. Slowly and imperceptibly however we began to acquire the dexterity necessary to work the lead sheet into such forms as 'herringbone flashings' and 'apron flashings', to make the 'lap joints' to vertical weathering and we learned how to round off a lead pipe with either a 'taft' or a 'lip' (Figs 18 & 19).

It has to be conceded that much of the delight we experienced in Harry's Tin Shop was due, how shall I put this, to Mr. Parkin's *relaxed* style of discipline — that is to say, his more-or-less complete lack of discipline! In short, we exploited his good and kindly nature. Our frolics took a variety of forms. A favourite diversion was to beat our bossing sticks in unison upon the surface of the metal-clad workbenches. The ensuing rhythmic cacophony was enough to rival the sounds of a drop hammer — I'm sure that there were occasions when the din must have disturbed the rehearsals in the Lyceum Theatre just round the corner! In vain would Mr. Parkin blast on his whistle to establish order — the sounds of his whistle not being audible above the noise. Silence would eventually prevail — even silly boys have their limits — and a red-faced, exhausted Mr. Parkin would give us a piece of his mind. Perhaps it was our youthful, excessive boisterous behaviour which precipitated Mr. Parkin into hospital — for quite a period. Regrettably we Builders thereby missed many of our favourite workshop classes.

Mr. Parkin was, first and foremost, a master craftsman, and it would be an injustice to his memory, and capacity as a teacher, to portray his classes as being an endless lark. This is far from the truth. I recall many times when the class grouped around him in total silence as he demonstrated a technique with a blow torch or soldering iron, with the practiced facility of an expert — leaving us tyros lost in admiration. Perhaps the apogee of his

technical expertise was the wiping of a lead joint, created by pouring molten solder from a ladle. In order to give his demonstration, the two parts of the joint — the spigot and socket — had to be first held in a clamp. With some ceremony Mr. Parkin went to the back of the workshop and returned with an amazing-looking contrivance which he deliberately threw down onto the metal-clad workshop bench to demonstrate its robustness. He then said: "If you ever invent anything, don't invent something like this — it will never wear out. Invent something that does wear out and has to be replaced"! The subject of this little piece of homespun philosophy was a universal clamp made from numerous cast-iron sections — it could secure just about anything in any position. He then secured two pieces of pipe and proceeded to make the required joint by pouring molten solder over the two parts and then working it into shape using a moleskin cloth — masterfully! "Would anyone like to try?" he asked — after having given this perfect demonstration of his skill. We collectively shrank away from the workbench shaking our heads. Our timorous reaction prompted Mr. Parkin to tell us a rather harrowing tale of the occasion, some years previously, when I boy had risen to the challenge of attempting to make such a wiped joint. Horrendously, he poured the ladle of solder over his fingers instead of the joint! He had forgotten to pick up the moleskin cloth! On hearing this we fell into a respectful silence, each of us examining our fingers trying to imagine the consequences of such an accident — there was no larking about that day!

I am prompted to recount another tale — rather horrific and not for the squeamish. We used blow torches in the workshop which were provided with a supply of mains gas and compressed air from a generator The air increased the temperature of the flame considerably — as we discovered when we made the ends of our soldering irons incandescent and waved them about like swords! It was tempting to disconnect the air supply pipe and to blast the powerful air jet over an unsuspecting neighbour — a sort of 'blow job' you might say! One day our fooling about induced Mr. Parkin to switch off the compressor — which was very noisy — and to have us gather around him. We new a cautionary tale was imminent. "You must understand that compressed air is very dangerous", rebuked Mr. Parkin. He then told us of some boys, at another technical school, who had inserted a compressed air pipe down the throat of a hapless boy, thereby inflating him causing massive internal injuries. This horrific tale produced the desired effect; we looked at one another sheepishly and never again played about with the air supply pipe. There is a corollary to the story. Mr. Parkin confided in me that the circumstances were in fact more grave than he had recounted. The victim had had the air pipe forced into his rectal orifice, rupturing his bowels and associated internal organs precipitating his protracted agonising death. My apologies for inflicting this story upon you.

Let me change the mood with a light-hearted anecdote. One day the Lyceum Theatre announced a forthcoming attraction in the form of a play called *The Black Widow*. I remember this for the reason that, on the same billboard, was a list of operas to be performed by the Carl Rosa Company — of which more later. The play came up in conversation with Mr. Parkin who told me that he and his wife had been to see *The Black Widow* — in anticipation that it was about the peccadilloes of an errant lady. "We were wrong", confessed a chastened Mr, Parkin, "It was all about a goldfish"!

In addition to working with lead, we also learned to fabricate objects from sheet tin. Perhaps that is how the premises derived their popular name as *Harry's Tin Shop*. As a Builder, I made only a very few objects from tin. I do recall learning how to solder and to manipulate a soldering iron. Mr. Parkin was insistent the iron, more properly the copper head, should be moderately heated — and no more. "You must look after your tools", urged Mr. Parkin — the ambiguity of his wording provoking some mirth in the class. Inevitably, one boy, by the name of Caunt, raised the temperature of his soldering iron almost to melting point. Seeing Mr. Parkin approaching, he hastily concealed the glowing iron under his bench. To this day I remember how Mr. Parkin, suspicious that something was amiss, came over to have a look at what was going on — placing his foot within a cat's whisker of the hot iron! It was a narrow escape for all concerned.

Here is a nice little story to end this section with. A number of years after the events I have been describing I had occasion to pay a visit to Mr. Parkin in his workshop — I was entrusted with the delivery of a message and a piece of equipment. On entering the workshop nothing much appeared to have changed; boys were rhythmically bashing away at their lead sheets and generally larking about. As I was about to leave, Mr. Parkin beckoned me over to a cupboard which he was sorting out. It was full of specimen examples of good work done by various boys over the years. "Look at this", he said, offering me a beautifully crafted pipe complete with spigot and socket joint and curved lip (Fig. 11). I admired the piece and commented on the high standard of workmanship. Mr. Parkin smiled and turned the pipe around — to reveal my own name!

I hope the surviving spirit of Mr. Parkin will forgive us our levity and youthful frivolity. Ours was non-malignant pleasantry. Allow me to say I took leave of Class 5X with the Plumbing Prize, gift of the Sheffield and District Branch of the Federation of Master Builders.

Brickwork

Class 3Y

I think most Builders had something of a love-hate relationship with brickwork classes. We undoubtedly enjoyed constructing walls and cutting bricks, but we all disliked intensely the effect of the sand-lime mix on our hands; it made them turn dry and wrinkled. Little use was made of cement so that our constructions could be dismantled and used again — re-cycled in today's parlance. The brickwork workshop was immense. It was located in the basement of the Bow Building and ran the entire length of the premises — below both Drawing Office DO1 and the classroom at the end.

I suppose only a technical school could ever have been equipped with a brickwork workshop. Ours had a concrete floor appropriate to the heavy rough work that went on in the place and daylight entered by means of rather dingy windows, set in the pavement of West Street (formerly Bow Street), which were covered over with thick glass lenses. We stored bricks at one end of the room and at the other was a supply of sand. Just outside of the main workshop was a changing room

equipped with lockers. It was here that the need for our boiler suits became apparent. We changed into these for our brickwork classes. I recall seeing one or two boys going home wearing their boiler suits in combination with their school blazer — a rather bizarre sight to say the least. Leading off the workshop was the teacher's office. His window overlooked the school playground but it was masked with frosted glass. The workshop could be a cold place but when full of lads it was a hive of activity with the air resounding to the sounds of shovels scraping the floor, trowels tapping bricks into place and boys chatting as they will when they are enjoying their work.

Brickwork was taught to us by Mr. James Bolton who, co-incidentally, came from Bolton — and he had a pronounced accent to prove it. He lived somewhere up Chesterfield Road — in the direction of Woodseats — and drove to school each day in a stylish green Riley car. He used to cast a glance at the queues waiting at the tram stop and if he saw a CTS boy standing he would give a toot, pull in and offer a lift. I arrived several mornings to school this way, often in the company of one or two other CTS lads. As a consequence I got to know Mr. Bolton quite well. He had been a bricklayer for several years before being attracted into teaching — there can only have been very few jobs in secondary education for bricklayers! Mr. Bolton had a mechanical turn of mind. One day, driving along, he drew my attention to an elaborate brass mechanism below the steering wheel. "I made that", said Mr. Bolton proudly, "its a gear selector". "Really!", I responded — with obligatory admiration. It appears this device could be used to pre-set the gear which the driver next required — or something of the kind.

From Mr. Bolton we learned the terminology of the bricklayer — quoins, headers, stretchers and the like — and acquired the skills to bond bricks in the time-honoured manner of mixing cement, applying it to the trowel — called cutting and culling — then laying the bricks and testing them with a spirit level. We realised that it was all ten-times more difficult than it would appear when you observe professional bricklayers at their work. From the simplest exercises, which consisted of little more than laying one brick upon another, we progressed to learning about the intricacies of bonding bricks together and of the different names by which the bonds are known, principally Stretcher bond, English bond and Flemish bond— but not James Bond! We even practised some special techniques such as toothed ends and racking back.

The skills of which we did not gain any practice, nor which were ever demonstrated to us, were those of the plasterer. Evidence that the skills of this trade had once featured on the CTS Builder's curriculum was to be found in a basement room off the main workshop. Here, scattered like fossilised remains, were to be seen fragments of ornate plaster cornices, decorative mouldings and console brackets — all relics from a bygone era of domestic architectural fashion. A large plasterer's bench occupied the middle of this room upon which stood a trough partly filled with brilliant white rock-hard plaster — abandoned by the boys who last did plaster work. I found this spectacle rather moving and evocative. It was all somewhat sad and neglected and told of previous generations of lads who had worked there and had moved on — as we in our own turn would.

The shear physicality of brickwork often commended the subject to us, no more so than when we were required to cut bricks in half with a club hammer and bolster. One day, when discussing the relative strengths of bricks, Mr. Bolton mentioned 'Staffordshire Blues'. These are bricks of such density they were used in the nineteenth century as damp-proof courses to houses, and in arch construction to railway bridges. After extolling their virtues, Mr. Bolton remarked: "Don't ever try to cut one of these in half, it's impossible"! He added: "I've seen grown men throw down their tools and walk off the building site when asked to cut a hole through a wall made of Staffordshire Blues!" We listened attentively and I, for one, to this day have never attempted this apparently impossible feat.

Instruction in brickwork was not confined exclusively to practical work in the basement workshop in Bow Building. We also undertook a parallel course of study based on drawing-office practice. In this we became more familiar with the bricklayer's tools and equipment by drawing them in our exercise books with related tasks being set for homework. We also made more detailed studies of brickwork bonding, than would otherwise be possible in the workshop, by drawing different bonding techniques and wall intersections (Figs 20–22). By this means we progressed to study door and window openings in walls and, one of the ultimate challenges in brickwork, namely arch construction.

We were exhorted by our teacher to take a wider interest in our subject than that afforded by lessons alone. For this reason I went along, one Saturday afternoon, to an Open Day held at the Salmon Pastures College of Building — or some such institution. It was located close by the River Don and I recall reading an extract from an ancient Charter which stated: "Boys shall not be fed salmon more than three days per week"! — lucky lads! On display was the most wonderful collection of City and Guild project work that I have ever seen. This included examples of arch construction in gauged brickwork — i.e., finely jointed geometrically shaped bricks, of soft texture, set in the most intricate of curved forms. There was also an exhibition of drawing instruments which included a T square more than ten feet long normally used by naval architects for drafting the side views of ships. Large display cases of drawing instruments were also on view. This reminds me; do any of you recall similar displays of Sheffield tools being on show down at the Sheffield Midland Station? For years they could be seen in display cases mounted in the elevated passageway over the main line. I remember being taken, as a little boy, to see a similar display, on an even grander scale, at the Cutlers' Hall — for the record this would be about 1948.

Our brickwork studies did not continue into Class 6X. Mr. Bolton left the CTS, presumably finding it more rewarding to lay bricks than to try to educate them. Be this as it may, his departure was a loss to the school; he was a skilful artisan and a most affable teacher.

Art

Classes 3Y and 5X

The teaching of art, in my time at the CTS, was entrusted to Mr. Edgar Grantham. One might say he presided over the subject since his statuesque form towered over all around him. I well recall an occasion — a field trip to Haddon Hall — when Mr. Grantham, the tallest member of staff, was in the company of Mr. Parkin, the shortest member of staff. The sight of the two of them together invoked the image of the prop taking the peg for a walk — as the old expression used to go. I will find it difficult to conceal my admiration for Mr. Grantham. I owe much to him since it was, as I will show, his enthusiasm for architecture that kindled my own interest in this subject.

Our art classes were held in DO1, appropriately since we were able to use the spacious desks set out in the room which also served, as I have previously remarked, as a drawing office. In having Mr. Grantham as our teacher, we were fortunate in being taught by a professionally trained artist. I recall how, after school, he once showed me a selection of his student work. His portfolio contained a fine display of life studies and drawings of plaster casts of sculpture derived from classical antiquity. Most vividly however I remember Mr. Grantham's self-portrait, titled, appropriately, *The Artist as a Young Man*. The work was about life size, rendered in oils and captured perfectly Mr. Grantham's youthful features.

Our first-year course soon revealed Mr. Grantham's personal enthusiasm for architecture — and his scholarly disposition. Within a few weeks each member of the class had been issued with a cyclostyled sheet titled *Glossary of Architecture*. From this we were required to learn the meanings of selected architectural terms which were set out in alphabetical order — *Abacus, Abutment, Aisle … Wall-Shaft, Weathering* and *Wheel-Window*. We were also required to illustrate several of these terms as an aid to our learning (Figs 23–25). Each Monday afternoon we presented our sketches to Mr. Grantham for his inspection and we had to be ready to define the meanings of selected words. Repeated failure would induce Mr. Grantham into a mild rage, provoking his favourite recrimination — 'blockhead'!

Mr. Grantham's instruction was by no means dry and formulaic. Accompanying his glossary was a series of large-format illustrations tracing the development of habitation from the earliest times to the mediaeval period in the sequence; caves, huts, Saxon dwellings, Norman keeps, castle plans and the English house (Figs 26 & 27). As part of his instruction we digressed to study selected architectural forms such as timber roofs, arches and chimneys (Fig. 28). Remember that this highly ordered, and specialised curriculum, was for boys of age only twelve to thirteen. We were required to copy Mr. Grantham's illustrations into a special large-size grey-backed jotter designated 'Upright Drawing Book'. A friendly rivalry sprang up, between myself and a few others, to see who could reproduce the illustrations the most faithfully using mapping pen and Indian ink. Another of Mr. Grantham's enthusiasms was for hand-drawn lettering. We drafted a series of studies using the block-letter style of alphabet beloved of all art teachers (Fig. 29). For setting out the curved letter-forms we used our newly acquired drawing instruments. What could be achieved in class however was inevitably limited to the time available. Consequently, about half way through First Year Mr. Grantham let it be known he was keen to establish an Art Club, the idea of which was to promote an enthusiasm for art and architecture for those who were sufficiently interested. It is no exaggeration to say that my participation in the work of this club was to determine the future direction of my career.

The Art Club met on Tuesday evenings after school in DO1. Initially there were about a dozen and a half members who gradually dwindled to myself and three or four others. Even this little group of stalwarts diminished until I was the sole survivor and received Mr. Grantham's undivided attention in the form of him setting me tasks which I would complete in my spare time — I will say more of these later. Concerning the Art Club, in its early days Mr. Grantham would often talk about various matters related to art and architecture and occasionally the small band of enthusiasts would draw and model small sculptures in clay. Let me give one example — from many — of our work. One Tuesday evening, Mr. Grantham introduced us to the architectural achievements of the Roman Emperor Trajan and to the famed Doric column erected in his memory. The classical style of lettering adorning this column — usually described as Antique Roman (or Roman for short) — forms the basis of most formal inscriptions adorning traditional buildings and monuments. Mr. Grantham considered we should master the intricacies of this beautiful script which presents a considerable challenge in setting-out and compass work. To understand the style and layout principles of the letters some of us purchased a handsome art sheet of the Roman alphabet — it cost me my week's pocket money — designed by a Bradford artist called E. Sanderson. The reason for my saying all this is that as far as my art lessons were concerned I had now found my *raison d'être* and I completed all the required Roman-letter exercises with enthusiasm (Fig. 30). Indeed, my enterprise led to my receiving my first 'artistic commission' as I will now relate.

Mr. Grantham was a member of a group of fellow art teachers who were representative of various towns and who met from time to time to talk about curriculum development in art. As a backdrop to their meetings it was the practice to have a small exhibition of pupils' work representative of the various participating schools. Mr. Grantham had made a selection of such work — modesty precludes my saying how much of my own material was on display — and he wanted a caption, in the Roman style of lettering, to proclaim the name of our school at a forthcoming meeting. He asked me to undertake the work. I set about the task with enthusiasm, first outlining, and then filling in with Indian ink, Roman letters — two inches high — proclaiming:

THE
CENTRAL
TECHNICAL SCHOOL

The meeting in question was held in Leeds. I was invited to go with three other boys, travelling in Mr. Grantham's small green van. It was a Ford and had neither windows nor seats in the back. I have good reason to remember this van — let me explain. The day came when Mr. Grantham wanted my 'artwork' for the impending exhibition. It so happens that he lived at Norton Lees Road not too far from my home in Valley Terrace. By way of interest you could get a good look into Mr. Grantham's sitting room from the top of the bus on its way to Graves Park — the walls were lined with pictures befitting the home of an art teacher! So, almost being neighbours, Mr. Grantham gave me a lift home in his van to collect my (beautiful) lettering on the way. But we didn't get very far! We went to his van which

was parked in the small CTS car park; I got inside and then, on closing the passenger's door, I attempted to pull it shut with the 'winder' for the window — instead of the handle. The consequence was the mechanism came away in pieces — spring, washer, securing nut etc. We had to virtually dismantle the interior to find all the pieces. An awkward silence followed as we got under way! The mood soon changed though and, prompted by me, we fell into conversation about how you qualified to become an architect. Until that time the word architect had just been to me another word — although one that required a little extra care to pronounce correctly. I did learn a bit more about the profession through my CTS friend John Mastin whose father was an architect. I recall once asking John if he had ever thought of becoming an architect himself. John looked at me bleakly and replied: "If you'd been dragged round as many churches as I have"! So I didn't pursue the matter any further with John. But Mr. Grantham's information was very welcome. He had, very obligingly, written to the Royal Institute of British Architects (RIBA) to obtain their guidance notes on this subject. He explained to me how it required seven years to become an Associate member — it sounded like a prison sentence! I recall asking him how you became a Fellow. He just laughed and remarked: "Don't worry your head about that"! He was right. It took me twenty-five years to be elected to my Fellowship. I duly collected my lettering from home and passed the rolled-up sheet to Mr. Grantham through the now jammed-open passenger's window — pretending not to notice the collection of chrome parts on the seat which would have to be re-assembled!

The eventual journey to Leeds in Mr. Grantham's little van was memorable for the following reason. As we had driven home I had noticed how near to the roof interior was Mr Grantham's head — but then he was, as I have already remarked, a man of considerable physical stature. This observation is significant for the following reason. We boys who went on the journey were required to sit in the back of the van on small stools — with the exception of one lad who sat in the front passenger seat. Needless to say he was exhorted not to dare close the door with the winder for the window — which by now was repaired! Those of us seated on stools now found our head perilously close to the roof interior. I have reason to remember the ensuing journey well since a banged my head on the roof at periodic intervals all the way from Sheffield to Leeds and back! This may indeed account for certain aspects of my subsequent behaviour in later life!

By the way, I very nearly was not allowed to go on the journey at all. My mother, hearing of the proposed trip objected and remarked: "You're not going away to Leeds in a van with a strange man"! I prevailed by protesting: "Mr. Grantham isn't a strange man, he's a teacher"! I will leave the reader to ponder if my reply was entirely logical.

On arriving at Leeds we found the various schools' art work was on display in a gallery located within a park. I felt proud to see my lettering introducing the pictorial work of the group of boys from the CTS who had their creations exhibited on the walls. The main exhibit from the CTS was an underwater scene. It portrayed a pearl diver swimming amidst colourful sea plants with tropical fish cascading all about. Whoever had created this little masterpiece — was it one of you CTS lads reading this? — had perfectly captured the aquatic atmosphere of slightly blurred colours and fragmented light. It was so good the group of us who had travelled to Leeds just felt rather envious! As far as my CTS lettering study was concerned — I never did get my sheet of artwork back.

Whilst Mr. Grantham took part in the meeting, we boys who had accompanied him were left to have a look around Leeds — ostensibly to study the civic architecture. Prompted by Mr. Grantham, we went to see the pioneering post-war circular plan-form block of flats which, regrettably, some years later started to became plagued by social problems — they were demolished a few years ago. There being limits to the extra-curricula enthusiasm of even good and diligent boys (!) I suggested that we should all go off to the Central Station — to do some train spotting. Eventually discovering where we had spent most of our time, Mr. Grantham remarked: "So you now know all about the engineering of large roofs in cast iron and glass"? We nodded sagely, relieved, however, that we were not required to produce our sketch books in evidence. In due course we made our way — bumpty bump — back home to Sheffield.

I will stay with the theme of Roman letters a moment longer in the form of a short digression. In my First Year of university art classes, which formed part of the architecture curriculum — held each Saturday morning — we were required to draw a text in large format antique Roman letters. For this exercise, I made use of my CTS Sanderson style-sheet which one morning fell under the gaze of the studio master — the name accorded to the art-class instructor. To cut a long story short he (Mr. John Wilson A.R.C.A. by name) told me how he had studied with E. Sanderson, mentioning at the same time his personal friendship with the rather better known Yorkshire artist-sculptor Henry Moore. So, by a rather round about route, my CTS lettering sheet gave me a connection with my First Year studies in architecture at the University of Sheffield.

Roman lettering featured in the design of the CTS school badge which underwent a number of transformations over the years. It so happens I can claim to have influenced the final version of the design. This is how it happened. Mr. Grantham held a competition to solicit ideas for the new design and the outcome was that he adopted my motif of three wheat sheaves for the lower part — see Fig. 86. To be honest, I got the idea from the Sheffield coat of arms painted on the side of tramcars. If you remember this design, you will recall that Vulcan (god of metalworking) is portrayed wielding his hammer — it is in fact Vulcan who surmounts the cupola of the Town Hall. I used to imagine Vulcan going home to tell his wife what a hell of a day he'd had slaving over a hot anvil!

Occasionally the Art Club was augmented by others for the purpose of going on field trips. These activities took the form of excursions to country houses. They were popular and some of you may remember taking part in these visits. For example, I have a group photograph taken on a visit to Haddon Hall which includes no fewer than 34 boys. We also made excursions to Hardwick Hall, Chatsworth House and Nostell Priory. I have a number of particular memories of my visit to the latter mansion house. A small group of us travelled by bus to the house which is situated near Wakefield. On this occasion we were in the company of Mr. Grantham and Mr. Parkin. I remember the journey well for the reason that I lost my return ticket and had to pay the fare twice. On approaching the house we contemplated the front elevation whereupon Mr. Grantham turned to me and said: "Well, Russell, what style of architecture are those columns"? "Doric Sir", I replied confidently. "Ionic", replied Mr. Grantham laconically. "Shit", I thought and I silently reproached myself because I did in fact know the answer — as you will be able to infer from what follows shortly. Later that day we lads were free to wander in the grounds and another pupil — Ken Taylor — took my photograph. I still have this amongst my little collection of CTS memorabilia. My notebooks also survive from this period (1954–56) and it is from these that I have extracted the following short essays that I wrote for Mr. Grantham as part of his encouragement to master the classical language of architecture and to develop the skills of architectural description. In the following essays, spelling has been corrected and the punctuation has been improved, otherwise the texts which follow are exactly as I originally conceived them in 1956.

Hardwick Hall
An Essay for Mr. Grantham
Terry Russell
1956

Hardwick Hall was built by Robert Smithson. It is a typical English Renaissance country house. It is unusual in plan, consisting of a rectangular block with added bays. The house is made famous by its large mullioned and transomed windows which have given rise to the saying: "Hardwick Hall more glass than wall".

The external façade is pierced by three storeys of windows of unusual conception in that they grow higher towards the roof. Surmounting the cornice is a low balustrade which combines with ornate scroll work containing the initials 'E. S' — Elizabeth Shrewsbury. Apart from providing decoration, the balustrade assists in concealing the chimneys which are, however, well executed.

The front porch, running parallel with the famed Long Gallery (166′ 4″), is covered so as to form an arcaded walk, the roof of which is supported by eight Doric columns. These are rather miniature but retain the delicate entasis and entablature of this order. The frieze of the entablature is plain but incorporates metopes and triglyphes which occur at regular intervals.

On entering the large entrance hall the visitor passes between a portico of Doric columns supporting a small gallery to accommodate an orchestra. Above the chimney piece is a large amount of strapwork decoration showing the crest of the house. It is executed in plaster and was probably painted while wet as in the case of fresco painting. The state room is reached by climbing a 'hanging staircase' constructed from honey coloured sandstone and is decorated with tapestries similar in character to the famous Bayeux work. The state room door has a glass tympanum crowned by a marble pediment and since it is viewed at an angle its edge is chamfered. The main feature of the room is the chimney piece which is also surmounted by coloured strapwork. The cornice is supported by two small unfluted Doric columns alternating in black and white local stone.

The ceiling is of pure white plaster heavily decorated in folded and spiral forms, but the frieze has many paintings from the hands of the masters. The floor is covered by large rush mats — as are to be found throughout the house. These are supported on floorboards more than twelve inches wide which appear to have been shaped with an adze. Adjoining this room is the Long Gallery which possesses a fine fireplace worked in alabaster. Throughout this gallery many beautiful paintings are hung; others are painted directly on to the plaster or wooden panels. Other rooms are similar in style but always throughout the house the typical English Renaissance style is dominant.

Chatsworth House
An Essay for Mr. Grantham
Terry Russell
1956

Chatsworth House was built by William Talman and is famous for its priceless treasures of art and literature and for the gardens laid out by Joseph Paxton. The main, longitudinal, façade is confronted with a wide sweeping staircase of Baroque style having a low balustrade. This leads to the main entrance hall. The first storey is of rusticated masonry, the other masonry being covered with a stucco-plaster finish. The façade is pierced by two storeys of mullioned and transomed windows which are separated by Ionic pilasters and which are surmounted alternately by triangular and semi-circular pediments. A balustrade is placed above the cornice as at Hardwick Hall.

Inside, above the entrance hall, is an orchestra balcony where the players could accompany dancers in the spacious hall beneath. Below the Long Gallery is the library which is situated at the junction of two long oak-panelled corridors. In these corridors are displayed many fine paintings by the masters together with beautiful pieces of pottery; these interiors are furnished with flowered carpets rather than rush mats as at Hardwick Hall. At the end of the main corridor is a crypto porticus or enclosed colonnade which overlooks the entrance hall — opposite to the orchestra balcony.

The chimney pieces throughout Chatsworth House are very large each having a breast about eight-feet square; these are decorated with figures and mouldings. Each cornice is supported by columns of the Composite Order and have their own small stylobate which protrudes to form a seat.

The Long Gallery is reached by mounting the grand staircase with its carved newel post, radiating steps, and pierced balustrades — all of which gave a dignified approach to the rooms above. The gallery is not as long as that at Hardwick Hall but [nonetheless] runs the length of the house and is decorated with ornate chimney pieces, panelled or tapestried walls, large mullioned windows and a modelled plaster ceiling. It was used to display the treasures of the house and served also as a covered promenade to reach the bay rooms.

The music room contains, as one would expect, many musical instruments but it served also as a living room and hence has in it bookcases, chairs, tables and many other fine pieces of English, French and Italian furniture — of which it had become a hobby to collect.

On the east side of the house there is another large hall which is reached by means of the library. This hall is lit by means of a glass roof and large French windows and throughout all the beauties of Hellenic art are expressed in the form of columns, arcades, high-relief mouldings and sculpture. Besides these there are many fine heirlooms and possessions — for example, armour, weapons, portraits and even the family stagecoach!

In the basement of the house is the chapel with its hammer-beam roof and high altar lit by tiny windows with reveals two-feet thick. The foundations of the house pass right into the chapel and are supported upon tall, slender octagonal piers that are decorated with many architectural designs as well as the banners and shields of the house.

Nostell Priory
An Essay for Mr. Grantham
Terry Russell
1956

Nostell Priory was built about 1730 by the Adam brothers and is famous for its collection of Chippendale furniture and paintings by Rembrandt. The entrance to the main façade is approached by a sweeping staircase evolved from the baroque style having a low pierced balustrade constructed from honey-coloured sandstone. On each side

of the doorway are a number of Ionic pilasters forming a portico which supports a typical Greek pediment, the tympanum of which is filled with figures.

Below the entrance, the masonry is rusticated whereas above it is plain ashlar pierced by Georgian style windows which have alternating triangular and circular pediments. The skyline is broken by a small cornice which is not accompanied by an architrave but which has dentils as are found in all Ionic and Corinthian cornices — which correspond with the mutules of the Doric order.

Below the main entrance hall is a secondary entrance which gives access to a basement hall wherein four mighty isolated piers can be seen and which carry the greater part of the weight of the house.

Inside the hall is a minstrel gallery, similar to that at Hardwick Hall, supported upon small Doric columns where coats-of-arms and regalia hang on display. From the hall there is a hanging [cantilevered] staircase designed by Adam when he was a mere nineteen years old; it leads to the head-of-state bedroom which is furnished with fine cabinets. The ceiling in this room is heavily worked in plaster and has several famous paintings let into it. However, the chief features are the Italian and Venetian inlaid ornamental cabinets and the large painting of an architectural composition by Rembrandt — reputed to be worth £20,000 [at the time of writing, namely, 1956].

The Long Gallery is not maintained in this house, as was the custom of the late English renaissance, but is sub-divided into small bedrooms and chambers. The first of these is curiously decorated with Chinese wallpaper some 180 years old, having all its panels of different design and again hung with the work of Rembrandt. Further within the room is a semi-circular table designed so as to be placed beside a wall and made of marble which is inlaid with many coloured stones. In an adjacent chamber is a large chimney piece worked in yellow and white alabaster of rusticated design — this too was designed by Adam.

Nearly all the furniture in [the rooms just described] was designed by Chippendale and includes: a pair of tallboys made from rosewood, incorporating a broken-pedimented top; an ornamental clock with secret drawers operated by a wooden mechanism; a backgammon table; and a complete suite of chairs with accompanying table. In the library the bookcases are also by Chippendale and, particularly fascinating, is a door completely covered with the backs of books so as to disguise it when closed. The ceiling has a wonderful circular painting in the centre by Rembrandt [?] about which radiates a plaster ceiling [motif] designed by Adam.

Another matching staircase, similar to the one designed by Adam, gives exit from the state bedrooms and leads to a museum in which are displayed many old family treasures including the plans of the house, ancient pottery, tapestries and the old armour of bygone Dukes.

Looking back on these youthful efforts, and reading them through, they seem to me to be not too bad. I now realise how very fortunate I was to receive Mr. Grantham's undivided attention and personal supervision. My surviving sketchbooks are covered with his red-ink drawings that he created in the margins of my essays by way of elaborating a point of architectural detail prompted by my own observations (Fig. 31).

In addition to the writings on the country houses which I have just cited, Mr. Grantham also required me to make more detailed studies of selected features of 'building elements'. His list included; wrought iron work, plastered ceilings, chimney pieces, columns, doors and windows. All this work was duly completed and, once more, I benefited from Mr. Grantham's critical assessment of my work (Figs 32–35).

Our art classes were occasionally enlivened by visits to the Graves Art Gallery — again under the direction of Mr. Grantham. He led us through the various galleries selecting a picture, here and there, for comment. I recall that subjects most frequently discussed were the artists' use of colour, light and shade, and architectural perspective. More entertainingly, on one occasion, Mr. Grantham, observing our gaze fixed on a portrait of a well-endowed young woman — in a state of décolletage — remarked: "Her dumplings are boiling over"!

It was during one of our visits to the Graves Art Gallery that Mr. Grantham drew to out attention the curious optical illusion typically to be perceived in portrait painting. I am referring to the effect which the gaze of the subject has when the pupils of the eyes are placed centrally in a face which confronts the viewer as it were 'full frontally'. The gaze of such a subject has a disturbing capacity to follow the viewer as you move before it, left to right or right to left. On having this explained to us we could not resist testing every picture we approached for this effect. For the casual onlooker this must have appeared quite comical since the collective effect of our enthusiasm resulted in about thirty boys passing to and fro before the canvases as though we were taking part in some form of dancing lesson — slow, slow, quick, quick, slow! The Gallery Keeper looked somewhat perplexed at our antics and Mr. Grantham maintained a discreet distance clearly impressed by the effect his instruction had upon us but mildly embarrassed at the same time!

My most notable visit to the Graves Art Gallery was to hear Mr. (later 'Sir') Basil Spence talk about his recent (1955) design for Coventry Cathedral. This was an evening lecture to which Mr. Grantham had drawn our attention and had programmed into the activities of the Art Club. As it happened, I was the only one to go. It was my first lecture on an architectural subject and it remains my most memorable. Spence illustrated his presentation with colour slides derived from his drawings — which were truly remarkable. About ten years later, on a visit to the Royal Institute of British Architects — of which I was by then a member — I saw a selection of these self-same drawings and appreciated them even more — because by then I had a better professional understanding of them and was more fully equipped to appreciate Spence's genius.

On one occasion, Mr. Grantham took us on a study-visit to Sheffield Cathedral — where, it so happens, I was christened. He discussed the modern extensions and then encouraged us to draw selected architectural details. I recall how it was a lovely sunny day and most of us contrived to develop our skills at sunbathing in preference to freehand drawing!

I was helped in my orientation to architecture, to some extent, by following in the footsteps of another CTS boy, namely, Alan Pagan. Alan was about two years older than myself and, I believe, held the post of School Vice Captain; we were both members of Telford House. Mr. Grantham helped Alan to prepare for admission to the Department of Architecture at Sheffield University by coaching him in the competition for an Edgar Allan Scholarship which was available in architecture. (Edgar Allan was a benefactor who endowed several such university scholarships.) I recall how one evening a few of us remained behind in DO1 to go through some past scholarship papers with Mr. Grantham. He sat at a drawing board, soft pencil in hand and read the instructions to us: "Candidates are required to design a throne and rostrum for use on ceremonial occasions". He then treated us to a bravura demonstration by creating a sketch design — an *esquisse* as we call such

creations. We stared in silent admiration as his thoughts evolved 'before our very eyes' as the comedian Arthur Askey used to say. I don't think Alan secured a scholarship but he was awarded a place to study architecture at Sheffield University. We were contemporaries and I have fond memories of observing Alan careering about on his motorbike.

Now let me tell you how something quite significant occurred one day in Mr. Grantham's art class — in its way no less than a 'defining moment'. Mr. Grantham trusted me with his personal copy of Sir Banister Fletcher's *A History of Architecture on the Comparative Method*. All scholarly disciplines have a 'standard work' and this, in its way, is the architects' key reference to the architectural styles of all the principal nations. I was allowed to take this precious book home and the moment I opened it I was mesmerised by the profusion of drawings I found therein — more than 4,000 — and I was in awe of the all-encompassing scholarship of the author. So far as any single volume can chronicle the diverse branches of architectural endeavour throughout the ages this volume has succeeded — it is still in print after more than a hundred years and 'umpteen' editions. This book, more than any other, decided me in my choice of career. I still have my own copy, awarded as a CTS prize, under circumstances I will describe later.

The study of art at the CTS did not continue beyond Third Year, i.e. Form 6X, and, even had it done so, Mr. Grantham would not have been around to teach the subject since he left the CTS to take up a career in commercial art. Mr. Albert Fairbrother eventually replaced Mr. Grantham as art teacher in September 1957 but I did not have any lessons from him. I seem to recall from a conversation with Mr. Hughes that he was a jazz enthusiast — I believe Mr. Fairbrother had no fewer than 3000 records in his collection. With Mr. Grantham's departure I lost my mentor and my active study in art ended. About two years later I discussed with Herbert Wadge the possibility of my taking art at O.L. but this, much to my disappointment, was not possible. Notwithstanding, I have much to thank the CTS for in general for giving me such a good grounding in art and in particular for Mr. Grantham for all his personal attention and enthusiasm.

History

I enjoyed school history. I gradually came to realise that history was not all about 'dates' and 'kings' and 'battles' and 'who was born when and when they died'. I could see the importance of these, for example, in defining 'periods' and for establishing the origins of 'movements' but I began to be aware of the larger picture that the study of history sought to portray. This was often concerned with very great people and their reforming ideas, voyages of discovery, the colonisation of new lands, the advent of technological innovation and so on. But there was also the lesser picture to be studied about ordinary people concerning their lives and their social conditions. In my own professional work history has given me — and continues to give me — a great deal of pleasure within the more specialised field of architectural history. In addition, during my time at the University of Sheffield, I did a year of Economic and Social History for which my historical studies at the CTS, albeit in their modest way, provided me with a good foundation. So I have never ever felt any sympathy with Henry Ford's observation that "History is all bunk"! Indeed, perhaps a law should be passed forbidding anyone, say for the next one-hundred years, from quoting his silly words — then people might quietly forget that he ever said them!

One of the tricks of the trade in the teaching of history, for young people at any rate, is to get them to illustrate their work. This is not as trivial as it may seem. So much can be learned through the visual image; visual images help to fix in one's mind such things as epochal events, defining moments and the salient characteristics of historical periods and styles. Elsewhere in my narrative I recall the time when I was at Junior School in Class 3B and made a study of Hampton Court; I am sure that particular circumstance is fixed in my mind so clearly because I made a drawing of the main façade of the building. So it was with history at the CTS. History was made enjoyable for me through the opportunities that its study provided to illustrate the different aspects of the subject. I have reflected this in the selection of illustrations which accompany this section of my narrative. When we studied lands that had been colonised, we drew a map of the subjugated territories; for our better understanding of the 'Age of Discovery', more maps were required to portray the circumnavigation of the globe; our study of the life and times of people-past called for sketches of their homes; lessons about technological innovation required illustrations appropriate to the technology — highway, steamship, railway engine, motor car and so on. In this way history was brought to life for us. What could have been just so many desiccated facts and figures became part of a rich tapestry of past events — in short *History*.

We commenced our study of history in the time-honoured fashion by making reference to 'The Romans in Britain' — I will remember the names *Ermine Street*, *Fosse Way* and *Watling Street* as long as I live! True to the ideals I have outlined above, we made illustrations of how the Romans laid out their towns and constructed their highways using technological methods that would not be improved upon until the age of Thomas Telford — now there's a name to stir the hearts of many CTS lads! The colonisation of Britain was more fully outlined with reference to the Angles, Saxons, Danes, Picts, Scots — all that rape and pillage! And all this endowed our memories with yet more names — even if we may now feel a little insecure as to precisely from whence some of these marauding characters actually came! Our study of Norman Britain gave me the chance to have a go at drawing a castle of the period which I see from my surviving sketch earned me a mark of ten out of ten (Fig. 36).

For me history took a big leap nearer to our own times when we studied the Mediaeval period which was all about manor houses, lords and serfs and especially the system of farming. Here is Terry Russell's version of these events circa 1954:

The Manor

A manor usually comprised a village with the land belonging to it being ruled over by barons and a small number of the king's most trusted friends. The village contained two big buildings, the church and the lord's manor both of which were usually made of stone. Besides these were the homes of the serfs which were built of rough wood, straw and mud and were divided into two parts one for the serf and his family and the other for his cattle.

The farmland was divided into three great fields farmed under the three-field system. That is, one year two of the fields would be farmed while the other lay fallow. The next year the fallow field would be farmed and one of the other two fields would lay fallow. And so they carried on in turn. Two or three days a week it was the serf's duty to work for the lord in his fields and at harvest time too he had to help collect in the lord's crops. This overtime was called boon-work. Also, every serf was compelled to use his lord's flour mill and to leave behind some of his flour as payment.

Each serf was allowed about thirty strips of land separated by a yard of turf called a baulk. To allow fairness, for some parts of the field were better than others, the serf's strips were placed on both good and bad land. Some of the produce grown on this land was then given to the lord and special presents had also to be given on each of the great feast days at Easter, Whitsun and Christmas.

The most lasting impression all this made on me was the thought that it must have been great to have been the Lord of the Manor (Fig. 37)! This impression has been successively reinforced over the years on my many visits to venerable properties now in the custody of the National Trust — the *National Rust* as my son Thomas was given to calling it when, as a little boy, he was dragged protesting around yet another manorial residence! In fairness I should add that he is now a convert himself to the *NT* and all it represents.

Out study of Mediaeval domestic architecture was not just confined to manorial residences. We considered the wattle and daub system of construction adopted by the very poor for their houses and how the workmen converted planks for use in this form of building (Figs 38 & 39). The work of the 'harmonious' blacksmith also featured in our narratives (Fig. 40).

We made a study of a Mediaeval monastery which related well to the work we did in art (Fig. 41). In art, as I have shown, we learned about the architectural terms applicable to old buildings — nave, cloister and so on. In history we learned about the ecclesiastical and social functions of these spaces, who occupied them, what they did and why. It was all necessarily pared down and simplistic to make it digestible to our developing understanding, but there was always a certain intellectual rigour and challenge about our history lessons. In my time at the CTS our history teachers were Mr. Stanley Farsnworth and Mr. Donald Charlesworth. Their lessons always went according to the following plan. First they talked about the subject under study. With hindsight I now recognise how scholarly and erudite were their introductions — although these are not words that I would have used at the time to describe how teachers talked. Then came the hard bit. We had to read a set passage from books and then make notes of the key events. This was followed by the even harder bit. The challenge was then to re-cast our notes into the form of a short essay. This was usually accompanied by the pleasurable bit, namely, to make a drawing of some aspect of the subject under study. This is the part that enabled those of us who were keen (!) to show what we could do with our pen and ink. Two little texts follow to demonstrate these general points. One describes a scene from the Middle Ages and the other is a description of one of the great fairs typical of this era. The original sketches illustrating these short essays are shown in Figs 42 & 43.

A Scene from the Middle Ages

On entering the town I was appalled by the evil-smelling streets which lay deep in dirt and refuse. It was only by a quick step that I missed the contents of a chamber pot tossed from an upper window. A little further on I saw a strange-looking character driving two pigs which were content to wallow in the mud. I met several people bartering their wares at crude stalls which nestled amidst the alleys but not all the goods would have met the standards of the Craft Guilds. I chanced to see a thief caught by the hue and cry method. It was very fortunate for him that a friar was nearby to prevent the howling mob from tearing him to pieces.

A Fair in the Middle Ages

Many great fairs were held in the Middle Ages, especially at Stourbridge and Winchester; some could last as long as eighteen days. Traders went to sell their goods and attracted all types of people ranging from rich noble men to beggars, thieves and foreign merchants with pack horses. These merchants sold all kind of goods; leather, wool, glasses, Italian and French mirrors, carpets and many other fine goods. Side-shows were to be seen including jugglers, musicians and dancing bears. Plays were popular; these were sometimes religious and sometimes were based on true stories acted by members of a guild which suited their particular trade.

The study of 'The Age of Discovery' captured our youthful imaginations with its tales of exploration into unknown regions. My personal literary contribution to this subject however must be one of the shortest on record: 'In 1492 Columbus reached America aboard the *Santa Maria*, together with the *Pinta* and *Nina*, both of which never returned. He died in poverty in 1506'! I did though add a rather good sketch of the *Santa Maria* to fill-out my little piece (Fig. 44). I had rather more to say about the 'New World' and the Elizabethan Seamen, but I still managed, schoolboy fashion, to compress the endeavours of several centuries into a few sentences — although once more supplemented with an accompanying illustration (Fig. 45):

The Elizabethan Seamen

England was late upon the scene in the New World with only Newfoundland and Labrador to its name, discovered in the reign of Henry VII by the two Cabots — John and Sebastian. Henry VIII did something to remedy this by having ships built for the navy and encouraged men like William Hawkins to sail the Spanish Main. It was Sebastian Cabot who thought of getting to India via the North-East Passage of Europe and Asia. Cabot was too old to go himself but he did help Richard Chancellor to make the exploration in 1553. Chancellor made his way to the White Sea, landed at Archangel and was received in Moscow by the Czar. He failed however to discover a North-East Passage. Equally fruitless were the efforts of the Elizabethans to discover a North-West Passage. Martin Frobisher, a Yorkshire man, went on three voyages of exploration (1576–8) and William Davis followed him ten years later. In the next century, Hudson discovered the straits bearing his name but it was not for another two-hundred years that a ship found a way through the ice to the Pacific.

In 1562 John Hawkins, hearing that Negroes were profitable 'merchandise', made a voyage to the West Africa where he landed and captured 300 Negroes. He then sailed across to the West Indies where he sold them to the Spaniards thus starting the infamous Slave Trade which lasted for a hundred and fifty years. Philip of Spain tried to stop this but the Spaniards were only too willing to trade with Hawkins. Later came the Armada which Queen Elizabeth I had not wished but which her sailors had long desired. The large flotilla of Spanish ships sent by Philip, filled with soldiers, appeared off the Cornish coast on 20th July only to be met by gunfire and fire-ships. These, and a great storm, wrecked the Spanish fleet. The remnants were chased onto the rocks off the Hebrides and Irish coasts by the ships of Lord Howard, Drake and Hawkins.

We continued the theme of maritime exploration with our study of Australia. The following extracts from my homework of 24th May 1955 give an indication of the various themes we considered in this aspect of our work together with the obligatory map (Fig. 46):

The Discovery of Australia

Australia was first sighted by a white man by the name of de Torres in 1606 although he did not land in the country. Australia was more truly discovered by the Portuguese and explored by the Dutch throughout the period 1600–50. It was the Dutchman Abel Tasman who was sent on an expedition in 1642 by the Governor of Java Van Dieman. Tasman circumnavigated Australia, explored its north coast and discovered Tasmania and New Zealand. The Englishman James Cook was sent out by the British Government in 1768–70 in command of an expedition of scientists and explorers. This voyage resulted in the re-discovery of New Zealand which he completely circumnavigated; he also mapped out the whole of the eastern coast of Australia in 1770. One place where they landed was named Botany Bay on account of its profuse vegetation. Cook made two other great voyages in 1772–5 and 1776–9 but was later murdered by some natives in the Sandwich Islands (Hawaii).

After losing the American colonies, England decided to use Botany Bay as a convict settlement since it was the custom at this period to send men for seven years transportation — even for trivial offences. Captain Arthur Philip was the first Governor General of the convict settlement which lasted for a period of fifty years. He founded Sydney in 1758.

Concerning the gradual expansion of Australia, gold was discovered at Ballarat, Bendigo and Bathurst which caused thousands of foreigners to enter the country in seek of their fortune. Those of them who did not find gold finally settled down to a life of farming.

Australia became a member of the Commonwealth in 1901 and is gradually increasing its population today by influxes of immigrants.

We then appear to have made a study of the Guild System which once more gave me the opportunity to create a detailed accompanying pen and ink sketch (Fig. 47).

Our study of British colonial expansion included a survey of India — the 'Jewel in the British Crown'. We considered the early struggles for possession of the continent with the French and some of the key events that shaped British policy in India. Again, an essay was required to demonstrate what we had learned. Here are extracts from mine which, once more, is remarkable for compressing a huge chunk of British history into a few sentences:

India

As the Mogul Empire began to disintegrate (1700–50), the French under General Dupleix took advantage of the decline in central power to establish an overseas empire. In 1750 civil war broke out at Arcot and Clive, whilst still only a young clerk, dashed to the scene with a band of soldiers and changed the situation for the English who had been holding out for fifty days. In 1756 the Seven Years' War with France broke out and it was at this time that news of a terrible outrage at Madras was received. The British station at Calcutta had been taken by the infamous Surajah Dowlah — an example of the worst kind of Indian despot — and it was he who ordered 146 English prisoners to be confined to a small room from which only 23 survived. When news of this outrage became known, the Governor sent Clive to Bengal and it was he who induced Meer Jaffer, one of the Rajah's officers, to conspire against his sovereign. Clive promised him the throne of Bengal if the British should win the conflict. Battle ensued in June 1757 at Plassey and, at a critical moment, Meer Jaffer deserted to the British leaving the Rajah with a mass of panic-stricken men and horses.

General expansion in India followed under the direction of Warren Hastings who was the first Governor General (1774–85). He was confronted with the task of holding India together when our colonies were rebelling in America (1775–83) and we were, moreover, at war with half the great powers of Europe. Wellesley held India during the struggle between England and Napoleon in Europe (1798–1805). The French unsuccessfully tried to raise the princes of India against the English; it was Wellesley who brought southern India under British control by the following means: (i) an alliance with the Nizam (1799), (ii) war with Tippoo Sahib and (iii) annexation of the Carnatic region by England in 1800. Half a century later, the Indian Mutiny broke out when the towns of Delhi, Cawnpore and Lucknow fell into the hands of the Sepoys — the native soldiers in the British Indian Army. This mutiny was severely crushed.

In 1947 India and Pakistan were divided largely according to religious beliefs; they are both members of the Commonwealth. In our own times, these two countries continue to make great strides due to the advantages of the roads, railways, canals and communication by telegraph.

My school history exercise book has almost fallen to pieces, but amongst the pages which have survived the records appear to suggest that we were invited to write a short essay about the Commonwealth country of our choice. Here is an edited version of my choice which gives some indication of the related historical themes which we discussed in class:

Canada

The Commonwealth country I would most like to visit is Canada. Stretching for thousands of miles it offers a very diverse climate, varying from the warm sunny beaches of the south to the cold tundra forest in the north where bears are hunted. In this region one could visit the lumber camps — ["I'm a lumber jack and I'm OK"!] — and also the old log-stockades where Canadian history was made in the conflicts with France. Journeys could also be made on the Canadian Pacific Railway, stopping here and there to see something, perhaps, of the famous Royal Canadian Mounted Police. Further north still, the remaining old gold prospectors could be seen panning for gold in the trout and salmon rich rivers flowing between the rocky gorges. As I have remarked, bears are hunted in this region and some of the world's finest furs have been obtained by the old-time trappers of Northern Canada. The Great Lakes offer the traveller one of the most romantic inland cruises in the World. Extending for miles, their rock-strewn shores are often battered by gale force winds but are set amidst some of the richest mineral deposits in the world.

Nearer to our own time, we all enjoyed learning about the Industrial Revolution and the way in which life in both town and country was changed forever. I think part of the appeal for this period of history was the industrial legacy that was all about us within the City of Sheffield itself and the immediate environs. It was therefore quite natural for us to learn about developments in the exploitation of iron and coal and their use in the smelting of steel. Together with these key themes we also studied developments in land transportation, including road and canal building, and the advent of the railways and steamships. As I have remarked, we were encouraged to illustrate our written work with visual images representative of the subject under consideration. Examples of the sketches we did for our work concerning the Industrial Revolution are shown at Figs 48–50. The tramcar illustrated in Fig. 51 is remarkably similar to those on which I travelled each day to and from the CTS!

I don't recall being able to study history to O.L. in my time at the CTS. Be this as it may, my study was confined to the first two years of school (Forms 3Y and 5X) and one term only in Form 6X. I am very grateful for this however, since, at the University of Sheffield I went on to take a First Year course in Economic and Social History for which my CTS grounding in history essay-writing was a considerable help.

Geography

Geography was taught by Mr. Geoffrey Firth in the end upper room on the second floor of the main CTS building — co-incidentally the Firth building. Mr. Firth was feisty and quick tempered and in some respects he was the Clint Eastwood of the classroom. By this I mean he had a deadly aim. With a piece of chalk he could silence a chatterbox at twenty paces! And in the case of a particularly naughty boy he could throw the blackboard rubber with equal effect. What must also be added is that he was razor-sharp intellectually. In my view Mr. Firth was one of the most intellectually able teachers at the CTS, as befits a graduate of the University of Cambridge — Mr. Firth was an M.A. Cantab. Something of the strictness of Mr. Firth's pedagogical regime is captured in the very first words we had to write down for him. These were his six-point 'General Instructions' for the proper conduct of our work in geography. Here they are:

1 Begin each piece of work on a fresh page unless otherwise instructed. Do not leave blank sides.
2 Give title (underlined) and date and rule off at the end.
3 If signs or colours are used on a map, give a key.
4 Spelling errors (marked /S) are to be corrected three-times each. Wrong answers are to be corrected once.
5 Neatness counts. Unsatisfactory work will be repeated.
6 The first job every homework is to correct the last-marked work and complete any unfinished work.

The formal tone of these strictures gave us a clear indication that Mr. Firth was starting out as he intended to continue — there was to be no messing about!

We commenced our First-Year course in geography with the study of mother Earth — 'Not a true sphere but flattened at the poles'. We learned how to describe any point of location on the Earth's surface by means of latitude and longitude, considered the Earth in relation to the solar system and drew diagrams to show how the Sun determines all things bearing upon climate and weather. This led us to consider rainfall and wind which we were told was 'moving air' — useful to know when you are gripped by indigestion!

Mr. Firth's geography lessons were far from static and he sometimes moved about from one topic to another. So it was we learned about 'The Aborigine'. This is what I wrote for my homework in June 1954:

Living in the northern part of Australia lives the tall, dark-skinned Aborigine. He lives the life of a nomad wandering here and there usually collecting his food which consists of locusts, caterpillars, beetles and other insects but his main diet is wallaby which he catches with a spear. As these food-collectors, as they are called, never stay in the same district for a long-time the demand for a well-furnished house is not necessary but they do use a bark or skin-covered shelter fastened onto a wooden frame. If a really severe storm should blow up they retreat to the shelter of the countryside. As the Aborigine lives in northern Australia where it is very warm, the need for clothes is minimal. When they are used the material is the skins of animals.

I suppose if I were to compose that text today it would have to be revised to take account of the contemporary Aborigine's awareness of his civil rights and make some reference to the transistor radio and popular culture — viz.: "Hold me kangaroo down sport, hold me kangaroo down"!

Turning nearer to home we made a detailed study of maps including those of the Ordnance Survey. This was my first introduction to these popular maps and I enjoyed drawing examples of the typical symbols used in the O.S. convention (Fig. 52). In fact I was sufficiently enthused to go and purchase 'Sheet 103' in the old 'One-Inch Series' depicting the Peak District. I used this regularly at weekends when out walking with my cousin and a school friend. In fact it is the only map I have ever worn out through regular use.

Our study of the surface features of the land extended to considerations of the representation of physical topography — plateaux, valleys, escarpments and such like forms. Some of these are shown in Fig. 53. This is a significant illustration for the following reason. It was drawn on 1st September 1954 by which time I had been at the CTS for almost a year. A certain style of friendly rivalry was beginning to emerge within Class 3Y, my form at the time, as to who could draw the best diagrams and Fig. 53 is my response to this development. It is not exactly a masterpiece but it is the first time that I had drawn such a diagram for geography in the medium of Indian ink. To achieve it I bought a large supply of this ink in a special stone bottle which cost me half a crown. This was a great deal of money, in schoolboy terms, for the period. It was a good investment though and lasted me throughout my entire career at the CTS.

Mr. Firth was far from being a dry pedagogue and urged us to take an interest in the peoples of other nations and their ways. His lessons therefore typically made reference to the physical characteristics of other people, their dress, habitations and above all how they worked (Figs 54 & 55).

I will make a brief digression from our curriculum at this point and pass a few remarks about our First Year geography exam. There are two points I want to make; one serious and the other amusing. First the serious bit. Mr. Firth explained the importance of revising for an exam and how to go about it — 'exam technique' I suppose you would call it. Whilst we take such things for granted now (and isn't it nice not to have to worry about exams any more!) our CTS First-Year exams were really the first of their kind which we had experienced at that time in our young lives — i.e., exams to a prescribed syllabus, extending over two or three hours and complete with a printed exam paper. The Eleven-Plus Exam and CTS Entrance-Exam were rather different, as were the 'tests' we had each of us taken at our various secondary schools before gaining a place at the CTS. So

Mr. Firth took all this very seriously. In the geography exam itself we were set questions about the Earth, rainfall, wind (!), the different types of rock and so on. Now I come to the funny bit of the story — although I have to admit it is somewhat to the detriment of a then fellow pupil by the name of Howard Baw — forgive me Howard if you are reading this. We had made a study of the planets, the solar system and the influence of the Earth's axial tilt on the seasons and climate. These subjects also came up in the exam in the form of a number of questions, one of which was: "What do you understand by the expression *heavenly bodies*"? I dutifully set about making diagrams of the Earth, tilted on its axis by 23.5°, intercepting the rays of the sun — etc. I glanced over in the direction in which Howard was sitting only to see him drawing — the silhouette forms of beautiful young women! They were rendered in Indian ink and looked lovely but were not quite what Mr. Firth had in mind as representing heavenly bodies — at least I don't think so!

I can't recall how Mr. Firth reacted to this interesting interpretation of *heavenly bodies*. In fairness I owe it to Howard to add that he was a naturally gifted artist. I also recall that he was very proud of his father who had gained the degree of M.Sc. by research. This prompts me to recount an achievement of a somewhat similar nature concerning Mr. Firth. It was revealed to us one morning in assembly by Mr. Wadge. Herbert was, as usual, exhorting us to do our best and then, by way of offering us an example, cited the recent success of Mr. Firth in — I believe — being elected to a Fellowship of the Royal Geographical Society. I can't be absolutely certain — it is after all more than forty years ago — but I do remember how the whole school gave Mr. Firth a round of applause.

As in the case of our study of history, our learning about geography was made more interesting by our being encouraged to illustrate our work. I suppose school geography rather lends itself to this. Be this as it may we drew lots of coloured maps of foreign countries (Figs 56–59). In this way we acquired a textbook knowledge of the continents, their mountain ranges, principal rivers etc. Looking back through my geography exercise book is a reminder to me what a zealous critic Mr. Firth was — nothing, in the way of errors, appears to have ever escaped his attention. The red-ink annotations on my work — including my ink maps — required me to insert missing names, re-direct the course of wrongly flowing rivers, supply missing information and, inevitably, highlight spelling errors. But there are also compliments in the form of 'good', 'neat work' and the award of an occasional 'merit'. Do you recall the pleasure it gave you to receive a merit, and how they were recorded, at the end of the lesson, in a book by the Form Monitor? Happy days!

Most lessons at the CTS were of the 'chalk and talk' kind but Mr. Firth was one teacher who used to innovate with the epidiascope — that's the name for the now obsolete optical instrument which enabled the illustration in a book to be projected on to a screen or wall. Mr. Firth made use of this when discussing Canada — a rather large subject! To be more precise the lesson concerned the Niagara Falls. In the darkened room, the projected image looked sharp and made the subject seem even more dramatic. Mr. Firth described the nearby Goat Island which prompted a boy, by the name of Dearden, to ask if the name derived from a population of goats resident there. It was a tongue in cheek question made all the more absurd by the fact that any such animals could only ever have colonised the island by navigating a stretch of water moving with the speed of an express train! Mr. Firth responded — by hurling the blackboard rubber across the room — at about the same speed as the rapids above the Niagara Falls! Mr. Firth was not one to be fooled with! Later in the year our geography exam contained the following question: "What are the *two* movements made by the water descending over the Niagara Falls"? It was a typically ingenious question — Mr. Firth was, as I have remarked, a bright chap and never asked a 'straight' question. Have you worked out the answer? Here it is. The water *descends* — obviously — and also moves *backwards* — very, very slowly as the rock face is eroded! Clever! Here is another of Mr. Firth's questions — a little less mentally taxing: "Does Grimsby smell like Pittsburgh or not"? You may think there's something fishy about that one — groan!

One day we were given a vivid insight into just how much geography personally meant to Mr. Firth. As the class was about to start he came into the room holding a big new shiny book. It had just been published and he had been dipping into its contents and was clearly eager to share some of his enthusiasm with us for this splendid-looking tome. The subject of the book was North America and, in effect, its theme was *How the west was won*. As he enthused away he sat on a desk near the front of the class and displayed some of the book's large-format illustrations — the National Parks, Rocky Mountains the vast cornfields and so on. But it was when he started to read from the book that he became most animated. He read extracts about the exploration of the country, the early settlers and how North America has been perceived in popular culture — notably the cinema. He could scarcely contain himself with his boyish excitement. It is a truism that enthusiasm is infectious and, slowly but surely, the class became captivated by the vivid prose style of the book and Mr. Firth's reading of it. We could not have wanted for a more compelling introduction to the study of North America and we duly settled down to learning about the country's climate, natural resources, land use and all the rest — not much of which, I have to confess, was quite as glamorous as Mr. Firth's introduction.

It was from Mr. Firth that I first became aware of the problems of what we now call the 'developing countries'. In one of his lessons he talked about the general issues that mankind faces if population is allowed to grow unchecked. We made a particular study of East Africa and its population and our homework was to draw a large-scale chart (histogram) of the relative populations of Uganda, Kenya and Tanganyika. This gave me the chance to draw my chart in black ink using a specially wide drafting pen I had recently acquired. I showed some daring and allowed my chart to extend over two whole pages of my exercise book (Fig. 60).

Another practical problem we discussed in geography was the question of land reclamation in the Netherlands. This was the kind of geography that many of us liked most of all — looking at a practical problem that embraced several issues. In this case the problems we considered were the design of sea defences, land draining and the ecology of the soil. We made a particular study of the Zuider Zee and the great embankments needed to secure the 'Polders' from encroachment by the sea. On an even grander scale we considered the proposals by the German engineer Sörgel to re-claim vast tracts of land in the Mediterranean — to

be called *Atlantropa* — by creating a series of immense barriers across the Straits of Gibraltar, and elsewhere, which would enable the level of the sea to be lowered by about thirty feet (nine meters)! An interesting aspect of this lesson was the discussion we had of the possibility this imaginative scheme offered for the generation of electricity by tidal movement — which is very much of course a topical issue forty years later.

During my time at the CTS the A.L. curriculum had already expanded to include maths — pure and applied, physics, chemistry, technical drawing, metalwork and woodwork. This is quite an achievement for a relatively small school whose original 'charter' was for the technical education of boys for the engineering and building trades. The only expansion of the A.L. curriculum that I can recall was in fact the inclusion of geography — doubtless in response to the initiative of Mr. Firth. Two of my contemporaries stayed on to take their A.L. geography and one of them was involved in a most unfortunate circumstance. After all his study he was not allowed to sit the exam. The reason for this was an oversight on the part of a member of staff — who shall remain anonymous — who was then responsible for the registration of candidates. Let me explain what used to happen — it was quite a complex process. The school registered each candidate for his list of O.L. and A.L. subjects, paid the fees — I suppose that was the responsibility of the Education Committee, then we received our candidate's exam number, the timetable was published — and we sat the exam(s)! The vital bit in the process was to be registered by the school. There was a 'late entry' system, which incurred an extra fee, but if you missed the final deadline you were debarred from taking the exam — until a later date. It must be every school's nightmare to leave someone off the list. And this is precisely what happened to my class contemporary. By an oversight, the member of staff in question had forgotten to add the name of the boy to the list of candidates. This is one of the very few incidents I can ever recall of the administrative arrangements at the CTS being flawed. It was a very unhappy moment for all involved. Doubtless the matter was resolved by the individual concerned taking his A.L. geography in the autumn 'resits'. I can recall that the following year (1959) the registration of candidates for the A.L. examinations was entrusted to Mr. Thompson — a very safe pair of hands.

The story I have just narrated is not a very happy one with which to end this section. So I will conclude by saying that my relatively short course of study of geography at the CTS was very rewarding. I now appreciate maps more than I ever imagined was possible — especially old ones which invoke a sense of history by recalling things as they once were. Moreover the global and environmental issues that now confront all countries and all mankind give geography, taken in its widest meaning, an unprecedented place in human affairs. Thank you Mr. Firth, concerning these matters, for doing your bit for us.

Mathematics

As I leaf through those of my maths books that have survived — I binned most of them years ago — I can scarcely recognise the work they contain as being my own. The symbols appear to belong to a different hand from mine — especially the work done for A.L. pure and applied maths. Moreover the abstract propositions they enshrine now just seem like so much 'mumbo jumbo'. Nevertheless I do recall that I enjoyed maths at the CTS and was generally quite good at the subject — at least in my early years. Later, as I progressed beyond the more fundamental stages and started to do work for A.L., I began to reach my natural limits and for me the subject lost some of its appeal. This was certainly not the case however for several of my more mathematically gifted contemporaries who went on from strength to strength and eventually took university courses in maths as part of their B.Sc. curricula.

In this section I will discuss the subject by following my established plan of starting at the beginning with a discussion of first year maths and will then progress to a discussion of the maths we did at various other stages in our time at the CTS.

Class 3Y

First Year maths was taught by Mr. Frederick Frow in Bow Building — the same room in which, three years later, we received instruction for O.L. English from Mr. Hughes. Mr. Frow was one of the more youthful of our teachers and I assume that at the period of which I am writing (1954) he was a recent graduate. At the risk of being over complimentary, there was just a hint, in his youthful features, of the matinee idol Dirk Bogarde! I seem to recall he drove a Triumph Mayflower car to school — that was the car whose bodywork was modelled on the Rolls Royce. For this reason, I believe it was a very expensive car to have repaired. With Mr. Frow we worked our way through such foundation subjects as the properties of triangles — sines cosines and tangents, the calculation of the areas of regular figures and circles, the computation of the volume of prismatic solids, the plotting of graphs and, of course, logarithms — does anybody, I wonder, use 'logs' these days. It so happens that I live within half a mile of where the inventor of logarithms, John Napier, lived. Every time I walk past his house — in actuality Merchiston Castle — I can't help thinking: "Thanks a bundle John for all the torment you gave us"!

Mr. Frow's lessons were well organised and disciplined. In the case of a particularly errant pupil he would occasionally inculcate the precepts under consideration by rhythmically tapping the skull of the unfortunate lad with his index finger. He also had recourse to some memorable expressions as, by way of illustration, when making the distinction between quantities ('x + y') and products ('x.y'). He would say: "If you mix cocoa and nuts you don't get cocoa nuts"! Very true.

I enjoyed Mr. Frow's lessons and his style of teaching. I recall how he always wore his academic gown. I must say, based on the occasions that I have worn my own gown, they do help to keep you warm. Perhaps that was the attraction, to some members of staff, in wearing their academic gown especially on a cold winter morning when some of the classrooms, particularly in the Bow building, could feel very chilly and send a veritable draught right up your Khyber Pass — so to speak.

I was good at elementary maths — that's what's called damning yourself with faint praise — and my competence once prompted Mr. Frow to comment: "Have you done all this before Russell"? In part, I had indeed covered some of the maths syllabus back in my days at Anns Road School and, remember, I was about a year older than the average age for boys in my class — that's what's called being disarmingly modest. I regret that, on occasions, I allowed myself to lead some of my mathematically weaker brethren astray — as on the following occasion. I sat next to a boy called Michael Porter — he was a tall, well-built lad who left the CTS to become a policeman. Mr. Frow, gazing at Michael one day, asked him: "How do we find the square root of a number"? Observing Michael's consternation, and sitting next to him, I whispered the misleading suggestion: "Divide by two", which Michael, trustingly, relayed to a not very impressed Mr. Frow who, shaking his head ruefully, retorted: "Fools rush in Porter, where angels fear to tread"!

There were occasions — very rare — when Herbert Wadge acted as a 'stand-in' teacher, presumably to fill in gaps in an emergency. One such morning, I recall, instead of finding Mr. Frow waiting for us we beheld the intimidating form of Herbert himself. We took our seats, beneath his baleful gaze, feeling about as relaxed as I imagine an antelope must when attempting to graze in the presence of a hungry lion. Notwithstanding, the class passed without incident.

Classes 5X and 6X

Second and Third Year maths was taught to Builders by Mr. Leonard (Len) Shipley, at Cathedral School in one of the classrooms on the upper floor. 'Killer' Shipley was, as his sobriquet implied, an intimidating individual. His reddish hair and red-brown jacket further enhanced his feisty character. One day, finding myself alone with him, I ventured to mention his nickname. He grinned, revealing his somewhat worn-down teeth — resulting from years of clasping the stem of a pipe — and he explained his simple theory of class control: "On your first day with a new class you scare the little buggers to death. After that you don't have any trouble"! Well, Len's philosophy may lack pedagogic refinement, but it certainly worked. But there was far more to Len Shipley's lessons than cosmetic wrath. He enunciated mathematical precepts with carefully studied eloquence, often pacing about the classroom as we sat attentively trying to take in that which he was expounding.

We learned to cope with Mr. Shipley's fulminations by adopting a variety of strategies. One of these was to keep a look-out posted by the door who, on seeing his approach, would exclaim: "He's here" — or, more accurately, " 'e's 'ere"!

Under Mr. Shipley's tutelage, our knowledge of maths expanded considerably to encompass more advanced algebra, theorems in plane and solid geometry and what I will call 'practical applications' of mathematics. Mr. Shipley was good at making maths 'come alive' by stressing its usefulness and applicability to everyday life. This was, in part, doubtless a way of securing our interest and also recognition of our intended destiny as future participants in the professional side of the building trade.

Early on in our course of lessons, Mr. Shipley somewhat startled us one day by saying: "I am now going to consider the principles of *mensuration*"! Had we heard correctly? — mensuration or menstruation? We listened eagerly: "Mensuration", stated Mr. Shipley, "is the application of geometric principles to the calculation of measurements such as length, area and volume". We slumped back in our seats — disappointed.

As the time of our Building Diploma examinations approached we sat what could be called trial exams.

Concerning the maths exam, Mr. Shipley urged us — "to be on our toes and to keep our wits about us"! I thought this a little bit odd since I was of the opinion that such an approach was always required with maths. When we duly sat the paper however I saw what he meant. The exam was held in the Dining Hall — the rather grand expression for the CTS communal feasting trough! I sat over to the left by the windows. I remember at the start of the exam a boy called Norris earned a reprimand for having removed his tie — this was the era when: "Ties must be worn at all times!" — or, as Herbert Wadge might have put it: "We have ways of making you wear ties"! Mr. Shipley's paper contained a number of traps for the unwary — hence his caution to be on our toes. I will cite two examples from the geometry part of the paper. We were confronted with a diagram of bewildering complexity — lines, angles and symbols were scattered all over the place. The question was simple enough — find the length of the side of a triangle. The challenge was to disentangle the triangle from the mass of information provided — 99% of which was redundant. Mr. Shipley was deliberately trying to lead the unwary down a false trail — naughty! The second question was cast in a similarly deceptive style. We were provided with the diagram of a clock face depicting the sixty minute sub-divisions and the hands set to a certain time. The question required the angle between the fingers on the clock to be calculated; this necessitated sorting out that a circle contains 360° and therefore that each minute of clock time is represented by 6° of angular rotation. But Mr. Shipley had more deceptive tricks up his sleeve. The question went on to assume that a specified interval of time had elapsed, with consequent change of position of the clock fingers. "What", asked the second part of the question, "is the new angle between the clock fingers"? To add further confusion. Mr. Shipley required the answer to be calculated to 'minutes' of angular rotation — not to be confused with minutes of clock time. I hope you have paid close attention and followed all that!

A few days later after the maths prelim exam the following incident occurred. We were quietly working away at our maths when I was rather startled by Mr. Shipley barking at me, in the aggressive tone he normally reserved to admonish an errant boy for doing something wrong — Len Shipley was not called 'killer' for nothing. "Russell!", he snapped, "Stand up"! I did so, somewhat startled — because I was working away in my normal virtuous fashion with my customary diligence (!) — and therefore wondered what was the matter. A slight grin appeared on Mr. Shipley's face and I knew then that he was play-acting. He startled me by paying me the compliment of informing me that I had been awarded a Third Class Diploma for the mathematical part of my Building Diploma! I was totally perplexed. We had not yet taken our final exams and, in any event, I was hoping for something better than a Third Class Diploma — a category reserved for the slackers — with apologies to all the lads reading this who got a Third Class. At the end of the lesson Mr. Shipley had a private word with me — his enigmatic smile now a big grin. I had apparently made a little bit of school history by accumulating sufficient marks, on my class work, to qualify for a Third Class Diploma without even taking the exam — the Diploma being awarded on an aggregate of class work and the results of the final examinations. So I went home that evening feeling quite proud of myself.

I have previously remarked how Herbert Wadge occasionally took lessons. He was also given to 'looking in' on classes. I am not sure if his motivation was intellectual curiosity or intimidation — I suspect a mixture of both. His presence in the classroom certainly concentrated one's mind. On one such occasion however two boys allowed their concentration to wander — with frightful consequences. One day when Mr. Ken Westnedge was taking our class in strode Herbert. He immediately assumed control and confronted us with questions concerning sines and cosines, demonstrating how quickly he could distinguish between 'opposite over adjacent' etc. To their misfortune, two boys — Gordon Swan (my good friend from Anns Road Secondary School days) and another boy called Dearden — passed some casual remark. · I think it was concerning Ken's rather remarkable features which have just a hint of the Chinaman about them. (Sorry about that Ken — I don't really mean it and, in any case, you know we all love you dearly!) The outcome of the disturbance in class was that Herbert administered a caning — of a harsh kind. The ritual involved the doomed individuals being required to select which cane was to be used. An armoury of canes was shelved in Herbert's study in an alcove that was normally shrouded by a green curtain. When open, a boy's petrified gaze was ineluctably drawn to these instruments of torment and Herbert's study assumed the atmosphere of a chamber of horrors. Gordon and Dearden, ashen faced, survived their ordeal — the severity of which would not pass unchallenged in our more litigious times.

Let me follow that by now portraying the compassionate and caring side of Herbert Wadge's nature. No former CTS lad needs to be told that Herbert Wadge gave every atom of his being in support of his school; he palpably identified with every aspect of daily life and work. Here is one small illustration of this. As examination time approached, one of our maths lessons was interrupted by Herbert convening a special meeting in the School Hall to discuss exam revision and technique. Unusually he sat in the gallery, just below the big windows, and we boys sat in our normal fashion crossed legged on the floor. Herbert's message was a simple one, although delivered at his normal one-hundred decibels tone of voice: "Boys! If you can't complete a question, don't waste time but go on to another. Remember, two half questions are as good as one whole question" — and so on. I remember being impressed by Herbert's facility to say the same thing a dozen times! But his exhortations had their desired effect and we eventually left somewhat dazed but resolved to do our best — which is just what he wanted.

I will now briefly reflect on an incident which revealed Len Shipley's kindly nature. The circumstance was the sudden death of my mother — to which I will make fuller reference later. Seeing me wearing a black tie, Len came up to me and said — in a gentle voice with his hand on my shoulder: "Terry, I'm sorry to hear about your mother lad". He cast a sympathetic look in my direction and then left me to my thoughts. This was the one and only occasion during my entire time at the CTS that a teacher ever called me by my first name. I was touched by Mr. Shipley's expression of feeling and from that day on I regarded his nickname 'killer' as signifying my inner bond of affection for the man.

Some years later when I was doing A.L. maths with Mr. Bee — of whom more in a moment — Mr. Shipley requested a rather unusual favour of me. He asked if he could look through my school maths exercise books adding, by way of explanation, that he was interested to see how his colleague, Mr. Bee, approached the teaching of certain aspects of more advanced maths. On returning my books, he expressed his admiration for Mr. Bee's mathematical ability and went on to confide in me — remember I was a mere schoolboy at the time — how he regretted not having a university degree himself. He said he felt quite the equal of those of his colleagues who were graduates and resolved to do something about it by, perhaps, taking the London University degree externally — the Open University was not then in existence. There is a sequel to this story — for which I had to wait more than forty years. On the occasion of Herbert's funeral, I met Mr. Shipley and we exchanged friendly words of greeting. Len opened the conversational remarks, revealing his wicked sense of humour, by saying: "I often wondered what had happened to Terry Russell. I never heard much about you and I didn't think of checking her Majesty's prisons"! I did not respond in kind but asked if he did ever get his degree. Len looked a bit startled that I had remembered our conversation of forty years previously but answered: "No. Herbert Wadge obtained promotion for me without it being necessary — so I didn't bother — too much work at my age"!

Those who were at Herbert's funeral will recall that Len gave a moving oration for the man to whom the CTS owed so much — the text of Len's oration is reproduced later in the section of my narrative specifically concerning Herbert Wadge. My reason for my mentioning this here is as follows. It so happened, after speaking his affectionate tribute, he resumed his seat by my side, turned to me and asked: "Was that all right"? I put my arm about him — as he had done to me four decades before — and replied: "You did us proud lad"! Len just smiled.

O.L. and A.L. Maths

Instruction in O.L. and A.L. maths was entrusted to Mr. Ronald Bee — a name that should always be accompanied with the doom-laden opening chords of Beethoven's *Fifth Symphony*! Mr. Bee's glacial expression, concentrated gaze and intimidating demeanour could collectively chill the marrow in a fraction of the time required to recite the theorem of Pythagoras. He entered the classroom like a praying mantis, his very appearance subduing the class in an instant. With a mere glance we felt like captives before the judgement seat of Julius Caesar. Terse utterances issued from him with the unambiguous authority of the pronouncements of the Oracle at Delphi. But there was more — far more — to Mr. Bee than class discipline. He was, pe-eminently, a scholar of considerable intellectual standing. As a boy he had secured a coveted Edgar Allan Scholarship to study maths at Sheffield University — I will reveal how I know that shortly. He was also co-author of one of our class textbooks — *Co-ordinate Geometry*. You could not be in the company of Mr. Bee without feeling that you were in the presence of a man of academic stature — if, also, of a somewhat forbidding personality. In a confiding moment, Mr. Davis once said to me: "I'll bet his own children have to put up their hand, when they want to speak to him, and say — 'Please Sir' "!

From my very first lesson with Mr. Bee, it was evident that we were leaving behind the secure realm of maths as applied to everyday propositions — such as the calculation of the areas and volumes of regular forms etc. With Mr. Bee we entered the more abstract domain of algebra, probability theory, co-ordinate geometry, differential and integral calculus etc. At our first lesson, our consternation was evident to Mr. Bee who, at the close of the class remarked: "From now on you will find mathematics (he never said 'maths') somewhat more challenging than what you have experienced before". Mr. Bee did allow himself an occasional smile but it must be said that his sense of humour was somewhat rarefied, as exemplified during the lesson when he explained: "Parallel lines converge at infinity — but you can't go there to check"!

An atmosphere of strict formality pervaded all our maths lessons with Mr. Bee including how we pronounced numbers when doing calculations with logarithms. You may recall we used 'four-figure' log tables — there were such things as 'seven-figure' log tables but we never used those at school thank goodness! It was tempting to regard the four-figure numbers as dates — '1199', '1450' and so on — but Mr. Bee insisted we enunciate each digit as a separate figure and would fly into a rage if we breached that principle.

We had our O.L. maths classes in the classroom in the Holly Building overlooking the City Hall. This is the very classroom from which CTS lads could get a very good view of the 1950s' era pop star stars arriving early for their rehearsals. Many of you will recall the minor sensation of seeing Buddy Holly arrive in this way some time in 1958. I just missed seeing him myself but I heard about it afterwards as everyone went about humming the themes from *That'll be the day*, *Peggy Sue* and *Oh boy*! Sadly, the work that went on in this classroom was of a more serious nature. In this context let me now tell a little story which will invoke, in a rather unusual way, a practical application of the theory of mathematical probability.

The desks in our O.L. maths classroom were used by various boys as lockers in which to keep their books and personal possessions, consequently they were each secured with a padlock — except the desk where I sat which was locked with a very impressive brass combination lock. Let me tell you about this lock — and how I cracked its combination! It was constructed from eight octagonal pieces of brass — a bit like those poker handles you see made from assembled brass nuts. Each of the eight octagonal facets was numbered 1–8, giving 8x8x8x8x8x8x8x8 possible combinations! I will leave you to work out what the actual number of combinations is. I often fiddled with this lock as Mr. Bee gave his lesson (!) but of course I never got anywhere — with the lock I mean. I even thought of applying the 'r x n' principle that Mr. Bee taught us in his 'probability and theory' lessons — I'm glad I didn't or else I would still be sitting there at my desk now! So how then did I crack the combination? Here's what happened. One day I noticed the lock had been left with the octagons all 'smooth' and lined up. I reasoned the owner had been in too much of a hurry to scramble them. But the lock was still secure. This is the clever bit. I assumed the lock had first been closed and had then been only partially scrambled. I reasoned I could open the lock by simply reversing this process. I therefore grasped four of the tumblers in my left hand and the remaining four in my right hand, I turned the latter counter-clockwise and — hey presto — the lock clicked open! I looked inside the desk to find — one pair of stinky plimsolls! Hardly worth all the effort!

Sitting behind me in the O.L. maths class at this period was a lad called Smith — M.A. Smith. He once achieved the remarkable feat of getting Mr. Bee to smile. It happened like this. We were required to demonstrate a proposition in geometry using one or other of Euclid's theorems. Smith could not produce the correct solution by Euclidean reasoning and so instead demonstrated the required proposition by making physical measurements and then stating that the basis of his proof was ' by my ruler'! "Ingenious", remarked Mr. Bee — with just the hint of a smile — "but not what is required"! I should add, in mitigation, that Smith was a very bright lad indeed and, I believe, accumulated no fewer that a staggering eight A.Ls.! Some years later I met him walking down West Street with a big grin on his face. He had just been told that he had been awarded a B.Sc. degree with first class honours — a distinct improvement on 'by my ruler'!

Looking back it is remarkable to contemplate the extent to which our lives once revolved around certain activities concerning books and their authors which have long since slipped away from our conscious memory. So much so that we are inclined to forget to what an extent they formed so large a part of our daily routine at the CTS. For example, who now remembers Borchardt, Brown, Durell, Mayne, Robinson and Tranter? Not many I suspect, yet these are the names of the authors of our maths textbooks which were once on the tip of our tongue. So much so that back in out CTS days Mr. Frow, Mr. Thompson and Mr. Bee had once simply to say: "Take out your Borchardt", or "Take out your Tranter" for it to be instantly comprehensible as to what was required. Now all this is buried in the sediment of school history and is probably best left there since I suspect the majority of us, if now asked to take out our Borchardt's and Tranter's, would not be able to make much of their contents — with apologies to the mathematicians among you who actually do know a thing or two about mathematics.

My O.L. maths exam was held in the dining room down at Cathedral School. The dinner tables were cleared away and were replaced by examination desks. It occurs to me, looking back, that someone must have been responsible for all this organisation which we simply took for granted as part of normal school life. I can still remember some of the questions but I won't bore you with the details. More vivid in my mind is the recollection that half way through the exam I wanted to go to the bog very acutely. I held out as long as possible but in the end, bladder at bursting point, I asked to leave the room — which you were not supposed to do during an exam. Mr. Hill, who was invigilating, raised no objection and I was able to obtain the required relief — what my medically qualified son calls "through evacuation of the bladder". I resolved henceforth that on the day of an exam I would abstain from drinks so as to get through the three hours without further urinary discomfort.

After morning assembly, Mr. Bee invariably made his way to the Holly Building by walking up Bow Street — shrouded in his gown, his stride purposeful, demeanour serious, and his hands clasped behind his back. Incidentally, I recall that you had to be a prefect before being allowed to take the pavement route between school buildings — as opposed to walking through the playground. Presumably this convention was to protect the citizens of Sheffield from being jostled into the gutter! In the classroom, as I have already implied, Mr.

Bee's teaching style was that of the strict disciplinarian. He addressed us with carefully measured eloquence, enunciating propositions with definition-like clarity. Mr. Bee's style demanded absolute concentration — blink, at the wrong moment, and you ran the risk of missing a piece of blackboard demonstration critical to understanding some aspect of calculus. 'Buzz', as he was known, was especially in his element when acting as interlocutor of the theorems of Euclid — complete with diagrams and proofs. Through his instruction, we strengthened our understanding of algebra, co-ordinate geometry and calculus which formed the basis of the A.L. curriculum — and ensuing examinations!

Brief intervals would sometimes occur in Mr. Bee's classes which he would fill with what I will call 'philosophical reflection' — perhaps this is a little grand but Mr. Bee was given to making cryptic rather perplexing utterances. One such went along the following lines: "Do mathematicians *discover* mathematics or *invent* it"? The proposition asks us to decide either, if the realm of maths is 'out there' externally of our minds waiting to be discovered, or if maths is a property of the imagination and creativity of the human mind and merely expands with the dawning of new intelligence in this subject. What do you think?

In my time at the CTS, classes in A.L. maths (and applied maths) were held in a small classroom on the first floor of the Holly Building on the front part of the premises almost above the main entrance. This prompts me to recall that the premises were used in the evenings for a variety of evening classes. The evening-class teachers were very sensitive about the blackboards being left clean ready for their use — discrete chalk messages were occasionally left as reminders of this. One morning I remember entering the classroom, the morning after an evening class had been held, to find written on the blackboard in bold prominent characters the following words: 'pox', 'syphilis' and 'gonorrhoea'! Some evening lecturer had clearly lost his patience and was taking revenge. Moments later Mr. Bee entered the room, clearly saw the words — he could not do otherwise — but, quite unfazed, he merely erased the offending text and started the lesson in his normal methodical fashion.

In my final year at school, Mr. Bee gave tangible expression of his desire to 'improve our minds' by initiating a series of debates. The intentions of these exchanges were to encourage us to formulate opinions — usually on matters of topical importance — and then to argue our case before our peers. Guess who was asked to arrange all this? When I had twisted sufficient arms, I established a list of speakers, subjects and a programme of events. We stayed behind after maths, on Thursday evenings, and duly practised our debating skills. Mr. Bee presided but not omnipotently — he sat, unassuming, in the midst of the class seated at a desk — contributing a word now and then anxious to let us take control. I recall how, on one occasion, he spoke to a motion supporting the need for personal courage in life. He reflected, with passion and eloquence, on his own youth and how he had had to make his way in the world by his own enterprise and application. In making his case, he cited an exchange between Pyramus and Thisbe as occurring in Shakespeare's *A Midsummer Night's Dream*. These evening debates revealed a more kindly and approachable Mr. Bee. If we faltered, he would encourage us without trying to imply that he had all the answers.

During the academic year when we held these debates (1957–58), the former Soviet Union launched its Sputnik series of Earth-orbiting satellites — to an astounded world. This was the period of the 'cold war' which was at its height. Such was the political tension at this time that the government issued a pamphlet titled *Russia the Atom and the West*. I read this publication and was pessimistically convinced that civilisation would cease by the end of the century in a spate of mutual destruction. Many others were similarly inclined — remember, this was the epoch of the Aldermaston Marches and the 'CND' campaigns which were actively supported by the ageing philosopher Bertrand Russell. The advent of the Sputnik served only to define Russia's pre-eminence in space research and, thereby, to heighten the east-west tension. Mr. Bee, alert to topical issues, suggested that we debate the question of space exploration and whether the money should be spent on other things — a theme which remains relevant today. The excitement we felt in those early days of space exploration cannot be overstated — even the mathematics of space projectiles which featured in our curriculum helped to strengthen our enthusiasm. But, if there was to be a debate, someone had to oppose the motion so I volunteered. My second was a boy called Norris and proposing the motion for space exploration was a boy by the name of Benson. Benson, I believe, developed a very deep religious conviction at this period and expressed the wish to become a clergyman. Interestingly, about four years later (1962) when I was at the University of Sheffield, I saw Benson working as a laboratory technician but I did not get an opportunity to talk to him. Concerning the debate, Benson carried the motion easily — we were all in favour of space exploration.

As I have remarked these debates took place on Thursday evening and the time eventually arrived when Mr. Bee passed the management of the proceedings over to myself. This required me to sit at the front of the classroom at Mr. Bee's desk seated in his high chair — a somewhat unnerving experience. We had several of these debating sessions and my recollection is of a number of boys speaking with considerable passion on subjects they cared about. But we had to follow the strict formal conventions of debating procedures. To put it rather grandly, we were developing our adult minds and it is to Mr. Bee's credit that he did so much to nurture these qualities.

A recollection from this period comes to mind which, although not directly connected with maths, may stir certain memories. One of the great medical scourges of the post-war period was the dreaded viral disease poliomyelitis — 'polio'. The very word was sufficient to send a shiver down one's spine — appropriately since the disease was a condition of the spinal cord that induced paralysis. Our awareness of this disease gripped our attention as does the subject of Aids today. As remarked, this was the post-war era and we had all seen newsreel pictures of President Franklin Roosevelt, a victim of the disease, in his wheel chair and we were well aware of its awesome consequences. In 1954 Jonas Edward Salk had devised his 'Salk' vaccine and this was all the talk of the day. We asked ourselves: "Would you take the therapy or not"? Our dilemma was that, pioneering as the vaccine was it remained controversial for being only 80–90% effective. In short, you could contract the virus from the treatment — although the probability remained very low. Herbert Wadge took up

the cause for vaccination in morning assembly with all his usual crusading zeal — he was after all a scientist by training and was disposed to 'scientific method'. I don't think an aural vaccine was then available to us and the treatment was consequently in the form of a vaccination of the upper arm. I mention this since injection resulted in temporary inflammation of the injected area with some swelling — we were exhorted to take great care until these symptoms had passed. My justification for mentioning all this here is that several of us resolved to have the inoculation after school following a maths lesson. The effort was made easy for CTS boys since a medical centre had been set up to administer the vaccine in Leopold Street opposite the Firth Building — this facility normally functioned as a NHS dental suite. (I know because I once had a tooth extracted there when I was in Class 5X!) On arriving at the centre we joined a long queue of like-minded 'sixth-formers' all emboldening one another how "We would be all right"! — it cannot be overstated what an emotional challenge it was to take the Salk vaccine. After about ten minutes of waiting a medical official emerged — suitably white coated — and called out: "Would any school teachers present please come to the front of the queue" — to receive priority treatment. Lo and behold, Mr. Bee emerged from the shadows — I should add that all this was about December (1958) and it was consequently a dark, cold evening. A few boys made the obligatory 'buzz' noise (Mr. Bee = 'buzz') but I remember very clearly being seized by a quite different reaction. I inwardly reflected, amidst the chatter of the crowd, how, notwithstanding our status in life, we are all made equal — 'levelled' as it were — by commonly shared adversity. Be this as it may, we had our injections, experienced some swelling of the upper-arm, duly recovered and survived to continue with our maths classes — to which I will now return.

It became obvious to me that Mr. Bee was in his element with the minority of boys who had a natural aptitude for maths and who were potentially capable of taking the subject to university level. This rather select group did not include myself — I could cope with A.L. pure and applied maths but that was about my limit. By way of interest, at this period A.L. maths and A.L. applied maths could be studied in two ways. The route for non-specialists was to combine the subjects as pure-and-applied-maths which were then taken in two exam papers. For the more mathematically inclined pupil — contemplating a university or college course in science — the subjects could be taken separately in four exam papers — and were known colloquially as 'full pure' and 'full applied'. It was with some reluctance that I entered for the latter courses of study. Some aspects of the curriculum did appeal to me. I enjoyed the work we did for conic sections which embraced the loci of the circle, ellipse, parabola and hyperbola and finding points of intersection with lines that had such fascinating names as asymptotes, vertices, major and minor axis and — best of all — latex rectus (plural latera recta). For all I can recall now of these mathematical properties, the latter might just as well describe a portion of the lower bowel! But at the time I found the experience of this aspect of maths stimulating; it required you to think in three dimensions, especially when we progressed to studying the volumes of shapes rotated about the x and y axes. Probability theory I found too abstract for my comprehension.

The most mathematically able boys stayed on an extra year to take 'S' Level or Scholarship Level — as I have remarked there were only a few boys in this category. Those successful could style themselves 'State Scholars' and, if proceeding to further study at university, they received an extra allowance on their Local Education Authority (LEA) Maintenance Award. Similar awards were offered by the National Coal Board (NCB) as an incentive to becoming a scientist or engineer with the NCB. These were very good awards indeed and I know of one CTS lad who secured one. He went on to work with, of all people, Prof. Jacob Bronowski — of TV (*The Ascent of Man*) fame — to do research on the combustibility of coal dust. This prompts me to recall a music-hall joke of the period which went as follows. A man goes into a sweet shop and asks for: "A bar of chocolate, and two ounces of *nutty slack*"! The latter was the commercial name for coal dust. The NCB had a surplus of this (well they would wouldn't they) and their scientists attempted to combine this material with weak cement which, when compressed, produced a more-or-less combustible substance that was retailed under the name of 'ovoids' — because they were oval in shape. We tried them at home on the kitchen fire and every now and then one would explode sending hot shrapnel about the room. Little wonder they did not take on with the public. But back to the study of maths.

A consequence of boys staying on at school to do an extra year in the sixth form was that some attained the remarkable age of twenty! Such an honour, if so it can be construed, fell upon — and I hope he will not mind my disclosing this fact — Richard 'Charlie' Prime. Charlie, as he was known at school, become School Vice Captain and has remained a life-long friend. (Indeed, had certain affairs of the heart turned out differently, Charlie might well have become my brother in law — but that is another story.)

One of the most gifted of the select group of mathematically able boys of my generation was Jack Glossop to whom I have made previous reference. I will elaborate a bit here about Jack and link what I have to say about him with Mr. Bee. In his last year at school (1958-59) Jack suddenly emerged from 'obscurity' to distinguish himself in both athletics and mathematics. In the latter he was coached by Mr. Bee for an Edgar Allen Scholarship to read for a B.Sc. degree at the University of Sheffield. (I will make a brief digression here to say a few words about William Edgar Allen. He was the founder of the original Imperial Steel Works and is now remembered, by the older citizens of Sheffield, as the benefactor of the Edgar Allen Institute for Medico-Mechanical Treatment. He also founded the Edgar Allen Library which formed the basis for much of the Library of the University of Sheffield.). In addition to taking papers in maths, candidates for an Edgar Allen award were also required to demonstrate proficiency in the writing of 'scientific English' — for which Jack Glossop received tuition from Mr. Dove. Jack duly sat the papers in advanced algebra, co-ordinate geometry and calculus and the English paper. From conversation with Jack, I recall the latter contained the question: "What do you understand by the term *ketones*?" The sequel to all of this is twofold. A few weeks later Jack was reading the evening paper (*The Star*) and discovered he had won one of the coveted awards — the letter informing him of this personally had been delayed in the post. The next day Jack naturally went along proudly to inform Mr. Bee of his success who, in return, confided: "When I was a lad I got one of them"! Mr. Wadge was duly informed and Jack's success provided Herbert with the theme for one of his morning 'sermons' as to how hard work and physical exercise bring their rewards! Jack had his photograph taken later on in the Summer Term. It still survives in the CTS Album for 1958–59 showing Jack resplendent in his crew-cut hair style which was fashionable at the time.

Mr. Bee's lessons were sometimes relieved by him circulating a magazine called *Mathematical Pie*. This consisted of maths problems disguised so as to make them fun — some hope. But there were occasional good jokes of the kind: "Ten monkeys are playing about in the trees when a hungry lion snatches one for its lunch. How many are left?" Answer: "None — those remaining are so frightened they all run away"! For some reason *Mathematical Pie* made occasional reference to the writings of the Anglo Saxon scholar the Venerable Bede — I think his fame concerns his computation of the calendar and the date of Easter. My point in stating this is to recall that the Venerable Bede became known to us affectionately, if somewhat impiously, as the *Venereal Bede*! I regret this reveals more about our state of mind at this period than it does of our inclinations to mathematical scholarship.

I recall how one day Mr. Wadge secured our attention in morning assembly by telling us about Einstein's 'Clock Paradox' — which will take us back to Mr. Bee. As I recall it Herbert's narrative went as follows. "Two identical twins each hold a clock set to the same time. One remains on earth but the other travels away at the speed of light. The clock with the latter now shows a different time from the one remaining back on Earth. From this it can be deduced the twins no longer have the same ages — and are therefore no longer identical"! (Mr. Wadge was very good at securing our attention with remarks of this kind which then formed the basis of some morality tale or personal exhortation.) Our curiosity roused, we questioned Mr. Bee about the clock paradox. Mr. Bee gave one of his enigmatic grins — they were quite unfathomable — and said, if I can paraphrase him correctly after all these years: "Time is recorded by clocks which give a measure of the events which elapse (clock time). This is true for all observers in the immediate vicinity of the same clock who, by definition, experience time simultaneously. The Theory of Relativity however undermines the concept of simultaneity with regard to a clock travelling away from the observer at the speed of light". Silence! We were perplexed and continued to puzzle over the proposition during morning break. It so happens that Mr. Bee returned to Einstein's Theory of Relativity a few weeks later — by which time the A.L. maths exams were over and there was some time to fill-in before the end of term. He announced how he would give us an introduction to the subject which he anticipated would last about half a dozen lessons — on Tuesday and Thursday afternoons to be more precise. My memory is clear to about lesson three by which point we had reached the part of the theory which requires the application of three-dimensional space-time co-ordinates. Charlie Prime I recall, and a few others, were taking it all in their stride but it was too advanced for the majority of the class — which was quite small. Mr. Bee, observing our perplexity, became rather irritated, finally stopped and told us to get on with some other reading. Talking later with the few boys who were in class doing 'S' level maths, I gathered that the previous year (1957-

58) Mr. Bee had filled-in the extra time at the end of term with a series of talks about the Greek philosophers. Perhaps some of the select few who took part in these classes can remember these talks?

My grades in the subsequent A.L. maths exams were sufficient for me to be admitted to study at the University of Sheffield for the Diploma in Architecture but were not high enough for me to be admitted to the honours degree course — my preferred choice. I would have to improve them. How I achieved this will be disclosed later. For now I turn to the sister subjects of mechanics and applied mathematics.

Mechanics and Applied Mathematics

Class 3Y

I have remarked previously that on our first day at school Mr. Dove, then our form master, had listed 'mechanics' on our timetable — for which we all assumed our boiler suits would be required. It was therefore with some small disappointment that, on making our way to the Holly Building for our first mechanics lesson, we entered a large room on the first floor furnished with long tables — I think we had been expecting to be taken to a garage. The mechanics room, you will recall, was a hybrid between a classroom and a laboratory. On the walls were black painted pieces of equipment — mostly pulleys and similar mechanisms. Waiting for us was a small somewhat rotund gentleman with a round face and freshly scrubbed countenance. We soon discovered how red faced he became as his apoplexy rose in direct proportion to our mischief. I am of course referring to Mr. Alfred Simpson — dear Alf. Boys rapidly develop an intuition for realising when they can take liberties with a teacher. With Mr. Simpson it took us about five minutes. From then on, as far as discipline was concerned, it was all downhill. To put it more candidly, we teased and tormented Mr. Simpson most cruelly. I look back on these transgressions with a tormented conscience — not that I was ever myself the cause of any disturbance please understand! However, somehow, this most kindly of teachers did impart to us the rudiments of his subject which we rapidly discovered was nothing to do with repairing broken-down engines. Mr. Simpson introduced us to the four basic principles in mechanics, namely, the inclined plane, the lever, the pulley and the screw — to which he added the wheel and axle and the cog and gear. In our study of moments and the turning effect of a force I recall how he caught our imagination with the saying of Archimedes: "Give me a fulcrum and I shall move the Earth"! We then entered the realm of statics with its branches of the parallelogram of forces, the triangle of forces and ultimately the polygon of forces — do you remember all those lovely diagrams each culminating in a 'resultant' force? We occasionally undertook simple experiments to give physical expression to these concepts, one of which is illustrated in Figs 61–62. From statics we progressed to dynamics with vector analysis, graphs of velocity and acceleration; we found it hard to grasp the concept of 'feet per second per second' no matter how often we repeated the expression.

The prevailing impression that remains with me of Mr. Simpson is of a most kindly individual. Moreover when class order was restored, after a session of larking about was finally quelled, he always impressed me by the quality of his teaching. He was a clever man who had the coveted A.M.I.Mech.E. qualification — I learned that from Mr. Bill Davis when once asking him about the qualifications of different members of staff. (Bill Davis, by the way, was an A.M.I. Prod. E.) Mr. Simpson was also a gifted organist — I learned that from my life-long friend David Dickson — a former CTS lad to whom I have made previous reference. (David is also an organist and once when at school borrowed some organ music from Mr. Simpson which is why I know about the musical side of his nature.) On rare occasions we had an opportunity to experience Mr. Simpson's piano playing in assembly when Mr. Hughes was indisposed.

It is a truism that smells are evocative. The merest trace of a scent or odour can bring to mind related associations from years ago. This prompts me to comment that I have an olfactory memory of Mr. Simpson, namely, that, when in close proximity, he always smelt very nice — as though freshly scrubbed with strong smelling soap! In personal conversation he could be a little hard of hearing — perhaps self induced through shouting so loud at errant boys. One consequence of this was a little speech trait which went: "Beg your pardon" — when asking you to repeat something. A lively twinkling gaze was another of his distinguishing characteristics. To digress a moment longer from mechanics, I seem to recall Mr. Simpson making announcements about the Old Boys' Association in Assembly — usually to say that a meeting was forthcoming or that a good time had been had by all the previous night. I suppose this was to help to promote the standing of the OBA. I will take leave of Alf Simpson here — although he will reappear later when I reflect on religious instruction. For now I will record my appreciation of the efforts of this warm-hearted teacher and, if there be such a thing, to ask his surviving spirit to 'forgive us our trespasses'. Amen Alfred.

Class 5X

When we progressed to Class 5X another teacher entered our lives by the name of John England Barton. What a patriotic middle forename! Curiously, in all my time at the CTS I cannot ever recall Mr. Barton being styled as 'Dick Barton' — in imitation of the radio character *Dick Barton and his special agent*. Perhaps, like me, you used to listen to the radio programme of this title which was serialised and broadcast on Saturday mornings in the late 1940s. It became well known for its signature tune — *The devil rides out*. What I can say, concerning Mr. Barton's style of address, is that we initially called him by his alias 'JEB' — until the novelty wore off when we reverted to the more conventional 'Mr. Barton'.

He presented a somewhat Edwardian appearance with his hair parted centrally just as I like to imagine was the case with the principal characters in Jerome K. Jerome's *Three Men in a Boat*. His entry into the classroom followed a predictable routine. On arriving he would place his attaché case (bearing his initials in black-ink block-capital letters) on the desk, open it — the catches making a rhythmic snap, remove the required books and papers and then fix his gaze upon us — the latter made all the more piercing by the lenses of his spectacles. Our days of larking about in mechanics were clearly over! I formed the opinion very early on that Mr. Barton was a born teacher. Indeed I once shared this view with another boy — Brian Lister. Brian just looked at me, rather perplexed, and contented himself by muttering darkly about teachers in general. Let me justify why I formed so favourable an opinion of Mr. Barton the pedagogue.

He had a no-nonsense style of teaching, the hallmarks of which were thorough preparation, clarity of delivery and punctilious attention to detail. More than these he was a committed and enthusiastic interpreter of his subject, in the case in question, mechanics — I will discuss Mr. Barton's contribution to the teaching of physics later. He was an animated teacher given to bodily gesticulations and movements of his arms. He, as I have remarked previously of Mr. Bee, frequently wore his black academic gown and could be seen most mornings, after assembly, striding purposefully along West Street to the Holly Building with his gown billowing in the wind. (Whilst on this subject, two other gown wearers and regular Bow Street walkers — rather a good pun — were Mr. Clarke and Mr. Gregory. The former progressed sedately along the pavement and the latter rather rolled along as though his somewhat spherical form had been captured by the breeze that always seemed to blast round the corner of West Street.) In the classroom Mr. Barton was particularly resourceful in making full use of any available equipment — and if none was to hand he would improvise. Let me give an illustration of the latter. One morning in mechanics he selected two tallish boys and then singled out a small boy — but only after ensuring he was wearing leather-soled shoes. The two big boys were then required to take the arms of the small boy and to pull them at an angle of 45°. This of course had the effect of dragging the lad along the floor — his leather-soled shoes offering little friction to the floor boards (no fitted carpets in those days). "There", said a triumphant Mr. Barton, "You now see the effect of the resultant of forces"! Not satisfied with this demonstration, Mr. Barton then required the two big boys he had selected to pull *him* along the floor as well. Having extolled Mr. Barton's pedagogical virtues (some of them) I will balance the picture by telling a story somewhat against him. He must hold the CTS record for procrastination concerning the marking of books. It was during my time in Class 5X that we handed in our class books; we did not receive them back until the following year — by which time we were in Class 6X!

Physical demonstrations in mechanics did not typically take the form of boys pulling one another about — that was usually reserved for the school playground. Class demonstrations were undertaken with the assistance of the rather remarkable equipment that was fastened to the walls of the room; in effect the mechanics classroom in the Holly Building was a well equipped laboratory. You may recall there was an assortment of block and tackle and pulleys of various types. With these facilities we studied the mechanical advantage and velocity ratio of simple wheel and axle systems (Fig. 63), the same properties for systems of pulleys (Fig. 64) and the mechanical behaviour of the more complex differential wheel and axle (Fig. 65). We all found practical work in mechanics very absorbing — especially when JEB was not looking and you could overload the pulleys sending their weights crashing to the floor!

A.L. Applied Maths

The days of playful innocence in mechanics passed all too soon and, on progressing to A.L., the subject was studied under the aegis of applied maths. The course extended over a period of two years the first of which was the responsibility of Mr. William (Bill) Davis whom I recall as being extraordinarily friendly and approachable. He always had a broad grin on his face and a kindly word. (I will digress here and add that, by way of co-incidence, Mr. Davis was a friend of my uncle John — my mother's younger brother — but the friendship came to an untimely end in 1955 when my uncle was killed in a car accident. This was my first 'adult' encounter with the pain of loss imposed by death, not least the effect on my mother — who was herself to die two years later.)

Mr. Davis's speciality was the action and reaction of forces imposed on vehicles moving in circular motion on an inclined plane. He became very animated when talking about centrifugal and centripetal forces (action and re-action being opposite and equal etc.). More generally the A.L. syllabus included the kinematics of particles moving with uniform energy, concepts of work and power, momentum, the impact of spherical elastic bodies (familiarity with which has increased my enjoyment of TV snooker), simple harmonic motion (which I found to be far from simple), the oscillation of a pendulum, projectiles (familiarity with which increased my enjoyment and understanding of NASA space rocket exploration) and — lots more — but that's enough to be going on with.

One afternoon, immediately after lunch, Mr. Davis started his lesson by telling us how he had been endeavouring to explain the concept of mechanical efficiency to a perplexed Mr. Dove. It seems Mr. Dove had passed some innocent remark concerning the power of a steam engine. (To make the point it will be useful to insert here, by way of a reminder, that mechanical efficiency is the useful work achieved expressed as a function of that theoretically possible — remember?) It appears Mr. Dove was incredulous to learn from Mr. Davis that the thermal efficiency of a steam engine is only of the order of 6%! "But steam engines are so powerful", protested Mr. Dove, "Yes", retorted Mr. Davis, "But that does not make them efficient"! Later on, in physics, some of this was explained with reference to Carnot's 'heat cycle' and the equation $(T1-T2)/T2$, where $T1$ and $T2$ are, respectively, the hottest and coldest parts of the engine. But this is getting too serious. I will close this little reflection by concluding, just a little wickedly, that the powers of application to work, of the average CTS pupil, bore an uncanny relationship to the restricted thermal efficiency of a steam engine!

The second year of my AL course in applied maths was taken by Mr. Gilbert Thompson. He was short in stature, went everywhere shrouded in his black academic gown and generally manifest a calm reserved demeanour. His image had just a hint of a military character that was enhanced by his carefully trimmed moustache. Mr. Thompson did not lend himself in any way to caricature. His style was strictly professional. His only mannerism which I can recall that remotely lent itself to parody, was a tendency, when at the blackboard, to roll a stick of chalk backwards and forewords in the palm of his hand. This calls to mind the following incident. We were being introduced to a geometrical proposition which required a demonstration of the Euclidean proof that the sum of the angles in a triangle is 180°. Mr. Thompson looked at me — here we go I thought — and then asked me to step forward to the blackboard to produce the required proof. I got about half way before having a lapse of memory. I paused to think — and, lo and behold, I caught myself rolling the chalk, Thompson fashion, backwards and forwards in my hand!

My reference to Euclidean proofs further calls to mind the manner in which we were required to complete a geometrical proposition with the designation 'QED' — which of course signifies *quod erat demonstrandum* — 'which was to be demonstrated'. Explaining this procedure Mr. Thompson observed dryly: "You only put 'QED' if you have in fact QED it"! — which I suppose is in itself, like so much of Euclid, an axiomatic truth. Humour was generally absent in Mr. Thompson's lessons but I do recall an incident of a light-hearted kind — albeit somewhat rarefied. Some of you will remember (?) from your co-ordinate geometry and calculus that when an increment *dx* is rotated around the x axis, so as to intersect with a parabolic curve, a solid of revolution is generated. In demonstrating this one day, Mr. Thompson said: "Let us first take an incremental strip" — at which point he stopped, turned to the class and added — "I suppose my reference to 'strip' has made you think of the *Reveille*"! The latter, you will recall, was the tabloid newspaper of the day which was dedicated to the promotion of the undraped female form. To say the least we were rather taken by surprise at this uncharacteristic throw-away line coming, as it did, from so orthodox a teacher.

More seriously, my reference to mathematically derived solids of revolution brings to mind a little incident which demonstrates how able a mathematician was my good friend and CTS contemporary Richard *Charlie* Prime. You may remember that we 'rehearsed' our forthcoming A.L. exams by taking practice tests — known as 'prelims'. Now, one of the questions on the applied maths prelim paper concerned the calculation of the hydrostatic pressure exerted on a submerged sphere — whose volume had to be calculated. We were supposed to know the formula for deriving the volume of a sphere, but Charlie confessed to me that in the exam he had a lapse of memory about this. So what did he do? According to his testimony, he simply derived the formula from first principles, using calculus, in the margins of his exam paper! The significance of this observation is that this very proposition often cropped up in A.L. maths as a half question. Let me enlarge on this story to make a generalisation. One day, several years later, I was relaxing listening to the radio programme called *The Brains Trust* — remember it? The chairman asked the philosopher and logician Professor A. J. Ayer how he would define intelligence — a good question (care to work out an answer?). Without blinking an eyelid Ayer quipped back: "Intelligence is best defined in terms of the manifestation of intelligence". How true — have a little think about it. Now my generalisation. I regard Charlie Prime's deriving of his required formula as a good illustration of Ayer's contention — but I have to add that I also suspect that Charlie was just too lazy to bother to learn the formula in the first place!

Together with his air of calm Mr. Thompson seemed always to be in total command of his subject. No problem ever seemed to perplex him. He demonstrated abstruse propositions with clinical efficiency. In short, he was a clever man who appeared to take each day as it came quite unfazed. The only circumstances I ever recall that gave a slight hint of Mr. Thompson outside of the realm of applied mathematics, were his occasional visits to the woodwork shop to borrow a tool from Mr. Hunter — prompting him to confide in me the observation: "I think Mr. Thompson must be good at woodwork judging by the tools he borrows from me"!

There was one occasion in class when Mr. Thompson was clearly impressed by the achievements of two of my contemporaries, namely, John Miles Mastin and Keith Healey. But it was for their achievement *outside* the classroom that they had earned Mr. Thompson's admiration. You could say these two boys — young men — had distinguished themselves by giving practical expression to the quantities of time and velocity. This is what I mean. John's father was a member of my profession; he was an 'L.R.I.B.A.' — Licentiate of the Royal Institute of British Architects. As admiring fathers will, he had bought John a motor bike — a 'track bike' with heavy duty tyres. For a few weeks John would arrive at school on his bike at full throttle coming to a screeching stop in Holly Street. Then came the day he exchanged the bike for a white sports car — could it have been an MG TF? This brings me to my point. John and Keith started to take part in cross-country-rallies — requiring high speed driving and dead accurate navigation. John was the navigator and Keith the driver. In addition, John had to calculate average speeds using his slide rule — the slide rule was then 'state of the art technology'! The weekend came when these two characters won a rally — and got their names in the papers! Mr. Thompson duly read about them and, as I have said, was suitably impressed.

There was almost a tragic ending to this tale. When out on a drive with another CTS lad Peter Watts — 'Watts for power' as we used to say — John misjudged a bend and overturned his lovely car — I believe it was 'a write off'. I recall Peter telling me how he had gone to see the wreck the next day parked at a garage. He heard two lads remark: "We're glad we weren't in that"! To the startled pair Peter remarked: "I was"! Mercifully neither of the CTS pair were injured and survived their experience. Indeed, I believe Peter maintained an affectionate correspondence for many years afterwards with the family who had looked after him immediately following the accident.

Our work in A.L. applied maths progressed to include such topics as — to name but a few — centroids and the centre of mass of irregular shapes, the motion of an object sliding down an inclined plane (with and without friction), projectiles (with trajectories intercepted by flat and inclined planes) and the hydrostatic pressures imposed on the surfaces of submerged cylinders and spheres. The mathematical technicalities of all these, and much more, were communicated to us by Mr. Thompson with, as I have already implied, his cool logical efficiency. Notwithstanding, my personal disenchantment with applied maths continued to grow as I realised the subject and its ramifications were not for me — I was inclining more towards the arts. Nevertheless, I duly sat the A.L. exam in 'full' applied maths — I remember to this day the location of my exam desk in the school hall (I wish I could forget it!). I also recall a number of the questions. Here, to give a flavour of the summer paper in 1959, is one — on a favourite theme of the examiners: "A small spherical projectile [of specified velocity, trajectory and coefficient of restitution] impacts with a smooth surface at the top of a flight of steps. Describe the motion of the projectile and demonstrate that, after an interval of 't' seconds as it descends the steps the sum of its successive horizontal trajectories conforms to an arithmetic series". I remember staring at the exam paper bleakly. Afterwards I found myself in the company of Jack Glossop to whose mathematical abilities I have already paid tribute. We were supposed to be doing extra study for technical drawing in the little back room near to Mr. Hedley's drawing office to which I have also earlier referred. Instead, Jack treated me to what I can only describe as a bravura performance by going over the entire paper, from memory, outlining every feature of the required solutions. He must have achieved a distinction. I obtained a more modest grade which was not sufficient to allow me to progress to the honours degree in architecture — a precise parallel with my achievement in pure maths. Something more was required of me to improve my position — all will be revealed in due course as to how I achieved this. But now it's time for a change of theme.

Science and Physics

Class 3y

How wonderfully simple life seemed to be all those years ago when we could innocently label our school exercise books 'science' with little concern for which precise branch of study this term was meant to encompass. I dimly recall being told, in those distant days, that science was concerned with observed material facts and the knowledge of natural and physical phenomena — or something of this kind. But to our youthful imagination prescriptive definitions of subject boundaries had little relevance. We were more imbued by the fascination of 'doing things' which involved the touch and feel of apparatus and measuring things and then recording 'results' in our stiff-backed large-format exercise books. In our various ways, we had all made some acquaintance with elementary science before our arrival at the CTS. In my case I had studied science at Anns Road Secondary Modern School for one year when the subject was a mixture of biology, physics and chemistry. I have particular reason for remembering the latter — I knocked over a glass bell jar during an experiment to 'collect' oxygen. You could say the consequences were shattering.

At the CTS the first acquaintance that Builders of my generation made with science was through the good offices of Mr. William (Bill) Gregory. Appropriately, we labelled our exercise books 'Building Science'. Allow me the following brief digression. Do you recall how our school exercise books were in two formats. We had a small-format book which we used for maths and language-based subjects and a large-format book which served for science and technical subjects. Both were inscribed on the cover: 'City of Sheffield Education Committee'. Above these words appeared the city's coat of arms depicting two bearded gentlemen, of goodly stature, each resting with an arm on a large shield. I have one of these images before me as I write this. One of the gentlemen — doubtless a god of foundry work — stands before an anvil whilst his companion — doubtless also a related god of manufacturing — rests, in time honoured fashion, on his sledge hammer. Both of these icons of industry are clad in a form of male mini skirt. I must say this visual imagery passed before our gaze so frequently we ceased to take any notice of it or its symbolism. But back now to science.

Mr. Gregory took Class 3Y for building science in the laboratory located on the first floor down at Cathedral School. This was a long room equipped with parallel rows of teak-topped benches with arrays of gas and water taps positioned at intervals. There was a fume cupboard on the right, as you entered, equipped with a lead covered surface. I don't ever recall this being used. At the rear was a preparation room which we seldom entered unless it was to gain practice in reading the Fortin's barometer which hung on the wall just behind the door. (These so-called mercury 'stick' barometers are now very valuable — they retail for about £1000 or more.) The laboratory was well provided with cupboards containing apparatus of various kinds. In my first-year science classes I sat next to a boy called Michael Porter. Our bench position was by a window which overlooked the adjacent premises. The proximity gave a good view into what I think was a kitchen area. This circumstance has left a vivid impression of my first day in the laboratory because I recall a canteen lady making ham sandwiches which made me feel very hungry. An even more vivid impression was that created by our teacher Mr. Gregory — 'Pop' Gregory.

I am being generous if I describe Mr. Gregory's appearance as somewhat untidy — dishevelled would be nearer the mark. He wore a baggy jacket from which a number of buttons usually hung loose; its capacious pockets were crammed full with miscellaneous articles — including a long length of brown-rubber Bunsen-burner pipe which he used from-time-to-time to spank the bottoms of errant boys. His muddy shoes conveyed the impression he had recently tramped across an open field. Mr. Gregory was usually to be seen in possession of a fisherman's keep-net in which he used to carry piles of exercise books. Even more remarkable were the vehicles in which he arrived at school. He had a penchant for large battered vans with thick-tyred wheels — caked in mud — the doors of which were secured with lengths of rope.

At our first lesson Mr. Gregory, rosy cheeked from the effort of climbing up all the steps to the lab, greeted us in his high-pitched voice. His eyes seemed to sparkle behind his spectacles and his hair stood in disarray as though electrostatically charged — there was definitely an air of the mad professor about Mr. Gregory. He exhorted us as to the virtues of hard work and reminded us that our working day was not much longer than that of children at junior school — although his reasoning didn't allow for homework! He often returned to this theme and would lampoon certain members of the class as being like 'Weary Willie' or 'Tired Tim' which was usually enough to stir the more sleepy members of the class back into wakefulness. But we were to discover that he had other, more forceful, ways of securing a class's attention!

Perhaps my most abiding impression of Bill Gregory is of his eloquence. He possessed considerable powers of oratory and was a natural raconteur, frequently enlivening his lessons with colourful imagery. Let me give an example — from many. In describing the hydrostatic principle, that the pressure exerted on a liquid acts uniformly in all directions, he drew a parallel with a man whom he had once found shot on the field of battle during some harrowing war-time experience. "Only a small bullet wound could be seen in the man's chest", remarked Mr. Gregory, "but when you turned him over there was a large symmetrical cavity blown away — demonstrating that the force of the bullet had acted uniformly in all directions on the fluids in the man's body"! We were impressed but sat in silence feeling slightly sick. With that vivid image established in our minds, Mr. Gregory proceeded to describe the functioning of the hydrostatic press. This, he informed us, was invented by Joseph Bramah; he was a local man who was born near Barnsley. We were told, in vivid terms, how the hydraulic press made practical use of Pascal's law to the effect that when pressure is exerted on the smaller of two pistons, connected and filled with liquid, a greater force results on the larger one. Mr. Gregory was always at his best when combining formal instruction with anecdotes and references to our industrial heritage. Let me provide an illustration. For some reason we were instructed into the metallurgical differences between pig iron and steel — this was doubtless considered to be essential for lads born and bred in Sheffield 'the home of steel'. This theme provided Mr. Gregory with the opportunity to outline the industrial achievement of Henry Bessemer and his method of making steel from pig iron. Our ensuing homework — that was always the downside of interesting lessons — was to draw a Bessemer converter and to describe how the blast of high-pressure air oxidises the slag impurities in molten iron and converts it to steel.

I have made a passing reference to Mr. Gregory and his war-time experience and this prompts me to recall an amusing interlude in a lesson when he reminisced briefly about this period in his life. It appears that a urine sample was required — doubtless part of a medical-fitness inspection. He described the colour of the 'samples' of his young soldier companions — in appropriately disparaging terms — then, holding before us a glass beaker that was ready to hand, he proclaimed: "My sample shone like golden glory"! We rolled about in mirth savouring the moment, enjoying Mr. Gregory's narrative style and the convivial atmosphere he had created between himself and the class — surely one of the hallmarks of a good teacher.

I am mindful that I am digressing from my allocated subject of science, but I will linger a moment longer with Mr. Gregory the raconteur. One of his recurrent exhortations was to drink milk which, of course, was provided daily in the form of a small glass bottle containing, I believe, one gill — or a quarter of a pint. To decline this daily provision of a free bottle of milk was, in the eyes of Mr. Gregory, a major sin. To emphasise the point he recalled the days of the Great War which required the first mass medical inspection of young men. This revealed the mal-nourished state of many young lads, resolving the government of the day to improve the diet of children with a daily supply of milk — and a low-cost school dinner. That anyway is how Mr. Gregory recounted this little bit of social history back in 1954. "So you see", he raged passionately, countenance reddening and eyes gleaming "how important it is for you to drink your milk"! Despite such exhortations — which must have lasted a full fifteen minutes — several members of the class, with a pathological aversion to milk, declined. I admired their courage since Mr. Gregory, when at the height of his passion, could be very persuasive and would positively quiver with rage.

The health of the nation's children was one of Mr. Gregory's favourite themes and I recall him several times digressing from the scheduled class to give it an airing. I will elaborate since it will shed light on the public spirited and compassionate side of Mr. Gregory's nature. From what I can gather he made frequent visits to sick children in hospital to entertain them by showing films on his cine projector. On one such occasion he told us the film came off the spool and he was left with about 1000 feet of film all over the floor of the ward! But the point of his hospital stories was to inculcate, in yet another form, the virtues of drinking milk. He would vividly describe the appearance of consumptive children — "Spewing up their guts into an enamel bowl"! Then he would add, in the same breath: "Now, who does not want his milk"? The unfortunate juxtaposition of 'guts' and 'milk' was enough to put anybody off! But now I should get back to Mr. Gregory as our teacher of science.

We made good use of the laboratory facilities in our First-Year science classes to undertake simple experiments. One of these required the burning of magnesium ribbon. Its combustion bathed the laboratory in eerie, brilliant white light. The process also produced considerable heat as one class member was to discover when, despite Mr. Gregory's exhortations to take care, he shattered a ceramic dish by allowing it to come into contact with the hot magnesium ribbon. Mr. Gregory flew into a rage and gave the class its first demonstration of how a length of rubber tubing could be used for reasons other than connecting to a gas supply!

Our lessons in elementary physics encompassed a diversity of subjects of which mention may be made of the following: the osmosis of a tree and the production of chlorophyll and sugar; and the concepts of density and specific gravity — complete with the story of Archimedes leaping around calling out 'Eureka!'. Pressure in a liquid was demonstrated by means of water being allowed to escape from a tall cylinder through a set of tubular orifices — which conveyed the visual impression of little boys having a pee! We were introduced to a host of similar propositions. These were all enlivened by the vivid powers of Mr. Gregory's narrative style to which I have made mention. Incidentally, should our concentration wander, one of his teacher's devices to secure our attention was to elevate his voice to a curious high-pitched tone; if that failed out would come the length of gas pipe!

After about a term, our study of physics with Mr. Gregory soon settled into a regular routine centred upon the familiar syllabus components of heat, light, magnetism and electricity — although not all these were studied in our first year, the latter topics being covered, as I shall explain shortly, by Mr. Thornton. Our study of convection gave Mr. Gregory scope to compare the flow of heat in air and water with the functioning of a domestic hot-water system (Fig. 66). Next came the measurement of temperature and the calibration of thermometers (Fig. 67). In this series of lessons we also studied the effects of thermal radiation and absorption using discarded chalk boxes as thermal containers. We occasionally used more sophisticated apparatus such as Leslie's cube (Fig. 68). I clearly recall spending an afternoon determining the coefficient of linear expansion of copper — and then having to spend a couple of evenings drawing the equipment (Fig. 69).

I have implied that in his teaching of science Mr. Gregory endeavoured to emphasise the practical aspect of the subject. One such example is to be seen in my illustration (Fig. 66) of the simplified working of a domestic hot-water system. Mr. Gregory's description of the heating and ventilation system originally installed in the Firth Building, to which I have made previous reference in my comments about the CTS buildings, also derives from these lessons to Class 3Y concerning the principles of heat. I can offer a further example of Mr. Gregory's teaching style, namely, when he outlined how a house loses heat through the building fabric. He explained how he had undertaken these calculations in connection with his own home. Such matters are commonplace today — but all of this was back in 1954! I remember Mr. Gregory concluding his lesson by remarking: "If you ever want to know how to do this for your own house one day I will help" — a typically friendly gesture.

There were other convivial moments in Mr. Gregory's lessons when he endeavoured to show us how to get on in the world and improve ourselves. Let me explain what I mean, although it will lead us away from the subject of physics for a moment. I recall him saying, with his typical passion: "The secret of getting a job done is to get on with it. Don't procrastinate! When you've finished one job get on with the next"! Well, I now know what Mr. Gregory was driving at — I believe it's called time management but I have to confess his advice is not always easy to follow — especially when sloth, the enemy of achievement, beckons in the form of a comfortable armchair — with *Match of the Day* about to start!

Mr. Gregory would sometimes enlarge on the theme of the virtue of being industrious, and tantalise us with the prospect of the financial rewards we might expect if we followed a professional career rather than that of a manual worker. He cited the typical monthly remuneration of the former in contrast to the more modest weekly wage of the latter. He furnished his arguments with figures even to the extent of the financial benefits which would accrue over a working lifetime. Much of his reasoning went over our youthful heads but there is no denying Mr. Gregory's sincerity in urging us to be industrious and hardworking.

I recall the time when our end-of-year exams were approaching and this afforded Mr. Gregory a further opportunity for him to show the supportive side of his nature. This time his theme was how to approach revision for examinations. This may not sound very glamorous but the concept was a somewhat novel one at that stage in our school careers. Most of us had not taken any significant examinations at that stage in our lives — with the notable exception of the (dreaded) eleven-plus exam and the 'tests' we had taken at the various secondary schools we had attended before entering the CTS. So Mr. Gregory, for our benefit, took all this very seriously explaining about planning time properly, not spending too long on a particular question and so on. Then he made a digression, which is the primary reason for my invoking the memory of this episode. He explained how his own son had recently (1952–53) sat the University of Cambridge Entrance Examination for which he had helped by analysing previous papers — which was another of Mr. Gregory's pieces of advice. So I dutifully settled down to my revision a consequence of which, allow me to say, was that I was awarded the First Year Science Subjects Prize.

Class 5X

The teaching of Second-Year science to CTS builders was the responsibility of Mr. Thomas Thornton. He had a distinctive hollow-cheeked consumptive look about him which was not enhanced by what I imagine was a two-packets a day rate of cigarette consumption. The brown-stained fingers of his right hand certainly conveyed this impression, as did the alacrity with which he disappeared after a lesson into the prep room behind the lab to 'light up'. His smoker's cough added a general air of fragile health to his physical demeanour. Mr. Thornton's gestures were also rather slow and deliberative as though he was seeking to conserve his limited stamina. I recall he walked with a steady pace, his posture somewhat stooped as though bearing the cares of the world. He usually went about shrouded in a woolly cardigan presumably to keep his rather lean frame warm. This is not a very flattering portrait! Let me add some complimentary features. Mr. Thornton had a most gentle nature and a twinkle in his eye. When a boy asked a 'stupid' question he never lost his temper; he merely allowed himself a brief look of despair, accompanied by a shake of his head, and he would patiently explain whatever was required all over again. When a boy raised his hand to ask a question, Mr. Thornton's invariable response was to say: "Yes Sir"! I must have caught this habit from him because I frequently find myself responding to my own students' queries in a similar manner. Mr. Thornton once confided in me that he had the Higher National Certificate (HNC) in physics. This personal disclosure came about as a consequence of my asking him, at the end of a lesson, how people studied science at night school. As for Mr. Thornton, he certainly made the fullest use of his powers in what were always well-prepared lessons.

At the period of my time at the CTS, Mr. Thornton's son was also a pupil at the school. He bore a striking resemblance to his father — although I should add, hastily, of a more youthful and animated being. Some years after leaving school I recall seeing Mr. Thornton Junior working in the Booking Hall at the Midland Station. I recall how he once had occasion to call into our classroom to see his father when one of our lessons was in progress. I expected to hear Mr. Thornton's normal friendly salutation "Yes Sir?" but instead his son was received with the somewhat bleak greeting: "And what do you want?" — followed by the slightly ominous: "I'll see you later"! I suppose it must have been rather awkward for both father and son to be in the school at the same time.

Mr. Thornton carried on our science lessons where Mr. Gregory left off — but by now we labelled our exercise books with the subject-heading 'physics'. Mr. Thornton was particularly accomplished at drawing neat representations of apparatus on the blackboard, from which we made faithful copies. By way of emphasising the standards of illustration he required he would, from time-to-time, remove a carefully preserved exercise book from a drawer in his laboratory bench. This book contained the work of a former pupil that I can only describe as being breathtakingly accomplished. Mr. Thornton smiled as we gasped — literally — with amazement at the sight of so many carefully coloured Indian-ink drawings of scientific apparatus. We marvelled, albeit rather enviously, that school work could be undertaken with such care. For me it was, as the expression goes, a 'defining moment'. From that time on I resolved to emulate the work I had seen — which of course was the purpose behind Mr. Thornton's little scheme. The immediate consequence of my good intentions was the series of sketches I have used to illustrate this part of my account. Try as I could, I never achieved the standard of draughtsmanship to be found in Mr. Thornton's 'exemplar'. This prompts me to ask who was it who could draw so well? He would be a Building pupil in his Second or Third Year at the CTS round about 1952–53. Whoever you are, or were, three hearty cheers. If I ever meet you at an OBA evening I will buy you a drink for inspiring me as you did — but don't too many of you claim to be the mystery man!

Continuing the theme of illustrating school work, I can reveal how my own studies in physics did reach a certain standard sufficient to earn Mr. Thornton's admiration — I hope that does not sound too immodest. One day this had the following consequence. Mr. Thornton alerted the class to the fact that one of Her Majesty's School Inspectors would be 'sitting-in' on our lesson very shortly. He did not make a great fuss of this but stressed the importance of our being on our best behaviour and of the need to pay attention. (I will remark in passing that it is a measure of Mr. Thornton's skill that he did not have to exhort us unduly to achieve what was required — and, in any event, we generally enjoyed our physics lessons.) On the day the Inspector called (as J. B. Priestley might have said) Mr. Thornton asked me for my exercise book and showed it to the dark-suited and important-looking official. He turned the pages with an occasional expression of approval and then cordially returned the book to me. I think I had nearly, but not quite, attained the standard of work in Mr. Thornton's carefully preserved exemplar to which I have made mention.

Mr. Thornton, having informed the inspector of the stage we had reached in our studies — with the assistance of my book as just described — then resumed his teaching. An embarrassing incident duly occurred which every teacher must dread when an 'HMI' is sitting-in on the class. A boy by the name of Cosgrove — my apologies Mr. Cosgrove if you are reading this — asked Mr. Thornton: "Sir, is this the same work as we did last week"? Now that may seem an innocent enough question but it was, in fact, a real clanger. Let me explain the sequence of events which led to Master Cosgrove's confusion. We had, in time-honoured fashion, made a study of Boyle's Law, remember: 'With the temperature remaining the same, the volume (V) of a given quantity of gas is inversely as the pressure (P) which it bears — such that PV = constant'. You all had that on the tip of your tongue didn't you! We then proceeded to consider Gay Lussac's Law which states — remember — 'In a given mass of gas if the volume remains constant then the pressure varies directly as the (absolute) temperature'. We then drew the apparatus (Fig. 70). And so to our lesson in the presence of the school inspector. "Today", said Mr. Thornton, "we will consider Charles' Law which states — 'All gases expand part of their volume with rise in temperature if the pressure remains constant' ". You may now appreciate why Master Cosgrove was somewhat confused — and doubtless a few more along with him. I was, of course, in full possession of these essential distinctions between the gas laws and the manner in which a volume of gas may be altered by change of pressure as well as change of temperature — clever clogs (!). On hearing Cosgrove's question, Mr. Thornton cast a look of despair and exclaimed: "Young man, you have as good as told me you have not understood a word I have been saying for the last three weeks"! "I have Sir, honest!", protested Cosgrove. Mr. Thornton shook his head ruefully and I discerned just the flicker of a smile on the face of the HMI. The incident passed and we went home to draw the apparatus (Fig. 71).

I have a more light hearted story from this same period which, in its way, must have been typical of similar incidents enacted daily in a dozen other boys' schools up and down the country — after all, do we not say 'boys will be boys'! Mr. Thornton had begun his lesson; I was, of course, dutifully paying attention but this was not the case with two or three boys seated at a bench behind me. As Mr. Thornton endeavoured to make progress with his discourse on the gas laws, I could hear subdued conversational murmurings along the lines: "Let me have a look!", "Wow!", and "Let me see". I could but deduce that these boys were not exactly striving to gain a better scrutiny of the blackboard but were feasting their eyes upon some other genre of visual material! Mr. Thornton's way of gaining the attention of errant boys was to stop what he was saying, place his hands on the bench before him, lean on them, incline himself forward and then fix the wayward lads with his admonitory gaze — made all the more concentrated by the dark cast of his sunken eyes. This little repertoire took all of several seconds to complete and was usually sufficient to achieve its objective. On the occasion in question, Mr. Thornton said — in a dead-pan voice: "I don't know if those are pictures of Jane you have there under the bench but if you don't pay attention I'll come and confiscate them"! Silence then prevailed. (Jane, of course, was the young heroine of the day who appeared regularly in a daily strip cartoon — an appropriate expression — and inevitably concluded her exploits in a state of deshabille.)

Whilst on a somewhat light-hearted theme, I will ask if you remember those tall three-legged laboratory stools on which we used to perch? Of course you do, they were rather uncomfortable. Do you also recall how they had a small hole cut in the seat to form a means of grasping them? Now, boys of my generation — I should qualify this by adding, of a certain lowly and disorderly inclination — discovered that, by inserting their fingers through the hole they could tickle an unsuspecting boys testicles. Many is the time I have observed a boy rising suddenly from his laboratory stool — in reflex action — prompting me to think: "There goes another victim"! This calls to mind the following. When I was a little boy I remember how my grandfather would take me upon his knee and whisper — with sage-like gravitas: "He who sits upon a red-hot poker shall surely rise again"! I merely looked at him perplexed, but now I could add: "And when sitting on a CTS lab stool granddad"! That's enough of being silly. It's time now for more physics.

Our studies of light included reflections in mirrors (Fig. 72), refraction in lenses (remember the lens law and the perplexing sign convention?) and, best of all, the colour spectrum — do you recall all those lovely colours — red, orange, yellow, green, blue, indigo and violet? We learned how to take a photograph with a pin-hole camera (Fig. 73) provided the subject could remain still for about four hours! The principles of the solar eclipse were explained and how the umbra and penumbra are formed (Fig. 73). Magnetism was fascinating. We 'played' with bar magnets, learned about their properties and studied the laws of magnetic attraction and repulsion. Do you remember the little piece of iron put across the north and south poles to help to keep all the molecules correctly aligned? In the case of the set of magnets that I used at school the manufacturer had cleverly inscribed the words from Holy Scripture: "I am my brother's keeper". The study of magnetism induced by electricity took us into the realms of fields of force which we plotted with the help of iron filings scattered on sheets of paper (Figs 74 and 75).

Our end-of-term Class 5X exam in physics was sat in drawing office DO1 in the Bow Building. I sat at the back of the room in the second row of desks. In front of me was my schoolmate John Butcher from Carfield Secondary School days. After the exam John said: "The sound of your pen scratching away is enough to put anybody off"! There was a question on the paper concerning the three 'effects' of electricity. Outside in the playground Jack Timms asked me: "Are these conduction, convection and radiation"? I had to disappoint him with the correct answer — remember — heating, chemical and magnetic effects. "Oh ****!', exclaimed Jack! As for myself — allow me to say I took leave of Class 5X with the Science Subjects Prize.

O.L. Physics

In O.L. physics we continued the study-themes of the previous two years. Our work at this time may be divided into two branches; we had lessons about what I will call ideas and concepts and there were parallel lessons concerned more with calculations — to test our grasp of the concepts. The ideas and concepts lessons always fascinated me most. They frequently included reference to the great discoverers in science. Messrs Gregory, Thornton and Barton (the latter of the trio to be mentioned in a moment) were all good at bringing their physics lessons to life by making mention of various individuals from science's 'Hall of Fame'. Here is a scattering of some of the things we were told to stir your memories.

We all remember Robert Bunsen and his famous Bunsen burner (Fig. 76), but remember also his grease-spot photometer? Then there was Humphry Davy and his miner's safety lamp (Fig. 76). Who remembers Evangelista Torricelli and his water barometer — over thirty feet tall? (It would be difficult to fit one of those in your front hall!) The story of Count Magdeburg's hollow brass hemispheres captured my imagination; remember, when evacuated of air the pressure exerted on them required two horses to pull them apart. The reference to horses prompts me to call to mind the story we were told of James Watt and his determination of horsepower. He used such strong dray horses for his experiments that Watt's standard unit is now considered to be about 50% more than can be sustained by a typical horse for a working day. Who remembers their study of the electric cells of John Frederic Daniell and Georges Leclanché (Fig. 77)? The latter led us directly to an explanation of the working of the electric doorbell with which it was commonly associated (Fig. 78). Our study of the measuring of electrical current became more advanced as we progressed to learning about the tangent galvanometer (Figs 79 & 80). Other sensitive equipment I recall using included the dip circle to plot the magnitude and direction of the Earth's magnetic field (Fig. 81). Do you recall the story of Luigi Galvani who discovered how to make a dead frog's leg twitch by application of electrolytic stimuli? Then there was Gauss whose name cropped up frequently in magnetism and electricity. And of course there was our good friend Isaac Newton. Such a list could go on and on. But that's enough of being serious, this is not supposed to be a comprehensive history of school science.

Instruction in O.L. physics was given, in my day, by 'Pop' Gregory. His classes were held in the laboratory perched on the top floor of the Firth Building. Mr. Gregory's lessons assumed their customary rather mad-professor frenetic style. His appearance never changed — windswept hair, jacket pockets bulging with papers, muddy shoes — and his clapped-out ex-army lorry parked in the streets nearby. Notwithstanding all of this eccentricity, a certain quality of intelligence and fiery enthusiasm permeated his lessons — interwoven with his endless exhortations to become strong and healthy by drinking milk! Let me now say something a little controversial. I began to have some doubts and misgivings concerning what I will describe as the 'unorthodox' nature of Mr. Gregory's teaching of physics. To come to the point, I thought he made too many digressions — at least to my rather orthodox way of thinking . I hope this does not sound too judgmental and censorious. Be this as it may, it's how I felt — at the tender age of sixteen. I suppose we all think we know best when we are young. (Do you recall what Mark Twain had to say about this? — "When I was fourteen I considered my father new nothing, but by the time I was twenty-one it was amazing just how much he had learned"!) Well, my doubts about my progress in O.L. physics felt real enough at the time — and they prompted me to take steps which, looking back, seem quite extraordinary. I will now reveal a closely kept secret — although the tale is a little convoluted.

In the recollections of my early life at Carfield Junior School, to which I make reference elsewhere, I mention my cousin who passed the eleven-plus exam. Barrie Bancroft, by name, attended Carfield Secondary School which, as I explain, subsequently moved from Meersbrook to Norton and was re-named Rowlinson School. By way of a little digression, I recall being invited to attend an Open Day for parents and friends. The headmaster was called Mr. Kay — known by the pupils as 'Man Yak'. He proudly spoke of the new building — set amidst its rolling acres of green fields. I remember walking about the corridors glancing in at the classrooms and workshops with their new equipment and shiny floors composed of interlocking wooden blocks — oak no less. It was an occasion to make everyone feel proud.

Sometime after making the visit to Rowlinson School I asked my cousin if I could borrow his school physics exercise books. He duly obliged and — wait for it — I copied out all his year's work, complete with line drawings and coloured diagrams! To this day not a soul has seen these. Let me briefly describe this work because I even made my own exercise book. It consists of forty pages each 11″ x 8″; every page is hand numbered in red crayon and all the lines are ruled out by myself in pencil. There is an Index Page on which I have listed no fewer than twenty-five subjects. I won't weary you with the full list, but here is a selection of the topics; the mechanical equivalent of heat, the relation between mass and acceleration, the colour spectrum, the law of inverse squares applied to light, latent heat and the electric motor — I will stop there. This work is carefully preserved in its original folder. There were a number of occasion when I wanted to show this book to my more close CTS companions — but I never dared for fear of ridicule. Even now I can't make up my mind if all this 'extra-curricula' activity is a monument to industry or misplaced enthusiasm. I will leave the reader to decide (Fig. 82).

The day of our O.L. physics exam duly arrived — one day in June 1957. We sat the exam — written paper only, no practical — in the upper classroom in Cathedral School (the room in which members of staff had their lunch — or should I say dinner). I will recall three of the question for you as follows: "Give two examples of how physical pressure causes ice to melt". I cited (i) the manner in which the ice beneath the blade of a skater's boot is momentarily turned to water and (ii) how a weighted wire, placed over a block of ice, will in time pass through the block — which is evidence of the ice progressively melting to allow the wire to pass. "Illustrate how evaporation causes cooling". Concerning this question I made a drawing of a glass beaker, containing some ether, standing on a glass sheet with a film of water trapped between the two. I showed the ether evaporating by being blown through a straw. The effect of the latent heat of cooling chills the film of water and turns it into ice — sticking the beaker to the glass. And the experimenter would probably collapse onto the floor anaesthetised!

I will conclude that my additional private study of physics paid off. Allow me to take leave of O.L. physics by saying that I was duly awarded the O.L. Science Subjects prize with which I purchased Charles Dickens's *Dombey and Son*.

A.L. Physics

Mr. Vincent McManus took the First Year of my A.L. physics course (1957–58). He was by then nearing the end of his career so I suppose he would be in his mid sixties. Indeed it eventually fell to me, in my capacity as School Captain, to make a farewell speech to Mr. McManus on behalf of the school on the occasion of his retirement — of which more later. Notwithstanding his advanced years Mr. McManus was very sharp and possessed a demeanour that manifest authority and intellectual standing in his subject. At the period concerned Mr. McManus looked rather elderly, was of modest stature with an inclination to be rather portly, had a reddish countenance and a deep voice — the latter becoming severe if his patience was tried (which no one dared).

My first encounter with Mr. McManus pre-dated the study of A.L. physics by several years. He would occasionally appear before the whole school to take morning assembly, presumably when Mr. Wadge was too pre-occupied with other matters. Mr. McManus's domain was the laboratory situated on the first floor of the Firth Building. This room was a veritable time capsule; its appearance must have remained unchanged for decades. Such was the pervasive feeling of antiquity in Mr. McManus's laboratory that at any moment you half expected Michael Faraday himself to appear from the prep room at the back! In this laboratory we had both our theory and practicals. We perched on our high three-legged stools — of the kind already mentioned with a hole in the seat (!) — which were disposed around large teak-topped benches. These were supplied with direct current which was required for performing certain experiments.

The theoretical part of the syllabus for A.L. physics was all-encompassing to the extent that leafing through the pages of my surviving physics exercise books makes the subject now seem positively intimidating. Did I really learn all this I ask myself? Probably not, but I must have assimilated a good amount because my result in A.L. physics was considerably better than that in A.L. maths and applied maths. The course extended over two years and began with *Heat* — the thermal behaviour of solids, liquids and gasses; conduction, convection and radiation; hygrometry; calorimetry and the theory of gases which culminated in the kinetic theory of gases. To be slightly frivolous, my memory from this time is clearer concerning a popular song which had the lyric: "I got steam heat 'ss' 'ss', I got steam heat 'ss' 'ss"! — remember it? Then we progressed to *Light* — mirrors, lenses, refraction, geometrical optics, the eye and vision, physical optics and the wave theory of light. I will insert here that physics was taught to us by Mr. McManus only until Christmas 1958 when, as I have previously remarked, he retired. Mr. Barton then took over for a short period until a new teacher was appointed. He was called Mr. George Nichols. I will leave my comments concerning Mr. Nichols until later and for the moment confine my narrative to Mr. Barton.

Mr. Barton was good at making conversational asides in his lessons so as to engage our minds with the wider implications of the subject under consideration. Here is an example. Do you recall Fizeau's terrestrial method for determining the velocity of light? Here's a quick reminder. Light, passed between the cogs of a rapidly rotating wheel, was reflected back from a mirror, placed several miles away, such that it could be deduced that the light took the same time to travel between the apparatus and the mirror (and back) as it did for the cog to move one interval of rotation — clear? Now this is point; not satisfied with this explanation, Mr. Barton went on to elaborate with comments about the Michelson-Morly experiment — and how this had set Albert Einstein on the road to the Theory of Relativity. This was just one of Mr. Barton's typical digressions. I should add that Mr. McManus was more orthodox and inclined to keep to the point.

Continuing my summary of A.L. physics, we devoted some weeks to *Magnetism* — including, initially, the properties of magnets. Gone were the days of simple experiments with red-coloured bar magnets and iron filings. A.L. physics was more seriously concerned with the study of the mathematical properties of magnetic substances — poles, forces of attraction and repulsion, magnetic fields, flux density and the power of magnets (remember the *dyne* as a small C.G.S unit of force — and what does C.G.S. stand for?). Then we progressed to the larger considerations of Terrestrial Magnetism — the distribution of magnetic fields across the surface of the Earth, declination, annual and diurnal magnetic variations and the mariner's compass (remember the function of the pair of large iron balls — sorry, spheres — placed on each side of the compass to neutralise the effect of the ship's magnetism?).

I will make a brief digression here to express a few remarks about the study of A.L. physics at Cathedral School. Our laboratory was on the ground floor and was entered through the cloakroom — in which we all used to queue at dinner time when the weather was bad. This room was modestly equipped with benches, and a raised dais at the front, which supported a large demonstration bench. I wonder if anyone who used this lab can remember what was to be found on the floor immediately upon entering the room? The answer — a map of the United Kingdom outlined in brass tacks. What was its purpose and who put it there? My own guess was that it may have been used in some experiment concerning terrestrial magnetism — does anyone have a better suggestion?

At this time (1958) the laboratory had no blackboard and consequently one had to be provided. It so happens this was the year when I was studying for my A.L. woodwork and Mr. Hunter requisitioned a 'task force' to accompany the technician Mr. McLean to construct the desired article. I volunteered — naturally — and set to work with several others to construct the necessary wall-support battens which we then surfaced over with hardboard. Mr. McLean supplied the finishing coat of special paint — colour green. Some weeks later, during a physics lesson, my mind wandered — nothing unusual in that — to musing not so much about what was written *on* the blackboard but about the blackboard itself. I recall thinking: "I helped to make that"!

Those of you who used this laboratory may well recall the waxy nature of the surface of the bench tops. Frequently, large lumps of pink wax could be found adhering to the bench and, intriguingly, one day someone discovered a partial set of wax false teeth! We knew they could not be Mr. Barton's because he had a fine set of knashers! All was revealed one day when we were told that the lab was used in the evenings by students learning to be dental technicians. They just weren't very good at tidying up.

I will recall an incident in this laboratory which, although rather trivial and school-boyish, leads me to an important moral generalisation. We were receiving instruction from Mr. Barton concerning the functioning of different types of photometer — those of Rumford, Bunsen and Wheatstone and another called the flicker photometer. Gordon Swan, who was taking notes by my side, missed the name of the latter and turned to me for guidance. Now, I have earlier confessed that I was not averse, on such occasions, to leading my contemporaries astray. Being in that frame of mind I whispered — "The *knicker* photometer". Gordon, recognising some similarity that the wedge-shaped apparatus had with the profile of a certain ladies' nether garment, succumbed to a fit of the giggles. These were overheard by Mr. Barton who was not amused; he reproached us with the observation that he was working hard on our behalf — and expected our attention. We felt somewhat chastened. Now for the moral part of the tale — which reflects well on Gordon. He looked at me reproachfully and, at the conclusion of the lesson, said to me: "I think we should apologise". Such an observation, a few years earlier following, say, one of Alf Simpson's more riotous lessons, would have been unthinkable — taking liberties, after all, was part of being a schoolboy. The mature nature of Gordon's remark in Mr. Barton's lesson illustrates how we were becoming more responsible for our actions — and not before time! So we duly apologised to Mr. Barton for our indiscretion. He was clearly touched by our sincerity.

Next on our A.L. physics curriculum came *Electricity* — cells, Ohm's law, electrolysis, electro-magnetic induction and much more — most of it of a mathematical nature. Do you recall Flemming's Left-Hand Rule whereby, *Thumb* indicated motion, *Fore Finger* the field and *Second Finger* current? And what about Maxwell's Corkscrew Rule which states: "When a bottle of wine is opened it makes an inviting pop"! — well that's Russell's version!

Mention must be made of *Electrostatics* and the Whimsurst's machine for the following reason. First, a quick recollection of the machine — necessary to enjoy the story. Whimsurst's machine is an induction mechanism capable of generating a powerful electrical discharge. Two well-varnished circular glass disks have strips of tinfoil around their perimeter. When rotated, brushes collect an electrical charge which is then stored in Leyden jars. At a certain voltage, this charge passes, with considerable force, across the gap maintained between two brass spheres. Considerable caution is required when demonstrating this machine! Now, I have made previous mention of the twitching of Galvani's frog's leg — but that is nothing compared to what was experienced by a certain teacher by the name of Mr. Woolhouse. I have said already what a kindly and amenable soul he was — to which I should perhaps add that he was a little susceptible to suggestion. I am indebted to my contemporary Peter Watts — a source of unimpeachable integrity — for the following account. It appears that one lunch time a number of boys had gained access to Mr McManus's lab and had fully charged a Whimsurst's machine — of course, in the interest of science! Who should then walk past the lab but Mr. Woolhouse — his normal bodily swagger even more pronounced than usual. He explained how he had a gammy leg adding; "The doctor's can't seem to do a thing with it". The group of boys hearing this urged Mr. Woolhouse into the lab on the pretext they could possibly help with a little 'electro-static therapy'! Amazingly, Mr. Woolhouse was persuaded to put the tender part of his leg between the two spheres of the Whimsurst's machine. With a few deft cranks, about 20,000 volts of static electricity duly surged through Mr. Woolhouse's knee cap! I am told — and I can quite believe it — that he momentarily became airborne and hovered above the bench! I have no precise record of what he said! I think he called out "Christ"! Be this as it may, it appears he left the room hastily with his leg fully restored!

We spent some of our time studying *Sound* — standing waves, wave motion, the vibration of air in pipes, the velocity of sound, reverberation and the acoustics of buildings. The latter was of particular interest to me given my developing interest in architecture. I wonder who will recall the method of determining the velocity of sound in a solid medium? Here's a quick reminder. A glass rod is attached to a long hollow glass tube containing lycopodium powder. When the rod is gently clasped and drawn with a leather cloth, vibrations are induced in the tube which settle the powder into nodes from which wave lengths can be calculated thereby allowing the velocity of sound to be determined — just like that, as the late Tommy Cooper would say! Now, the point of resurrecting all this in your mind is to say that teachers had evident embarrassment when naming the equipment which was called — *Kundt's* dust tube. I'm still trying to figure out what the problem was.

The theoretical part of A.L. physics concluded with a broad survey of the subject called *General Physics* — properties of matter, gravity, equilibrium, force, motion, work, power and energy. We then proceeded to simple harmonic motion, the oscillation of bodies and moments of inertia. One day, when discussing hydrostatics and viscosity, Mr. Barton made a little aside which revealed that teachers did in fact have a life outside of the classroom. "Bubbles", he remarked of the subject we were then discussing, "is the nickname of my friend's girlfriend"! — at least that's what I think he said. I will add here, by way of a little digression, that I received my first instruction in wave motion when I was about three years old. I should add this took place every Monday afternoon at about tea time. This was the time of day that my mother took in the washing line at the end of wash day. She stood by the door, where the clothes line was hooked to the wall, then give it a flick, sending a beautiful sinuous wave down the clothes line, whereupon it detached the hook from the clothes pole! I believe this also illustrates what is known as the principle of least effort!

Of the following Mr. Barton story there can be no room for doubt. It is really a story concerning Jack Glossop to whom I have already made reference. Here's how the two come together. At the end of a long lesson, Mr. Barton said, in an almost 'throw away manner': "See who can derive the transformation of energy equation for a fly-wheel". For the assiduous, this proposition will be found on p.77 of Book II of Nelkon's *Revision Notes In Physics*. Former students of A.L. physics will have good reason to remember these orange-backed books which gave a condensed view of the subject — ideal for exam revision. I took one look at the equation and decided it was not for me! But not so in the case of Jack Glossop. At our next lesson Mr. Barton, with his typical zeal, asked if anyone had been able to derive the equation; there was general shaking of the head together with expressions of bleak pessimism — until Jack spoke up: "Yes Sir"! Jack was a man of action and few words! He explained how he had used calculus and an array of other mathematical techniques to solve the problem. A clearly impressed Mr. Barton then took up the challenge and developed the formula himself on the blackboard. It was a bravura performance that occupied him for the best part of an hour. Throughout, he called out to Jack Glossop to check if his working-out tallied with Jack's — the rest of the class just looked on like so many spectators! I will add here that when satisfied with himself, Mr. Barton had the little mannerism of placing his tongue in the corner of his mouth, pursing his lips and then allowing himself a smile. This was such an occasion! I left the lab feeling that I had witnessed an able teacher rise to the challenge of a very able pupil.

It so happens that a remarkable visual image of Jack Glossop featured in the back cover of my copy of Nelkon's *Revision Notes in Physics*. Here's what I mean and it will throw more light on another aspect of Jack Glossop's accomplishments — albeit in a rather unconventional way. I purchased my set of 'Nelkon's' from my friend John Mastin; let it be said for the tidy sum of half a crown — CTS lad's always struck a hard bargain over such matters! Now John was something of a caricaturist — I could add, more generally, something of a character! In my second-hand copy of Nelkon, I discovered John had drawn a magnificent spoof of Jack Glossop along the following lines. Jack was portrayed as a gorilla, clasping his slide rule in one hand and holding the branch of a tree in the other. The gorilla imagery was a testimony to Jack's athletic prowess which was as evident as his accomplishment in physics — to which subject I will now return.

It would be overstating the mark to say that Mr. Barton delved into the philosophy of science — as I have shown that Mr. Bee attempted in mathematics. But there were occasions when he explored with us what I will call the fundamentals of science and scientific method. Here are two examples. It was Mr. Barton who introduced us to the 'MLT' system — Mass-Length-Time — for checking to see if a formula 'balances'. All physical units of measurement can be reduced to one of these basic properties and we were encouraged to adopt this system to check our calculations — you might like

to try it out when you next attempt to sort out your Income-Tax Return! The other example concerned what Mr. Barton called 'errors of the personal equation'. By this he meant that when we observe and measure, the accuracy of our results is, in part, influenced by our personal physical limitations. We were therefore encouraged to qualify any measurements we derived by making reference to 'experimental errors'. Alas, my results included a number of such errors and, even worse, the older I get I find the errors of my personal equation seem to increase!

Mention of experimental errors leads me to say a few words about our A.L. physics practicals. To record the results of our lab experiments we were each of us provided with a thick, hard-backed book — the most voluminous we were ever given in our time at the CTS. I still have mine; in new money it weighs in at three centimetres thick. It is crammed full with carefully recorded experiments, all dutifully checked off with Mr. Barton's little red ticks — and occasional remarks of the kind: "Explain!", "Your 3% error is too high"!, "Doubtful"!, "Give theory"! — but on 2nd May 1958 I was rewarded with the observation: "Good —JEB"! It's a bit late to say it but — "Thank you JEB"!

Our first year of A.L. practicals took place in what I suppose was, in effect, Mr. McManus's laboratory in the Firth Building. Instructions for each practical were typed out in orderly fashion on instruction sheets which had been pasted on to rectangles of thick card. Generations of boys had quite obviously used these since, in places, the typed sheets were worn through to the card. This could, as a consequence, be rather frustrating. A typical instruction sheet, with blanks, would read: "From which it can be seen (?)", "Calculate (?) and thereby derive the expression (?)", "What value of (?) gives (?)". I may have exaggerated slightly but you can see what I mean. As we busied ourselves at our tasks, Mr. McManus, who was then our A.L. physics teacher, would circulate about the room peering here and there offering well intended advice such as: "Measure to the top of the meniscus"!, "Don't confuse positive and negative"!, "Take care with that galvanometer boy"! and a few dozen similar offerings. When writing up our results, one of 'Mac's' most frequent exhortations was: "Remember to get the decimal point in the right place"! Observing that simple piece of guidance saved me from blundering on more than one occasion.

A moment in Mr. McManus's lessons was beautifully captured one afternoon by my class contemporary David Moran. If I remember correctly, the subject of the lesson was wave theory applied to the propagation of energy in a liquid medium. In order to explain this, Mr. McManus drew an elaborate diagram on the blackboard — which required all his concentration. This provided David with several moments to surreptitiously create a fantastic pencil sketch of 'Mac'. I recall how it captured to perfection his portly form and double chin. Just how much David took in of wave theory I don't know — but he did go on to pass his A.L. physics — and to get a B.Eng. degree.

In our second year of A.L. physics we undertook many of our practicals down at Cathedral School in the small lab to which I have already made reference. This did not have its own supply of direct current and so a car battery was frequently used for this purpose. Mr. Barton used to provide this, from the lab in the Firth Building, but the afternoon came when he had left it behind. He asked me if I would mind going to fetch it and, of course, I duly obliged. However, I had no experience of car batteries in those days — and of how heavy they are. About twenty minutes later I returned — comprehensively knackered! I had just sufficient energy left to lift the battery on to the bench. An appreciative Mr. Barton said "Thank You" and I sank limply upon my lab stool to recover. Now, let me tell you that I am, as they say, rather long in the arms — which always becomes apparent when I buy a shirt. I have often wondered if this has anything to do with the day I carried that heavy battery for JEB?

I will make a little digression here from physics to say that about two years later (1961) I was walking up West Street on my way to the University and who should I meet struggling across the road but, my former teacher of English, Mr. Brennan — with a car battery! My arms still felt funny from my own previous encounter with the said object so he had my instant sympathy. I recall saying: "They're rather heavy!" — I believe that is what is known as a self-evident truth. "Beasts!", exclaimed Mr. Brennan — the veins standing out in his temples like so many tree roots. He put the battery down on the pavement and we had a brief chat about how I was getting on. I then politely asked him how things were back at the CTS — he rolled his eyes heavenwards, smiled diplomatically, took a deep breath, lifted the battery and went his way calling out "Cheerio"! That was the last I ever saw of Mr. Brennan.

Back at the Cathedral School physics lab, life maintained its steady rhythm of young minds delving into the secrets of nature under the guidance of Mr. Barton. In passing may I ask if you are familiar with these wonderful words: "Nature and Nature's laws lay hid in night. God said, *Let Newton be!* and all was light"? These were written by Alexander Pope as an intended epitaph for Sir Isaac Newton. Two-hundred years later, the writer J. C. Squire could not resist adding: "It did not last: the Devil howling 'Ho! Let Einstein be!' restored the status quo"! My reference to Newton is deliberate because it leads me to the afternoon we considered Newton's law of cooling — the best practical expression of which is: "When a can of beer is put inside a fridge it assumes its optimum condition"! — with apologies to the great the man. What Newton actually said was, as if you didn't know: "The quantity of heat lost or gained by a body is proportional to the difference between its temperature and that of the surrounding medium". We verified this by taking the temperature at intervals along the length of a copper rod which was heated at one end. There are two observations to be made here concerning Mr. Barton's diligence. First, thorough as ever, he insisted we acquire a grasp of the theory of an uninsulated bar (Forbe's experiment) and of an insulated bar (Searl's experiment) — these require quite elaborate experimental and theoretical treatment but I'll spare you the details of all that. Second, we gained an insight into Mr. Barton's own care in writing up lab reports for the following reason. Spread out before us, on the lab bench, was Mr. Barton's own First Year university lab book — beautifully written up with careful pencil diagrams. I know the book belonged to his university days because I asked him. On doing so, he seemed a little abashed and modestly put the book aside. There were two sides to his demeanour: when teaching at the blackboard he was flamboyant and expressive; when in more personal conversation he was modest and retiring. This leads me to the generalisation that all good teachers need, at times, to have recourse to a little theatricality —

but not too much. Michael Faraday, a very popular lecturer at *The Royal Institution*, once wrote in a pamphlet titled *Advice to a Lecturer*: "A lecturer should not angle for claps" — i.e., should not show off. Mr. Barton was expressive but never showed off.

It would be quite wrong to convey the impression that we transacted our physics practicals as though we were the pious disciples of Isaac Newton eager to carry the torch of light into the darker corners of unexplored science. Far from it — after all, as I have already remarked, 'boys will be boys'. So, here now are a few 'confessions'. It will be useful first to invoke the ancient Chinese proverb, that I am just about to make up, which states: "You can lead a horse to water — but it's not half as much fun as watching one have a pee"! The connection with what I am saying is a little tenuous but my inference is that boys, of a certain temperament, will, when introduced to a proposition, undermine order if they can — and there were plenty of such lads about in the CTS! This proclivity occasional manifest itself in our physics practicals. There was the afternoon when we used Foucault's pendulum to demonstrate the rotation of the Earth. Allow me a few words of explanation. Mr. Barton suspended a weight of about 10 kilograms from the ceiling of the lab; for this he used special square-section wire to make the suspension free of torsion. He set the weight in motion, like a pendulum, and drew a chalk line on the floor immediately below the path of oscillation of the gently swinging weight. This was at the start of our lesson — afternoon lessons commenced at 1.20 p.m. remember? "Now, let us forget the pendulum", said Mr. Barton and we did our best to concentrate on the blackboard leaving the big weight to tick silently away. At break, Mr. Barton invited us to examine the path of the pendulum. To our amazement it now no longer swung above the chalk line but in a direction displaced from it by several degrees. Mr. Barton explained: "On a stationary Earth, a Foucault pendulum would always swing in the same vertical plane but on a rotating Earth this vertical plane slowly changes". We were much impressed. Now for the silly bit. We were urged to take care and let the pendulum continue to oscillate so that we could observe it's further progress after the break — our physics practicals took up the whole of an afternoon. During break, whilst larking about, someone inevitably disturbed the weight. We tried frantically to re-set it so as to restore its motion — but to no avail. One thing led to another and we thought — the experiment ruined — we might as well have some extra fun. We therefore twisted the weight about its wire suspension some several hundred times and let it go, taking delight as it madly spun round — all thoughts of Monsieur Foucault now right out of our minds. The problem came when we tried to stop the damned thing! This was impossible! We had cranked up so much torsion into the wire that, as soon as we stopped the weight spinning, it resumed its merry oscillations — doubtless in accordance with some other law of Foucault. We had no alternative but to let the weight spin. Our break over Mr. Barton returned, doubtless refreshed by his mid-afternoon cup of tea, and dutifully continued his work at the blackboard. No one dared to so much as glance at the weight for fear of revealing what had happened. But, of course, Mr. Barton in due course did just that — only to see the weight still turning madly and his careful experiment ruined. "Oh you silly boys!" he exclaimed. We felt rather foolish — but the incident did not deter us from committing a further indiscretion as I will now relate.

One afternoon a group of us had arrived early at Cathedral School for a physics practical, and our minds took to creatively wondering what would happen if someone lit a gas tap. "There'll be a bloody explosion!", "Don't!", "Go on!" and "JEB might come in!" were typical responses to this proposition. Of course, someone had a match and it was not long before the tap was lit — tentatively at first and then with the gas at full pressure. The effect was impressive, not least on the shellac varnish covering the surface of the bench and the wax residues left by the dental technicians to which I have previously referred. Further pyrotechnics were suspended by the sound of Mr. Barton approaching. The gas tap was extinguished, *allegro vivaci*, and we all sat innocently on our stools — with a smoke pall hovering above our heads. In walked Mr. Barton, nose discernibly twitching and made instantly suspicious by our subdued demeanour. I will conclude this little episode in the style of the physics questions to which we were supposed to be turning our minds. "A group of errant boys light a gas tap supplied at normal town mains pressure". (i) How far does the searing flame extend across the bench surface? (ii) How long does it take the teacher to ask: "Can anyone smell something"? Answers: (i) About three feet. (ii) About ten seconds!

The study of physics did not lend itself to 'extra-mural' activities in quite the same way as, for example, I have described that we were able to enjoy art, by visiting galleries, or the study of architecture, by visiting large country houses. There was an annual event however in the field of science that enabled enthusiasts to enjoy their subject, namely, the *Faraday Lecture*. This was named, you hardly have to be told, in memory of Michael Faraday — 'creator of classical field theory'. With no mathematical training he discovered the laws of magnetic induction — and a few dozen other things. His contemporaries used to say of him: "Faraday can smell the truth"! — the rest presumably just smelled. Anyway, in 1957 it was the turn of the Faraday lecture to be held in the Sheffield City Hall. It was given by the pioneer of computing Sir Leon Bagrit — later Lord Bowden. his subject was '*Machines that can Think*'. This was a popular way then of describing the newly evolving computers — another expression you will recall from this period was 'Electronic Brain'. Bagrit had a massive contraption mounted on the platform of the City Hall and with this he demonstrated how it could be 'programmed' — which was a quite novel term for the period — to sort a random collection of coloured balls (about the size of beach balls) into orderly sets. Let me briefly describe the experimental set-up. The 'machine' was placed before a large black curtain. We saw the balls, in their random order, disappear through a hole at the top of the curtain, only to re-appear at the bottom through a series of similar holes but in an orderly procession of colours — red to the right, green in the middle and yellow to the left. As this took place there was an impressive clanking of gear wheels and traps. After a little while Sir Leon asked for the machine to be stopped — we thought something had gone wrong. "Now!", he said, "I know what you are all thinking. You don't really believe it's the machine that's doing all the sorting out. You think I have a lot of little men running around behind the curtain pushing the balls out of the correct holes don't you"? This prompted laughter from the audience. "Well now watch this!", he said. Whereupon he had the curtain drawn aside to reveal his contraption in all

its Heath Robinson splendour. Then he commanded it to be re-started revealing, to our shear delight, how the machine did indeed direct the balls to wander this way and that until finally finding their way to their allocated aperture — without there being any little men in sight! The audience erupted in enthusiastic applause at the sight of all this applied electronic wizardry.

I had attended the lecture with my CTS contemporary Charlie Prime who, as it so happened, went on to study electrical and electronic engineering at the University of Manchester — one of the great UK pioneers in computing. I think the evening lecture could well have helped to influence the subsequent direction of Charlie's career.

I have said that Mr. McManus retired and his post was taken by Mr. George Nicholls. I believe he took up his post as Deputy Head and Head Teacher of physics early in 1959, also taking over the teaching of final year A.L. physics from Mr. Barton. I will introduce Mr. Nicholls more fully when I write later of the time that I was School Captain. For now I will confine my remarks to Mr. Nicholls' teaching of physics. He was a very experienced teacher, which presumably explains why he was promoted to the post of Deputy Head, and on arriving he immediately threw himself into his work with great commitment. Since our final A.L. physics exam was approaching, his first responsibility was to set the 'mock' exam — or 'pre-lim' exam as some people call these things. To do this he made a painstaking survey of all the University of London A.L. physics exam papers for the preceding five years or so. He then went through our class performance in the mock exam and discussed with us the possibility of certain questions coming up in the actual final exam — trying to back the winners as it were.

We soon discovered that Mr. Nicholls was a highly disciplined teacher, both with regard to his personal style of teaching and his expectations of the members of his class. In this connection I recall him muttering to me darkly a few days after our mock A.L. exam — by which time he had marked our papers: "You'll have to work hard you know!". Since I was already working hard it was not the kind of encouragement I needed!

The day of reckoning for A.L. physics duly came in the form of the final exams — two written papers and the practical. The former were sat, as so often, in the dinning hall at Cathedral School. One boy I remember came to the exam wearing two wrist watches in case one broke down — which was a somewhat unnecessary precaution since part of the exam ritual was for a clock to be placed at the front of the exam room. But exams inevitably made us all nervous and, on this occasion, I recall trying to write without having removed the top from my fountain pen — which was a *Parker 51*. More seriously, concerning the exam itself, what stands out in my mind is the style of the last question on the paper — question eight. This was always a written question — no less than an invitation to write a short essay on a set topic. I never knew enough about the subjects under consideration to even contemplate attempting this question but I distinctly recall how my friend Charlie Prime, imbued with the study of science, could natter on at length about atomic theory, Van der Waals' equation or a host of similar topics. The practical for A.L. physics was held in the lab in the Firth Building. What may be of general interest is that the experiments had to be set-up the night before the examination was to take place. In theory, the lab technician was therefore at liberty to tell the members of the class, about to take the exam, what equipment he had set out — thereby enabling them to conjecture what the experiments were. To ensure absolute confidentiality, the lab technician — a young lad not much older than ourselves — remarked, after the exam, how he had been required, by Mr. Nicholls, to swear an oath of confidentiality on the Holy Bible. For the practical itself we had to perform two experiments. One was concerned with latent heat and the other was the determination of the velocity of sound by the method of a column of water and tuning fork — so familiar to you all as to require no explanation! All went well and I subsequently passed A.L. physics with a creditable performance.

It is time now to take leave of A.L. physics and to do this I will return briefly to Mr. Barton — get your handkerchief out because I am about to indulge in a little emotional gush. I have good cause to remember his last words to me at the CTS because he bade me a fond farewell. But before I come to that I will re-iterate a point of view about Mr. Barton that I have expressed already, namely, that he was assuredly borne to teach. Doubtless some teachers acquire the skills of pedagogy and others more-or-less have them thrust upon them as a result of not being able to think of what else they might do with their lives. In Mr. Barton's case neither of these two propositions could be further from the truth. I could almost believe that he sprang forth into the world clad in academic gown and mortar board clasping a stick of chalk — such was his natural disposition to teaching! And now to my point. On my last day at the CTS — or a day very close thereto — chance conspired that I should meet Mr. Barton. He exchanged a friendly greeting which extended to a kindly expression of good wishes for the future culminating in — "God Bless". So, forty years on let me say: "Thank you John England Barton, alias 'JEB' for all that you did for us at the CTS". And allow me to re-iterate your own words — "God Bless"!

Chemistry

I have only a little to say about chemistry at the CTS even though it formed so important a part of the school curriculum. I had just one formal lesson in chemistry during my entire five years of schooling at the CTS. What I have to impart therefore is mostly derived second-hand from others. Nevertheless, here goes.

Builders did not take chemistry as part of their studies for the Building Diploma — with the exception of some elementary lessons called 'Building Science' to which I have made previous reference. These were given by Mr. Gregory and were largely concerned with the chemical properties of such materials as lime and cement. At this time I used to hear about chemistry from my CTS friend and contemporary David Dickson. Elsewhere I explain that David and I attended Anns Road Secondary Modern School at the same period and after school there were several times that we conducted a few chemistry 'experiments' in David's kitchen with a chemistry set he had for Christmas. I remember we succeeded in making some noisome smells which made his mother cross! But David got rather hooked on chemistry and, after leaving the CTS, he became a metallurgist — until ill-health from the industrial fumes compelled him to find other employment. But whilst David was at the CTS, I used to

hear stories from time to time about various goings on in the chemistry lab. Here are two. Chemistry was taught by Mr. Ernest Clark — 'Nobby' Clark. He was the archetypal chemistry teacher — tall, thin, bald and academic looking. I heard one day how he splashed some acid on his suit and fled into the prep room to scatter some powder on it — doubtless the chemists among you will know what this 'antidote' would be. More amusing, if the tale is true, concerns the character who dropped a piece of phosphorous onto the floor. Even my limited knowledge of chemistry extends to the awareness that this is a highly volatile substance which ignites spontaneously with air and must consequently be stored under water. It appears that one day a certain CTS lad, seeing the fallen piece of phosphorous burst into flame on the floor, attempted to extinguish it with his foot. This action simply transferred the phosphorous to his shoe — and promptly set fire to it! Well, that's what I was told forty years ago.

My CTS contemporary David Dickson is, I know, just one of many CTS boys who left school to work in the metallurgical industry. Sheffield's steel manufacture was then all-powerful and offered secure employment prospects for scientific chemists. Leaving school though was just the beginning and I know of several lads who went on to study at evening school to get their HNC. This leads me to say that I learned from an HNC student that Mr. Clark used to teach evening classes and had, by all accounts, the reputation for being a very clever man. By a rather indirect route I can confirm this with the following observation. One day I recall seeing an envelope addressed as follows: 'Mr. Clark M.A. B.Sc.'. I did not know somebody could be both a master of arts *and* a bachelor of science. I was most impressed.

I have previously remarked that I had one chemistry lesson only at the CTS. This was from Mr. Gregory at the start of O.L. I decided one lesson was enough for me and transferred to O.L. woodwork. I had to obtain special permission to do this from Mr. Wadge. He said that maths, physics and chemistry was an ideal combination. I agreed — adding, if you want to be a scientist — "But I don't Sir". He generously conceded the point and allowed me to join the woodwork class. Mention of Mr. Gregory calls to mind a quite dramatic incident during morning assembly which some of you may also remember. It was early November and Guy Fawke's Night was approaching; consequently our minds were turning to thoughts of fireworks and pyrotechnics. This was the subject of Mr. Gregory's intervention in the formalities of our morning assembly. It appears that Mr. Gregory had got wind of the fact that a number of boys had evolved a formula for creating an explosive compound! From high up in the balcony he gave an impassioned warning of the perils of meddling with such volatile substances. It was a remarkable piece of oratory — dramatic, eloquent and scholarly. It certainly secured our attention. I don't know of any subsequent untoward consequences arising from anyone attempting to make their own fireworks!

At a later period I used to hear choice items from my friends about chemistry when they were taking the A.L. course. There was a time when they went on about something called 'the brown-ring test' which they used to call by another description — upon which I will not elaborate. I believe the first year of the A.L. chemistry course was taken by Mr. Frow. The day came when he was involved in a minor incident — although not exactly concerned with chemistry. This is what happened.

Several of my close friends, who were taking A.L. chemistry, had just returned from a school trip to Paris. They had brought back with them a number of 'souvenirs'. Amongst these was a collection of a certain genre of subversive writings — of the kind normally confiscated by the customs officials! One of these pieces of subversive 'literature' consisted of rhyming verses describing the exploits of a lady called 'Eskimo Nell' — aboard the good ship *Venus*! One day the temptation to look at this text in class proved too irresistible to some boys — a chemistry class, no less, taken by Mr. Frow. He appears to have observed the book being passed around and duly confiscated it! What would be the outcome the lads in question asked themselves? For a short while the fate of several of my contemporaries — and their reputation — hung in the balance. But all was well; Mr. Frow took a generous view of the incident and returned the 'offending material' with the caution it should not be brought back to school. There was no need — my wayward friends had committed the verses to memory and took to reciting them on every possible occasion — until the novelty wore off!

Mr. Gregory taught some A.L. chemistry but his style of teaching was not apparently entirely to every one's preference. I say this for the following reason. One day I was in the Prefects' Room when in came a group of lads who had just had a chemistry lesson — they were clearly very animated. A minor sensation had just taken place. One boy, whose name escapes me — perhaps it's just as well — had erupted in class and called Mr. Gregory — "A bloody fool"! Remember, we were now age eighteen so such a remark could not be dismissed with a flourish of Mr. Gregory's gas pipe. It was a serious happening. This boy was disgruntled with the progress being made in class and from that day on resolved to follow his intuition and study by himself. As far as I can remember, Mr. Gregory allowed this moment of 'anarchy' to pass — and I believe the lad concerned went on to get top marks in the subsequent A.L. chemistry examination. His class companions will recall the circumstances better than I can.

I will take leave of chemistry here. I am mindful that I have not said much of any significance about this important subject. So I will conclude, more respectfully, by observing with what outstanding laboratory facilities we were provided at the CTS for the study of chemistry. As an architect I can say these are difficult facilities to design with their complex building-service needs of gas, water, electricity, fume cupboards and waste disposal. We took all these things for granted when we were boys. It is only looking back that you realise how outstandingly well designed and equipped were our school buildings and facilities.

This is the point in my narrative when I take leave of making reference to the formal parts of our academic curriculum. From now on I will concentrate my reminiscences on more general themes. But, before I do so, I will offer a few remarks about the CTS Diploma.

The CTS Diploma

As all former CTS boys well know there were two styles of CTS Diploma, one for the Engineers and one for the Builders. There were three classes, namely, First, Second and Third — presumably you could also Fail. To be serious here for a moment, Herbert Wadge maintained so tenacious a grip on the discipline of our school that he was not averse to exercising his ultimate sanction of having a boy expelled. Indeed, in my time at the CTS I recall how on two occasions Mr. Wadge, with measured gravity, announced to the whole school in morning assembly that a boy had indeed been expelled. Concerning the Diploma, I think most boys managed to scrape together sufficient 'Brownie Points' for at a least a Third Class. To enter into a little more detail, the Diploma listed the standard of attainment achieved in each subject, namely, *Pass*, *Credit* and *Distinction*. You may recall that when reflecting on *Mathematics*, I briefly mentioned that I had learned from Mr. Shipley that the Diploma was awarded in part on marks based on the continuous assessment of our course work and in part on achievement in the end-of-session examinations. I think the proportions were 30%/70% — or something of that order. What is of more general interest is that Mr. Wadge, with the support of the Board of Governors, had persuaded Sheffield's principal industrialists to accept the CTS Diploma as an 'official' qualification of some recognised academic standing. (In passing I will add, with admiration, that some CTS lads have subsequently gone on to become distinguished industrialists in their own right.) If I wanted to be disparaging, which I certainly don't, you could say that the CTS Diploma was a glorified 'Leaving Certificate'. (Incidentally, at the period we CTS lads were leaving with our coveted Diplomas, at the rather more exalted level of Eton College, boys who did well there could leave with the Eton College Certificate which conferred admission to the universities of Oxford and Cambridge. I have put that in to wet your appetite for other things I have say later about this famous public school which featured so frequently in Herbert Wadge's personal reflections on his own school days.)

We received our Diploma on Speech Day. You may remember that on the morning of Speech Day we had a rehearsal of the principal events. This included going up on to the platform, from the right stair (as viewed from the audience), and leaving by the left stair. Now, on the morning of my rehearsal, the proceedings were organised by Mr. Bill Davis — in his usual animated, whistle-blowing manner. He told us that, to save time in the rehearsal, we should ascend the platform, as I have described, by the right stair but to leave the platform down the *centre* stair. For me this sowed the seeds of confusion in my mind because, later that evening at the actual event, I dutifully left the platform by the *centre* stair! What a twit do I hear you say? Well, let me redeem myself by adding that I was awarded the CTS Diploma in Building *First Class*. My Diploma certificate still survives and is reproduced in miniature in Fig. 83. This is not for the purpose of showing off but to tell the following story. If you look at Fig. 83 closely you will see that I did not achieve a clean sweep of Distinctions — nearly but not quite. For Building Drawing, one of my best subjects, I attained only a mere Pass standard. So what went wrong? I will approach what I have to say with a point of general interest. One day in morning assembly, Mr. Wadge informed the school that he had obtained approval from the Board of Governors that certain subjects, taken at O.L. in the GCE, could count as the equivalent in the CTS Diploma. His action was intended to reduce the number of examinations we had to sit. In point of fact we were offered a choice; we could sit both the Diploma and GCE exams if we wished, or make the substitution. I opted for the latter course of action. But this proved to be my undoing as far as Building Drawing is concerned. Here's what happened. I took the GCE O.L. exam in Technical Drawing, as I have already described, and agreed to substitute my mark for Building Drawing in my Diploma. So far so good. However, as I have previously explained, I made a mess of the O.L. Technical Drawing exam. You will recall that I said the exam paper required candidates to draw the front elevation of an engineering casting in combination with two cross sections — viewed from the left and the right — and that I muddled the latter. It was an expensive mistake and cost me my distinction in Building Drawing on my Diploma. Sad is it not?

Here is another point of general interest for Builders of my generation. I have previously described how our teacher for Brickwork left the CTS and, in fact, was not replaced — does this suggest a scarcity of educated teacher-bricklayers at this time? The consequence was there was no instruction in brickwork at the CTS for the period 1955–59. This circumstance prompted Herbert Wadge to make an announcement concerning the effect of all this on the status of the Building Diploma. His statement, in the Spring Term of 1956, went something like this: "The Board of Governors have agreed that the Building Diploma, which ordinarily includes Brickwork, can be awarded without this subject — with no loss to its status". I can't say I had been losing much sleep over this ever since but I thought I should recount the episode by way of general interest in illustrating how very thorough Herbert Wadge was in the formal conduct of the school's academic affairs.

Allow me to take leave of this subject by saying that I was awarded the prize for being First in the Building Diploma Year and was awarded the Gift of the Sheffield and District Branch of the Federation of Master Builders. With my prize I purchased *A History of Architecture on the Comparative Method* by Sir Banister Fletcher. It remains a treasured possession, although now somewhat worn with usage — like its proud owner!

General Studies

My heading *General Studies* will probably have significance for only a few CTS boys of my own generation. Let me explain why. During my first year of A.L. study (1957–58), Herbert Wadge announced that certain class periods were to be set aside for non-specific study so as to give more balance to our scientifically oriented maths-physics-chemistry curriculum. This was a refreshing departure from the strictly prescribed timetable and I, with my growing inclination to the arts, anticipated this development eagerly. Two periods each week were assigned for general studies. One of these periods could be described as current affairs. We were invited to discuss topical issues of the day with the member of staff assigned to take the class. An illustration will describe the type of activity in which we participated. One morning the class was taken by Mr. Arthur Hill. He was by training an historian, being no less than an M.A. of the University of Oxford. He was a very versatile teacher and a good sportsman. If I remember correctly, as a student he had played centre forward for *Pegasus* — a football team combined of players from the universities of Oxford and Cambridge — for that information, I am relying on my memory of

an announcement that Herbert Wadge made in assembly about 1956 just before Mr. Hill arrived to join the CTS. With Mr. Hill we were obviously in good and capable hands. Our class was held in one of the upper rooms in the Firth Building. I mention this for the following reason. A glass-fronted bookcase stood by the window on the wall overlooking Leopold Street; inside it were about forty copies of *Outline of British Economic History* — and guess who was the author? — our very able teacher Mr. Arthur Hill. The class I am recollecting started with an invitation from Mr. Hill to suggest a topic for discussion — he was good at improvising extended answers. Now, very topical at that time (1958) was the so-called *Benelux Treaty*. This, you will not have to be reminded (?), was an economic union between Belgium, the Netherlands and Luxembourg. The aim was to achieve economic integration and mutual trade between the three countries. I suppose this was a precursor to the Common Market. So, mindful of Mr. Hill's knowledge of these matters, which I had deduced by peeping inside the bookcase to which I have referred, I asked him to lead the discussion on this subject. About an hour later he had finished! He answer was a masterly performance — more in the nature of college lecture than a class discussion.

Another of Mr. Hill's General Studies classes which stands out in my mind is the time he talked about Adolph Hitler and the rise of the National Socialist German Workers' Party (the *Nazi Party*). For much of his account, if my memory serves me correctly, he drew on the experience and direct observation of a friend of his who had been in Germany during Hitler's rise to power. He told us how his friend had attended one of the rallies of the Nazi party that we have seen so often captured on archival documentary war films. The chilling aspect of the story is that Mr. Hill's friend, even though he was a mere bye-stander at the rally, had admitted to finding himself falling, almost mesmerically, under the magnetic influence of Hitler's oratory. More specifically I recall Mr. Hill discussing *Mein Kampf* (*My Struggle*) and him saying how he found it to be a maze of contradictions.

More congenial to me was Mr. Hill's discussion of the development of European politics during the 1930s. The reason is that in so doing he mentioned Poland and, thereby, her Prime Minister Ignace Paderewski. He was, of course, a distinguished concert pianist as well as being a statesman. Mr. Hill had actually heard Paderewski play and he gave us a vivid description of the pianist's appearance including his famous mass of red hair. As I will later explain, the music of Paderewski had particular meaning for me — so Mr. Hill's observations had special significance.

In effect Mr. Hill's classes were seminars and they gave us the opportunity to develop the skills of debate and discussion that we would be required to demonstrate later at college and university.

My mention of the music of Paderewski leads me conveniently to a companion set of classes which ran in parallel with those of Mr. Hill. I said there were two periods a week set aside for General Studies. The second series of classes was taken by Mr. Hughes. His theme was a musical one — pun intended. In effect, he gave us an outline of the history of music and the origins of musical form. We were given a little blue exercise book in which to make notes. Mine has now been lost but I recall we discussed several of the early English composers such as Orlando Gibbons, Thomas Morley and Henry Purcell. These composers were merely names to me at the time, but I am grateful to Mr. Hughes for introducing them to me since, a few years later — as a member of the Sheffield University Madrigal Group — I sang several of their works. Mr. Hughes also provided us with an outline of musical form and structure. My memory-list of musical forms includes *Binary, Ternary, Compound, Sonata* and *Rondo* — I'm not sure if I have the order correct but my list gives some idea of the things we discussed. Blackboard illustrations formed part of Mr. Hughes's expositions and included letter sequences of the kind 'A – B - A' to describe the musical structures under consideration. This was all beginning to make sense to me since I was becoming acquainted with such things in the programme notes written for the Hallé series of concerts by a certain Dr. Linstead D.Mus. — more about the Hallé concerts shortly.

We made gradual progress with Mr. Hughes through the evolution of music and eventually reached my favourite period, the Romantic Movement — and in particular the Viennese School of Mozart, Schubert and Beethoven et. al. I was in my element. I remember thinking how I wished I was doing all this for A.L.! In fact, at about this time, it did become possible, in some schools, to take General Studies at A.L. It so happens that I subsequently discovered some of my university friends had indeed combined their more formal academic curriculum with A.L. General Studies — lucky people. But for me and my class companions, General Studies suddenly stopped! The classes came to an end without any warning or prior notice and we reverted to our normal timetable. I was mortified since the break these classes afforded from our normal routine was a welcome relief. We could still enjoy our music at the CTS in other ways though as I will now describe. But before I do, let me take leave of this section by saying that I was awarded the Class Prize in General Studies with which I purchased Volume II of *Simpson's History of Architectural Development*.

Music

Music permeated our life and work at the CTS even though it did not constitute a formal part of the academic curriculum. For this legacy, I am personally deeply grateful. Music is more important to me than anything else in life — except, of course, close personal relationships. It means more to me even than architecture, notwithstanding that my profession can proudly be described as 'the mother of the arts' and 'the hand-maiden of society' — to cite a couple of expressions found in history books. Often was the time, in morning assembly, when I thought to myself that I would give my right arm to be able to play the piano like Mr. Hughes — even though that would have confined me to performing the repertoire for the left hand!

Personal Musical Development

Before I discuss music at the CTS let me say a few words about the origins of my own musical development — they are very modest. My mother played the piano but, it has to be said, with more enthusiasm than technical skill — but her heart was in it which is what really matters. She would take me, as a little boy, to Canns' Music Shop in the old Sheffield Market where she would buy sheet music of the popular melodies of the day. My head is still full of the tunes I heard her play. Moreover, she could whistle! If anyone can remember the entertainer Ronnie Ronald then my mother could whistle in his style. I attribute my own enthusiasm for whistling to my mother's influence. Recent research now suggests that the musical disposition of a child developing in the womb may be influenced by the music it receives via its mother — so: "Thank you Mum for all your whistling"! My mother influenced my musical appreciation in other ways. I will give one example which may stir fond memories for other CTS lads. My mother was an admirer of the Northern Ireland tenor Joseph Locke. In the immediate post-war period his interpretations of such songs as *Hear My Song, Violette; Down in the Glen; I'll Take You Home Again, Kathleen; Goodbye* and a host of others, were immensely popular. As a family, we listened to these songs on the 'wireless' and I committed the melodies to memory and they became a part of my musical inheritance. Let me add that when I was a little boy on holiday one year at Blackpool, I heard Joseph Locke sing and he afterwards signed my autograph book.

As for my father he was a typical workman whose strong hands gave intimation of his heavy manual work. But he was fond of 'good music' and, as a young man, had taken a course of violin lessons after work. Indeed, I once heard him play an arrangement of Handel' *Largo* — honesty requires me to add that once was enough! But he did own a Stradivarius violin! I confirmed this one day, when as a little boy, I peeped through one of the little scrolls in the body of his instrument and read: *Antonio Stradivarius — made in Birmingham*!

To bring my narrative closer to the CTS, I will mention here, once more, my good and lifelong friend from the CTS David Dickson. In the more personal part of my reflections (see later), I explain how David and I were at Anns Road Secondary Modern School together and it is from this period (1951-53) that I have memories of listening to David playing the piano. Two works had a formative influence upon me. These were Joseph Hadyn's *Gypsy Rondo* and Ignace Paderewski's *Minuet in G*. The influence of these works on me was that I took up the piano, had lessons with David's teacher and eventually played duets with him — I recall crashing our way through a four-hand adaptation of Wagner's concert overture *Die Meistersinger von Nürnberg*. So, I joined the CTS in January 1954 with a strong disposition to music but no knowledge of the repertoire. But as my years at the CTS progressed my knowledge of music grew, not least, in response to the influences to which I and my contemporaries were exposed. It is these I will now discuss.

There is a moving story concerning Beethoven to which I will here make brief reference. Towards the end of his life he completed his mighty setting of the solemn mass — *Missa Solemnis in D*, which is contemporaneous with the well known *Choral Symphony*. On presenting the manuscript to the publisher it is said the Editors, on leafing through the pages, stared in wonder at the grandeur of what they saw portrayed therein. One of them, mindful of Beethoven's deafness, took a pen and wrote: 'Finished with the hand of God'! Beethoven, only too mindful of the personal tribulations the creation of the work had caused him — he was all of seven years late in delivering it to the publisher — took the pen and added: 'Man! Help thyself'! I have a number of reasons for narrating these events. The first is as follows. I read about the Missa *Solemnis* towards the end of my time at the CTS (1958) in *Thayer's Life of Beethoven*. For a while this vast work, in four volumes, became my Bible and I took Beethoven's words — 'Man! Help thyself' — as my personal motto. More generally, my enthusiasm for Beethoven become all encompassing and I resolved, when I left school, to travel to Vienna to visit the places associated with him. I will return to that episode in my life later in my narrative. Another point I wish to make here is that at about the age of sixteen I purchased a stiff-backed, red-coloured Cash Book. In this I started to list all the pieces of music I heard and liked. It became a sort of personal diary. Over the years the list of works grew and I added 'Opus' numbers and 'Köchel' numbers and such other musicological paraphernalia. By this means, and enthusiastic listening to concerts and radio broadcasts — and, it should be added, enjoying music at the CTS — I developed my love of music.

Five years after joining the CTS my enthusiasm for music was much more consolidated and my knowledge of the repertoire was firmly established due, in no small measure, I wish to re-iterate, to the influences I experienced at the CTS. Today, I am a member of the Schubert Institute and can take pride in that I had some responsibility for bringing about the recent publication *Schubert Studies*. With those preliminaries out of the way let me turn now to music at the CTS.

Music in Morning Assembly

I have made the claim that music permeated our life at the CTS. Now let me prove this — mathematically! Consider the following. Our terms had the following durations: Spring Term, 1st week January to last week March; Summer Term, 2nd/3rd week April to 2nd/3rd week July; and Autumn Term 1st/2nd week September to 2nd December. This gives a total of about 42 weeks; at five days per working week we therefore have 210 days. And now to the point. Let us assume we sang one hymn per day, every day. This is a reasonable assumption; hymn singing was an indispensable part of morning assembly. Let me take my calculations a stage further — and I hope you are paying attention! A period of 210 days yields 210 hymns per year which, for a typical CTS period of study of five years yields no less than 1050 hymns — sung by each CTS lad! Let me press on further. Assume each hymn had five verses and took five minutes to sing; this a conservative estimate — some of our hymns went on for 'ages'. But, at a duration of five minutes for each hymn, I estimate we sang our way through no fewer than almost 90 hours of music — or the equivalent of nearly four days of non-stop choral singing! Shall we spare a thought for the pianist — for the greater part of our music-making this was Mr. Hughes. If we sang for 90 hours it follows that he played for this length of time. It gets better. Over a period of twenty years he must have played the piano in morning assembly for the equivalent of 16 days! Do you not agree now that music permeated our lives at the CTS! That's what I think Mr. Thompson would call *QED*! But that is more than enough of being silly. Let me now pay a more respectful tribute to our CTS musical heritage.

The music we sang for morning assembly was invariably chosen by Herbert Wadge as an integral part of his meticulous daily preparations for school. Singing in morning assembly of course embraced his own vocal contributions. With little prior notice the musical part of morning assembly would commence with Mr. Hughes

sitting down at the piano to play whatever music was required. There were times when Mr. Wadge requested the music to be played in a different key to that printed in the music. Without hesitation, Mr. Hughes would rise to the challenge and transpose the music to a lower register to make it easier for us to pitch the notes. This is a *very* difficult thing to do. I remember several such occasions which always prompted Mr. Wadge to pay Mr. Hughes a compliment on his skill.

I think most of us enjoyed singing a particularly rousing hymn such as Arthur Sullivan's *Onward Christian Soldiers*. The assembled concourse of about 650 boys and staff could certainly make a splendid sound which was clearly audible outside in West Street. I know this for a fact since on a few occasions, when I was School Captain, my duties detained me and I heard the proceedings, as it were, from a distance. I like to think thereby that our communal singing each day in assembly not only elevated our own spirits but also those of a least a portion of Sheffielders favoured by passing our school as they went about transacting their own daily labours!

Another advantage of being School Captain, in the context of morning assembly, was the privilege — if it can be so described — of listening to Herbert Wadge sing! You will recall that the School Captain sat but a few feet away from the headmaster on the dais at the front of the hall with his Vice Captain to his right. In my year (1958–59) there was one Vice Captain only — my good friend Richard *Charlie* Prime. In previous years, I believe it was more typical to have two Vice Captains. Be this as it may, for a whole year I was, in a manner of speaking, just a heart beat away from the great man himself and had plenty of opportunity to hear him in full voice — the hearing in my left ear has never really recovered! But I have a serious point to make here. Herbert always sang the bass-baritone harmony line to our hymns — never the melody. And I can vouch that he was bang-on secure in pitching his notes which sonorously rose and fell like the diapason of an organ. He sight-read the music from his personal copy of a large, black-backed book with gilded lettering; I think it was *The Congregational Church Hymnery*. It was a well-worn and much used text which bore his pencil-note annotations — evidence of the care with which Herbert made his musical preparations.

I will add a little detail here about Herbert's preferences in music, at least as far as I, a schoolboy developing my own musical tastes, was able to fathom them. I would describe his preferences as being strictly orthodox. Concerning religious music he was rooted in the harmonised melodic tradition of the Anglican Church, as his well-worn hymnal confirmed. Outside of religious music I formed the view that Herbert's tastes were conventional — but I don't mean that in a pejorative sense. I recall occasions when he made reference to Bach and Mendelssohn, the latter concerning the *Dresden Choral* as it occurs in the *Reformation Symphony*. Herbert would sometimes make little musicological comments relating to some piece or other which we had sung, or were about to sing, and would seek confirmation of his views by casting a glance in the direction of Mr. Hughes. I can't recall the latter ever disagreeing — although he may have allowed himself to look a little doubtful sometimes!

About once per term, morning assembly was dispensed with in favour of evening assembly. This was to enable a choice of more reflective service to be held

— looking back, as it were, on the day that had just passed over us. On these occasions the hymn we sang would reflect this aspect of our deliberations. Favourite hymns for such circumstances were: *The day Thou gavest, Lord is ended/The darkness falls at Thy behest*, and *Abide with me; fast falls the eventide/The darkness deepens; Lord, with me abide!* Very exceptionally, we sang these, or similar hymns, in morning assembly, Herbert Wadge justifying the reason for doing so on the grounds that we otherwise would not have the opportunity to enjoy them. Herbert rarely blundered in his choice of matching words and music but there was one memorable occasion. Who will remember when, in the middle of the Summer Term we found ourselves singing some sober words of moral improvement to the tune of *Hark the Herald Angels Sing?* Never was a hymn sung so heartily!

Herbert Wadge would occasionally play the piano himself in morning assembly — in a manner of speaking! To be close to the piano when Herbert Wadge was playing was rather like standing by the open door to an iron foundry. He did not so much as *play* the instrument as *assail* it. His endeavours were a triumph of enthusiasm over musical limitation. When Herbert played the piano it was indeed a case of *The Lost Chord* — or, more precisely, lots of lost chords! I recall at this time there was a craze, amongst university students, to see who could dismantle a piano, using a sledge hammer, in the shortest possible time. Dear Herbert should have had a go — he would have been a serious contender for the prize! According to the testimony of Mr. Hughes, Herbert's colleagues, on hearing him play the piano, were inclined to remark: 'Where's your shoe Bert'!

More accomplished stand-in pianists, if that is how I may describe them, were Mr. Alf Simpson — as I have previously acknowledged, an accomplished church organist — and Mr. Arthur Hill who taught history. But, as I have shown in my calculation (!), Mr. Hughes was our ever-faithful servant when it came to playing the piano. I will just add the further observation that if I allowed my attention to wander from what Mr. Wadge was saying — and he could go on at length sometimes (!) — I might occasionally catch sight of Mr. Hughes silently passing his hands over the keys to establish the best fingering for the piece he was about to play.

Some members of staff made outstanding vocal contributions to our morning singing. In this context special mention must be made of Mr. Barton. He could be heard most mornings in assembly contributing heartily to our hymn singing. He never failed to make a solo contribution whenever we sang *Cwm Rhondda* — from *Hymns Ancient and Modern*. Do you remember: *Guide me O thou great Redeemer* — etc. — *Feed me now and ever more* — "EVER MORE"! The latter repetition would come in bang on cue sung volubly by Mr. Barton. I believe Mr. Shipley also made his contribution. He sat close by Mr. Barton under the balcony near to the entrance through which Herbert Wadge would ceremoniously appear each morning.

After leaving the CTS I did in fact see Mr. Barton — I should say *hear* him — on several occasions. By this I mean, I used to go regularly to the Hallé Orchestra concerts at the Sheffield City Hall. Choral music often formed part of the repertoire including such well known items as Handel's *Messiah* and other works of a similar oratorio kind. These were performed by the Sheffield Choral Society and Sheffield Philharmonic Choral Union

— or some such groups — and who was to be seen, looking splendid in evening dress, but our JEB!

If you have paid close attention to what I have so far written (!), you will recall that I said that Mr. Hughes had a tenor voice. One morning he gave an illustration of its vocal qualities. A space was cleared for him at the front of the Hall and he gave a rendering of Ariel's song from Shakespeare's *The Tempest*:

> *Full fathom five thy father lies;*
> *Of his bones are choral made;*
> *Those are pearls that were his eyes:*
> *Nothing of him doth fade*
> *But doth suffer a sea-change*
> *Into something rich and strange.*
> *Sea-nymphs hourly rang his knell:*
> *Hark! Now I hear them —*
> *Ding-dong, ding-dong bell.*

He received a terrific ovation for his efforts!

There were other occasions when morning assembly was enlivened by musical departures from our established routine. During my time at the CTS we were fortunate enough to have a gifted pianist in our midst. He was Brian Smith and was at that time already at the Associated Board *Grade 8* standard of piano playing — that's as high as you can go before taking your Diploma in music (LRAM or similar qualification). Mr. Hughes gave his youthful protégé every opportunity to shine and as a result Smith performed solo piano pieces at morning assembly a number of times. I recall him playing the first movement of Beethoven's Piano Sonata No. 8 the *Pathétique*. I recall quite distinctly how Mr. Hughes made a distinction between the contemporary meaning of 'pathetic' and the late eighteenth-century connotation of *Pathétique* = 'sublime'. And sublime was young Brian Smith's playing.

Mr. Hughes was no musical elitist. He would champion the cause of music in whatever shape or form it took — and it certainly took some strange forms. No more so when there was a craze for *skiffle* music. You will remember the essential requirement for authentic skiffle music was a tea-chest base. This was constructed from, as the name implies, a tea chest — which acted as a resonating chamber — to which was attached a broom handle and a length of taught string — the chest being held in place by the performer's foot. Pressure on the broom handle varied the tension on the string, and thereby the pitch of the note which was achieved by twanging the string — boom, boom, boom etc. Melody was produced by a vocalist who strummed away on the obligatory guitar. The rhythm department was a metal-surfaced scrubbing-board animated by the player's fingers being tipped with thimbles. That anyway is how a group once appeared in morning assembly in 1955 under the auspices of Mr. Hughes. They rocked away — man — with an amazed Herbert Wadge looking on in silent wonderment. He probably thought that civilisation as he knew it was coming to an end, but he went along with the performance and clapped heartily with the rest of us when the piece came to an end. I should add that this was long before the days when former CTS pupil Joe Cocker achieved fame!

Wind Band

It would be about this period when Mr. Wadge announced one day in morning assembly that a sum of money had become available to purchase a set of brass instruments for the school. This was a major development in the musical life of the CTS and over the following few months a wind band was formed. As far as I know, all the players started from scratch and they achieved a good performing standard — in fact their standard was very good indeed. They gave occasional performances in assembly and on more set-piece occasions such as Speech Day. I recall a particularly rousing performance of a march by Handel. Standing at the front of the School Hall by the piano when the band played, as I did a few times when I was School captain, was a remarkable experience. The power of the band was such as to set the strings of the piano vibrating — in sympathy as it were!

Under Mr. Hughes's baton the band was in capable hands. He once told me that, during his student days, he had played the trumpet in the university orchestra but had subsequently given it up as a consequence of, as he put it in 1955, "Having lost my lip — you need a firm lip for the trumpet". Very true. In my student days I took up the clarinet and found it difficult to acquire the *embouchure* — to use the posh word for a stiff upper-lip.

My mention of the clarinet is deliberate because it enables me to make a brief reference here to a most gifted clarinettist. I can't recall his name but he was at the CTS round about 1955–56. He had a staggering jazz-style technique. I heard him play one day at lunch time during dinner break. "Man, could he chew that liquorice stick!" — I believe that's what aficionados say.

Recorder Group

I have said that Mr. Hughes was prepared to champion music in all its forms and I benefited personally from this. A number of us asked if we could form a recorder group — not very original but at least it showed some initiative. For a while about six of us used to meet at lunch time in a classroom in Bow Building — the first room to the left on entering from the playground. Mr. Hughes had a tin locker in this room in which several instruments were stored. I had the Tenor instrument; I think the rest of the group played Treble. One or two of the lads were quite good and give a lead. Mr. Hughes was encouraging and let us each have the loan of a little music tutor to help us on our way. This contained transcriptions of several well known tunes with Johann Sebastian Bach making an inevitable appearance. Mr. Hughes was very tactful and always left the room to let us get on with our practice. Our problem for him was that whenever he returned we stopped playing — we were so embarrassed! I think in the end he resorted to listening to us through the keyhole! We did make some progress but we were never asked, thank goodness, to gave a 'public' performance.

Following these Recorder Group meetings Mr. Hughes would fall into conversation with us as we were drying out our instruments and generally putting things away. I recall him saying how much time he spent writing out musical notation for school productions and what a boon it would be if someone would invent a form of musical shorthand. It was on one such occasion as this that I learned a little about Mr. Hughes's own personal academic achievements. I fell into conversation with him and he remarked how he had once played the trumpet — of which I have already made mention — as well as the piano. He told me he had first studied for a B.A. degree — I think in English and Music. He had then followed this with the B.Mus. degree at the University of Sheffield. Now, it so happens

that when I was an architecture student at the University of Sheffield, I used to spend some time in the Music Department — I became a member of the Sheffield University Madrigal Group. One day, standing before the Music Catalogue, I decided to see if there was an entry for Mr. Hughes. This is what I found: "Hughes, Roger: B.Mus. Degree, *Variations on an Original Theme*". So, our Mr. Hughes had skills in composition as well as musical performance.

Singing Lessons

It is not entirely true to say, as I have previously, that music did not feature in the formal part of our curriculum. We had singing lessons. That is a rather grand way of describing periods which more resembled the letting off of steam! I recall a number of members of staff took us for singing lessons. I suppose the essential qualification was to be able to play the piano — and to be enthusiastic. In this category I will place Mr. Bill Gregory — but only just; his piano playing was about as limited as Herbert Wadge's. But he made up for lack of technical competence with enthusiasm. He typically played with two or three fingers, occasionally casting a searching glance in the direction of us boys. This latter action was necessary to keep order! It was a case of give us a crotchet and we would take a minim — the musical amongst you will be able to work that out. For the rest I will give an illustration of what I mean in more specific terms. There were times when we sang *Shenandoah* which, you will recall, has the line: "*Oh Shenandoah I love* your *daughter*". The temptation to modify this verse proved too much for a certain group of boys — of a low demeanour — who corrupted it to: "*Oh Shenandoah* I ******* *your daughter*". Mr. Gregory, with his alert ear, on suspecting that he had heard a departure from the set text would leap up from the piano — gas pipe flailing in the air — as he searched our countenances for signs of misdemeanours. But, by then it was too late; orthodoxy prevailed and the wayward lads sang away angelically so as to conceal their errant ways. I could add, by way of further illustration, how certain CTS lads were able to modify the words to *Barbara Allan* but I will refrain — I have made my point.

There were a few occasions when we had music lessons from Mr. Clark — ordinarily associated, as I have explained, with teaching chemistry. In fact Mr. Clark was quite musical and I saw him a number of times at the Hallé Concerts. He could play the piano reasonably well, at least adequately enough to give us a few singing lessons. True to his rather scholarly nature, he was not content that we should idle the time away by exercising our vocal chords and so we had to 'work' as well. This usually took the form of learning about the rudiments of music — somewhat different than being with Mr. Gregory when, as I have indicated, we were more interested in the 'rude-iments' of music! So Mr. Clark introduced us to such musicological technicalities as note values and key signatures — it was not much fun.

Mr. Hughes took us for singing at the Cathedral School. A small upright piano was stored in the Dining Hall for this purpose. It was invariably locked but Mr. Hughes had the knack of opening it with a nail file which he carried about with him. He also usually had a tuning fork 'at the ready' in his breast-coat pocket. The tendency for lads to subvert Mr. Hughes's singing lessons usually proved as strong as I have described when Mr. Gregory was in charge. But Mr. Hughes had more subtle ways of channelling our youthful exuberance than the flailing of Mr. Gregory's gas pipe. I will illustrate what I mean. One of our favourite songs was the American marching song *Marching Through Georgia*. The line "Hurrah! Hurrah! We bring the Jubilee!" proved too tempting for some boys who modified it to: "Hurrah! Hurrah! We bring the Jubilee — STOUT "! You will recognise the addition 'Jubilee Stout' as being the name of an Irish beer — CTS lads could certainly be inventive! But Mr. Hughes was not one to let such anarchy prevail in his lessons. He struck a compromise; we could modify the song — but on his terms. For the 'Hurrah!' chorus, he divided the class into two groups — roughly, those to the left and those to the right. He then introduced us to singing in *syncopation* — a form of off-beat accentuation. So those to the left sang 'Hurrah!' and, in quick succession, those to the right sang 'Hurrah!' but with more emphasis. This gave a terrific zest and spatiality to the music. It was a good example of a teacher using psychology to divert the unruly energies of lively boys to more productive ways.

I can offer a further illustration of how Mr. Hughes was prepared to humour us by accommodating to our wishes during singing lessons. First, a reminder of one of the popular 'hits' of the 1950s:

> *You load sixteen tons and what do get?*
> *Another day older and deeper in debt.*
> *Saint Peter don't call 'cause I can't come,*
> *I owe my soul to the company store.*

One afternoon we asked Mr. Hughes if we could sing this pop tune — but he didn't know the melody. So two or three lads duly obliged by providing the refrain. Mr. Hughes quickly got the hang of it — he had a good ear — and we were soon singing away: "*You load sixteen tons And what do you get?*". After that we settled down to the more orthodox part of our singing lesson.

Music at the City Hall

Mention should be made here of the vital part which Mr. Dove contributed to music-making at the CTS. This was most apparent at the period each year when Speech Day was approaching. He would train a choir of selected boys who invariably achieved a remarkable standard of singing. I will reserve my comments about this for later when I come to consider Speech Day as a particular item. For the time being, I will recall another aspect of Mr. Dove's contribution to the musical life of the CTS, namely, his championing of the Sheffield Philharmonic Series of concerts which were held weekly at the City Hall, usually under the auspices of Sir John Barbirolli and the Hallé Orchestra with contributions from visiting orchestras. Mr. Dove was unfailing in his drawing to our attention of the forthcoming programme. On occasions he would cite the name of an artist of particular renown. It so happens that an alert CTS lad walking along Leopold Street, past Wilson & Peck, could have read all about this for himself on the bill-board placed on the street corner for this purpose. But Mr. Dove's observations, always delivered on a Monday morning in assembly as part of the regular announcements, served as timely reminders of what was happening — musically speaking — and identified Mr. Dove with the musical life of the school. I started to take notice of these concerts round about 1957 and attended the Hallé series regularly thereafter for several years. Let me single out a particular concert. I went to hear a young pianist called Richard Farrell; I believe he played Rachmaniov's *First Piano Concerto*. I should add, by way of further information, that the Hallé series of concerts took place alternately on Friday and Saturday evenings; the former were more eclectic and the latter were of a more popular kind. Farrell played on the Friday evening and, the following Monday, I read of his untimely death in a car accident — he was still only a young man in his thirties. I happened to mention this to Mr. Dove who went on to lament the death earlier in the year of the young horn player Dennis Brain who also died (age 36) in a car crash — enthusiasts still speak about Brain's consummate horn playing.

At the Hallé series, Mr. Dove could always be seen sitting in the Circle on the right, facing the platform, about three rows from the front. I became familiar with the standard repertoire at these concerts. Later on, when I was at the university, I kept up my concert going for over five years. I used to get in free by helping to sell concert programmes for Wilson & Peck. Not only did I go to the classical concerts but I also went to the pop concerts as well. At the latter I saw, should I say heard, Cliff Richard, The Shadows, Dusty Springfield, Tommy Steele, Cilla Black, Akka Bilk and, yes, the Beetles — on no fewer than three occasions. (On one of these occasions I was *all alone* with the four lively lads for a few minutes outside the *artistes'* entrance — I must tell you more about that sometime.)

A number of other CTS lads shared my enthusiasm for music and went along to the Hallé Concerts. One Friday evening I chanced to meet School Captain Gerald Craven — a very gifted lad. The first half of the concert included Max Bruck's *Violin Concerto No 1* — just about the most popular violin concerto in terms of the public's estimation. If you are familiar with the piece you will be aware of how elegiac it is in character. Gerald picked up on this and, after the performance, he commented: "That's the most sleepy piece of music I've ever heard". This may not be very musicological in its terminology but Gerald's judgement was spot on.

A CTS lad whom I remember as having a good strong baritone voice was Geoff Gray. He could out-voice all of us in morning assembly during hymn singing. I believe he sang for his church choir at the weekends. He was a Senior Prefect in 1958 and left the CTS that year to read for a B.Sc. at the University of Sheffield. In fact about two years later I heard Geoff giving demonstration of his vocal powers at the university in a student production of Gilbert and Sullivan's *Yeomen of the Guard*.

A few weeks later I chanced to meet Mr. Frow and Mr. Clark at a Friday evening City Hall concert. Amazingly, this was the one and only occasion that I ever exchanged any words with Mr. Clark in my whole time at the CTS. Mr. Frow introduced me to Mr. Clark — if that is not too grand a way of putting it, as follows: "This is Russell? Do you know him? He is one of the famous ones"! Mr. Clark, I have to say, just shook his head — as well he might. *Famous ones* indeed — but I am still working on it!

There were times when Mr. Hughes also made announcements in morning assembly about forthcoming Hallé concerts. I have just described these as being either eclectic or popular. Mr. Hughes had a novel way of making this distinction; in his terminology concerts were variously described as being highbrow, middlebrow, lowbrow — and sometimes he would make subtle distinctions of the kind: "Just above the middlebrow". One morning, after making such an announcement, I approached Mr. Hughes with a question — in the spirit that teachers known everything! On TV the previous evening BBC had screened what was the first Chopin Piano Competition — Chopin being 'The Prince of the Piano'. At the close of the programme, the winner played one of the works which had secured him the prize. I asked Mr. Hughes if he knew what this was. With disarming candour he replied: "I've never even heard of the Chopin Piano Competition — sorry"! I now know the answer, just in case any one of you have been trying for these last forty years to identify the piece in question, it was *Étude No 42 in A minor*.

The approach of Christmas was always marked by the Hallé Orchestra who invariably performed Handel's *Messiah* under the baton of Sir John Barbirolli. This was almost a social event in the life of the City of Sheffield and each year tickets were soon sold out. In December 1957 I was a Junior Prefect and happened to see the placard near to Wilson & Peck announcing the forthcoming Hallé production of *Messiah*. I did not have a ticket but the opportunity immediately presented itself to obtain one — here's how. I had been assigned to prefect's duty at the Holly Building to look out for late-comers and to 'book them'. As I stood sentinel-fashion by the door, I decided I would be more profitably employed abandoning my post (!) and joining the queue at 'Willy Pecks' for a ticket for *Messiah*. It so happens that the queue stretched way back along Leopold Street — almost to the Education Offices. It took some nerve to stand there being so near to the CTS main building. This was one occasion that I was grateful that Herbert's morning service extended for its typical legendary length! I just purchased my ticket in time to resume my post at the Holly Building before the lads staggered out from assembly — looking for all the world like the dazed prisoners in the scene from *Fidelio* when they emerge from their prison cells into the open to enjoy the sunshine!

Personal Reflections on Music

I have another personal recollection to call to mind. Mr. Hughes used to go home by tram to Woodseats — the same route taken by myself. There were times I would meet him, by chance, at the tram stop outside the Peace Gardens just by the Town Hall. These were occasions when I showed an excess of youthful enthusiasm and, instead of leaving Mr. Hughes to his own thoughts, I intruded with remarks and personal observations of my own about music. Mr. Hughes, true to his genial nature, always responded to my enthusiasm with his own. Let me give an example. One evening, I asked him about the principle of equal temperament — devotees of classical music will know this has significance in Bach's Forty-Eight Preludes and Fugues *für Das Wohltemperite Klavier* — 'for the well-tempered Clavier (keyboard)'. What a question to be asked after a hard day's work! Unabashed, Mr. Hughes patiently explained how equal temperament is an adjustment in tuning in order to reduce the inaccuracy in the intervals between certain notes on the keyboard so that all keys can be played in harmony together — that will have to suffice even though it's an oversimplification which leaves out half a dozen pages of mathematical acoustics. At this point in our conversation the tram came and Mr. Hughes was able to make his escape!

It was on such a similar journey home that I once more chanced to find myself in conversation with Mr. Hughes. This time the subject of conversation was Franz Liszt. I had just 'discovered' Liszt's piano transcriptions of the Beethoven symphonies and would talk about them to anyone prepared to listen. Once more Mr. Hughes was the 'victim' but he gave me his attention and made several illuminating remarks — sorting out a few of my misconceptions on the way. Then he asked me: "Have you heard this: 'The abbé Liszt plays with his fist' ", He then went on to explain the origin of the remark and I thereby added a bit more to my growing store of musical history. There is an interesting sequel to this episode. About three years later when I was a student at the University of Sheffield, I was having lunch with the pianist Dennis Matthews. He had just given a lunch-time recital to the students which I had helped to arrange as a member of the university's *Music Committee* — I got a free lunch for my efforts. I happened to raise the subject of Liszt's transcriptions of the Beethoven symphonies with Dennis Matthews which, it so happens, had been recently (1962) performed on what was then the *Third Programme* of the BBC. At that time these works were almost totally neglected — not least because of the technical skills required to play them. I happened to say how enterprising it was of the BBC to promote these works and to give them an airing. Then Mr. Matthews said: "Thank you very much. As a matter of fact it was me who persuaded the BBC to create the programmes and I was the Producer for the series"! So I was rather relieved I hadn't said anything derogatory about them or I would have really put my foot in it!

Perhaps there were times when I wonder if Mr. Hughes did indeed think there was no escaping from Terry Russell and his enthusiasm for music. My reason for saying this is as follows. About two years after leaving school I went to the Lyceum Theatre to hear a performance of Rossini's *The Barber of Seville*. Afterwards whom should I meet in the foyer but Mr. Hughes. Now, the stage-set designer for this production had made use of false perspective to achieve the visual effect of foreshortening — what architect's call *trompe-l'oeil*. I made an observation about this to Mr. Hughes who, on this occasion, resorted to tact, observed how late it was and quickly made his escape to get back home!

Let me tell another evening-at-the-opera story from about this same period. This time the work I had gone to hear was Mozart's *The Marriage of Figaro*. Whom should I meet at the theatre this time but Mr. Gregory! Mr. Gregory, by the way, used to go to the Hallé Concerts and always sat in the Balcony immediately above Mr. Dove; this is a good place to sit, incidentally, since the acoustics in the City Hall are at their optimum at this location. My chance meeting with Mr. Gregory occurred during the interval by which time I had a glass of beer in my hand. I said "Hello" and then made the observation that my glass of beer was a distinct improvement on a bottle of milk! Mr. Gregory shook his head questioningly and diplomatically disappeared into the crowd!

There were times when I shared my interest in music with other boys. Here are a few instances. Some of you may recall that round about 1955, BBC TV screened an adaptation of *The Quatermass Experiment* in six episodes on Saturday nights — they electrified the nation. The introductory music was *Mars* from Holst's *The Planets*. My CTS friend Gordon Swan, to whom I have made previous reference, became so enthusiastic about this he bought the record. I went round to his house one Sunday afternoon to listen to it. Also at this time, BBC TV screened a sophisticated panel game called *Animal, Vegetable and Mineral*. This was, in effect, an archaeological programme chaired by a man by the name of Glyn Daniel who was Professor of Archaeology at the University of Cambridge. The star of the programme was Sir Mortimer Wheeler — a scholar-archaeologist with a quite remarkable memory. So sage-like was he that for a time it became a catch phrase to say in conversation: "Well, Sir Mortimer what do you think"? Guests would occasionally take part in the programme. One regular guest I recall had the splendid moniker 'Emeritus Professor Thomas Bodkin' — he was sharp! Now, the point here (double pun) is the programme opened with a solo violin playing to the visual image of a turntable rotating to display the title of the programme and an archaeological artefact. Gordon and I were captivated by the violin tune and went off one evening to see if we could obtain it on record from Wilson & Peck. Gordon sought my advice but I messed things up which resulted in Gordon purchasing *Tilting at Windmills* which I believe comes from the *Don Quixote* Suite of Richard Strauss — sorry about that Gordon! I now know the music we were trying to identify; it was the celebrated *Chaconne* from the *Partita in D* by Johann Sebastian Bach.

My personal enjoyment of music served, indirectly, to inform my wider appreciation of literature. A couple of examples will illustrate what I mean. Working my way through the standard musical repertoire, I became familiar with Tchaikovsky's concert overture *Francesca da Rimini* and its sound-world portrayal of the tale of illicit lovers — condemned to eternal anguish and lamentation. Tchaikovsky's turbulent music captures the rise and fall of their successive hope and despair to perfection. This stirred my youthful imagination and led me to find out more about Tchaikovsky's sources of influence. In due course, by searching about in the Central Library, I learned about Dante Alighieri's immortal epic poem *The Comedy*. My other illustration concerns the musical treatment of the legend of *Faust*, a name which occurs throughout music, to give but one example, in the work of Hector Berlioz — viz. *The Damnation of Faust*. This time my library researches led me to Johann von Goethe's equally immortal epic poem *Faust*. I now have the texts of *The Comedy* and *Faust* in my collection of poetic writings and I am so thankful for the formative experiences I enjoyed listening to music when I was at the CTS, not least for opening my mind to ever wider vistas.

Let me give a further illustration of how incidental TV music enlarged my understanding of the classical repertoire and helped me to establish a bond of friendship with another CTS lad. This time the programme was for children and was called *The Silver Sword*. This sword had magical properties, rather like King Arthur's *Excalibur*, and conferred great power on its custodian. The background music had great dramatic power and I made a mental note to find out what it was. After painstaking research — just like Sir Mortimer — I established that the music which had so captivated me was *The March to the Scaffold* from the *Symphonie Fantastique* by Hector Berlioz. I purchased the music on Decca's then low-cost *Ace of Clubs* label. The CTS friend to whom I wish to make reference, concerning this piece of music, was Ian Glasby who was on the

Engineering side of the school. One night I went along to Ian's house and we played through my record and swapped musical stories. At this point I will digress from music for the following reasons; Ian has two claims to CTS 'fame'. First, he is one of the very few lads whose brother also attended the CTS — namely Stuart Glasby. Ian's other claim to fame is more macabre! It concerns a circumstance worthy of Berlioz's *March to the Scaffold*. On his first day at work, soon after leaving the CTS, he discovered a human head lying at the foot of a railway embankment! Some poor wretch had decided to end it all and it was Ian's misfortune to find the deceased's mortal remains by the side of the track. Naturally, Ian wasn't feeling too well when he eventually turned up for work! — which by the way was Arthur Lees. He was met by a kindly man who said: "Cheer up lad. You look as though you've seen a ghost"! Ian explained that he more-or-less had! Now let forty years pass — the story has a remarkable sequel. A few years ago I recounted these events to an uncle of mine who had just retired. He listed attentively and then remarked: "I was the 'kindly man' who met your CTS friend all those years ago at Arthur Lees"! It is indeed a small world.

Lunch-Time Recitals

In 1958 some of you may recall that a series of Lunch-Time Recitals commenced in the Basement Lecture Theatre at the City Library. These were recitals given on recordings and were intended to provide office workers a pleasant mid-day break. The authorities were enterprising and encouraged participants to bring along their sandwiches. I went along to several of these concerts with my CTS contemporary Brian Lister. Concerts were of the kind that Mr. Hughes would have described as being 'middle brow'. Indeed, he frequently made reference to forthcoming concerts in this series in his announcements in morning assembly. A typical concert consisted of an overture, a piano concerto and a symphony. These concerts were most enjoyable and helped me to learn more about the standard repertoire — they also provided a welcome alternative to walking about in the rain!

Opera

If you have been paying close attention to what I have been saying — and I hope you have because you may get a test on all this (!) — you may recall that I made a previous reference to the *Carl Rosa Opera Company*. I gave a pledge to return to this topic and now that time has come — hold tight, this bit is going to be serious. In the academic year of 1957–58 I made one of the great musical 'discoveries' of my life which has enriched it immeasurably. Whilst reading Thayer's *Life of Beethoven*, to which I have referred, I learned about the gestation and creation of Beethoven's only opera — *Fidelio*. The experience elevated my musical appreciation to a wholly new level. The moral grandeur of this work, and the resplendent musical language in which its themes are enshrined, place this work — in my opinion — at the very pinnacle of human aesthetic and intellectual achievement. I will resist the temptation to elaborate and will confine myself to what happened back in 1957.

My first action was to obtain a copy of the piano score (Novello edition) of *Fidelio* and to work my way through the music — very slowly using one or two fingers only to pick out the melodies. I soon had the principal themes by heart — declamatory Overture, First

Act Quartet *Mir ist so wunderbar* (*A wondrous feeling fills me*), Prisoners' Chorus — and so on. If I may use a metaphorical construction; the dye my mind took from this score has remained permanent and the themes have stayed in my heart ever since. Now let me get back to the CTS connection with all this in 1957. Following a visit to Harry's 'Tin Shop' in Arundel Street, I noticed that the Carl Rosa Opera Company was scheduled to perform *Fidelio* — the very opera I had just been learning about one-finger-one-thumb fashion on the piano (my mother's piano). I enthused about this to my CTS friend Brian Lister, gradually wore down his resistance and duly persuaded him to go along with me to hear the production. In fact Brian was as enthralled as myself — and became a *Beethovenian* too!

There's a little bit more to tell. Not satisfied with my own efforts on the piano I got my CTS pal David Dickson to call round to see what he could make of the piano score of *Fidelio*. Poor lad, accomplished as he was at the keyboard — especially the organ — all he could manage was to struggle mightily with the first few pages of music which were filled with the fists full of notes that abounded on every page. I put him out of his misery and asked him to stop. We finished off our musical evening by David playing through some sections of Handel's *Messiah* which, being an accomplished church organist, he more or less knew by heart. A good time was then had by all.

More Personal Musical Reflections

In my personal discovery of music during my time at the CTS, I should briefly mention some of the concert venues I attended. One of these was Firth Hall at the University of Sheffield where it was possible to hear the Sheffield Bach Choir and the Chamber Orchestra. I am grateful to Mr. Hughes for introducing me to this musical circle. Indeed, in March of 1959 he even secured a ticket for me to go to hear Handel's *Israel in Egypt* — he phoned the concert secretary for me (Mrs. Denman) and I collected the ticket at the door. Another concert venue, which will have meaning for many CTS lads was the Victoria Hall — the connection with the CTS being, of course, that it was the hall where we held our Speech Day. The Sheffield Choral Society performed several concerts at the Victoria Hall. Two concerts stand out in my mind. One was a performance of Handel's *Messiah* in December 1958. I still have the programme and what may be of interest is that it bears my pencil annotations. I made these when preparing a 'reading' for Telford House, as House Vice Captain, early in the Spring Term of 1959 — more details later. The second concert I wish to recall included a performance of Schubert's *Miriam's Song of Triumph*. Miriam, you may remember from Holy Scripture, was the sister of Moses and urged the people to rise up against their oppressors — "Strike your timbrels Hebrew maidens, Miriam bids uphold the lay"! These are the opening words of this oratorio-like piece which stirred me so much all those years ago. I resolved then and there to become a *Schubertian*. I have to say that I was not only enamoured of Schubert on the evening in question but also of the lovely young soprano singer who sang the title role. She was called Avril Roebuck. Where are you now Avril?

To my CTS days belongs the purchase of my *Pye Black Box* — a then state-of-the-art record player. I saved up for this with pocket money given to me by my father. It cost £40 in 1958 — a considerable sum of money in those days. My father, realising how long it was taking me to accumulate the required amount, increased my weekly pocket money to £1. I used to pay this into a savings account that was administered through the school. At some time in 1956, Herbert Wadge made a very big issue of saving. Thrift became the *credo* of his morning discourses in assembly. Just about every boy at the CTS took out an account and put aside a few shillings. The money was collected by our Form Master on Monday mornings; entries were recorded in a little blue fold-out pass book. At this time Mr. Donald Charlesworth was my Form Master and he was assisted in collecting the money by Mr. Firth. I recall one Monday morning Mr. Firth remarking to Mr. Charlesworth, seeing me deposit yet another £1: "Do you think he flogs peanuts as a side-line on Saturday evenings to the picture queues"! I just explained I had a generous father. In fact, very generous; at this time he earned £11 per week — I know because I used to help him to complete his Income Tax Form!

Having spent all my money on my record player it was weeks before I had accumulated sufficient money to buy any records to play! I did however eventually make a very significant purchase. The record company Vox had just started to publish the complete chamber works of Franz Schubert. I was still 'discovering' Schubert — I still am — and I purchased *Vox Box No 6*. It is before me now, still cared for and fresh looking. It contains two treasures that, for me, occupy the high musical territory occupied by Beethoven's *Fidelio*. The Schubertian's amongst you will intuitively anticipate that I am referring to: — The Quartet in D Minor *Death and the Maiden* and the Great Quintet in C Major. Here is my way of expressing my high estimation of the latter work — hold tight, I'm going to be serious again. Suppose one day the Supreme Being, The Eternal One — God — asks humanity to give account of itself. Let five musicians play the sublime music of the *Adagio* of Schubert's C Major Quintet. It will be sufficient to convince our Master that humanity has served Him well.

I still have my *Pye Black Box* and use it to play my collection of ancient '78s' — I have treasured recordings by Enrico Caruso and other comparable artists. My final remark here is a little gratuitous but I want to exercise the proud father prerogative. This is what I mean. It is my great pleasure that my daughter shares my love of music. Rosalind is an M.A. of the University of Oxford and has the music diplomas ALCM (Performer) and LLCM (Teacher). I can't persuade her to be a *Schubertian* though — but you can't have everything!

I have other remarks I wish to make about music at the CTS but I will reserve these for the section which follows.

Speech Day

Speech Day is a set-piece occasion in the annual cycle of events of most schools. It provides an opportunity for the school to celebrate its achievements and those of its pupils under the admiring gaze of benefactors and devoted parents. The CTS was no exception and Herbert Wadge and his entourage of colleagues made every effort to ensure that it was not just a success but a triumphant occasion. During my period at the CTS, Speech Day was always held at the Victoria Hall which provided ample seating and stage facilities for pupils, staff, parents, distinguished visitors, Guest Speaker —

and, of course, the ever dominant figure of Herbert Wadge himself. Commandingly centre-stage he presided over Speech Day like a god. He was clearly in his element and he manifestly took pride in having the achievements of his school publicly extolled — and bathed, thereby, in the reflected glory.

I have made reference to the staff of the school, since, of course, Speech Day was not a one-man show. Many staff contributed to the success of the evening, especially the musical part of the activities to which I will shortly make reference. Speech Day was the one occasion in the year when members of staff, who were graduates, could wear their full academic robes, including their colourful hood and formal bow tie. Staff who were not graduates looked very smart in their best suit. Some staff acted as 'chaperons', receiving families at the door welcoming them and seeing them to their seat — it was all good public relations.

Music

Music was an essential part of the Speech Day proceedings and preparations commenced weeks in advance. They began by Mr. Dove selecting a choir from the classes of First-Year boys. The criterion for selection was if a boy's voice had broken or not. To find out, we were all lined up in the Dining Hall at Cathedral School and, as a class, we had to sing a set piece of music. For this we stood in rows and, as we sang, Mr. Dove listened intently to each of us in turn. All boys who still retained their treble voice were touched on the shoulder. This was the hand of fate! These boys were destined to be the choir for that particular year — and were required to devote many hours of practice to perfect their choral skills. It was a rather pragmatic way of making an audition but it worked and was the precursor to some truly lovely music-making that earned much admiration from the audience.

There were times when the school was fortunate enough to recruit from the ranks a lad with a particularly fine boy-soprano voice. This enabled Mr. Dove, in collaboration with Mr. Hughes, to plan a work for solo voice as part of the evening's proceedings. I recall one such occasion. The choir sang a setting of the *Magnificat* with its stirring words — *My soul doth magnify the Lord*. A boy, with a particularly fine voice, contributed a solo — very movingly — this would be about 1954–55. Messrs Dove and Hughes clearly gave a good deal of thought to their programme planning, doubtless with an ear to the capabilities of the boys and with regard to the tastes of the audience. I assume Herbert Wadge would have to be consulted and give the selection of music his own seal of approval.

One Speech Day the music featured a selection of melodies from the Broadway show *Oklahoma*. All the boys in the school participated in a number called *When I take you out in my Surrey, my Surrey with the fringe on top*. A Surrey, we were told, was the name of an open-top carriage with a canvas roof — complete with a fringe. But what made this number so memorable was that someone had the bright idea of getting all the boys to whistle. Now this took a good deal of practice in morning assembly before Mr. Wadge was satisfied we were all whistling in tune. I remember he flew into a rage on several occasions until we got things right. Poor Messrs Dove and Hughes simply had to go over things time and time again. In passing, it should be remarked here that Mr. Dove was a very accomplished violinist, at least, according to the opinion of Mr. Hughes — and he

should know. And Mr. Dove's daughter was an accomplished performer on the French horn.

At one of these rehearsals, Mr. Wadge actually had the proceedings stopped claiming that he could here a single boy whistling out of tune! "He's somewhere up there!", he bellowed — pointing up to the gallery by the windows — "If he's standing by you tell him to stop at once"! How discerning Herbert's ear really was I can't say, but his intervention had the desired effect of getting us all to whistle in unison like so many song birds.

These occasions were very demanding — and especially so for Mr. Dove. Indeed, I recall how during the rehearsals for one of our Speech days Mr. Dove was absent for some time due to illness — I could well imagine induced by all the exertions he made in exhorting us to improve our standard of musical performance!

Let me call to mind another occasion in morning assembly when Mr. Wadge took a close interest in the proceedings. On the day in question we were rehearsing Elgar's *Pomp and Circumstance March No 1*. This is the one which contains the word - setting that includes the line — *God is drawing his sword*. Mr. Wadge stopped the proceedings and complained that our diction was unacceptable. He raged: "The way you sing makes it sound as though God is drawing his *saw*"! This of course induced universal mirth — which was not the intended reaction and served only to prompt Herbert into fresh paroxysms of rage. These were not easy occasions for Mr. Dove who showed much forbearance and patience as he responded to Mr. Wadge's imprecations and strove to coax the best from us. Let me recall another circumstance concerning our Speech Day rehearsals. This time we were singing an aria about Tubal Cane. In Holy Scripture (*Genesis*) he is a smith or metal worker but in the piece we sang the poor man is condemned to labour in Hades, or somewhere equally unpleasant, and sings the refrain: "*So now you know, So now you know, So now you know, Why I am down here below*"! These innocent seeming words had to be deftly articulated to a complex musical rhythm. If we sang those lines once we sang them a hundred times — but we got the hang of them in the end. We always did under the highly professional tutelage of Messrs Dove and Hughes — and the baleful gaze of Herbert Wadge!

I have a further recollection of our practice-singing for Speech day which will call to mind, at least for some of you, the patriotic fervour that frequently characterised our vocal productions. One year we were required to sing *The Yeomen of England* form Edward German's *Merry England*. Perhaps the mention of this circumstance will call to mind the refrain: 'Where are the yeomen. the yeomen of England?'. To which the response was: 'In homestead and in cottage, they still dwell in England'. The whole school gave expression to these loyal and nationalistic sentiments as though our young lives depended upon it — which they probably did when Herbert Wadge was sitting at the front of the school hall listening attentively to our efforts!

Herbert Wadge was a very shrewd man and one day, at the period when I was School Captain — as Speech Day was approaching — he confided in me how politics and social relationships played a part in the proceedings. He was hinting at the subtle art of influencing people — and of advancing the cause of the CTS thereby. He told me the following circumstance. Our Guest Speaker was to be an old *Harrovian* — a former pupil of Harrow School. So what better way then of charming your way into this man's heart than by having the CTS lads sing the stirring lines of Harrow School's famous Song — *Forty Years On*. Herbert certainly new how to 'play to the gallery'. And the charm worked its effect on our Guest Speaker who, on the evening of Speech Day, sang away heartily on the platform along with the CTS lads who were standing in rows before him. I can vouch for this because, for reasons which will shortly be revealed, I was also seated on the platform that evening, not far from the Guest Speaker, in my capacity as School Captain. By way of further comment, the reader will now be able to deduce from these circumstances the origins of the title for my *Reminiscence*.

The saying; 'It will be all-right on the night' does not always hold true. This, alas, proved to be the case one year with what was intended to be one of our Speech Day set-piece musical items; Mr. Hughes will not thank me for recalling this little debacle. The musical item in question was the so-called *Toy Symphony* of Leopold Mozart — or perhaps the composer was Joseph Haydn. The very inclusion of such a work in our Speech Day music-making, it should be noted, is a good illustration of Mr. Hughes's valiant efforts to promote the endeavours of lads with relatively modest musical skills. Concerning the *Toy Symphony*, its instrumentation calls for a warbling bird-song effect. At the performance on our Speech Day this was supposed to be achieved by a lad blowing air across a small water-filled instrument inside of which a pea-sized sphere was animated to produce the warbling effect. That was the general idea! Sadly things did not go to plan. I think the lad, in his enthusiasm, blew too hard and expelled all the water from the instrument in a single jet! The consequence was his 'instrument' produced the kind of plaintive sound that I imagine might be made by a wounded albatross! This had, shall we say, a disturbing effect on the rest of the performers. I will not elaborate save to say the performance more or less ground to a halt — to Mr. Hughes's despair.

Let me draw a veil over that evening and narrate the details of a circumstance altogether more complimentary to Mr. Hughes.

There is another saying; 'The show must go on' and this held true for us one year when Mr. Wadge told us in assembly, the very day before Speech Day was due to take place, that Mr. Hughes had hurt his finger — rather badly. I believe he had lost the entire nail of one finger — it must have been very painful. In the true Yorkshire spirit — although I believe Mr. Hughes was only a Yorkshire man by adoption — he had his finger bound up and, on the evening of Speech Day, played quite undeterred. Herbert Wadge paid him a particularly warm compliment for his efforts the following day. I can add a little more shine to this story by recalling another event when the musical honours, at least in the piano department, went once more to Mr. Hughes. This time the musical fare for Speech Day included the engaging setting of Benjamin Britten's *The Merry Hearted Ploughboy*. The piano accompaniment requires a deft touch with lots of trilling and ornamentation in the upper register to convey the high spirits of the happy ploughboy. Mr. Hughes imparted these to perfection — and duly earned another compliment before the whole school from Herbert Wadge.

I have remarked how hard the choir worked at their rehearsals to achieve the remarkable standards that eventually gave so much pleasure. For their reward I recall they were allowed an afternoon off to go the cinema. I believe one year they saw a light-hearted film featuring Danny Kaye. I remember this because Herbert Wadge went on about Kaye's acting skills in assembly concluding: "In his way the man's a genius". And, in his way, Herbert was right.

The day after Speech Day was always good fun since we were given an opportunity to hear all the music a second time in morning assembly on a tape recording. Someone — I wonder who — made a recording of the principal musical events including some of the speeches. The tape recorder used to play the music was a remarkable machine being vast and cumbersome by today's standards — and all glowing inside with hot valves! It was carefully trundled into the centre of the School Hall where Herbert manipulated the controls, with occasional help from Mr. Thompson — perhaps it was he who made the recordings? The re-plays of Speech Day music was one morning - assembly whose inordinate length we did not mind as we re-lived the events of the preceding evening on which so much effort had been expended. Herbert Wadge was again in his element, extolling the virtues of his beloved school and enlarging on the theme that virtue brings its own rewards. It was very easy to be swept along in all the euphoria. On one occasion this proved too much for Bill Davis — here's what happened. A piece of music had been played through and, as the recorded sound of the audience clapping commenced, Mr. Davis absent-mindedly joined in! There was an embarrassing moment followed by the good-natured mirth of the whole school — who then spontaneously joined in the applause and all was well!

I must say a few words concerning the CTS School Song and what I know as to how it came about. In my final year as School Captain I was forever being asked to sort things out concerning prefects and their duties and such like matters. These circumstances would take me away from the classroom for short periods. Following one such occasion, I was returning to the Holly Building to resume my lesson in applied maths. Whom should I meet on the stair but Herbert Wadge. He asked if I had a moment to listen to something on which he had been working. Then, to my amazement, he began to sing — the echo of the tiled walls giving added resonance to his already mighty voice. He quickly checked himself with the observation: "I think it might be more appropriate to go to my room, I don't want to make a fool of myself here"! "Quite right, Sir", I responded dutifully and off we trekked to his room — making me wonder what musical experience lay in wait for me! In his room he explained that he had for some years entertained in his mind the idea of the CTS having a school song and that he had been recently working on such a project. He cited the Eton College *Boating Song* as evidence of how words and melody could stir patriotic feelings — *Jolly good boating weather* etc. For a moment I seriously wondered if Herbert had composed a song about the CTS lads and the River Don! But he allayed all such thoughts by invoking the idea that when CTS lads leave school they scatter far and wide. This realisation, he observed, had provided him with the initial inspiration for his text. He explained to me how he had embodied the idea of geographical diffusion in his word-setting by selecting particular locations, viz. — Cheviots (north), Dover (south), Wash (east) and Milford Town (west). I listened respectfully, nodding at appropriate intervals whilst not really being sure where some of these places actually were! Then the exciting bit occurred.

Herbert treated me to a personal rendering of his creation, no less than a song in four verses with chorus. Here are the words:

> From the Cheviots down to Dover,
> From the Wash to Milford Town,
> Yea and all the wide world over,
> Men are singing thy renown,
> Thy renown, O Spartan Mother,
> CTS our pride and boast,
> Here's good luck to one another
> Here's a rousing loyal toast.
> Chorus — "Flourish CTS for ever!"
>
> In remote and rural stations,
> 'Mid the busy haunts of men,
> In the service of the nations,
> Wielding skill of tool and pen,
> Ne'er to duty turning traitor,
> Looking trials in the face,
> Sons of thine, dear Alma Mater,
> Share the manhood of the race.
> Chorus — "Flourish CTS for ever!"
>
> Some alas! their labour ended,
> Now have passed within the veil,
> Some 'gainst foe their land defended,
> Died that freedom might prevail.
> These were they who prov'd not craven,
> When the call of duty came,
> Now the roll in bronze is graven,
> To preserve their honour'd name.
> Chorus — "Flourish CTS for ever!"
>
> Alma mater! may their story,
> Nerve us in the age-long fight,
> For the triumph and the glory,
> Of a world of truth and light,
> Once again then Spartan Mother,
> CTS! Our pride and boast,
> Here's to all who hail us "Brother",
> Here's once more the Grand Old Toast.
> Chorus — "Flourish CTS for ever!"
>
> Chorus "Flourish CTS for ever!"
> Pass the word along!
> Here's a hand and there's the other
> Friendship's pledge to one another
> Shake for Auld Lang Syne my brother,
> Shout the good old song,
> "Flourish CTS for ever!" "Sheffielders,
> Hurrah!"

Herbert's personal rendition to me of these partisan sentiments was full-voiced and impassioned. To judge the effect this had on me, I will ask the reader if he has ever stood in a church belfry with the bells going at full tilt? "You see!", said Herbert — as he sang away to me in full voice, "Do you see the imagery?" "Remarkable!", I replied which, although ambiguous, was true. Herbert was manifestly pleased with himself and resolved to introduce his song to the whole school at the earliest opportunity. Perhaps some of you remember rehearsing this masterpiece for Speech Day?

There is a little corollary to my tale. After he had given his rendition, Herbert picked up on the words 'Shake for Auld Lang Syne my brother'. He said he thought it would be good idea if, at these words, the whole school should join hands and swing them in rhythm to the music! Again, he asked my opinion. This time I decided to be more candid — which took a lot of courage I can tell you. I replied: "Do you not think that would appear rather emotional Sir"? For a moment Herbert looked as though he had walked into a brick wall. He was clearly surprised at my reaction and added: "Possibly so, possibly so". On the evening in question we never did link hands and I have to say that I have chastised myself ever since for not entering fully into Herbert's sense of the theatrical.

Now, before I leave the subject of music at Speech Day I wish to fulfil a self-imposed obligation. I wish to express my debt of gratitude to Mr. Hughes for, at least in part, setting me on the road to musical appreciation and, again in part, for helping me to establish my musical credentials. I will not overstate the case, nor try to put him on a pedestal. (This calls to mind the story of the people of Rossini's home town who once had a collection to create a statue in his honour. On hearing this Rossini remarked: "Tell them to give me the money instead and I'll go and stand for an hour each day in the town square myself!") So, concerning Mr. Hughes: "Thank you Roger for all you did, in general, for the musical life of the CTS and, in particular, for, as I have just intimated, elevating my own musical appreciation.

Prizes

The award of prizes in recognition of achievement was an integral part of Speech Day. Indeed some schools, in recognition of this fact, call their Speech Day 'Prize Day'. This was one of the highlights of the evening when recipients of prizes could enjoy their brief moment of fame which typically lasted about 30 seconds, or rather longer for a prize-winner who had won more than one prize — there were a few select individuals in this category (!). Let me remind you of this aspect of our Speech-Day procedure. Boys who were to receive an award lined up at the foot of the stage in the strict order that had been established earlier in the morning at the rehearsal. This was vital to ensure that the correct certificate and prize were issued to the rightful recipient. All this required a considerable amount of planning and it is a tribute to the members of staff responsible for the organisation that everything ran as smooth as clockwork — most of the time! I know of only one disaster. Reflecting on Speech Days in the past, Mr. Davis told me that there had once indeed been an almighty cock up. On the evening in question the sequence of boys had run out of synchronisation with the issue of the prizes resulting in a shambles. All the prize-winners had to stay behind after the ceremony until the mess was sorted out. But this was the exception and, as I have remarked, our Speech Day was, in general, a model of disciplined organisation.

Mr. McManus usually announced the prizes following which the award winner mounted the central stair to the platform to receive his award — usually a book. The steps were very steep and had to be negotiated carefully if you were to avoid taking a fall before receiving your prize. Mr. Davis issued the prizes by first removing them from the table on the platform and then passing them to the dignitary — the Guest Speaker — who issued them to the recipient. There were variations on this procedure and, by way of illustration, on one of the occasions that I received a prize the awards were handed out by Mrs. Wadge. I remember her as being of slight physical stature — certainly when seen against the towering figure of Herbert Wadge himself. Mrs. Wadge remained in the background as far as school life was concerned, although I can well imagine that there were occasions when she must have thought that she was married to Herbert Wadge *and* the CTS. I can give one illustration of her devotion to the life and work of the CTS. This observation comes from the time when I was School Captain; Mr. Wadge disclosed to me that it was in fact Mrs. Wadge who wrote out all the citations on the Prize Certificates which were issued to the prize-winners. For this reason I have reproduced one such of my certificates in Fig. 84. You can see from this copy what a neat hand Mrs. Wadge had. There must have been thirty or forty prize-winners at a typical Speech Day, so it was no small undertaking to write out the details of all those awards in her copper-plate handwriting. Note also in Fig. 84 the pride with which Herbert Wadge has signed the certificate — complete with his own honours listed after his name. By way of additional interest, Herbert Wadge used to individually sign a boy's Class Report — provided he was top of the class (Fig. 85).

The brief moment of fame to which I have referred was not confined to prize winners. Every CTS lad had his moment of glory. All boys returned to Speech Day to collect their Diploma, although I assume some lads obtained theirs *in absentia*. So each year the ranks of those receiving applause were swelled by the proud *Diplomates*. This is a good time to reflect that we had to work very hard to get a good Diploma. My mentioning this is a little contrivance to allow me to say that I was awarded the prize for being First in the Building Diploma Year in 1958 for my three years of study over the period 1954–57. For interest I have reproduced my Diploma in Fig. 64. I have often thought I should hang it on the wall like you see barbers display their certificates in their shops but I haven't yet got round to it!

Speeches

Speech Day would not have been Speech Day without its obligatory speeches. In this respect there were two highlights to our Victoria Hall proceedings. One was Herbert Wadge's annual review of the activities of the school and the achievements of the boys — not forgetting also, on occasions, those of some members of staff. It was a major achievement if Herbert Wadge could secure the services of a distinguished person to fulfil the role of Guest Speaker. I know he give much thought to this because he told me so personally one time as Speech Day was approaching. I recall two Guest Speakers. On one occasion this role was taken by the Vice Chancellor of the University of Sheffield, Dr. Whitaker FRS. As well as being a senior academic administrator he was a very distinguished mathematician who had been made a professor whilst still a young man. In fact he retired early from the university to devote his remaining energies to mathematics. His Speech-Day address was, I have to say, a rather dry affair. He discussed the role of engineering and architecture in society — the latter being of particular interest to myself. I will say here that the essential pre-requisite for a good speech is a joke — at least in some part of the proceedings. This is a cue to let me share with you a humorous observation I once heard at one of my daughter's speech days. The guest speaker promised he would be brief, if only for the reason of a remark he had once read on a hand drier which he had used when he was visiting a college at the University of Cambridge. A student had written: "For a short address from the Dean, press the red button"!

Another Guest Speaker at our Speech Day was the Director of Education — I believe Mr. Stanley Mofffat M.A. He did indeed make us all laugh with the following observation. First, you will recall that the Education Offices were next door to the CTS, indeed our premises were all one continuous building. The Director remarked that his office was located close to the party-wall separating him from our School Hall — in which, of course, we held our Speech Day rehearsals. Consequently he had plenty of opportunity to, as it were, listen-in on our preparations. Notwithstanding the thick walls, he observed at our Speech Day how audible our efforts over the preceding weeks had been! There was general laughter as he said all this which culminated in an outburst when he remarked: "I nearly didn't bother to come since I'd heard all the music so often"!

It is fitting that I should pay tribute here to another distinguished speaker on the occasion of, I believe, Speech Day in 1957. This time I am referring not to a Guest Speaker but to our very own former School Captain and now, even more distinguished, Lieutenant Colonel Ron Saville. I intend to refer to Ron's contribution to the life of the CTS later so I will confine my remarks here to the Speech Day in question. Ron had remarkable poise and eloquence for a schoolboy — qualities that were manifestly evident on the occasion of his address as our Guest Speaker at the OBA Annual Dinner in 1999. Clearly, Ron's aptitude for public speaking had come to Herbert Wadge's notice, doubtless in morning assembly when Ron made his various School Captain's announcements. So it was no surprise then that Herbert, with such talent so to speak by his side, should make use of Ron's abilities. At our Speech Day Ron made a rousing speech worthy of any School Captain or Head Boy in the land — and I include in that generalisation our famous public schools. He received a terrific ovation from the audience composed, as it was, of admiring mums and dads.

Let me turn now to a similar, though I have to say somewhat less exalted, circumstance involving myself. I have remarked previously, albeit briefly, that there was an occasion when I became involved, as School Captain, in the formal events of Speech Day and I gave an undertaking to explain how. Here's what happened. In their way the events in which I found myself embroiled could scarcely be more dramatic. I arrived at school on the morning of Speech Day (1959) to be received by a somewhat animated Mr. Davis. Dear Bill Davis always did have an air of agitation about him on 'official' occasions; doubtless this was a consequence of the fact that he was usually in the thick of all the preparations and organisation. I was not unduly perturbed therefore by Mr. Davis's excited demeanour until he called out: "Mr. Wadge wants to see you immediately"! Now I was by then a grown up lad and, as School Captain, I had already had a number of 'audiences' with the great man. Notwithstanding, the command to go and see Mr. Wadge still had the power to make you feel anxious — especially with morning assembly just about to begin. I mounted the stair to his room wondering what was about to unfold. I found Herbert in some agitation surrounded by sheets of paper which, from all the crossings out they bore, looked like the rough drafts of a speech. That indeed was precisely what they were as I was shortly to find out. "Now!", said Herbert in his typically forceful way — he always spoke to you as though you were standing across the opposite side of the street — "You may wish to sit down as you hear this — before you fall down"! These, I vouch, were Herbert's precise words. That's a great beginning I thought as I frantically searched my mind for some imagined wrong-doing of which I expected to be accused. "These things happen", continued Herbert, "and when they do we have to rise to the occasion"! But there was still no intimation of what this was all about. Then Herbert explained. An hour previously — it must have been about 8.00 a.m. — he had received a phone call from the Guest Speaker to say that he was indisposed and much regretted that he could not now give his planned address to the school. "We must therefore do something about it", said Herbert. I looked about the room to see who else was there and, finding ourselves alone, the realisation dawned that I was implicated. He explained that he had been able to find another Guest Speaker but in the short time available it was not possible for this person to write an elaborate speech The Guest Speaker would therefore confine himself to a few remarks of a general nature and would distribute the prizes. Consequently, Herbert explained, he would expand his own remarks by way of compensation. But, he added, something else was required in addition! The School Captain would have to speak himself on behalf of the school! I was given no opportunity to react. "Here", said Herbert, "is a draft of what I want you to say"! I took from the papers on his desk a neatly written text which he had just finished compiling. At that point the 8.45 a.m. morning bell sounded. Herbert explained that I was to accompany him into assembly, that he would explain to the school the unusual circumstances and that I would have the chance to rehearse my speech by reading it to the school from the text he had just provided.

In assembly, I had a few feverish minutes to read through the text provided for me as Herbert explained to assembly what had been taking place behind the scenes. Those of you who can recall these events may remember that at the end of 'my' speech I asked the school to rise and to give three cheers; this was all part of Herbert's plan — a typical piece of Herbert Wadge's theatricality. The events concerning the delivery of my speech later that evening were also not without a certain touch of dramatic theatricality as I will now explain.

In the evening, before leaving for the Victoria Hall, I read through my speech, laid the text safely aside, combed my hair, made sure that I looked presentable (!) and made my departure. Mr. Wadge had said to me, in the hasty morning briefing session, that I should take my seat on the platform just a few minutes before it was my time to speak. By way of interest he justified this on the grounds: "You now how it is — I sometimes have to speak confidentially to the guests and it's remarkable how much business gets done on these occasions". I suppose that's what we now call wheeling and dealing! As the evening progressed I duly took my seat on the platform, heart going boom boom, composed myself and waited for my cue. Herbert introduced me, I rose, stood by the lectern and gazed at the sea of pink faces before me — boys to the left, boys to the right and mums and dads up in the gallery. I reached into my pocket for my speech and — no! — dismay! — my pocket was empty! I had left my speech at home on the kitchen table!

I suppose basic instinct took over; I more or less knew my words by heart and, for the rest, I improvised. Half way through, when making some remark about the Guest Speaker — following the principle that flattery will get you everywhere — I inclined myself to look in his direction. To my amazement, the audience took it as a cue to burst into applause. The three cheers from the whole school went well — do any of you remember

them? — and my ordeal was over! And the moral of this tale? When you have to speak in public, concentrate on where you put your speech and don't spend so much time combing your hair!

Afterwards, I was invited to have a glass of sherry in a small room with the invited guests. I felt a bit like a fish out of water amidst the VIPs. Mr. Brennan came up to me and remarked that I had expanded my speech on the morning presentation. I explained the circumstances to him which prompted him to clasp his chest and make a humorous pretext of fainting. "Yes!", I said, "That's just how I felt"!

In Memoriam
Rose Russell
1914–1957

Allow me to make a few personal observations here about my mother. My justification for doing so is that the CTS Speech Day of 1957 was the last time she appeared in public.

My mother had been unwell from as early as the time of my entry to the CTS in January 1954. In 1957 she was eventually taken into hospital for a suspected heart condition — a leaking valve was diagnosed. It so happens that at this same period replacement heart valves were then being pioneered — the very operation had been shown on TV in the celebrated series *Your Life in their Hands*. Although very weak from a preliminary operation, the surgeon consented to allowing my mother to leave hospital to attend our Victoria Hall celebrations — an ambulance was arranged to take her. Naturally, she wanted to see me collect my prizes. I remember her saying, touchingly: "People won't mind, will they, if I don't stand to sing the National Anthem"? "I'm sure they won't", I replied reassuringly. After the ceremony she was taken straight back into hospital so I did not have the opportunity to discuss the evening's events — or anything else for that matter. The next day she had the operation but this proved too much for her weakened constitution and she succumbed.

At her funeral there were two poignant incidents which I would like to recall. As the funeral cortege progressed down Valley Road, it passed her place of work. Notwithstanding that it was a bitterly cold day, all the factory 'hands' were lining the pavement to pay their tribute. Then, as we made our way to the cemetery, we chanced upon some workmen who were wearing their cloth caps so typical of that period. As we passed them, they instinctively stopped their work and lifted their caps in respect — it was a simple but moving gesture.

My mother's passing impoverished my life greatly. From that time on I took meals with my aunt who generally also came round to clean the house and to care for me and my father. For my remaining time at the CTS family life was very austere. During the week I saw very little of my father who left the house in the morning, just after 6.00 a.m., and returned — physically exhausted — in time for his evening meal at my aunt's. As time passed by, we progressively circled about one another rather like two planets which are held together by mutual attraction but each simultaneously being destined to keep within its own orbit.

Although it is somewhat outside of my terms of reference, I will add here, by way of a happy ending, a further personal observation. My father eventually remarried and, in my maturity I acquired a brother — Adrian. He is now Dr. Adrian Russell B.Sc. Eng. (Hons. Class I) Ph.D. (University of Cambridge) and a distinguished Director of Astronomy at the Royal Observatory, Edinburgh.

But to return to my mother. I thank her for all she was and for all she did for me.

Requiescat In Pace

My Last Speech day

I have said already that boys who had left the CTS returned to collect their Diploma and various certificates — and some of us our prizes! It was my turn in February 1960 to enjoy this aspect of CTS Speech Day ritual. I was by then a student at the University of Sheffield studying architecture, so it was a simple matter for me to attend the evening celebrations. The 'swinging sixties' had not yet quite got under way but I had by then allowed my hair to grow well in advance of the CTS standard expectation of 'short back and sides'. Let me pause here and tell you why I say this. The previous year at the CTS, when I was School Captain, my inclination to the arts and Beethoven and Schubert and all that lot was already taking a hold on me and I started to grow my hair on the long side — like you do when you are romantically inclined! This proved too much for Herbert Wadge who summoned me to his presence one day and said — I should say thundered — "The School Captain must set a good example! Go and get your hair cut"! So I did. I had the regulation short back and sides — and I hope that those of you who were at the CTS at this period noticed and followed my good example! However, one year later, my hair was even longer and I remember thinking, defiantly, "Sod what Herbert Wadge thinks"! At the ceremony I took my seat amongst my contemporaries who had also returned to their *alma mater* to receive their awards. Sitting behind me were three of my old cronies, namely, John Mastin, David Moran and Peter Watts. One of them dishevelled my hair giving it a *bouffant* effect which I remember I couldn't smooth out. Now, you will recall the old Yorkshire saying of lads who need a hair cut: "When are you going to get a violin son"? I conformed somewhat to such an appearance when I duly mounted the platform to collect my prize. But it was my crowning glory — and I am not referring to my hair. Allow me to take leave of Speech Day 1960 by saying that I was awarded — and it is a source of great pride to me — the School Captain's Prize with which I purchased *A History of the World's Art*.

Holy Scripture
Religious Instruction

I have deliberately given this section two headings to reflect what I consider to be the principal means by which boys received guidance concerning questions of faith and religion during my time at the CTS. *Holy Scripture* was inculcated largely in morning assembly and *Religious Instruction* was assigned to a regular 'RI' period each week. I will now consider each of these separately.

Holy Scripture

Holy scripture was an integral part of morning assembly, indeed, in many ways it was the *raison d' être* for morning assembly insofar as we were a community of souls meeting each day to, as it were, transact our daily labours. It may be that it was, and doubtless remains, an integral aspect of a school's constitution under the Education Act to provide for guidance in spiritual matters as part of a school's larger obligations concerning the moral development of its pupils. Whatever the formal obligations may have been to take religious instruction seriously, there can be no doubt whatsoever of Herbert Wadge's personal commitment — no less than crusading zeal — to shepherd his CTS boys down the path of righteousness and virtue. It is, of course, open to question as to the extent to which we did actually accompany him down the path of righteousness and virtue! As a matter of fact I believe we did — we were too fearful to do otherwise! Herbert Wadge's desire to instil virtue within us emanated from his very being and morning assembly was his forum for disseminating his morally improving views — at whatever length was required!

I have already shown, perhaps a little light-heartedly, that within a five-year period at the CTS — shorter for some boys — we must have sung over a thousand hymns. Now, for each hymn we sang we also had a reading from Holy Scripture together with a 'sermon' from Herbert Wadge. You can do the calculations yourselves but they amount to a great many readings from the Bible and formal addresses from our headmaster!

Herbert was clearly seized not only by the moral grandeur of Holy Scripture but also by the resplendent style and language within which he considered it to be enshrined. This frequently disposed him to urge us to reflect not only upon the *message* inherent in, say a Lesson or Psalm, but also the use of particular words and stylistic constructions. He had favourite texts to which he would return time and time again. Of these, mention must be made of St. Paul's *Letter to the Corinthians*, Chapter 13. I believe this, of all scriptural texts, was closest to his heart. I must have heard him read it a dozen times, on each occasion listening to him elaborate on the meaning of the words *Faith*, *Hope* and *Charity*.

By way of recollecting the many texts we heard Herbert Wadge read in morning assembly, and as a token of respect for the man, I reproduce below the verses to which I have referred which I have come, through Herbert's influence, to cherish as did he:

> Though I speak with the tongues of men and of angels, and have not charity, I am become as sounding brass, or a tinkling cymbal.
> And though I have the gift of prophecy, and understand all mysteries, and all knowledge; and though I have all faith, so that I could remove mountains, and have not charity, I am nothing.
> And though I bestow all my goods to feed the poor, and though I give my body to be burned, and have not charity, it profiteth me nothing.
> Charity suffereth long, and is kind, charity envieth not; charity is not puffed up,
> Doth not behave itself unseemly, seeketh not her own, is not easily provoked, thinketh no evil;
> Rejoiceth not in iniquity, but rejoiceth in the truth;
> Beareth all things, believeth all things, hopeth all things, endureth all things.
> Charity never faileth: but whether there be prophecies, they shall fail; whether there be tongues, they shall cease;

whether there be knowledge, it shall vanish away.

For we know in part, and we prophesy in part.

But when that which is perfect is come, then that which is in part shall be done away.

When I was a child, I spake as a child, I thought as a child: but when I became a man, I put away childish things.

For now we see through a glass, darkly; but then face to face: now I know in part; but then shall I know even as also I am known.

And now abideth *faith, hope, charity*, these three; but the greatest of these is *charity*.

There was definitely something of the Jesuit about Herbert Wadge — and I intend that remark to be a compliment. His exhortations embraced the Jesuitical ideals of strict obedience, loyalty, compliance and the over-arching principle of respect for society — be it the small-scale society of the CTS or the larger one awaiting us when we left school. I believe the Jesuits *credo* went: "Give me a boy for seven years and I'll have him for life"! That could well have been Herbert Wadge's *mission statement* to use modern-day parlance. I mean by this, of course, that he sought to mould and fashion our character — with the support of his colleagues — to an imagined, but attainable, ideal. And by and large I think he succeeded!

There were occasions when Mr. McManus, in his capacity as deputy headmaster, used to take morning assembly. With all due respect, his endeavours were rather pallid in comparison to those of Herbert Wadge. He was sincere, yes, committed, yes — but he lacked Herbert's charisma. Herbert Wadge had few equals when he was in full voice on the podium before his assembled school.

Religious Instruction

We received our formal induction into matters spiritual through a weekly period of religious instruction — 'RI'. The member of staff I most associate with these classes was dear Alf Simpson. Now, what am I to say of his RI classes without being disrespectful to his memory? He was sincere, yes. He was punctiliously sincere, yes. He was reverentially and punctiliously sincere, yes. He was totally out of control, yes — and this of course was the problem. Levity, impiety and class disorder undermined his good intentions. It fills me with angst to think how much we ragged this good and kindly man who had so much to offer. Alf's problem was that his trusting nature allowed him to be easily led — down the garden path, as it were, to perdition. Let me illustrate with a typical example. One morning Herbert Wadge somewhat startled the assembled masses by reading the text from the Bible which tells of the incautious virgins who went forth into the darkness with insufficient oil in their lamps. It was very brave of Herbert to speak of virgins before so many pubescent, and impressionable lads. But that was typical of the man — uncompromising, in this instance, to the last drop of virgin's oil. Now, on the morning in question, Alf Simpson's RI lesson resumed where Herbert's 'sermon' had left off. Inevitably, some wit — to be more accurate an organised chorus of wits — set about dear innocent and unsuspecting Alf and asked him: "Sir, what's a virgin"? At this, Alf looked perplexed. He was clearly torn between two conflicting emotions. His intuition was to follow his kindly nature and to give a serious reply to the question; his teacher's instinct was to recognise that some wayward lads were simply trying to tease him. Alf's discomfort was of course our loss. In making a response he just got redder

and redder and mild chaos prevailed which gave little or no opportunity for him to examine and discuss the metaphorical imagery implicit in Herbert Wadge's morning lesson.

Slowly, but perceptibly — over time, things did improve in our RI lessons. I suppose we grew older, became more respectful and learned how to behave — to paraphrase *Corinthian's Chapter 13*: "As we became young men we did learn to put away with foolish things". Indeed as we entered what would be called the Sixth Form in other schools — A2Y and A3 at the CTS — there were moments when the class discussions in our RI lessons touched upon the central issues of the human condition — the meaning of life, the concept of the soul, immortality, the relevance of Christian worship and so on. Our school community consisted of a heterogeneous mix of 'believers', 'putative agnostics' and the inevitable band of 'don't knows'. Consequently, some boys were able to bring to our class-discussions the orthodoxy of their church beliefs, strengthened by regular church attendance — a few lads I knew were choir boys (Geoff Gray) and one was a church organist (David Dickson); other lads came from homes where their parents (including my own) never set foot in church unless to attend a wedding or a funeral; and some lads were genuine waverers in search of a belief — of these I believe at least one CTS lad did eventually take Holy Orders. So, as far as our religious inclinations were concerned, we were a typical heterogeneous group of mortals.

For a period our RI lessons were taken by Mr. Brennan. His approach was concentrated and serious. I recall how on one occasion a whole lesson was devoted to the question of the place of the church in society. On other occasions Mr. Brennan made us ponder such issues as the relevance of Christian teaching in contemporary society, the nature of miracles and their modern-day interpretation, the meaning of faith and the relationship between religion and science in the modern world. It was sometimes heavy going and he was not satisfied with simple answers; he made us think and debate amongst ourselves.

I recall one lesson in particular when he invited us to consider the concept of Eternity. He took as his starting point a moving line in Rupert Brook's poem *The Soldier* — which the reader will recall I said the whole school was required to learn by heart. The line in question was — "A pulse in the eternal mind …". "Let us try to consider Eternity" said Mr. Brennan, and he went over to the blackboard and drew a long straight horizontal line. On it he drew a dot and then remarked: "Let the dot represent the time scale of the entirety of human existence and suppose that the chalk line extends indefinitely in both directions and represents time outside of human existence". We stared in contemplation of the model he was offering us of Eternity. It had secured our attention and we had a good discussion on the fleeting nature of human existence within the great scheme of things.

Mr. Brennan's classes were towards the end of my time at the CTS and they prompted me to take religion quite seriously — although privately and without reference to, or even consultation with, close friends. I don't mean to suggest that 'I got religion' as the rather disrespectful expression puts it. But I did make a conscientious effort to find out more about religion and the basic tenets of Christian faith. And where better to hear these issues addressed than by going to listen to the

Bishop of Sheffield on Sunday evening? So it was to the Cathedral that I journeyed for several weeks in my search for enlightenment. I attended several evening services and listened with great care to what the Bishop had to say. I was impressed by his eloquence and imagery but found it difficult to embrace the basic tenets of the Christian faith. In particular I found it difficult to accept the proposition that we are each of us possessed of a soul which is a non-material substance that is the source of the body's life and that the origin of that life is God. I reasoned that it must follow that the person who recognises that his psyche and personality have their origin in the soul and in God must have an obligation to God. But I gradually worked out a position for myself whereby I would seek to exercise the rights of my personality independently of God but embracing what I will call the 'social contract' which is implicit in religious faith, namely, to be good and, within my powers, to do unto others as I would have them do unto myself. Forty years later my position remains largely unchanged. I subscribe to the view that man is by nature good rather than evil, that he is amenable to the guidance of reason and inclined to be humane and, as an educator, I would add that mans' condition is improved through knowledge, learning and understanding — but founded on reason and independent of miracles and personal communing in the form of prayer. So much for my personal views.

It is fitting that I should close this section with an additional reference to Herbert Wadge who was in so many ways, through his morning services, our mentor and guide on spiritual matters. As School Captain I had an opportunity each morning, in assembly, to closely observe his working methods — at least those which he practised at the lectern. For his daily reading from Holy Scripture he of course made use of the Bible; but there were occasions when he had recourse to a passage of prose which he considered memorable for its high moral tone and the style of its language — Herbert was a relentless educator. This leads me to recall a reading from a morning service in late December of 1958; Christmas was approaching and likewise the New Year. Herbert remarked how he had been moved some years previously by the words he had heard read over the radio by the late King George VI. I have tracked these down and have learned they were broadcast to the nation at Christmas in 1939 — which of course was a troubled period. I find the words very moving and they seem to me to embody the essence of trust that is implicit in Christian faith — in which I believe Herbert Wadge had such an unflinching conviction. Here they are:

And I said to the man who stood at the gate of the year: Give me light that I may tread safely into the unknown; and he replied: "Go out into the darkness and put your hand into the hand of God. That shall be for you better than light and safer than a known way".

The Literary and Scientific Society

The majestically named *Literary and Scientific Society* was a creation of Herbert Wadge — Fig. 86. It is my recollection that he first gave intimation of his wish that the CTS should be enriched by such an august body one morning assembly in the Autumn Term of 1958. I have a particular reason for remembering this circumstance; I had just taken up my duties as School Captain and the moment I heard Herbert give expression to his wishes a little voice inside me said: "Terence, this sounds like more work is coming your way" — and I was right! But more of that in a moment; for the present I will say a few words as to how the society came about and its general aims in the life and work of the CTS.

As I have just remarked, Herbert Wadge expressed his desire to see a society created which would in effect be a debating society. That he should want to have such a society is typical of his pedagogical enthusiasm by means of which his lads would improve their minds. He suggested various possible names for this fledgling creation — I believe *The Debating Society* was one of them but eventually he settled on the title which heads this section of my narrative. His intention was to choose a name which embraced both the arts and sciences — what C.P. Snow, a few years later, was to characterise as *The Two Cultures*. I have to say that in choosing the title that he did, I thought Herbert was suffering from a mild form of delusions of grandeur. I had by then gained some experience of organising school debates and had come to the rather bleak conclusion that most lads were happiest when talking about football or their latest girlfriend. So I felt instinctively that getting them to discourse on matters literary and scientific was going to be uphill work — and again I was right.

With the idea of a society established it fell initially to Mr. Bee to take the concept forward. This probably came about through Mr. Bees custodianship of his own series of after-school debates to which I have already made reference. I have also previously remarked that I helped Mr. Bee with the arrangements for his talks and so it came as no surprise to me that he should call me into his room one day and ask if I would be the Chairman of the new society — and arrange a list of speakers and suitable topics! In short, I had the job of getting the new venture started. My first action was to form a committee — not very original but I saw this as a way of distributing the work. The members of the committee are listed in Fig. 87. I held a number of informal meetings with several boys and, to my pleasant surprise, some came forward with constructive suggestions — it would serve no useful purpose for me to make reference to the non-constructive suggestions I also received! It soon became obvious to me that most potential contributors wished to participate as part of a group rather than to shoulder the full responsibility of an entire lecture. As a consequence the programme of the society fell under three headings: contributions from *Sections* which consisted of *Chemistry*, *History* and *Geography*; group events in the form of *Debates*; and individual Lectures. To legitimise all this I convened a meeting of several members of staff and students; this was held one evening in the Firth Building. We evolved an agenda and a list of contributors; these are shown in Figs 88 & 89. The little booklet from which this information is derived was designed by myself; you will see that the cover makes prominent use of one of the versions of the school badge. I believe the annual membership fee was one shilling — to help to defray the costs of publication.

The reader will see from the Christmas Term programme that the first two lectures were given by the so-called *Chemistry Section* of the new society. In fact they were contributed by Mr. Gregory. His presentations were a *tour de force* of the art of the lecturer. They were given in the school hall where he had assembled an array of equipment all of which was concerned with some aspect or other of the science of clay-pigeon shooting. I have previously remarked that Mr. Gregory was at this period in his life the National Clay Pigeon Champion — a remarkable achievement. The reader will also recall that I have commented that the stocks of his two guns were specially made for him from matching pieces of walnut that had been carefully shaped to his requirements by Mr. Hunter. These were on display and, moreover, we were allowed to pick them up and handle them. Needless to say they were unloaded!

A high point of Mr. Gregory's lectures was a simulation of the flight of a pigeon. This was achieved by means of an imitation bird which was suspended from an inclined length of fishing line. The line was attached to a point high up in the school balcony and descended to a few feet above the floor of the hall. At a signal from one of Mr. Gregory's helpers, a boy in the balcony released the imitation bird so that it descended down the fishing line — as though in flight. As this happened, Mr. Gregory demonstrated how he could track the flight of the bird finally discharging his gun at the right moment. He explained that the science of such shooting involved a knowledge of the principle of relative velocity; to be more precise, he explained how it was necessary to aim not *at* the moving target but some distance *ahead* of it. This took allowance for the speed of the bird and the time taken for the shot to reach its target. He then went on to talk about complicating factors such as wind speed and direction. It was a most impressive lecture demonstration by a very accomplished lecturer.

A few weeks later it was my turn! To be more precise, my lecture was scheduled to be the first of the Easter Term on 6 January 1959. I was somewhat nervous about giving a lecture — it was the first time I had ever done such a thing — but, as Chairman of the new society, I felt under an obligation to lead by example as it were. In the preliminary meetings we had held before creating the *Literary and Scientific Society*, we had discussed the kind of contributions that speakers might make. I now turned these over in my mind; music was my abiding enthusiasm — not, surprisingly, architecture — and so this became my chosen subject. But what aspect of music should I choose to talk about? I resolved to go along to have a chat with Mr. Hughes and seek his advice. I remember he asked me how long I planned to speak; "About three hours" I replied — at which he nearly fainted! Mr. Hughes tactfully explained that the art of lecturing is to captivate the listener — not to see how long you can go on talking! Somewhat chastened, I reduced the scale of my lecture plan; I would make a survey of the Romantic Period of music with special reference to the First Viennese School; in

short, I would say why I liked Mozart, Beethoven and Schubert — complete with musical illustrations.

I did not have all the records that I needed for my musical illustrations so I had to borrow some. I discovered that the Education Department had an Audio-Visual Unit from which such things as LPs could be loaned. That was not the only thing I discovered; working in the shop was a very pretty girl — so I contrived to visit the shop as many times as I could — each time creating a pretext that I would have to make a return journey. By this means I eventually secured the records I required — but, sadly, not the reciprocal feelings from the pretty girl behind the counter!

The night of my lecture duly came and I made my way in good time to the school hall to complete my preparations. Then I waited for the audience to turn up — and I waited — and waited. After about a quarter of an hour I had the grand total sitting before me of one person — Mr. Gregory. He looked at me sympathetically and said: "I'm very sorry but these things do happen sometimes". I appreciated his tact but it was obvious to me that not many other CTS lads shared my enthusiasm for the First Viennese School of the Romantic Period of classical music.

Undeterred, I rescheduled my talk for another evening. I should add that at this period I was the School Captain and it was my responsibility to announce the forthcoming meetings of the Society to the school in morning assembly. I therefore had the pleasure of introducing my own lecture — which I did with renewed enthusiasm. I offered would-be participants the prospect of hearing some lovely music. My power of persuasion worked; the second time round I had a good audience which included Messrs Gregory, Hughes, Brennan and Hill. It was something of an ordeal giving a lecture with four teachers listening intently — all of them, it so happens, very musical. But all went well. Indeed, at the end of my talk — which lasted well over two hours — two lads came up to me to note the details of some of the music I had played. So I went home feeling I had done my bit for musical appreciation at the CTS.

The following day two things related to my lecture occurred. By chance I met Mr. Brennan who paid me a compliment saying: "Why don't you take up lecturing Russell?". That was rather prophetic since it was in fact the career path I eventually followed. My second encounter was with Mr. Wadge; morning assembly was over and he had dismissed school but had stayed behind on the podium to talk to me. He did this from time to time to discuss school business, insofar as it affected the prefects and the general running of the school. He then remarked that he was looking forward to hearing my lecture — "When is it?", he asked. "Last night", I replied! Herbert first looked dismayed and then he reproached me: "But I was looking forward to that particular talk!", he remonstrated. I explained that I had made an announcement about the forthcoming event in morning assembly; this merely stirred Herbert's passion to new levels. He bellowed: "But my mind is very pre-occupied with many things during assembly". I saw his point and henceforth I sent him written personal notification of all the scheduled lectures. However, as far as I can remember, I don't recall Herbert Wadge ever attending any of the lectures of the *Literary and Scientific Society*.

A lecture in the series I do remember concerned budgerigars. Now, in my simple innocence, I had thought that all there was to the care of a budgerigar was that you bought one, put it in a cage, gave it some seed and water at daily intervals and kept it happy by saying things like: "Who's a pretty boy then?". But the lad who gave this lecture disabused his audience of all such simple notions. He told us how they get sick — something to do with distemper, how they reproduce — that was the best bit of the lecture; and it was explained if you work at it for about ten years you might breed a bird worth showing at exhibitions. It was all very interesting but I had the feeling that most lads left the talk resolved to confine their attentions to birds of a somewhat different kind.

My final recollection of the *Literary and Scientific Society* concerns Richard Charles Prime who was at this period School Vice Captain. Charlie, as we knew him, was an able pupil with a particular aptitude for science. He was considering nuclear engineering as a future career and he therefore took this as the theme for his lecture. Nuclear engineering was still in its early stages of development at this time (1959) and its proponents held out untold benefits for the generation of electrical power by this means. Indeed, I recall a contemporaneous TV documentary programme in which the speaker felt so enthusiastic about the new technology that he prophesied electricity would one day be so cheap that it would not be worth the bother and expense of installing meters in our homes! In his lecture, Charlie Prime did not allow himself to get quite so carried away, but he did give a most articulate and informed exposition of the subject. I have two reasons for recalling this particular lecture. The first is that I was the projectionist — it being an illustrated lecture. The illustrations were in the form of a continuous role of filmstrip and it was my job to co-ordinate the required image with the words of the lecturer. We had a screen set up in the assembly hall and attracted an audience of about forty boys. My second reason for recalling the lecture is that I collected the filmstrip for Charlie from the Education Department's Audio Visual Unit which I have previously mentioned. I thereby got to see the pretty girl, to whom I have also referred, one more time!

I have said that I do not recall Herbert Wadge attending any of the meetings of the *Literary and Scientific Society* but, as I have also previously remarked, it owed its existence to his personal energy and enthusiasm. I have no idea for how long the society flourished — I suspect it was a short-lived experiment. But it certainly gave me, and my fellow office-bearers, valuable experience of using our power of persuasion to get things done and to motivate others to make their contribution. It was hard work but lots of fun.

The House System

Houses are an integral aspect of the social structure of most schools. They contribute to a sense of communality and belonging and, of course, they foster the spirit of competition amongst the pupils. In addition, the names chosen for houses perpetuate the reputations and achievements of great men and women — presumably in the hope of inspiring successive generations of pupils to emulate their illustrious forbears. They also give selected individuals the opportunity to act as office bearers, typically in the roles of House Captain and Vice Captain, and enable others to shine and make their mark through achievement in sport and athletics.

Doubtless the origins of the house system can be traced back to the great public schools of the nineteenth century — or even earlier. Be this as it may, most of us will have come through our school days via the house system. In my own case I recall the names of the houses at Carfield Junior School as being called Chantrey, Eliot, Montgomery and Ruskin. I was a member of the latter house whose 'colour' was yellow — colours were, and doubtless remain, an indispensable means of designating houses. At Anns Road Secondary School I was a member of Nelson House. At the CTS I was a proud member of Telford House (blue), the other houses being, of course, Bessemer (green), Faraday (red) and Stephenson (yellow).

As I recall it, house meetings at the CTS were held each month. They provided an opportunity for all the members of a particular house, pupils and members of staff, to meet and to transact the relevant business. On these monthly occasions morning assembly was curtailed and we made our way to our various house locations. Telford House met in Mr. Hedley's drawing office in Bow Building, which was appropriate since he was Telford House Master. If my memory serves me correctly other CTS Telford House staff members included Messrs Frow, Hunter and King. Mr. Davies was, I believe, head of Stephenson House. It was the responsibility of the House Master, amongst other things, to regulate the conduct of his house and to lead morning prayers. An integral part of Telford House proceedings were exhortations from Mr. Hedley to do our best to look neat and tidy — some hope! Shoe inspections were occasionally held, the announcement of which inevitably precipitated much frantic furtive rubbing of the top of one's shoe against the back of a trouser leg in an attempt to induce an instant shoe-shine. Sam Hedley had, of course, seen it all before and would command everyone to stand still by way of subverting this practice. I also remember Mr. Hedley urging us to keep a nice crease in our grey-flannel trousers. This was not easy since the flannel did not retain a sharp crease like modern-day materials — so most of us went about wearing trousers that resembled a pair of old sand bags.

It was from Mr. Hedley that I first learned about the merit system for rewarding good work — and the de-merit system for punishment. Merits, and de-merits, were recorded in a class book on a daily basis and were then audited, first for the week and then for the month. By this means the cumulative totals were augmented and thereby contributed to the 'points' awarded to a particular house. points were also awarded in recognition of achievement in sport and athletics. I remember being the cause of some consternation during my First Year one morning in house assembly when it was revealed that I had been awarded a grand total of thirty merits for the month concerned. Mr. Hedley, on hearing this news, first looked perplexed and then remarked: "It sounds to me as though somebody's been rather generous". On hearing this Mr. Hunter, who was seated nearby, rose to his feet and commented: "Russell is a hard working boy". Well, I wasn't going to argue with that and I enjoyed my fifteen seconds of fame — Mr. Hedley, by now convinced that I had earned my merits, beamed proudly.

It will be recalled how the sum totals of all the points achieved by individual boys and teams were added up at the end of the Summer Term to give a final total for each house. The culmination of all this was the ritual of determining which house was the 'top' for that particular academic year. The ceremony was reserved for a special assembly held in the afternoon just before going home time. Herbert Wadge, after concluding his part of the proceedings, gave way to Mr. Davies who mounted the small podium at the front of the hall. Above the podium, fixed high on the wall for all to see, was a wooden display frame containing four columns of colours representative of the four houses — red, yellow, blue and green. The columns, which were in the form of continuous canvas bands, could be adjusted by rollers and it was Mr. Davies's responsibility to perform this task. To reach the frame, he had to stand on the wooden seats normally reserved for the School Captain and Vice Captain. Mr. Davies came equipped with a piece of paper, bearing the 'scores' for each house, which he consulted from his elevated position. He would first reduce the four columns to zero and then elevate each in turn to a level representing a particular house's achievement. As each coloured column rose, so did the chorus of approval of the various members of each house — to be replaced by groans and jeers if their house was overtaken. His exercise in showmanship complete, Mr. Davies would carefully step down from his seat and the podium and give one of his big smiles. This was sufficient to promote a round of thunderous applause from the boys of the successful house which was endorsed, perhaps a little grudgingly, by the members of the other three houses.

The formal business of house meetings usually commenced with a reading from Holy Scripture by the House Captain or House Vice Captain — at least that is how my own house, Telford, conducted these occasions. I was the House Vice Captain for my last year at school and had the responsibility of selecting the text and of reading it to the gathering of boys and staff. Let me insert here that Mr. Hedley asked my if I wanted to be the House Captain. I explained to him that since I was already the School Captain, I thought the honour of being House Captain should be bestowed upon my School Vice Captain Charlie Prime — a nice example of youthful chivalry! The more serious point to be made here is that for the academic year 1958–59, Telford House had the honour — if that is how it may be described — of conferring both the School Captain and Vice Captain from its ranks.

One month I thought I would be inventive and I compiled my required text from selected passages of the words to Handel's *Messiah* which, you may remember, were originally compiled for Handel by the clergyman Charles Jennins. This was somewhat novel and it went rather well since the lads were familiar with the words. Afterwards Mr. King came up to me and paid me a compliment; he then took me aside and offered me a few points of advice concerning speaking in public. He spoke to me about voice projection and of the importance of articulating certain words to add clarity. He concluded by saying: "I know you won't mind me telling you these things. I've been impressed by your readings in morning assembly and thought you would appreciate a word or two of advice". I certainly did not mind and considered Mr. King's guidance as being welcome and kindly.

Telford House meetings were always congenial and friendly even though Sam Hedley did sometimes inject into the proceedings brief moments of his own special blend of sergeant-major like authority, as when haranguing us to get our hair cut or to endeavour to get us to look more neat and tidy! I recall these meetings

with affection and I assume that other CTS lads feel similarly inclined towards their own house rituals and proceedings.

Physical Training

Physical Training, better known as 'PT', was a weekly event that most of us endured rather than enjoyed. It must be said however that some boys demonstrated a natural affinity for physical exercise and clearly enjoyed themselves — I was not one of them.

I imagine PT was introduced to the school curriculum by educational hygienists or health experts who believed in the Victorian precept — "If it hurts it's good for you". There was certainly a stoical aspect to PT. The discomfort commenced by our being crowded into the basement changing room where we removed our everyday clothes to be substituted by those wonderful blue flannel navy shorts — which were about as sexy as a hot-water bottle cover. On a hot day the sweat-charged changing room could feel like the Black Hole of Calcutta. When clothes-changing was over we each had to cram our clothes into a small metal locker. Anyone who wore a wrist watch removed it and gave it to the teacher — Mr. Robert Howell — for safe keeping. By the time he had collected in all our watches his desk resembled a jeweller's window display.

When arrayed in our shorts we made an orderly dash up the stairs into the school hall. On cold mornings goose pimples visibly rose from our shivering pink torsos. Mr. Howell would invariably call out: "Running on the spot — begin". And so we shuffled somewhat half-heartedly through our warm-up exercise — Mr. Howell, clad professionally in his green track suit, gave a much more convincing display of jogging. It occurs to me that Mr. Howell must, by the very nature of his job, have been the fittest teacher in the whole school — if not in Sheffield.

After some vocal exhortation, and blowing on his whistle, Mr. Howell would contrive to arrange us in a long line as a necessary preliminary to receiving his instructions as to how we were next to proceed. Sometimes these exhortations took the following form: "Chin up, shoulders back, stand upright, tummies in, breath deeply — come along, try harder!". To the onlooker we must have presented a remarkable spectacle — the flower of Sheffield's youth as it were on the threshold of manhood. After some time a curious and pernicious physiological effect would manifest itself. I refer to the desire we all felt to want to scratch our shoulders. This must have been something to do with the air reacting with our skin. The desire for relief was almost irresistible and each of us would surreptitiously cross our arms in an endeavour to rub our shoulders or to scratch away at our arm pits. This would invariably prompt Mr. Howell to snap: "Stop that — you look just like a bunch of monkeys"! And, come to think of it, I suppose we did.

The resemblance to a group of primates was all the more evident when we attempted to hang from the parallel bars that lined the walls of the hall. In this context, who can remember 'chin-ups'? You had to clasp a high wall bar and then attempt to lift your body weight until your chin was level with the bar you were clasping. It was a killer of an exercise. And that was only the start of the torment; the real challenge was to achieve half a dozen chin-ups or perhaps a dozen! I recall some lads, especially those of a lighter build, could indeed perform this feat — and more. Mr. Howell could do chin-ups with no apparent effort, going up and down like a coiled spring. But then, as I have remarked, he was a very fit man.

The wall bars were the only fixed pieces of PT equipment in the school hall. In this respect the facilities for PT at the CTS were somewhat inadequate, certainly compared with those to be found in any other typical school gymnasium. Nevertheless we did have some equipment. This was stored in a small room that was mid-way along the wall on the Leopold Street side of the school hall. By means of much ingenuity this confined space accommodated several long wooden benches, a leather clad 'horse' on wooden legs, fibre mats, a number of medicine balls, several dozen wooden hoops — of large and small diameters, and doubtless other things I have long forgotten. All these items had to retrieved from the store which required more exhortations from Mr. Howell and military-like discipline from teams of boys.

Our physical exercises were usually undertaken with the class organised in parallel rows of boys. When the rows were suitably arranged Mr. Howell would demonstrate the exercise he wanted us to perform. Mr. Howell's demonstrations were always a model of agile movement and lithe animation. Springing up on the tips of his toes he would show us what he required with supple and pliant physical gestures. Then it was our turn! Thirty or so boys would attempt to reproduce the exercise we had just observed. With arms and legs flailing we galvanised ourselves into more or less co-ordinated action. Sometimes Mr. Howell would maintain his demonstration to keep the rhythm of the class; on other occasions he would stand and watch our endeavours, interpolating suitable remarks of the kind: "Chin up; Hands above your head; Spring up higher" — and so on. A blast on his whistle would bring the exercise to a close and would herald the start of some new activity.

A competitive element sometimes featured in our PT classes in which we were organised into teams, occasionally wearing house colours — in the form of cloth bands circled over one shoulder. Typically we would leap frog over one another's back or dart between the legs of the boy standing in front. The winning team was the one which completed the sequence of movements in the shortest time. I recall how we took all this very seriously — and we did not take too kindly to any boy who faltered and thereby became the cause of one's team losing.

My personal achievements in physical training were unremarkable. But I did have one success — I eventually learned to do the handstand against the wallbars. I was very proud of this; in fact I was so proud of my achievement that one sunny day, about twenty-five years ago, I gave a demonstration of my athletic abilities to my children on our patio terrace. I have to say the shock to my nervous system was so great I have never attempted the exercise since — from now on I live by the precept that 'discretion is the better part of valour'! But like so many other aspects of life and work at the CTS, I would not now be without my fond memories of all that organised physical activity, of the sound of Mr. Howell's whistle, of his exhortations to do this or that, of the sounds of our hands and feet rhythmically beating out the tempo of our exercises — and even the sweaty atmosphere of the changing room! Happy days!

Sport and Athletics

Being situated on an urban site in the centre of Sheffield was a distinct setback for the CTS when it came to enjoying sport and athletics — for the obvious reason that there was no playing field or sports ground in the immediate proximity. Even the school's limited playground scarcely allowed for more than the occasional improvised game of football — played with a tennis ball! Cricket was completely out of the question in such a built-up area overlooked by so many windows. By way of a digression, this prompts me to recall how, after a snowfall, Herbert Wadge would allow snowballing to take place — after all boys will be boys — until he received news of the first broken window. The message then went round the school that all such 'winter sports' should cease forthwith!

So as far as field sports were concerned we had to journey out into the countryside. This was by no means a hardship. Each Wednesday afternoon, the day set aside for sports, two double-decker buses would arrive to transport two or three classes of boys out to the leafy suburbs and beyond to the extensive playing fields near Ringinglow. To be honest, I enjoyed these bus journeys more than the ensuing sports! You could sit lazily next to a friend and enjoy a good chat. In particular I recall how the bus would go up West Street past the University of Sheffield Union Building called Graves Hall. This, you may remember, had a garden outside its French windows which was frequented during the summer months by the students — especially the young women from the Arts Faculty! So we had a brief moment to catch a glimpse of the 'talent' as the bus went by. Let me add that a few years later, when I was by then a student myself, I spent many a happy lunch time at the Union — frequently going out into the garden — to enjoy the 'scenery'!

The playing fields at Ringinglow were well worth all the effort we had to make to get there. Several pitches provided ample scope for teams to play football and there was an extensive cricket ground. These were served by good, if somewhat Spartan, changing rooms. It could certainly be very Spartan in winter with several inches of snow lying on the ground and only the door to the changing room to provide protection from the cold — the rooms being unheated! The facilities did however include hot showers which were fine, for those who did not mind — how shall I put it — bathing in a state of nature; some boys were sensitive about such things.

I do recall how one games afternoon in my First Year — it would be the early spring of 1955 — the snow had fallen heavily making any games impossible. To their great credit the teachers hit on the idea of taking us all for a walk along the upper reaches of the river valley. It was idyllic. The sun shone brightly and the snow had drifted several feet deep in parts tempting lads to test the precise depth with their wellies. And of course the snowballs rained back and forth between different groups of boys like canon balls — despite much whistle blowing by the teachers in charge. In fact the teachers had the discretion to keep their heads out of the way or they could well have been the subject of some spirited target practice!

When the weather was particularly bad, by which I mean if it was raining heavily, games were cancelled and we had to stay behind in school. This made us all feel disgruntled, especially those lads who were really proficient at sport and who looked forward to having a good game. On these occasions there was nothing to do but to make the best of it. This usually took the form of having extra lessons from Mr. Howell. His favourite subject on these occasions was hygiene — he must have thought we were an odoriferous lot and were in need of some personal guidance. This observation calls to mind the contemporaneous advertisement for *Lifeboy Toilet Soap* — perhaps you will remember it. It depicted a forlorn looking chap who never got any girlfriends, until one day his best friend whispered to him — 'BO'! After which he started to use the magic soap and thereby attracted lots of attention from the fair sex. I must say it never worked like that for me! But Mr. Howell did his best to encourage us how to keep neat and tidy, how to trim our nails and to brush our teeth. Another theme for his wet-day lessons was the finer points of football — on-side, off-side, what constituted a penalty and so on. When he had exhausted this subject he would endeavour to explain the names of the fielding positions in cricket. I found these more baffling than algebra! I recall once being asked by an American to explain the rules of cricket; I only succeeded by adding to his confusion.

I never excelled at sport but I do recall once scoring a goal for Telford House — it made my day. Boys who had a natural gift for games soon established themselves as captains of their teams. For those who were not proficient at football or cricket an alternative was offered, in my time at the CTS, in the form of cross-country running. This did not require skill, merely stamina and a sense of application. Several of us took to this with some enthusiasm. This alternative did, I must confess, offer some scope for skiving. Notwithstanding, I recall how one afternoon I ran the distance to the so-called *Round House* and back — I am referring here to that curious octagonal building some miles from the CTS playing fields. I did this all alone, so there is no one to verify my achievement. On the way back, which was by means of a rough path known as the *Sheep Track*, I recall pausing for breath — like you do when you are knackered — and I discovered an amazing sight. As I stood gasping for breath there before me, lying on the ground, was a pile of contraceptives! Was this the scene of some 'orgy' I wonder? If you have any information about this, send your answers to me please because I am still curious — even after all these years!

The circumstance to which I have just referred calls to mind another rather extraordinary incident which may well be locked away in the minds of one or two readers who can cast their mind back to a Wednesday afternoon in the early summer of 1958. We had finished our games, had changed back into school uniform and were seated on the bus ready to be taken back to school. It was a double-decker as usual and I was seated upstairs. I was one of the last to get on board and I immediately detected a certain air of something unusual having happened — as when a group of boys are trying to conceal something but give the game away by casting knowing looks at one another. Well, innocent of what was going on, I took my seat and a few moments later a commotion started up. Mr. Woolhouse could be heard downstairs calling out, in an agitated voice: "They're disgusting! Throw them away! Has anybody here got any?". Then he came upstairs, visibly shaken and ashen white — as I had never seen him before — and he

repeated his remarks. All the boys around me shook their heads innocently and replied: "No Sir". Mr. Woolhouse, trusting as always, appeared to accept these responses and went down below still audibly remonstrating — "Disgusting!". When the bus eventually got under way I discovered what had been the cause of all the commotion. It appears the bus had parked near to where someone had disposed of a pile of pornographic magazines which the first boys to get on the bus had discovered — and had duly gathered up! I never did discover any more about this incident but if there is any one out there reading this who recalls the circumstances I would be interested to learn more — for strictly historical reasons of course!

I owe it to the memory of Mr. Woolhouse to follow that particular story with some rather more edifying observations. He was, first and foremost, a kindly man; secondly he was a fine sportsman. On the football pitch and cricket ground he was in his natural element; he became animated and self-confident in ways which revealed his natural aptitude for sport. His somewhat bow-legged swagger seemed to enhance his capacity to swerve and dribble a football past his opponent. At cricket I recall him giving a demonstration to some boys in the handling of a bat to improve their stroke play; it was a consummately professional demonstration. I also recall a wet-afternoon lesson with Mr. Woolhouse to which he devoted most of the time telling us about the finer points of cricket equipment, such as what to look for in a good bat — the grain of the wood, how the handle should be sprung and so on. Then the theme turned to physical protection, and in particular the nether regions — protective head gear was unknown in those days. Now this is a delicate subject and requires some self confidence — I would not myself relish the idea of standing up in front of a class of boys to tell them how to protect their 'sphericals' when playing a game of cricket. "Don't be embarrassed", reassured Mr. Woolhouse, "its all perfectly natural". Then he added: "If you go into a sports shop and you find it's a young woman assistant, just go ahead and ask for a *protector*". We were still trying to grasp this concept when some wit in the class chirped up and asked: "Sir, do they come in different sizes?". We all fell about laughing — including Mr. Woolhouse. But he was not to be outdone; the incident prompted him to tell us a story about a lad who was by all accounts remarkable for his sense of humour — of the kind with which I am presently concerned. This is how the story went. "One day", said Mr. Woolhouse, "I was refereeing a football match when a lad got the full impact of the ball between his legs and promptly fell to the ground in agony. A few moments later a voice called out — 'Don't rub em, count em' ". And once more we all fell about laughing — Mr. Woolhouse included

A great deal of sport took place each weekend when, depending upon the season, the CTS football and cricket teams would pit themselves against those of other schools. The results of these encounters would be announced the following Monday morning. I never took part in any of these events but I do seem to recall that our lads frequently acquitted themselves rather well. Honesty requires me to add, however, that there was an exception to his generalisation; I refer to the school's achievements in rugby. I have recorded earlier that Mr. Alfred Bunn was appointed to the CTS in September 1956 and he brought with him an enthusiasm for rugby. I should add that this game was not played at the CTS at this period but, undeterred, Mr. Bunn set about building up a team with the zeal of an army recruiting officer. By the shear force of his personality he eventually got enough stalwarts together to form a team. I have to say that I admired their courage — there not being much else to admire if I may be forgiven for saying so. Whether it was through lack of experience or the physical size of our team, things always seemed to conspire against us. This was evident when Mr. Bunn, reporting on the outcome of a match would remark, in a demeanour normally reserved for announcing casualties following a military conflict: "The CTS put up a good fight; the outcome was — CTS '5', opponents '250' "! I may have exaggerated somewhat but that is what it felt like. Nonetheless, Mr. Bunn bore each setback with commendable fortitude and always offered the promise that things would get better — which, to his credit they did; we eventually levelled the scores to more like CTS '5', opponents '150'!

Swimming was an activity which featured in the lives of many CTS boys, particularly those with a natural aptitude for the sport — and the dedication to sustain the demanding regime imposed by the regular training sessions. For our swimming we used the magnificent facilities of King Edward VII School which were situated at Clarkhouse Road beyond Glossop Road. Just visiting these baths gave a sense of occasion since they enjoyed the backdrop of the main school. King Ted's, as we knew the school, was built in 1837 to a design by William Flockton — whom I assume was the father of T.R. Flockton who, as previously stated, was the co-designer of Firth College — the CTS main building. So the CTS can claim some affinity with King Ted's! The latter's magnificent elevation, decorated with an array of Corinthian columns, always looked magnificent — especially when viewed across the extensive playing fields. On our visits to this school for swimming, we were strictly confined to the pool and its facilities. But once inside we were always made welcome but a strict regime of order and discipline prevailed. This commenced with a clean ankle and feet inspection; anyone found not meeting the required standards had to go to the slipper baths for a wash. We all had to take a preliminary shower as is now conventional practice in most swimming pools.

I remember the baths as being of Edwardian style with glass roof and parallel rows of seats for spectators; special seats were reserved at one end of the pool for distinguished spectators. As I have remarked, some boys swam regularly in response to their natural affinity for swimming. As for myself, and many others, we only participated when we had to. This usually came about each year when it was time to do our bit for our particular house. House points could be won by, for example, swimming a length, or, even better, by swimming several lengths. Through this incentive we all, more or less, went along for swimming once a week for a period of several weeks tallying up our house points — at least that was my experience. I am glad I participated because it revealed to me just how accomplished some boys were at swimming. Breast stroke, crawl, back stroke and butterfly were all in some boys' repertoire. All I could manage was a rather stately breast stroke, with head held high so as not to get my face wet — pathetic, but it earned me a house point!

The hard work and training on the part of the swimmers culminated at the end of the Summer Term in the form of the House Competitions. This was an opportunity for boys good at swimming to demonstrate their skills. Such boys, however, of my generation faced one small problem — in the form of a boy by the name of Brian Day. Brain was not simply a good swimmer he was outstanding even in comparison with other accomplished swimmers of his age throughout the country. At the CTS he dominated the sport completely. In one competition I recall seeing Brian complete almost three-quarters of a length under water before surfacing, by which time his fellow competitors were left far behind wallowing in his wake. Brian was a natural but he had to work at his skill by regular training and endless preparation. With Brian's achievements went a natural modesty; he was never triumphalist over his rivals — he simply swam them into extinction! Merely to list Brian's swimming records and awards would require a whole page in this book; suffice it to say that he was British Breast Stroke Champion in 1958 — a magnificent achievement for a schoolboy busy with his full-time school studies.

Outstanding swimmers enjoyed their moment of fame at Speech Day when they were presented with their cups. Supporters of a winning house cheered loudly as a particular trophy was handed over to an individual, either in recognition of his own achievements or on behalf of his team. Naturally, admiring parents joined in the applause. The fame of these lads is preserved for all time in the CTS archive of photographs.

Although tennis did not feature in the CTS games curriculum, mention of this should be made here if only to make reference to the quite outstanding achievements of Roger Taylor. Roger, it hardly has to be said, achieved great distinction nationally by playing for his country at Wimbledon and in the Davis Cup. He currently holds a position of importance as a senior British tennis official.

Pugilistics occasionally erupted in the school playground — very seldom in point of fact — but boxing, as an organised activity, may not have been experienced by many boys at the CTS. Indeed, in my time at the school I only ever remember a boxing competition taking place just once — this was in 1956. The boxing ring was set up in the school hall. Four posts were fixed into brass rings set into the floor and ropes were secured to them in the normal way to from the boxing ring. Boys who wanted to take part signed their names on lists which were displayed on the notice board behind the glass screens in the vestibule on the wall to the right of the side entrance to the main building. So that competitors could be equally matched, each boy had to give his height and weight. I recall that School Captain Ron Saville signed the list! My exclamation mark here is because Ron was just about the tallest lad in the school at this time and certainly the most well built. Little wonder that no one had the courage to take him on in the final draw of competitors!

When the bouts were finally announced I can't help but think that some boys had set themselves against one another to settle a few old scores. But that prompts me to add that I do not recall any bullying at the CTS nor malicious behaviour between the boys; things might get a bit heated at times but it seldom went any further than that. In the ring though, during the competition in question, things were rather different. The boys scrapped as though they wished to kill one another — their honour was at stake. To ensure some semblance of order prevailed, Mr. Thompson was made the Master of Ceremonies. He read out the Queensberry Rules for 'Pugilistic Physical Engagement'! For obvious reasons he disposed of the opening remarks: "My lords, ladies and gentlemen", and replaced them with: "Headmaster, members of staff and boys of the Central Technical School". This imparted an air of dignity to the occasion which otherwise ran the risk of resembling the Christians being thrown to the lions in a Roman amphitheatre! The referee was Mr. Dove, probably selected for being so inherently kind and gentle — he was very well named. After each pair of combatants had entered the ring, he passed a few obligatory remarks: "I want a good clean fight, break when I say so, no hitting low and if either of you do not rise after a count of ten the contest is over". These words appeared to have two effects: in some cases they emboldened boys to exert their maximum aggression; however, in other cases they chastened some boys into realising just what they had let themselves in for — they visibly turned ashen faced! Contests were limited to three rounds — which must have seemed an eternity to some boys. Where contestants were unequally matched, this rapidly became apparent and Mr. Dove stopped the match by raising the hand of the victor. On leaving the ring the vanquished received a hearty cheer for showing their courage. In a few cases pairs of boys put on a good display of boxing by parrying the blows, weaving and darting and making good use of the ring. As I have remarked, as far as I can recall this was a one-off event in the life of the CTS and it probably did some good in allowing the lads to let off a bit of steam and thereby to get rid of their aggression.

Having recalled what I believe was an isolated whole-school event, I will insert into this section another one-off activity which engaged the entire school. The event to which I am about to refer should more properly appear under a heading such as 'Recreation' rather than Sport and Athletics — but here it is.

At some time in the Fifties, a popular radio programme started up by the name of *Brain of Britain*. Quiz shows, in which competitors are required to demonstrate their recall of factual information, seem to have the capacity to capture the public's imagination. I believe some of the fun they provide is that the listener, or viewer in the case of TV shows of this kind, can pit his or her wits against the contestants. Be this as it may, the *Brain of Britain* programme was an immediate success. So much in fact that Herbert Wadge started to make reference to it in morning assembly. I remember on at least one or two occasion he took the programme as his morning theme, exhorting the assembled boys to take an interest in current affairs and to be alert to what was all around us — in emulation of the virtues of the contestants. In particular he singled out a schoolboy contestant who did indeed go on to become the youngest ever *Brain of Britain*. In his final round he answered all the questions correctly, save one; he did not know what a *rebate* is — which was just about the only question I could answer. If I remember correctly, this remarkable lad went on to study at St. John's College Cambridge and, some years later, took part in a *Brain of Brains* competition and won the title *Superbrain*.

Now, at about the period when Christmas was approaching in the academic year concerned — about 1956–57 — Herbert Wadge announced there would be a school competition styled along the lines of this radio programme. The first step was to select competitors. This was achieved by all the boys having to attempt to answer a set of about fifty 'general knowledge' questions. These were set in class one morning and

took the form: "Which is the longest river in the world?, Give the name of the highest mountain … ", and so on. I managed a score in the low thirties but some other lads did much better. The best of these became the eventual contestants.

On the day of the competition the whole school assembled in the hall. Mr. Wadge presided over the proceedings from the front, in his usual way, and members of staff occupied their normal seats along the side of the hall and in the gallery. The Quiz Master was Mr. Firth. Contestants came to the platform and were read a question which, if they could not answer, was offered to the other contestants. All went well for a while, until some of the lads in the audience started to get a bit excited and, when a contestant faltered, they could not resist calling out the answer — or what they considered to be answer. This agitated Mr. Wadge considerably: "Silence", he bellowed, by way of restoring order. But the temptation to intervene proved too irresistible to a few boys and the interruptions continued. Eventually Mr Wadge issued an ultimatum; if boys did not stop calling out he would have the contest ended and normal lessons would be resumed. The prospect of this chastened the audience and the contest resumed. But, alas, the point came when one of the contestants did not know the answer to a particular question which prompted someone, high up in the balcony, to provide a clue. This provoked Herbert into a final paroxysm of rage. He rose and condemned the whole school as being irresponsible. With that, he terminated the proceedings and ordered us to return to our classes.

This was an unfortunate end to what had been billed as a major fun event in the life of the CTS — one of the very few such activities of its kind. But the manner in which the proceedings were so forcibly terminated serves to further illustrate just how determined was Herbert Wadge to impose his absolute authority upon his school.

Back now to some final thoughts about athletics in the life of the CTS.

The culmination of the school's season of athletics was the *Annual Athletics Meeting*. This was a very well organised event indeed, complete with a printed programme and an official games co-ordinator who was given the grand title of *Mr. Starter* — in fact he was Mr. Cofield of Sheffield University. The other officials were: *Referee*, Mr. Wadge — who else?; *Chief Judge*, Mr. McManus; *Clerk of the Course*, Mr. Woolhouse; and *Chief Competitors' Steward*, Mr. Howell. Other officials held the roles of *Judges, Recorders, Timekeepers, Take-over Judges* and *House Marshals*. In Figs 90 and 91, I have reproduced my copy of the Athletics Programme for July 1957 which provides the names of the members of staff who fulfilled the various official roles that summer. I have not mentioned the *Announcer* who was Mr. Thompson. His voice, amplified over the loudspeaker system, informed us as to which event was about to take place and of the subsequent outcome.

If the reader looks over the list of *Records* which is preserved in the Athletics Programme for 1957 some very creditable performances will be noted. For example, in 1950 a lad by the name of Frost ran 100 yards in 11.0 seconds. Given the nature of the equipment in those days — heavy running spiked-shoes — and the nature of the facilities — cinder track — such an achievement is remarkable. Roy Tandy's Long Jump in 1956 of 18 feet 7 inches is no mean achievement. And in 1951 a lad called Jewitt managed to throw a cricket ball 83 yards 7 inches which is a colossal throw. So some CTS lads, as these records indicate, were no slackers! More generally what the records indicate is that no particular house, contrary to popular belief, dominated over the rest at athletics. Taking the period 1942–1956 the honour of *Champion of Houses* was conferred as follows: Bessemer (5), Faraday (2), Stephenson (4) and Telford (5). Poor old Faraday toiled a bit! The year 1950 is of interest insofar as three houses shared the honour of being equal champion.

I believe the CTS can be proud of the sporting and athletic achievements of its boys. That may sound like a rather predictably partisan statement but the school records substantiate this assertion. It also has to be emphasised, once more, that we had no playing fields of our own and boys with an aptitude for, or inclination to, sport had thereby to make a considerable extra effort to practice and develop their skills. Well done lads!

The Outward Bound School Ullswater

It is fitting that I should follow the section concerning *Sport and Athletics* with a reference to *The Outward Bound School* at Ullswater since the very *raison d'être* and ethos of the Outward Bound School was 'Character Training through Adventure'. This particular section of my account will however only have personal meaning for the relatively few CTS boys who actually attended one of the Outward Bound Schools. Even so I consider this does qualify as a legitimate subject for discussion, albeit relatively briefly.

The Outward Bound School system was established at Aberdovey on the coast of Wales in 1941. It was founded by the pioneering educationist Dr. Kurt Hahn, the Headmaster of Gordonstoun. The emphasis of this particular school was on seamanship with allied courses in athletics and cross-country expeditions. In 1946 the *Outward Bound Trust* was formed and from that period the so-called *Mountain Schools* were established at Eskdale and Ullswater in Cumberland. The training received there was severe and the discipline was stern; moreover there was a high conception of honour, team spirit and of the power within each individual to overcome his weaknesses. If all that sounds rather intimidating then let me confirm, on the basis of personal experience, that it was! Boys were taken to the limits of their physical capacity — but never beyond. From about the mid 1950s, it was the custom for just one boy to be selected from the CTS each year to participate in an Outward Bound School programme. From this it can be worked out that, as I have remarked, just a few boys only from the CTS participated in these adventure-training programmes.

I first heard of the 'OBS' one morning in assembly; Mr. Wadge outlined the aims of the system, much as I have done in the preceding paragraph — although he extended it to last about twenty minutes in his typical fashion — and then he announced the School Captain for that particular year had been nominated to take part. I remember thinking at the time: "Thank God it's not me!". A few years later the hand of fate pointed in my direction!

One morning in June, shortly after I had been elected as School Captain, I was summoned to see Herbert Wadge — always an interesting experience. "Congratulations", he said, "You have been awarded a place at the Outward Bound School at Ullswater". My bowels nearly turned to water! "Christ almighty" I thought to myself as I mentally anticipated the nature of the Spartan regime to which I would be shortly consigned. "Thank you Sir", I replied dutifully. Herbert compounded my anxieties by saying that much was expected of me, rather in the style of Nelson before the Battle of Trafalgar — 'England expects every man to do his duty'. I then experienced a typical piece of Herbert's capacity for theatricality. He explained that he would go first into morning assembly, whilst I stood outside, he would then make the announcement to the school at which point I was required to enter the hall — to thunderous applause of course. So I dutifully performed my part endeavouring to look outwardly calm whilst inwardly feeling like a condemned man.

A few days later something rather unique occurred. Herbert Wadge announced that the CTS had been fortunate enough to secure a second place at the OBS for the newly elected School Vice Captain, namely, Richard Charles Prime. This was most unusual to say the least and may owe something to Herbert's powers of persuasion, particularly since 'Charlie', as we knew him, was one of the grand old men of the CTS and was already beyond the limited entry age of nineteen years and a half. But it was good for us both to be going at once since we could make our preparations together. We were provided with an information sheet on the type of clothing we should take, the hiking boots we needed and, most ominously, a recommended programme of training to be followed so that we would arrive at the OBS in the required state of fitness! I don't recall complying with the latter!

The OBS at Ullswater, at the time of which I am speaking, was a magnificent Regency-period mansion house, called *Hallsteads*, which had been adapted for use as a training centre. Situated on the western shore of Lake Ullswater, this location is surrounded by mountain ranges to the south — Helvellyn, Striding Edge and Grisedal — and to the west by the high peak of Great Mell Fell — all of which we explored and rock-climbed. More generally, these ranges and hill tops, and Ullswater itself, provided the adventure-training area for the community of 96 boys who were divided, house fashion, into *patrols*. I was a member of Mallory patrol, named, of course, after the intrepid explorer of Mount Everest.

Charlie Prime and I journeyed by train to Penrith in the Lake District on July 28 1958 and duly met up with several other boys who had undertaken similar journeys from all over the country — the pride of British youth! The next morning we were soon introduced to the severe regime which prevailed at the school. A morning bell sounded at 6.00 a.m. at which we were required to leap out of bed as though we had been electrified. At a hurried pace we were marched to an area before an old stable block where we assembled in our respective patrols. It was then a matter of running several hundred yards through a forest where we gathered at a jetty by the waterside. What then followed was remarkable. Ninety-six boys leaped into the water — stripped-bollock naked, as the phrase goes. And woe betide those who hesitated, especially the poor devils who could not swim — they just got pushed in by the supervising officer. Moreover, I can tell you, Lake Ullswater is cold at 6. 00 a.m. in the morning — very cold! — in fact, positively scrotum shrinking!

Later in the morning, each boy was kitted-out with the following items of equipment: rucksack; anorak; primus stove and container for petrol; a 'volcano' kettle — a special device for heating water rapidly in the event of emergencies; a canteen of aluminium plates, cups, knives and forks; maps, protractor and whistle; sleeping bag; and — ominously — a set of field dressings and a guide to first aid! Later on each pair of boys was provided with a canvas tent and a set of bamboo rods with sturdy brass fixings — looking for all the world like equipment discarded from the era of the British Raj in India. In the afternoon the boys assembled to meet the Warden and Chief Instructor of the OBS, namely, Squadron-Leader L. Davies. He was, as his title indicates, a gentleman with a military bearing and demeanour. He explained the concepts underlying the course, why we were there and what was required of us. No departure from the school's rules and conventions would be tolerated and neither would anyone be released from the school save in the case of family bereavement — so now we knew what we were in for! Before the school was dismissed the Deputy Warden emphasised the rigorous nature of the training regime adding, at the end of his discourse: "If I can do it so can you — watch this". He then stood by one of the dining tables and, with seemingly no effort, stepped up onto the table top and back down again to the floor — and so on several times as though he were merely exercising at a doorstep. It was an amazing demonstration of agility and strength; don't ever try it yourself or you may do yourself an injury!

I will insert here a brief reflection concerning Squadron-Leader Davies which will be of general interest. He was a distinguished photographer who had accompanied several expeditions. This prompts me to say that you may recall that in the mid fifties tales started to be told of a strange hairy, ape-like creature that had been seen frequenting the lower slopes of the mountain regions in the Himalayas. We of course came to know this as the *Abominable Snowman* — known locally as the *Yeti*. Squadron Leader Davies had participated in the 1955 RAF expedition to Mt. Everest and had taken some of the earliest official photographs of strange, enlarged footprints which were alleged to belong to such a creature. One Sunday afternoon — the period set aside for 'recreation' — we had an illustrated lecture about all this by Squadron Leader Davies. His lecturing style and the nature of his subject thoroughly captured our imagination. He also earned our respect since he showed us illustrations of the severe terrain he had traversed to secure his pictures — at times almost life threatening. I remember we left the dining hall, which had been darkened for the lecture, exclaiming — "fantastic"!

A detailed description of the daily life and routine of the OBS at Ullswater lies outside the scope of my narrative. However, by way of further reflecting on my adventures, here are a few highlights.

What may be described as 'classwork' included training in map reading and first aid. Both of these subjects incorporated practical field tests which contributed to the end-of-course assessment and final award. Our most dramatic group work of this particular kind concerned an exercise in mountain rescue; we had to imagine that someone had fallen from a rock face and was to be taken off the mountain. To make the simulation realistic we were taken in a *Land Rover* to a location where rock climbing was practised. From there we continued on foot hauling a stretcher, ropes and all the medical paraphernalia required to save someone's life — assuming they were not already dead! At the summit our instructor, Mr. McCormack, asked for a volunteer 'patient' to be strapped into the stretcher. We all wanted this role since we thought how nice and cushy it would be to be carried down the mountain, snugly wrapped in a warm sleeping bag. But, as we soon discovered, there was more to it than that! A candidate was eventually chosen — a lad of small build so as to lighten our load — and off we set down the mountain. Our 'patient' could not resist beaming at the rest of us as we laboured down the rocky terrain bearing him and the stretcher — we just glared at him muttering: "You lucky bugger". But then Instructor McCormack drew the party to a halt above a precipitous drop saying: "We are now going to practice rope and stretcher technique over this cliff face — for which extreme care is needed"! Our patient went ashen faced and it was now the turn of the carrying party to beam at him. One or two lads could not resist facetiously calling out: "Have many boys been killed doing this Sir?". Mr. McCormack was not pleased to hear this — nor was our stretcher-case who by now had intimations of his own mortality.

Ropes were attached to each of the handles of the stretcher and it was lowered carefully over the cliff by a team of eight boys; the remainder of the patrol held on to safety ropes. The lad in the stretcher — by now looking petrified — gritted his teeth bravely, ignoring the advice of some wit who called out: "Pretend you're unconscious"! It took some time for us to synchronise the sequence of ropes and for an anxious moment the stretcher oscillated like a pendulum! After much manoeuvring we eventually reached level ground where we were allowed to release our patient from his confinement. His acknowledgement of our efforts was terse: "*You f...ing bastards*"!

On our second day we were introduced to 'circuit training'. This consisted of a sequence of physical exercises and 'obstacles' — in effect it was a form of commando training course the intention of which was to develop the stamina and muscular strength required to undertake the various, more extended, field and mountain adventures which featured in the OBS programme. Circuit training encompassed every ingenious physical challenge conceivable including ropes, nets, a wooden 'wall' some twelve feet high (3.6 metres), parallel bars, a plank spanning a deep trench and several other challenges. In particular I recall we had to perform a weight-lifting exercise using, as a weight, two concrete blocks embedded in the ends of a metal pole. The weights were so heavy the pole had bent about the middle! The supreme challenge for me was doing chin-ups from a rope suspended between two trees. This calls to mind how we also had to swing between the branches of trees like Tarzan. This particular demand was the cause of my having my only misfortune at the OBS; I let the rope slip through my fingers and suffered a quiet severe rope burn. This was nothing though compared to one lad I saw who had a rope burn across the entire length of his face.

The OBS had a version of abseiling that was positively alarming. A very long rope was tethered to a fixing at the top of a steep cliff face which then descended, in a catenary curve — as with the cable for a suspension bridge, to another fixing way below at ground level. You then attached yourself to this by a girdle of rope about your waist and then — wait for it — you leaped from the cliff and descended, at a hell of a rate, until you reached the safety of the ground below and — if all went well — the waiting arms of a team of helpers who stood by in case anything went wrong! It was seriously scary! Moreover, none of us wore safety helmets as would most certainly now be required under contemporary health and safety legislation. But we all survived.

Also surviving from this period is my OBS *Log Book*. It accompanied me on all my Lake District expeditions and now, as a consequence, it looks very crumpled and stained — with the marks of damp from the rain which poured down in August 1958. We undertook a number of these expeditions which were of one, two, three and four-day periods; these were completed in groups. We also made a solo excursion into the hills — called 'The Tod' — which was of two days duration. All of these expeditions required elaborate preparations including a full hiking kit, tents and associated equipment and, on one particular occasion, all the ropes and gear needed for rock climbing. Our individual rucksack was so heavy it could only be lifted into position on our back with the help of a companion. The great weight of these rucksacks — which were made from canvas fixed to a steel frame — made negotiating rough terrain very hard work. If we came to a river we were expected to ford our way across it. On one such occasion a boy in my patrol fell in and was nearly swept away until he freed himself from his rucksack. He then spent a miserable night trying to keep warm.

To give a flavour of our expeditions here are a few extracts from 'The Captain's Log':

Three-day Scheme
Day 1, 31 July:
Departed for three-day 'scheme' as expeditions are called. Fully equipped with tent, rations, rucksack etc. Route: Gowbarrow Fell, Dockray, Dowthwaitehead, Hart Side, Sticks Pass, and Brown Cove — our camp site. Pitched tent at 5.30 p.m.

Day 2, 1 August:
Rose at 7.00 a.m. Breakfast then departed at 9.30 a.m. Route: Catstycam, Swirrat Edge, Helvellyn (3,118 feet), Dollywagon Pike, Grisdale Tarn (met Watkins patrol), Fairfield, Hart Crag, Dovedale, Middle Dod, Kilnshaw Chimney, and Kirkstone Pass — our camp site. A strenuous day; the sea was visible from Helvellyn summit. We had some experience of screeing down mountain slopes.

Day 3, 2 August:
Rose at 8.00 a.m. and departed camp at 10.30 a.m. Route: Plane Fell, Martindale, Hallin Fell and east bank of Lake Ullswater. We were ferried by boat to the west bank and returned to the school. Dinner at 6.00 p.m. and lights out at 10 00 p.m.

4 August:
6. 30 a.m. morning jump in lake — now becoming part of routine and refreshing. Breakfast at 8. 00 a.m. The food here is very good. In the morning we did athletics. I ran half a mile across a hilly track in 2´ 39˝ and was awarded a merit. Dinner at 12. 45 p.m. In the afternoon we had a course in estate management and chopped a tree down. Late afternoon Circuit Training. Supper at 6. 00 p.m. Evening: principles of first aid and mountain rescue. Practised putting splints on fractures and how to inject morphine in seriously injured accident victims. 9. 00 p.m. cocoa and biscuits followed by lights out at 10. 00 p.m.

6 August:
Had school photograph taken. Practised principles of mountain rescue and stretcher technique with Mr. Holt. He is very demanding and outspoken.

7 August:
We were introduced to 'The Wall' — 12 feet high. All the patrol had to clamber over it. The OBS all-time record for twelve boys is 60 seconds — an Olympian effort. We were also introduced to 'The Beam' — a long log spanning between two trees. The OBS record for this is 18 seconds. Mallory Patrol could only manage 30 seconds.

8 August:
In the morning we ran the cross-country two-mile event for our OBS badge. To be awarded honours you had to do the course in 12 minutes 40 seconds; I could only manage 13 minutes (precisely) and so qualified for a merit award. In the afternoon we were sent out on our solitary hike called 'The Tod', the purpose of which is to test personal initiative. My route was: Watermillock, Nabend, Great Mell Fell, High Row and Deepdale where I bivouacked for the night — a tent and poles are too heavy for one boy to carry.

9 August:
Climbed out of bivouac at 7.00 a.m. Had a poor breakfast because primus stove was wet and failed to work. Kendal mint cake and dates form part of our 'iron rations' and are very good sustaining food. Resumed route: High Row, Dockray, Matterdale, Gowbarrow Fell, Green Hill and so back to school. It rained all day and I was soaked. Despite being exhausted the patrol went canoeing in the late afternoon. In the evening we saw a film of the 1936 Olympic Games. Supper drink and lights out at 10.00 p.m.

Four-day Scheme
Day 1, 12 August:
We have been told this will be our toughest assignment, involving rock climbing, fell walking and camping. My patrol was taken to the camping site at Dubb's Hut (mountain hut) where we pitched tents at 11. 00 a.m. and immediately set out with our climbing equipment for Pillar Rock. The weather was good but on the climb we were buffeted by driving wind and enveloped by mist. Mr. McCormack was our guide and climbing instructor and led us up the twelve-stance climb. The guide book describes the climb as difficult but I, and my companions, found parts of it very difficult. We returned to camp at 8.30 p.m. where the remainder of Mallory Patrol was camped. An evening meal concluded the day's activities.

Day 2, 13 August:
The worst day of all regarding the weather conditions. At 9.15 a.m. four of us set out on a fell walk. The route was: Hay Stacks, High Crag, Red Pike, Buttermere, Dale Head and return to camp. We walked as far as Buttermere but the weather conditions were so severe — we could not even stand up in the wind — that we were compelled to return to camp by an alternative easier route. At camp we attempted to dry out our thoroughly wet clothes. We were revived by a welcome hot meal.

Day 3, 14 August:
The day was spent fell walking in almost perfect weather. Our route was: Hay Stacks, Red Pike, Pillar Rock, Black Sail Pass and Great Gable where we struck camp. We resumed the walk but one of the party injured his foot and could only continue with difficulty. The weather continued fine and we enjoyed some of the finest views possible of the lakes and hills. Returned to Dubb's Hut at 6.00 p.m. and cooked an enormous meal. I thoroughly enjoyed the whole day's activities.
Day 4, 15 August: We rose early to make a quick departure. I was in the walking party to go back to school, the bus being reserved for those who were to go climbing. Our route was: Borrodale, Brigend, Thirlmere, Sticks Pass, Black Crag, Glencoynedale, Watermillock Common and the OBS *Hallsteads*.

16 August:
Morning work consisted of group patrol tests including: traversing a deep pit, surmounting an imaginary high-voltage power line, clambering over a wall and swinging

across a ravine. Our overall performance was good but we lacked harmony. The main event of the afternoon was a cross-country run of five miles which included Birk Crag, to the summit Swinburn's Park, Gowbarrow Fell (1,579 ft.) and Halfmoon Wood. It was a killer of a course. Officials were staged along the route in case any boy collapsed. I returned 74 from a field of 96. This was disappointing but good enough to earn me a merit.

Although I continued at the OBS at Ullswater for several more days, my Log Book ends at this point. I will however add here a little further detail from memory to complete my account.

My patrol built a canoe from plywood sections which we covered with layers of canvas. This was then waterproofed, left to dry and was duly 'launched' on Lake Ullswater to shouts of appreciation. One day the entire patrol spent an afternoon practicing canoeing skills on the lake. Each canoe held two boys and we had to journey from the west bank over to the east bank and back again. It is a considerable distance and proved to be very fatiguing. Interestingly, some months later I chanced to see a TV programme about the OBS movement which depicted just such a patrol of boys on the water singing *Shenandoah*. The sight and sounds of their singing made me feel very nostalgic.

One afternoon chance decreed that I should enjoy about fifteen minutes of fame. This is how it came about. My patrol was practicing rock climbing and, just as I was making my decent, the instructor called up to me to stay where I was — calling out: "Hold it there". So I did what I was told, clinging to the rock face as though my life depended upon it — which of course it did. An elderly gentleman then came into view down below me — a long way down below me! — whom I later discovered was none other than the famous Dr. Kurt Hahn, founder, as I have previously remarked, of the OBS system. He was making a film of the life and work at *Hallsteads*, Ullswater and I was required to descend the rock face in an orderly fashion as he filmed away. As I descended he remarked approvingly in a thick German accent: "Yah, good, ist good". By the time I completed my climb the great man had gone, but I like to think that my mountaineering efforts are preserved somewhere in his archives for the benefit of posterity!

Chance conspired on another occasion that I should find myself in the company of a distinguished member of the OBS movement. At about my third week at the OBS we had a visitor who was about to take up the post of Warden at the OBS in Devon. I believe he was called Captain Charles Keys R.N. and, to his great credit, he determined to experience for himself all the rigours of the OBS regime before taking up his appointment. Accordingly, he accompanied my patrol on our climbing expedition to Pillar Rock which I have previously described. He made his ascent with an instructor by an alternative route to that taken by my patrol but which approximated very close to us mid-way up the climb. It so happens I had reached the mid-point stance, to use the climber's terminology, when alongside me appeared Captain Keys. I recognised immediately that the climb was as great a challenge for himself as it was for me — there is no concealing fear — but he showed remarkable courage, especially for a man in middle age, in following intrepidly behind his lead climber. At one point he cast a glance across in my direction and we exchanged fleeting smiles of comradeship. Here we were, two individuals of different generations, several hundred feet up in the air, clinging to the rock face and our safety ropes both pitting our skills against nature and the elements. It made me feel good.

Our time at the OBS at Ullswater concluded in an Awards Ceremony. Achievement on the course was recognised by the award of a small badge bearing the following inscription:

"To Serve, to Strive and not to Yield"

These words are the motto of the Outward Bound movement and are derived, albeit in adapted form, from the epic poem *Ulysses* by Alfred Tennyson. By way of interest these words, in their original form — *To Strive, To Seek, To Find, And not to Yield* — were carved on a cross of Australian jarrah wood which was erected on The Great Ice Barrier close to the location where Captain Scott and his companions perished on their legendary, but ill-fated, return journey from the South Pole. I am pleased to report that all 96 boys of the OBS training course in the summer of 1958 survived their ordeal! A very few received the highest accolade of *Honours*. The rest of us received a Merit award which was conferred in one of three classes — *First, Second* and *Third*. I was awarded my badge with Second Class Merit for which I worked physically harder than I had ever done before in my life — and I do not expect to ever work so hard again!

I am mindful that I have made no reference to the experiences at the OBS of my CTS companion Charlie Prime. This is because we were in separate patrols and therefore went our own individual ways. I do recall that Charlie had a foot condition that precluded him taking part in several of the activities which he much regretted. For a fuller account of his own adventures readers will have to contact Charlie Prime themselves.

It is now time to conclude my narrative of the Outward Bound School; this can be quickly told. On returning to the CTS in, early September 1958, Herbert Wadge called me to his office to hear an account of my experiences in the Lake District. He first told me how much the area meant to him and his wife and how they frequently spent their holidays camping in the region. I then described my adventures more or less as I have outlined them above. He hung on to my every word, nodding with agreement when I bestowed praise on some view or fell walk with which he was clearly familiar, he interpolated remarks of his own, asked me numerous questions and chatted away in a convivial manner for the best part of an hour. I left his room wishing that I had achieved a First Class merit so as to be more worthy of the trust he had placed in me.

A few days later I met Mr. Brennan who greeted me with: "Well, and how did you get on?". Once more I outlined my experiences to which he listened attentively. When I had finished he inclined himself towards me and said: "One day, Russell, this will be the stuff of your future treasured nostalgia". And so indeed, forty years on, it is.

The Lunch-Time Break

It is stating the obvious to say that the primary purpose of our lunch-time break was to get something to eat. In this respect there were two quite distinct categories of CTS lads; there were those who had school dinner at Cathedral School and those who had a packed lunch seated on the balcony in the main building. I will first consider the category of those who, like myself, had a cooked school dinner.

Looking back on all this I now realise how the lunch-time dinner break was run like a military operation. In our First Year we had to assemble in the school hall and stand, regimental fashion, in rows according to our various classes. To be released to go off for dinner, all the members of the class had to stand unflinching bolt upright. If you were lucky the member of staff supervising this para-military exercise gave the word for the class to be dismissed promptly and off you went to get your lunch in the dining hall located down at the wonderfully named Cathedral School. Sometimes we had to stand to attention for ages before being allowed to depart for our dinner. Running was banned — until you were out of sight when you ran like the wind to get a good place in the queue. You will recall that when the weather was fine we formed a long queue in the yard between the toilet block and the dining room. If it rained the queue meandered round the cloakroom and up the stairs to the first floor where the classrooms and physics laboratory were located. Jumping the queue was something of an art and required both skill and the connivance of friends if you were not to be found out — which invoked a chorus of disapproval.

The dining hall was very adaptable; I have already described how it was used for both examinations and for music lessons. At lunch times, two rows of tables were arranged each consisting of sets of two tables giving a combined seating arrangement of sixteen boys, with a central isle which was patrolled by the teacher on duty. In this way I suppose about 150 boys in total could have their dinner at any one time. On entering the dining hall, which could some days entail a long wait, we handed in our dinner ticket to the prefect on duty who placed it in a small wooden box somewhat resembling those you see in churches when you buy postcards describing the stained glass windows etc.

Two prefects were usually on duty to regulate the dinner queue and to maintain some semblance of order. Being a prefect had two lunch-time privileges; one was that you did not have to wait in the queue and the other was you were able to eat at the prefects' table in relative peace and quiet. The master in charge bore the primary responsibility for supervising the dining hall and my recollection is that this duty rotated amongst some, but not all, members of staff. One member of staff who was a regular was Mr. Gregory who not only supervised but took his meal with us as well. He usually scoffed his dinner voraciously as he simultaneously devoured the *Fishing Times* or *Angler's Monthly* or some such journal devoted to huntin' shootin' and fishin'. Rumour held that after Mr. Gregory had taken his meal with us he went upstairs to have a second one with his colleagues. I have to say the only evidence to support this was Mr. Gregory's physique.

Having just been rather personal about Mr. Gregory's anatomy calls to mind the team of middle-aged women — the dinner ladies — who served our school meal through the large serving hatch at the far end of the dining room. To my youthful perception they had bodies like gorillas, their pink skin turned red from the heat of the kitchen. And they were strict in exercising their responsibilities; they never served any portion an ounce more than had been stipulated by the head cook — a positive orang-utan of a woman. Seldom did their vigilance slip in this regard but I did once benefit from a rare lapse of concentration — this is what happened.

Our favourite meal was being served — chips and fried egg. We had this about once a year; when it was on the menu news of it was eagerly relayed along the dinner queue — "It's chips and egg!" — "It's chips and egg!", and so on until about 100 boys were salivating like Pavlov's dogs. On the occasion of my unexpected benefit, the woman serving the fried eggs was deep in conversation with her companion 'on the chips' and she served me two eggs. I made a rapid departure before she realised her mistake!

Another favourite meal was meat and potato pie which we had quite often. Boiled cabbage was generally unpopular — I can't think why. The culinary all-time low was reached during a period when there was an acute shortage of potatoes. To give them their credit, the cooks attempted to make up for the deficiency by serving a potato substitute called 'pomme' which even the average CTS lad was able to work out was derived from the French *pomme de terre* — potato. This pomme we were given was so glutinous that it could not be detached from the serving spoon without the cook swinging her spoon down vigorously so as to jolt the consolidated mass of potato-like substance onto your plate. It landed with a splurge. I remember it was almost completely impervious to gravy which just washed around in your plate. We all found it revolting and it was returned in heaps on the waste plate. This prompts me to add that from each group of sixteen boys seated at a pair of tables, the boy unlucky enough to be seated fifteen had to return the waste food; it was the responsibility of the boy seated sixteen to return the empty plates and cutlery. Needless to say that pomme was so universally disliked it was eventually taken off the menu and for a period we were given a slice of bread to help to fill us up; this was the only time I ever recall bread being served at meal times at the CTS.

One day a boy told me how it was possible to get a better dinner than the one being served to the unwashed masses. This is how it was achieved. At the very end of the serving — this would be about 12.50 p.m. — the cooks frequently served up the left-overs of some delicacy that they had been reserving for themselves; for example roast potatoes were often available instead of boiled ones. But contriving to benefit in this way had its perils since it meant being the very last in the queue — and this meant running the risk of being late for dinner which was a bookable offence by the prefect on duty. I had one or two close encounters with the prefects in this way but always managed to get away with it.

My final comments on school dinners should be — perhaps a little grudgingly —that they were well balanced and nutritional. They certainly kept the pangs of hunger at bay until we got home for our evening family meal.

In my entire time at the CTS I never had a single packed lunch. I am therefore not very well qualified to comment on this aspect of CTS lunch-time social life. I know that boys gathered to eat their sandwiches on the balcony of the school hall. It is common knowledge that an adjunct to having packed lunch was to playing shove ha'penny. A few boys seemed to live for this and played the game fervently. It was necessary to scratch marks in the surface of the benches to establish goal posts. The consequence of generations of boys so scratching away was that there was hardly any paint left on the seated surface of the benches. This prompted Herbert Wadge to announce one day in morning assembly that there were sufficient marks on the benches and that henceforth no more should be made. I believe this was one of the very few occasions that the boys did not pay too much heed to what he had to say — they just carried on as usual.

It is a further statement of the obvious to say that our lunch-time break was not merely an opportunity to have something to eat; it was also a chance to relax with your pals or perhaps to do some shopping. Wet days were always a problem since they confined boys to indoors. On such occasions the school library was opened to provide us with some additional diversions — such as leafing through the mouldering, dog-eared back issues of *Country Life*. I recall one rainy day when I retreated to the library and became engrossed in the section at the back of *Country Life* devoted to houses for sale. I should add these were manorial residences located in their own grounds, complete with stable block and tennis courts etc. I recall that at the more modest and of the scale such a property could be purchased for about £5,000 — a considerable sum for the mid 1950s. After a while, as I turned over the pages of my magazine, I became aware of a tall dark figure standing by my side. I looked up to behold none other than Herbert W. Wadge! "You know", he said, "I could never afford to buy a place like that". And off he went. This remark somewhat surprised me since I had formed an impression in my mind that our headmaster must be quite well off, appearing as he did each day in his splendid-looking green *Jaguar* motor car. But at that age I had little idea of how much people earned or of how professional people were remunerated relative to each other. What I did know is that I was rather hard up — but so was everyone else!

My reference to the magazine *Country Life* calls to mind the somewhat controversial subject of the 'magazine fund'. This was a levy imposed on all boys of, I believe, three pence each week. It was supposed to be, as its name implies, a source of revenue from which to provide the school library with a supply of magazines. But, as I have intimated above, the physical condition of many of the magazines in the library was testimony to their great age — for the most part they resembled the well-thumbed collections to be found in a typical doctor's surgery. I was not the only CTS lad of my generation to mentally compute the weekly revenue to be derived from three pence times the number of boys in the school. It worked out at several new magazines per week — but they never materialised. What, I still ask, happened to all those three-penny pieces? Are they still accumulating interest in some long overlooked bank account I wonder?

I will stay on the subject of magazines a moment longer and ask the question: Who remembers the magazine shop — more appropriately described as the 'dirty book' shop — located near to the Graves art gallery on Surrey Street? Its window was crammed with those small-format magazines of the period which were dedicated to the female form. It was a source of some embarrassment to ever be caught looking in at this window during the lunch-time break — although I must add that I do not speak from personal experience on this matter! Naturally, such 'works of art' never appeared in the school library! What, I wonder, would have been Herbert Wadge's reaction if they had? He would I suppose have had instant heart failure.

Having taken the reader, as it were, to the threshold of the Graves Art Gallery let us now go inside. By this I mean to say that between the years 1956–59 I made many lunch-time visits to this gallery. I used to go alone — for two reasons; one, I could never find anyone else sufficiently interested to accompany me, and two, I actually preferred to go round the gallery at my own pace. I got to know the collections rather well and enjoyed most of them, with the exception of all those carved Chinese ivories. By way of interest, some years later I got to know the Director of the gallery on personal terms. He was called Dr. Singleton and acted as my external tutor in my final year of architectural studies at the University of Sheffield — this was in 1964. My thesis project was *Art Gallery Design* and Dr. Singleton helped me with such technical matters as the lighting of paintings and the environmental conditions required to safeguard them from damage.

My lunch-time visits to the Graves Art Gallery were the only occasion for my ever getting into trouble with the prefects during my five years at the CTS; here's what happened. I normally went to the gallery after I had had my school dinner. This usually left about 30–45 minutes for recreation if we had consumed our meal quickly; this typically was the case since we wolfed our meals voraciously. However, in the circumstance in question, I reversed my usual custom and went to the gallery first where I subsequently became immersed in the pictures and drawings. The outcome was that I duly turned up for dinner very late. The prefect on duty assumed I had been holding back in order to get the better type of dinner to which I have made previous reference. My protests that I was late due to having been to the art gallery cut no ice. The prefect just looked rather incredulous and then booked me to attend the forthcoming Prefects' Meeting. So I took my meal and contemplated my fate; as I did so I had an idea. It was Wednesday and so only two more days of the school week remained; I went up to the prefect, who was still on duty, and volunteered to wipe the tables for the next two days in exchange for being removed from the Prefects' List. The lad concerned looked at me somewhat suspiciously but agreed to my proposition. The following day the member of staff on dinner duty was Mr. Frow who, seeing me wiping the tables — which was a foul job — enquired: "What's all this about then Russell?". I recall he said this an air of: "What's a nice person like you doing in a place like this?". So I confessed to being late due to visiting the art gallery. It was now Mr. Frow's turn to look somewhat suspicious, used, as I imagine he was, to errant boys doing penance for such things as throwing empty milk bottles at the prefects — I exaggerate a little but you see what I mean. Henceforth I made sure I was never again late for my dinner.

There were occasions when a craze would sweep through the school. One such passion I remember was for the game of pocket-chess. This particular enthusiasm gripped the school like a fever in the spring term of 1955. Whoever sold us our miniature sets must have done very well since dozens of boys purchased them. I still have mine; it consists of small red and cream pieces mounted on a plywood base contained in a black coloured box — all dimensioned about 5″ x 6″. Some lads became very proficient at the game. I recall especially a boy in my Class 5X who was always difficult to beat. He also found it difficult to keep quiet when he was observing others at play. His favourite intervention was: "Hit it with your wellie!". For a while this became something of a class catch-phrase. Like all crazes, the passion for chess gradually faded away — but I wonder how many of you still have your set of pocket-chess tucked away on a shelf somewhere as a little memento of this period in your life?

Shoplifting can hardly be listed as a lunch-time recreation, nor would I, for a moment, ever make light of such a thing. But I will mention this here for the following reason. Being in the centre of town, surrounded by so many shops, the temptation to some boys to occasionally take something without paying for it proved irresistible. Such misdemeanours would therefore occur and doubtless the shopkeepers would inform the police and Herbert Wadge would in turn get to hear about it. On these occasions he was of course his typical uncompromising self, taking the opportunity in morning assembly to deplore such wrong-doing and to warn would be offenders to keep out of trouble. I'm pleased to say we usually did.

Sometime around about my third year at school, a group of boys told me how they had started to pay lunch-time visits to the Law Courts. Their motive, it has to be said, was entirely voyeuristic, by which I mean they had discovered it was possible to sit in the public gallery to hear other peoples' misery discussed. I have to add further that the particular misery that impelled these lads to take an interest in legal matters was of the kind normally reported in the *News of the World*. After hearing the lads concerned recount a number of cases on which they had eavesdropped, I relented and one day went along with them myself. My companions had become quite skilled in court procedure. They showed me how to check on the day's list of cases, how to decided which of the cases looked the most promising — by which I mean salacious — and how to find a particular court room. By these processes I let myself be guided along the corridors until we came to a particular court which we entered and where we duly took our seats in the public gallery. I will not elaborate further; it was all most embarrassing and I resolved henceforth never again to intrude into other people's misery.

Being located in the middle of town had the great benefit of allowing CTS lads freedom to roam the city centre for the best part of an hour. I will conclude this section by saying a few words as to how I made use of this opportunity in my first and second years. At this period I had two particular friends from my pre-CTS days at Carfield Junior School, namely, John Butcher, who was a Builder, and David Dickson who was an Engineer. John and David had a packed lunch, after which they made their way down to Pond Street. We had an arrangement whereby I would meet them at 12.40 p.m. provided I had by then finished my school dinner. Most days I kept the rendezvous and we would invariably spend sometime looking at the building work which was then in progress on what was to become the new Sheffield Polytechnic building. Our route was always the same; Pond Street, Calver Street, Pinstone Street and so back to the CTS. We chatted, as lads will, about what was going on, did our share of complaining, sometimes discussed school work — but not very often — shared what 'scandal' came our way and generally passed the time of day. I expect many of you did much the same.

Railway Excursions

The inclusion of a section of narrative concerned with railway excursions requires a few words of explanation. My sub-heading will have an immediate rapport with those boys who were at the CTS in the mid 1950s who were keen train-spotters. I am referring of course to the excursions several of us made with Mr. Pilling to enjoy railway-based outings of various kinds. I recall how they came about, but let me first say a few words about Mr. Pilling's enthusiasm for all things connected with railways, and in particular railway modelling

His interest in railways first came to my attention during the mid-morning break in woodwork classes sometime in my First Year. Mr. Pilling would invariably bring his cup of tea into the workshop, whilst we drank our milk, and would frequently leaf through that month's issue of *Railway Modeller* or *Model Engineer*. My bench was situated near to where Mr. Pilling took his tea break so I had plenty of opportunity to have a good look at what he was reading. My inducement to do so was that I was quite interested in railway modelling myself. I was a very close friend at this time of David Dickson (Engineer) to whom I have made previous reference — I should add that I am still a very close friend of David's. We created many 'OO' gauge layouts in his attic on a large billiard table that was installed there — you could say this is where much of our mis-spent youth was passed. So I had good reason to share Mr. Pilling's enthusiasm for railway modelling.

One day my curiosity got the better of me and I asked: "Are you interested in railway modelling Sir?" This is a good example of stating the obvious but it had the desired effect of prompting Mr. Pilling to confirm that he was indeed interested in railway modelling and that he had in fact been a keen modeller for several years. His interest was in the larger scale known as 'O' gauge. This, for those unfamiliar with such things, is twice the size of 'OO' gauge. The 'O' gauge scale was popular in pre-war times and for some years afterwards in the form of the legendary tin-plate Hornby trains — so much valued now by collectors. I discovered that Mr. Pilling had made no fewer than seven locomotives in 'O' gauge, all electrically powered and complete with rolling stock. He told me how he had converted his loft for the purpose of setting out his layout and running his trains. The time came when he invited me to his home to see his models running but I never managed to achieve this — much to my regret. Did anyone reading this, I wonder, also receive such an offer and actually go along to Mr. Pilling's house to see his layout?

I have a further recollection about Mr. Pilling's railway modelling interest. One day he told me that he was thinking of purchasing a fully working steam engine. The following Saturday he and his wife went all the way to Leeds to pay a visit to a railway modelling shop called *The Leeds Model Railway Company*. In its day this was a highly respected model engineering shop — by no means a toy shop — whose models are now sought after by collectors. Sometime later I asked Mr. Pilling if he had purchased his steam engine. "No", he replied in his typical abrupt manner, adding: "At £12 my wife considered it was too expensive". I felt very sorry for him! By way of interest, such a model would now cost about £2,000. It would have been a good investment.

It is time now that I said something about railway excursions; this is how they came about. One day during another mid-morning break in our woodwork class, Mr. Pilling asked me what I thought of the idea of taking part in an excursion to visit some engine sheds and locomotive-building works. "Do you think it would be a popular thing with the boys?", he asked. He might as well have asked me if I enjoyed Christmas! I must have endorsed his idea so eagerly with my — "Wow, yes Sir!" — that he actually smiled and remarked that he would think about it. I will pause here and add that I now realise, with the benefits of hindsight and experience, what a great deal is involved in taking a party of young people away on a day trip. There are the arrangements to make, the formal consents to be obtained, the money to collect, the transport to arrange etc. When you are a schoolboy, you take all these things for granted — you just expect them to happen. And so, in the case of Mr. Pilling's railway outings, they did. One day in the spring term of 1957, he duly announced his intention to take a party of interested boys to the Crewe engine sheds and works. He had no difficulty in getting the numbers required; he even allowed me to invite my cousin Barrie Bancroft, to whom I have referred earlier, to participate in the trip even though he was not a CTS lad.

We did not of course appreciate at the time that it was, in effect, the twilight era of the age of the steam-powered railway locomotive. Nor were we aware that a certain 'gentleman' by the name of Lord Beeching would soon put an end to so much of what we young lads were intent on enjoying. We were not concerned with the economics of the railways; we were captivated by the 'romance of steam' and the chance to actually see engines being constructed. So off we went to Crewe in a state of excitement clasping our 'ABC' guides to *British Railway Locomotives*. I wonder how many of you recall these little pocket-book publications by Ian Allan Ltd. They listed all the classes of railway engines according to the four major regions, namely: *Western*; *Southern*; *London-Midland*; and *Eastern, North-Eastern* and *Scottish*. Columns of numbers gave the numerical list of the locomotives in a particular class or grouping and a selection of photographs illustrated typical examples. Being located in the LMS region there were 'locos', as we used to call them, that we Sheffield-based lads had little chance of seeing unless we were away on holiday in another region where they were worked. Mr. Pilling's excursions therefore, in taking us further afield than we would normally travel — to go train spotting — offered us the prospect of seeing some 'cops', i.e., engines not previously seen and which could be recorded in our little ABC manuals.

Crewe was a fantastic place for a group of young railway enthusiasts to visit with its complex railway junctions, large marshalling yard, engine sheds and locomotive works. It was no less than a railway paradise. An average of one locomotive a week was built at the Crewe works — about 8,000 in total — of which the Coronation Scot streamliners were among the most notable. In its heyday, as many as an amazing 1,000 trains per day passed through the Crewe network and almost 10,000 people worked there. I recall how we were taken around the entire complex, looking in at the main fabrication workshops and the paint shops. In the big workshop we paused by a man operating a huge lathe. He was finishing a driving wheel of about six feet diameter (1.8 meters). I distinctly recall him saying that when the machining was finished its balance would be so fine that a penny piece, placed on one of the spokes, would be sufficient to gently tilt the wheel down! We just looked at one another in amazement.

In my memorabilia of this occasion, I have a photograph I took of Mr. Pilling on the station at Crewe with its famous junction in the background. We were a true bunch of 'anoraks', as train spotters are known — somewhat pejoratively I have to say — and we eagerly jotted down the numbers of locomotives as they passed by us in profusion. I was later to discover from Mr. Pilling that, despite him recording dozens of numbers on our trip, not one of them was a single cop; he had seen them all before — on more than one occasion! Another photograph I have in my collection, dating from this visit, was taken by Mr. Pilling inside the workshops and shows the last production line of steam locos ever built at Crewe — even then the writing was on the wall.

On another excursion we visited York. Architecturally the great attraction of York to the railway enthusiast was, and remains, its majestic through-station with its dramatic arched roof hovering above the sweeping curves of the platforms and track. However, the supreme attraction of visiting York station, to the train spotter, was the possibility of seeing a *Streak* — one of Sir Nigel Gresley's famous A4 Class of locomotives. And, sure enough, in my collection of photographs of this particular visit I have a picture of *The Union of South Africa* in full steam heading south. I can hear the CTS lads now chorusing to each other: "It's a Streak!", as we fixed our gaze on its classic curvilinear lines. Surely, Gresley's A4 Class of locomotives are arguably the most famous and most aesthetically satisfying class of all locomotives ever to have run in Britain — and indeed in the world.

Doncaster was always a favourite town for train spotters to visit; being not too far from Sheffield it was easily accessible for a day trip. The chief attraction of Doncaster station, to we train spotters, were the up and down main through-lines each separated from the platforms by two further lines of track. This, and the relatively straight approaches to the station, meant that through trains could negotiate the station at full speed. In fact they still do and Doncaster remains an exciting place for the railway enthusiast to observe high-speed trains, such as the 125 Class of diesels, travelling north and south at about a hundred miles an hour. Indeed, the north-bound track-bed is banked to about 10° to facilitate high-speed running — CTS lads who remember their mechanics will have no difficulty in recalling the relationship between the angle of banking and the speed of negotiating a curve.

At the height of locomotive building at Doncaster, the site covered about 200 acres with more than 60 miles of sidings. We were allowed to walk the length of some of these, looking in at various workshops which serviced the Great Northern Railway. Clattering past we saw steam locos hauling endless lines of trucks full of coal from the mines around Doncaster and Barnsley. What I recall most vividly, however, were piles of brass nameplates which had been removed from various engines. These were sometimes simply lying by the track, where they had been removed, or rested, one against the other, by the side of an engine shed. This was clear evidence of locomotives being taken out of service — the majority never to run again. I recall how some groups of boys attempted to lift these nameplates apart in order to be able to read their names, so they could then say they had 'copped a namer' — as we used to say. The lads soon discovered though that the plates were very heavy and only a few could in fact be read. It occurs to me to add, rather naughtily, that if we had shipped a few of these items of railway memorabilia home, they would now be worth a small fortune — original brass nameplates are now eagerly sought by collectors.

Darlington was the furthest that we ever ventured with Mr. Pilling on his day excursions. We had all learned in our history lessons that the Stockton and Darlington Railway was the first to be empowered by Parliament to convey goods and passengers by steam traction — thereby inaugurating the railway age. To remind us of this fact, George Stephenson's *Rocket* was on display at the railway station — subsequently removed, where it rightfully belongs, to the National Railway Museum at York. But our devotion to history soon gave way to railway enthusiasm as we were shepherded around the extensive works of the London and North Eastern Railway Company. The men in the works must have become accustomed to seeing lines of boys filing between the work bays because they seemed to accept our presence quite naturally. Perhaps they felt proud, as indeed they had good cause, since many of these men were highly skilled in the very trades being studied at the CTS, namely, engineering and workshop practice. In fact I recall how some men paused at their work to explain the action of a lathe or to tell us how a piece of work — a connecting rod or the steel tyre of an engine wheel — had to be finished to an accuracy of thousandths of an inch. And the most excited amongst us was Mr. Pilling himself. Perhaps, deep down, he was a schoolboy who had never grown up — like a lot of other men! Perhaps he simply enjoyed the company of young lads — who were the sons he never had. In this context he once told me, rather sadly, how, as he put it, "I am the last of the Pillings" — the family generation ceased with himself. Be this as it may, his railway excursions gave generations of CTS boys immense pleasure.

School Prefects

The school prefect system at the CTS was an integral part of the functioning of the school — as is the prefect system in many schools. This is doubtless a legacy of the public school era where senior boys held positions of minor responsibility — even administering physical punishment. According to my school records, the typical numbers of school prefects at the CTS were as follows: 1957 (20); 1958 (39); and 1959 (37). My source are the copies of my school photographs for these years and so they don't take account of any boys who for some reason or other failed to have their picture taken. After a year of being a prefect, the normal progression was to be elevated to the position of a senior prefect. This was a smaller group of boys, for example, in 1959 the number of senior prefects was 19.

The prefects were, as I have remarked, an integral part of the daily management of the life of the CTS. They contributed in many ways to the smooth running of the school and the maintenance of its discipline. Prefects kept a record of which boys were late in the morning, they helped to control the dinner queue at Cathedral School and generally exerted an influence by

their presence about the school. It is easy to look back with a certain smile on all this and to dismiss it as being of small significance. But that would be wrong. It was important at the time for the formative influence it exerted upon us — those, that is, who became school prefects. We were trusted with positions of responsibility and had to exercise our judgement. This could be difficult at times since it involved being firm and upholding the standards that were required of us.

Being a school prefect was not all self-sacrifice; it had its advantages. The most coveted of these was the use of the prefects' room. This provided a more personal place to arrive in the morning than the school hall which is where the rest of the school had to gather prior to morning assembly or the start of afternoon school. In addition, within the prefects' room, was a suite of lockers in which to keep books and items of personal equipment. I noticed, on the occasion of my visit to the premises at the time of the Education Committee *Open Day*, that they are still there — now freshly painted whereas in our time these lockers were stained with a wood finish. Having the use of a locker meant that you did not have to carry large numbers of books between school and home. I have quite a clear memory of the inside of the door of one boy's locker; he had decorated it — in the manner required by tradition — with pin-up photographs. This was in fact one of the few concessions to decoration in the prefects' room which was generally very austere. In fact there were two rooms. There was a room for the junior prefects which was accessed directly from the flight of steps leading from the school playground between the Bow Building and the Holly Building. Another room, overlooking this playground, was provided for senior prefects. I used this room daily in my final year at school. One day someone generously contributed to its decoration in the form of a number of holiday posters of the kind you see in the windows of travel agents. I recall that one of these posters was of a view of the snow-clad Matterhorn and it chanced to be the subject of conversation by none other than Herbert Wadge. One day during lunch time, without any prior warning, he suddenly entered the prefects' room. In my experience this was an unique event. Fortunately everything was in order — there was no litter on the floor or anything out of place — and he cast his gaze benevolently around the room. It duly alighted on the colourful poster of the Matterhorn, provoking expressions of approval. "I know that view", he exclaimed; "One year my wife and I visited Switzerland and walked in those very woods". On saying this he walked up to the poster and pointed to a wooded area at the base of the mountain. Believing what he said, those of us in the room — only two or three in number — nodded approvingly, estimating that he and his energetic wife must have ascended several hundred feet. Herbert then cast a look in my direction; I was seated on the widow sill which was broad and quite comfortable. Numerous boys had done this before me, with the consequence that the heels of our shoes had worn away the plaster on the wall immediately below the window sill. Herbert's gaze fell upon this and his jaw positively dropped with incredulity. He promptly raged on about the lack of respect for property, making me feel personally responsible for the accumulated wear and tear innocently created by several generations of boys. I recall jumping to my feet to explain — but it was to no avail. Herbert left the room grumpily and, the very next day, he resumed the theme of the need to respect school property with myself, as School Captain, sitting uncomfortably by his side. I endeavoured to look stoic and resolute as though such things could not possibly apply to myself!

The most visible manifestation of the school prefects being a collective group of senior boys was to be seen in the weekly prefects' meeting. These meetings were held each Wednesday after school at 4.15 p.m. The school bell went at 4.10 p.m. and we were allowed just five minutes to make our way to the Firth Building and up the stairs to Mr. McManus's physics laboratory where the meetings were held. There was an air of formality about these meetings consistent with their ritualistic agendas. This was further enhanced by the prescribed manner in which the prefects disposed themselves about the room. The School Captain and Vice Captain sat at the front of the laboratory on the raised platform before the blackboard; at their side was the Secretary whose responsibility it was to keep a record of the proceedings and to write them up in the form of minutes. The principal purpose of the prefects' meeting was to hear the cases made against boys who had been 'booked' for some alleged offence. These wayward, errant and capricious lads were known collectively as 'miscreants'. This was, to some extent, a misnomer since the dictionary definition of a miscreant is a 'wicked person', an 'evil doer' and a 'villain'. Now, it may be that in later life a few — I trust a very few — CTS lads graduated in crime to justify this appellation! But, during our time at the CTS, by no stretch of the imagination could any of us lads — even the most errant — justify being described as a 'miscreant'. Notwithstanding, this is the term that I initially used as School Captain until one morning Herbert Wadge intervened and bellowed: "We do not have any miscreants in this school!'. Henceforth I was required to use the term *wrong-doers*! I don't think this was much consolation to the lads who were duly summoned to the weekly prefects' meeting. They were required to stand outside the laboratory in the corridor whilst the case against them was put by the prefect who had, so to speak, apprehended them in the act of their wrong-doing. They were then called into the room to answer the charges made against them — for the most part bearing the countenance of the condemned.

I recall my first prefects' meeting very clearly — for two reasons. The first was the hapless nature of the first lad to be called into the room and the inherent seriousness of his offence. He had been caught smoking. Now this was a cardinal offence; in fact it could only be surpassed in gravity by a boy taking a swipe at a teacher — for which immediate expulsion from school was the inevitable consequence. As far as smoking is concerned, Herbert Wadge regularly railed against boys ever daring to light up whilst at school or even when travelling to and from school. I have to say that he was more concerned with the principle of obedience to school rules than with the contemporary issues of health and well-being. On the occasion I am recalling the boy concerned stood before the prefects with this serious accusation hovering over him like a sentence of death — to be more precise with the grim prospect of him being sent to see Herbert Wadge — which was just about as bad! What then happened provides me with the second reason for my recalling this meeting — I refer to the adult demeanour and remarkable eloquence of the School Captain presiding over the meeting. This was none other than Ron Saville.

He questioned the boy in the following manner. "You are accused of being seen smoking, is that correct?". The boy became evasive. Ron continued: "Now this was before you had consumed your school dinner?". The boy again confirmed these circumstances. "Nonetheless", said Ron, "smoke was seen issuing from your mouth but, since you had not recently eaten, it cannot have arisen from the processes of food decomposition!". At this the prefects erupted as one in laughter; the lad was left with no other option but to concede that he had indeed been caught smoking and to await the fate in store for him at the hands of Herbert Wadge.

As the end of our time at the CTS came ever nearer, and with the serious business of A.L. exams being over, we were left with some spare time on our hands — in effect we had some 'free periods'. I have already described how Mr. Bee continued his maths lessons in the form of additional classes devoted either to Greek philosophy or Einstein's *Theory of Relativity*. In my case I had to devote a lot of my 'spare' time to completing my A.L. woodwork project — you may remember, from what I have written earlier, that this was a record cabinet. Even so, I had my share of free time which leads me to say that some of this was spent in the prefects' room listening to records. One of the prefects had a portable record player which he had brought to school and had installed in the senior prefects' room. Other lads contributed by bringing in their favourite 45 rpm discs. By this time my musical tastes were more in the classical direction but I distinctly remember sharing in the enthusiasm when someone — I think it was Jack Glossop — brought in a collection of Lonnie Donegan's original Skiffle hits. These included *Rock Island Line, Don't You Rock Me Daddy O, Puttin' On The Style and My Old Man's A Dustman*! Enthusiasm, they say, is infectious and other boys contributed with their own 45s amongst which I recall the following that are included here to stir your memories: Acker Bilk playing *Stranger On The Shore* and *Georgia*; Anthony Newley singing *Do You Mind* and *Strawberry Fair*; and Tommy Steele singing *Rock With The Caveman, Singing The Blues* and *Sweet Georgia Brown*. With these 1950s hits we rocked away what remained of the Summer Term. Oh to have those days all over again — Man!

The School Captain

The School Captain at the CTS was far more than a symbolic figure with which to ornament the dais in morning assembly; the post carried considerable responsibility and the School Captain, as I was to discover myself, had to perform several duties. I have already described my first day at school and the part played in it by the then School Captain Rudd. I have also remarked how grown up he looked to my youthful gaze; five years later and I had reached the same age, doubtless looking similarly old to the junior boys. I have no idea how the School Captain was selected. Doubtless Herbert Wadge consulted with the staff and a name was brought forward and subsequently approved. Be this as it may, I recall arriving at school one morning late in the Summer Term of 1958 to be told that I was required to see Mr. Wadge immediately. Even though I was a senior prefect at the time, the summons to go and see Mr. Wadge still had the power to stir butterflies in the tummy. So it was with some trepidation that I knocked on his door and responded to the booming voice inside to enter. I remember how instead of remaining seated he rose, allowed himself a smile and then, walking towards me with outstretched hand, offered his congratulations on my being selected as School Captain for the academic year 1958–59. I was quite unprepared for this; there had been no preliminary discussion and certainly no mention of my being a possible candidate. Indeed, all the previous School Captains in my time at the CTS had been Engineers and I had assumed that this tradition would be maintained. So I was genuinely surprised at being chosen. Needless to say, I was not given any choice in the matter! That was it! I was the School Captain, elect, and I, like my predecessors, was expected to get on with it!

Herbert then said a few words to me about the importance of the office of School Captain in the life of the school, but at no point did he moralise or exhort me to do my best — I presume he took such things for granted! Following this event there was a pleasant little ceremony of initiation which took place at the next prefects' meeting. The retiring School Captain, Jack Badger, made a speech in which he thanked his fellow school prefects for their help and support over the year which had passed. He than removed from his lapel the captain's 'bar', that was worn above the school prefects' badge, and handed it over to myself. For a moment it felt like I was receiving the M.B.E.! It was then my turn to thank my predecessor for what he had achieved and to pledge myself to strive to follow his example. From this the reader will infer that our little ceremony was transacted very earnestly — it was in essence a test of public speaking. The school Vice Captains then followed with their own pious vows. It was all worthy of the arcane rituals of the Brotherhood of Masons!

My first administrative duty in the last few weeks of the Summer Term of 1958 was to allocate the responsibilities to be carried out by my fellow prefects. I consulted with Mr. McManus who had been through this procedure before with several other School Captains. I was grateful for his support since this undertaking was my first experience of exercising authority and it concentrated my mind. Who, I asked myself, should get dinner duty?; and who should monitor the entrances to the Holly and Bow Buildings in the morning for late-comers? In this way we worked our way through the list of duties to be performed during the academic year 1958–59.

By now the summer holiday was almost imminent when I was once more summoned to see Herbert Wadge. I have in fact already explained the reason for this in a previous section, namely, that I had been selected to attend the Outward Bound School at Ullswater. So, within a space of just a few days I found myself precipitated into two quite exposed positions and had to assimilate the meaning of Winston Churchill's words — "With leadership comes responsibility"!

My School Captain responsibilities began in earnest the following autumn when we all returned back to school. I was somewhat dreading the first morning assembly for the reason I will now explain. I duly took my School Captain's position at the front of the hall on the raised dais with my Vice Captain Charlie Prime seated at my side. Herbert Wadge went into overdrive with many exhortations to the new boys, seated just before me, to be good and to uphold the fine traditions of the school — and so on. As the end of his soliloquy

approached, I said to myself, "Will he introduce the newcomers to the CTS ritual of formal departure from assembly?". And, sure enough, he did. Thereby I found myself enacting the very same ceremony that, five years previously, I had seen performed by my predecessor School Captain Rudd. Furthermore I distinctly recall that as I called out, "School! Attention!", my legs started to wobble — just as I had seen Rudd's wobble all those years before!

The reader may recall that I have already remarked that Mr. McManus retired at Christmas 1958 — see the section concerned with *Physics*. This circumstance was eventful to me as School Captain since I was given the responsibility for arranging a collection from the prefects with which to buy a farewell present. I believe we each contributed one shilling — far more than its equivalent value today — and with the accumulated sum of about four guineas I went out shopping. I purchased an electric blanket! I have to confess that my selection of this particular present was deliberately contrived; let me explain why. When it came to the end of term a special assembly was held, late in the afternoon, at which I had to make a 'Thank You' speech to Mr. McManus on behalf of the prefects. Mr. Wadge first made a few remarks of an appreciative nature and then it was my turn. I recall thanking Mr. McManus for all that he had done for the boys at the CTS over his many years of service. In particular I remember saying: "The school hall in which we are now gathered could be filled many times with all the boys you have helped over the years". Then I reached my punch-line which went as follows: "On behalf of the prefects I would like you to accept this gift of an electric blanket — we all wish you a happy and a warm retirement!".

The late December end-of-term assembly meeting, to which I have just referred, was memorable to me for another reason; the circumstances are almost too embarrassing to relate but here goes. Earlier in the year Mr. Hughes had encouraged about half a dozen of us to meet at lunch time to practice singing; to describe us as being a small choir would be to unduly elevate our vocal accomplishments. But after several lunchtime practices, under the supervision of Mr. Hughes, we mastered the art of singing a number of melodies quite tunefully — and, let it be said, in four-part harmony. One week, with Christmas approaching, Mr. Hughes brought along the music for *The Holly and the Ivy* and with more practice this piece, at the risk of sounding rather grand, entered our repertoire. Then came the surprise that I suspect Mr. Hughes had long been planning; he suggested we should give a performance before the whole school! More specifically, he designated the occasion of the farewell to Mr. McManus as the occasion for making our public debut. We agreed, albeit with some trepidation but were nonetheless flattered by Mr. Hughes's implicit trust in our abilities. With about two days to go, in the midst of one our practices, Mr. Hughes sprang a further surprise by saying: "What we need is a solo. How about you Russell?". Now, you know what they say about being young and foolish — so I agreed! The outcome was, on the occasion of saying 'Thank you' to Mr. McManus, we entertained him and the school to a rendition of The *Holly and the Ivy*, for one verse of which I sang a solo! In this way I suspect I made a little piece of school history by being the only School Captain ever to have the nerve to sing before the whole school — that is in the capacity of a soloist!

Mr. McManus duly departed from the CTS and his

position as Deputy Head Teacher and Senior Science Master was taken by Mr. George Nichols — to whom I have already referred in the section concerning physics. He was not able to take up his appointment immediately which had a number of consequences to which I will now briefly refer. The most immediate of these was that there was a gap in the teaching of final year A.L. physics. This was filled for a period by Mr. Barton whose support for us in the teaching of physics I have previously discussed. Mr. Barton's temporary elevation to the teaching of final year A.L. physics left a gap lower down the school which also had to be filled. This post was taken, on a part-time basis, by Mrs. Marion Hill who was the wife of our history teacher Mr. Arthur Hill. Mrs. Hill, a science graduate from the University of Exeter, took up her post in September 1958 — precisely the same time that I became School Captain. The reason for my recalling these particular circumstances can now be told. Towards the end of term I received yet another request to go and see Herbert Wadge. As I entered his room he rose and greeted me with a look of some intensity — by way of preparing me for the seriousness of what he was about to say. He then remarked that he trusted my judgement and that he was in need of my opinion, adding that the matters which he wished to raise were confidential. He pledged me not to impart what he was going to say to anyone else — a pledge I have thus far upheld for more than forty years. He then came straight to the point and asked me how the boys were responding to Mrs. Hill's teaching of A.L. physics. Herbert justified his question on the grounds that he was mindful that she had had very little time to prepare her lessons — being thrown in at the deep end as it were — and that he was anxious that his boys should receive the best instruction and make good progress. Now, it so happens that my good friend Gordon Swan had remarked to me a few days previously how very conscientious and thorough Mrs. Hill was her in class preparation; she clearly took her work seriously and gave of her best. So I was able to impart these views to Herbert who appeared to be both relieved and satisfied. He then smiled and reaffirmed how people in his position sometimes had to make such requests of those around him — in the wider interests of his school. I made some form of acquiescence and duly departed. This experience was my first 'close encounter' with Herbert Wadge and it gave me some insight into the working procedures of our school — and a parallel insight into Herbert Wadge's own working methods and, more importantly, it offered me yet further confirmation of his absolute dedication to the CTS.

I have just mentioned Mr. Nichols and I will return to him for a moment since I had a number of occasions to work with him in my capacity as School Captain. Although a graduate of the University of Durham, Mr. Nichols came from Dorset — and he had a pronounced country accent to prove it. Shortly after his arrival he told me about the day of his interview for his new job. He told me how his train arrived at Sheffield via Rotherham; the furnaces were going full blast, the chimneys were belching smoke and it was raining! He looked at me and remarked: "I very nearly stayed on the train to go straight back home!". He had been the senior science teacher at a grammar school in the leafy south and the sudden transition to the industrial north was something of a culture shock. However, Yorkshire friendliness must have prevailed and, as I have intimated, he accepted the post on offer at the CTS.

Since everything was new to him he asked me to explain some of the 'ins and outs' of the school prefects system. Mr. Nichols did not take long to settle in to his new responsibilities and in due course we went on to collaborate on a number of occasions concerning such matters as the organisation of the prefects' meeting and the allocation of prefects' responsibilities. Our closest participation occurred some months later when Mr. Nichols consulted with me in the appointment of new prefects. He sought my advice as to who would make a good prefect and — more invidiously — who would not. This was my first experience of taking difficult decisions the outcome of which, in this particular case, would result in personal disappointment for some of the individuals concerned.

One of my most pleasant, and unexpected, obligations as School Captain was to represent the CTS on Civic Sunday. This was an annual event of religious thanksgiving — rather like Armistice Day. The event was, in effect, a ceremony of worship and thanksgiving. It took place one Sunday morning early in the Spring Term in the Cathedral where representatives from each of Sheffield's Schools gathered. After the service was over we processed from the Cathedral to the Town Hall. Once inside, still in formal procession, we ascended the main stair to the large banqueting-assembly room on the first floor. The school teachers amongst us were welcomed with a glass of sherry; the boys and girls were offered a cup of coffee. I found myself in the company of the Head Boy from King Edward VII School. We fell into conversation about which A.Ls. we were taking, as you do at that particular age in your life — now I suppose the equivalent subjects of conversation are the need for an hernia operation or a hip replacement. But on this Sunday morning such things were far from our minds, possessed as we were by youth and thoughts only of the immediate future. The latter prompted me to ask my King Ted's companion if he was planning to go to university. "Yes", he replied, adding "Of course". "Of course", I added myself — in recognition of the fact that what other destiny could there be in store for the Head Boy of King Ted's. Then I really let myself in for it by asking: "And which university are you planning to attend?". He contemplated me for a moment — as I believe a pigeon may do when deciding upon which innocent passer-by to deposit a load of shit — and replied: "Cambridge", adding "Of course". "Of course", I added. Whereupon I decided it was time to make my departure.

In the Autumn term of 1958 I found myself required to undertake further responsibilities as School Captain concerning the arrangements for the Entrance Examination, the very examination that I — and you other CTS lads reading this — had taken, in my case five years previously. The school was given a day off but I had to organise a small rota of volunteer prefects to help with various organisational matters. I recall how very young the boys looked who were sitting the exam — and I assume how grown up I must have appeared in their youthful eyes. At mid-morning there was a tea break for the prefect-helpers which took place in Mr. McManus's physics laboratory — he still had a few weeks to go before his retirement. A huge electric urn was placed on the laboratory bench and we stood around patiently waiting for it to come to the boil. Herbert Wadge made a brief appearance and, contemplating what was taking place, remarked: "You know what they say? A watched pot never boils!". We laughed, rather dutifully, and he disappeared back to his room. In due course the pot did of course come to the boil and we had our welcome cup of tea with a couple of biscuits. The best part of the day was school dinner. That remark requires a few words of explanation.

The Entrance Examination, being something of a special event in the daily routine of the CTS, inspired the cooks down at the Cathedral School to rise to the occasion by producing a meal somewhat better than their usual 'meat and two veg' bill of fare. On this particular day we had, amongst other things, roast potatoes and a choice of puddings. I recall how there were only about a dozen or so of us boys in the dining hall and having our meal in relative peace and quiet seemed very unusual — which of course it was since such a din usually prevailed at meal times that you had to raise your voice merely to have any chance of being handed the salt and pepper.

After partaking of this much better than average mid-day repast, we returned to the school hall to help out with the remaining afternoon session of examinations. I remember casting a benevolent eye over the young hopefuls, as they toiled away at their English paper, silently wishing them success. Perhaps some of you more youthful OBAs were amongst these self-same candidates?

One of my less agreeable duties as School Captain was to supervise the 'late parade'. A few of you reading this will doubtless not need to be reminded — from your personal experience — that the late parade was the punishment reserved for certain misdemeanours! The decision as to whether a particular boy should be required to attend the late parade was taken at the prefects' meeting. Similarly, the length of time that had to be endured on late parade depended upon the extent of the individual boy's naughtiness. Late parade took place in the main hall after school on a Thursday night. Boys were required to arrange themselves around the side walls facing close to the wall bars. At the command of the School Captain they then had to stand to attention and to maintain this posture for the stipulated length of time. Describing late parade in this way almost make me feel like a mediaeval tormentor! But that was the system and I, like my predecessors — and those who came after me — had to uphold this rather unedifying CTS tradition. Incidentally, I hope no lad who had to attend late parade under my auspices is thinking of taking his case to the European Court of Human Rights! I will personally settle out of court with any lad who thinks he was wronged as a result of my actions in the form of a free pint at the *President's Dinner*, no, on reflection I'd better make that half a pint — I may have too many claimants!

I have already intimated that I found the whole business of late parade uncongenial, not least for the obvious fact that the longer a group of boys were required to stay behind so had I! I would willingly have gone home and left the lads to their own devices! But the School Captain was required to set an example — as I was to discover one Thursday evening from no less an authority than Herbert Wadge himself! This is what happened.

As the term progressed I supervised several late parades, trying my best to be a martinet but I found I was not much good at it for the simple reason — if I may say so — that I found it difficult to be unpleasant! To explain just how I felt, let me digress a moment and recall a Peter Sellers sketch in which he portrays a reluctant sergeant major. He enters the men's sleeping quarters and, instead of barking out "Wake up you 'orrible lot!", says: "I say you chaps, look here it is getting rather late now — in fact it's almost the afternoon — do get up now — please"! I have to confess that I was just such a reluctant 'sergeant major'. Moreover, I could not bring myself to patrol round the hall by way of enforcing discipline in the form of my intimidating presence. In addition I wanted to make better use, as I saw it, of my time. The consequence of all this was that I contrived to do my homework whilst the unfortunate 'miscreants' stood to attention facing the wall bars. I did occasionally call out, to a lad whom I considered to be wilting somewhat, to stand to attention — "please". But I have to admit that my discipline was not of the most severe kind. The evening inevitably came when Herbert Wadge put his head round the door to see how things were progressing. I remember it well! A group of lads were standing to attention — well, more or less standing to attention — and I was engrossed in my applied maths homework — which concerned projectiles. There was strictly no talking on late parade and so absolute silence prevailed. This was suddenly rent by the sound of Herbert's voice which thundered: "Here, you! Stand to attention boy!". The effect was galvanic and his command was sufficiently general to make each and every boy in the room stand bolt upright as rigid as an icicle. I even myself endeavoured to assume a more determined posture, simultaneously sweeping aside all traces of my homework. Herbert came downstairs from the balcony and proceeded to patrol the hall issuing commands right and left which had the collective effect of stiffening the forms of the terrified lads even more. Then he came over to me and muttered certain dark imprecations concerning the need to maintain the strictest of discipline. "Yes Sir", I replied, and duly went home resolving to be more of a tyrant next time — not very successfully I have to add!

I have another Herbert Wadge story to tell, somewhat against myself, as follows — it comes from about the same period. I have already explained how my inclination was developing to architecture and the arts in general. This tendency must, somewhat subconsciously, have started to effect my appearance. I mean by this that I had allowed my hair to grow somewhat longer than the 'short back and sides' as required by strict CTS convention. Let it be added that my romantic inclination — if it can be so described — was several years in advance of the liberal-minded era of the 'swinging sixties' — and the long hair styles that were one of its hallmarks. Be this as it may, the day came when I received a summons to go and see Herbert Wadge — always an interesting experience as I have already remarked. "You asked to see me, Sir", I remarked on entering his room. Herbert contemplated me for a moment and conveyed an expression that intimated that he was wrestling with some inner conflict, in short, how to combine tact with candour. "Yes!", he replied — somewhat sternly. This prompted me to run through a quick mental check list; were my shoes nicely polished — yes, was I wearing the regulation school uniform — yes, was my tie neatly in place — yes. What then, I asked myself, was my solecism? I did not have to wait long for enlightenment, Herbert himself supplied the answer — in his normal commanding manner — as follows. "I have had occasion recently to reprimand a number of boys for their untidy appearance, in particular for their unkempt hair. To this they have replied — 'But the School Captain has long hair'. Now this makes it very awkward for me — you do see what I mean?". "Yes Sir", I replied, thinking to myself all the while: "But you're not much of an oil painting yourself". To be fair, Herbert gave a sort of kindly disarming smile and that was that — well, almost, because when I arrived home I had to pay an obligatory call on the barber for a CTS-approved short back and sides. The next morning, in assembly, Herbert mounted the podium in his usual manner and cast a searching glance in my direction. I have to say that I was the very embodiment of sartorial perfection! A fleeting smile of approval played across Herbert's countenance: "Be seated", he called out to the school, and I knew that all was well.

Another incident occurred in assembly a few weeks later which provides me with further reflections about Herbert Wadge. There are however a number of strands to this tale which I must first explain.

I have just mentioned my inclination to the arts and, at the period which I am recalling, this disposed me greatly to want to take O.L. Art — by way of preparation for my future study of architecture. The only problem was that O.L. Art was not on the CTS prescribed curriculum. I had several meetings with Herbert Wadge over this which, at times, became somewhat heated. I even suggested going for lessons at another school, but Herbert would have none of this. I will not elaborate on our meetings other than to add that they concluded by him telling me that I must do what I was told — which I greatly resented. Now, in the course of our discussions I had drawn to Herbert's attention that I had achieved my seven O.L. passes all at one sitting, without any 'resits'. This had quite impressed Herbert; in fact I was only the second boy, at this period, to achieve this feat the other lad being Gerald Craven — a former School Captain. I am not boasting when I say this because it is essential to my story in the following way. In the midst of our conversations Herbert looked through my school record — you may recall how all our school reports and personal documents were stored in a folder. He noticed my seven O.L. achievement and remarked: "Your parents must be very proud of you". Now, the reader will recall from the earlier part of my narrative that my mother had died the previous year, so I had to reply tactfully: "Yes Sir, my father is very pleased and, if my mother were still alive, I am sure she would be also". I added: "You will recall that she died last year". Dear Herbert looked mortified and apologised for his oversight. Again I tried to help things along by remarking: "I do understand; you must have many things on your mind". He smiled — but still would not relent and let me take O.L. Art! Now I can come to the main point of my tale which is what happened the next day in morning assembly.

At the close of assembly — a typical forty-five minute session — Herbert did something quite untypical. Instead of requiring the school to stand to attention as he made his departure — which was his normal procedure — he dismissed the school and remained behind. At the same time he turned to me and said: "Please remain Captain" — he frequently made reference to me in that style. Once more I wondered what I was in for and made another quick mental check of my appearance — hair, tie, uniform etc. — all were neatly in order. So what did Herbert want to say. Finally, alone in the hall, he turned to me, placed his right hand on my shoulder and said: "You know that was a *faux pas* of mine yesterday about your mother. I do apologise for my oversight". I was very touched by this show of remorse. Clearly, the misunderstanding of the previous day had played on Herbert's mind and he still felt the need to exonerate himself. Once more I thanked him for his consideration and we went our separate ways. I tell this little story to confirm — not that such confirmation is really necessary — how kind and caring a man was Herbert Wadge beneath his outwardly intimidating exterior.

Being School Captain had a number of privileges which I occasionally turned to my advantage. Let me describe one circumstance when I used my position of authority to good effect. It was lunchtime and I left the prefects' room to make my way down to Cathedral School for my dinner. In doing so I noticed a damsel in distress; to be more accurate the damsel was a middle-aged woman but she was clearly distressed. Her car, which was parked behind the Education Offices, had a flat tyre. As I passed she looked at me beseechingly, exclaiming "Oh dear". "Oh dear", I reciprocated, "You have a flat tyre". I realised that was not a very constructive observation but inspiration then dawned. "Wait a moment", I added, "I think I can help". Whereupon I made off in the direction of the Firth Building to find a group of 'volunteers'. It did not take me long to search out a small group of lads to whom I made a determined approach. Indeed, so determined was my approach that I momentarily put them in a state of fright — they instinctively thought that I was going to reproach them for some wrong doing. So I disabused them that I had any admonitory intentions by adopting my most beguiling manner, as follows: "Look lads, do you think you could help me out. There's a lady nearby with a flat tyre and she could do with some kindly help". "Yes Sir", they choroused in unison — I should add that they were a young group of boys who were typical of many others who, at that age, paid me the compliment of calling me 'Sir' — another one of life's small pleasures. So I led my band of helpers to the lady in distress, introduced her to my young companions, set them to work and then made off to get my dinner — feeling very pleased with myself!

I have another story to tell which reflects on the position of authority enjoyed by the School Captain, although this is rather an unedifying tale — indeed, it is something of a confession. To come straight to the point, one morning — during my period of being School Captain — I was late for school! I have no excuses to offer, I was quite simply late. Morning assembly was already under way so there was no chance of my sneaking into either the Firth, Bow or Holly Buildings since their entrances were already guarded by the very prefects whom I had appointed to watch out for late-comers! What then was to be done? Inspiration subsequently dawned. I first made my way to the prefects' room where I removed my coat and left it with my other possessions in my locker. I then assumed a look of calm authority and made a completely bogus tour of inspection of the Holly, Bow and Firth Buildings pretending that I was checking up to see how things were going. Since nothing of the kind had ever happened before, the prefects, on the lookout for late-comers, were rather startled by my presence. I smiled genially by way of intimating that I was not checking up on them! Then I said: "Good morning, well, I'd better be going now" and made my departure — leaving the prefects concerned in this little episode looking distinctly perplexed! But I still had to get into morning assembly. I waited outside the hall with my ear pressed close to the door listening out for the moment when Herbert announced which hymn was to be sung. When the moment came I entered the hall, disguising my entry amidst the general commotion of boys standing up getting ready to sing. I duly took my place on the podium a little to the surprise of Herbert Wadge who was by then getting into his full hymnal stride. Later in the assembly, whilst a member of staff was making an announcement, Herbert leaned over to me and remarked: "We missed you at the start of assembly. I took it you were busy with your other responsibilities". "Yes Sir", I replied — "I was just making sure that everything was going well with checking up on-late comers". "Ah", responded Herbert, "Just so". "Indeed", I rejoined, thinking to myself — with skills of deception like these I should become a second-hand car salesman!

I will stay a moment longer with the theme of punctuality and my journey to school since a circumstance in my life, at this period, somewhat changed my normal school travel arrangements. My cousin Barrie Bancroft, to whom I have made previous reference, had by now left school (Rowlinson Technical School) and worked for the Safety in Mines Research Establishment. Like many other lads of his age he yearned after, and eventually obtained, a motor bike — I was not to achieve this particular ambition until my second year at the University of Sheffield. In due course Barrie started to give me a lift right to the very entrance of the CTS main building. However, on cold mornings my cousin's bike could be distinctly temperamental — by which I mean, simply stated, the bugger wouldn't start! On more than one occasion I recall how, in making up for lost time, we rounded the corner of Leopold Street/West Street at about fifty miles an hour, inclined at about 45° to the horizontal — just as shown in Bill Davis's mechanic's diagrams portraying the angle of banking of objects in circular motion! On such occasions, to the accompaniment of screeching brakes, I would leap off the bike and make a hasty dash for the Prefects' Room, endeavour to regain my School Captain's composure, and then get ready for morning assembly. In fairness to my cousin, he tried everything possible to coax his bike into action, including pr-heating the bike's sparking plug in the gas oven! After a few months of all this excitement, I graciously declined any more such lifts to school and reverted to the more sedate mode of conveyance of the public tramcar.

My last official duty in my capacity as School Captain was to represent the CTS once more at Sheffield Cathedral. A special service of thanksgiving was held to which sixth-form representatives from Sheffield's secondary and grammar schools were invited. The principal theme of the service was an expression of appreciation, on the part of the clergy, for the work undertaken by the teachers for their pupils. The service also included some words of hope for the future for the assembled sixth-fomers who, like myself, were about to leave school. It was quite an emotional occasion — rather like being in the midst of a typical CTS morning assembly but on a much larger scale. A number of pupils had been selected to read verses from the Bible; interestingly, one of these was a close friend of my then CTS companion Brian Lister. This lad was called Barrie; he was attending one of Sheffield's grammar schools and he read his selected words with great conviction. Most memorable of all, for me, was the singing of Beethoven's stirring *Dedication's Hymn* the sentiments of which were well suited to the occasion.

I will close this section with a reference to the farewell speech that I made as School Captain — it involves a quite remarkable set of circumstances and coincidences. But, let me first call to mind the CTS tradition of the School Captain making his farewell speech.

On the very last day of the Summer Term the departing School Captain had the privilege of recording a speech which was later played back to the whole school. This event took place, as usual, in the main hall but at the untypical time of about 3.00 p.m. in the afternoon. It would be overstating the case to describe these recordings as being messages for posterity, but, as I will shortly reveal, at least a few of these recordings are still in existence. The most memorable and eloquent of all these speeches must surely be the one made by School Captain Ron Saville. I recall, from the end-of-term assembly held in the Summer of 1957, that Ron spoke affectionately of his time at the CTS making mention of all that the school had done for him. But what was so memorable about his speech was the manner of his anticipation of what his new school held in store for him; Ron was not strictly leaving school but was transferring to another school with a view to preparing to train to be a doctor — a plan subsequently abandoned in favour of a military career. If I remember correctly, the key phrase in Ron's speech — which stirred our collective imagination — was when he spoke of 'obtaining new furniture for the mind'. We all listened with rapt attention, engrossed in Ron's imagery and powers of expression — which were quite remarkable for a schoolboy. Such was the effect of Ron's speech that it prompted Herbert Wadge to rise from his seat, at its conclusion, and to congratulate him on his performance — for such it was. Since Herbert never lost an opportunity to 'moralise' he immediately upheld Ron's skill with words as an example to the rest of us, at the same time lamenting our slipshod ways and slack speech idioms. Poor Ron just had to sit and endure all this unsolicited praise! Now let me turn to the circumstances of my own farewell speech which I recorded two years later in the Summer Term of 1959.

I first wrote out a draft of my text and read it over, made various changes, tried very hard to emulate the style of my distinguished predecessor Ron and, realising that I never could, I eventually settled for what I had written. The actual recording was made in Herbert Wadge's room under the direction of Mr. Thompson. I was given a brief opportunity to record a few words to get the feel of things and to establish the sound-recording level. Then I recorded my speech and that was that. It was played to the school the next day on the ancient recording equipment that many former CTS boys will remember that Herbert Wadge used to record and replay the musical proceedings of our school Speech Days. In my Captain's speech I made a metaphor concerning my successor — a lad called Britton — and wished him, as School Captain, a 'fair sea and a prosperous voyage'. The words in quotation marks are taken from the *Overture* by Felix Mendelssohn which is known by these particular words; from all of this the reader will correctly infer that I was trying hard to make a favourable impression!

Over the following years, in moments of nostalgic reflection, I often had occasion to think about my farewell speech but it gradually faded from my mind as such things are wont to do. Then, quite remarkably, these events were recalled to my mind through what I have already described above as a remarkable combination of circumstances and coincidences.

Here is what happened.

Let me say first of all that I was a late developer as far as joining the CTS *Old Boys' Association* is concerned. My membership commenced in the mid 1980s — by which time the long arm of our then Secretary Stuart Green had reached out to me and secured my affiliation with the OBA. Nevertheless, being resident in Edinburgh precluded my taking an active part in the proceedings of the Association. My participation was confined largely to reading the *Newsletter* and making occasional phone calls to other OBA members. It was by means of the *Newsletter* that I eventually learned of the death of Herbert Wadge, in May 1989, from our then President Mike Ingham. Mike urged as many Old Boys as possible to take part and provided us with detailed instructions as to how to reach Huddersfield Crematorium where the funeral service was to take place. I discuss the circumstances of Herbert's funeral in some detail later. For now, I will confine myself to the particular circumstances that bear directly upon my narrative. As I was waiting for the funeral cortege to arrive, my eye alighted upon the tall figure of Mr. Ronald Underdown. Ron was appointed to the CTS in September 1957 to teach English and French — and, may I add, what a handsome young man he was as the school photographs that survive from that era bear testimony. Ron has not so far featured in my narrative for the simple reason that I did not receive lessons from him in either English or French. Nonetheless, I immediately recognised his still handsome features and we fell into conversation. It was thereby that Ron chanced to say what pleasure he had been experiencing in sorting out the CTS archive of sound recordings of Speech Day and the few remaining speeches recorded by former School Captains. At the mention of the latter, I naturally picked up my ears. Ron informed me that he had nineteen tapes in all dating from the years 1951–1961 of which about two thirds were, he said, of CTS Speech Days for the years 1952–1955 and 1961. Ron lamented the gaps in the recording sequence but told me it was of little consequence since the recordings had so deteriorated over the years as to be virtually unplayable. Ron then added that the surviving recordings of School Captains, and other school officials, dated from 1950 and continued through to 1960 — and, importantly, were of a much better quality — some in fact being quite audible. Ron then enthused by remarking: "It so happens that it was only the other night that I played through some of these recordings and I was particularly taken by the phrase used by one of the speakers". That must be the speech by Ron Saville, I thought to myself, and so I said to Ron Underwood: "Did the School Captain in question talk of 'obtaining new furniture for the mind' ". "No", replied Ron, "That wasn't it". Could it be, I asked myself, that Ron had been listening to a recording of *my own* speech? So I put the question to Ron: "Did the speech you are trying to recall include the phrase 'a calm sea and a prosperous voyage'"?. "That's the very phrase!", exclaimed Ron. Silence! I was quite astonished! I had not given active thought to my speech for many years and then suddenly I discovered Ron Underdown with a recording of it in his possession; moreover he had played it through, prompting me to recall a phrase from it — from more than forty years ago — which in turn helped Ron to identify the speech as being my own! I found this sequence of events quite remarkable. A few days later an audio-tape copy of my speech arrived through the post, by courtesy of Ron, and it is from this that I have made the transcription which follows — in effect my 'farewell' words to the CTS boys assembled in the school hall on the last day of the Summer Term in 1959:

Terence Russell speaking, School Captain and Telford House Vice Captain for the year 1958–59.

If, five years ago a certain rather tall, pink-faced First-Year boy had been asked to hazard a guess as to his lot in five years time he would have timorously replied: "I don't know"! Well now, those five years have seen many changes; four unshaven weeks at an Outward Bound School have seen the disappearance of the pink face forever and a treble voice — always suggestive of a distressed cat — has now become, I think Mr. Hughes would agree, a fairly passable tenor.

But, seriously now, I can say with all sincerity that my stay in the school has been one of reward and profit. I cannot however confess to any deep sorrow over my departure since the promise of a university course, and, more immediately, a month's stay at a camp in Austria are expectations too great to evoke any but feelings for the future. It would be wholly wrong of me though to let this opportunity pass without saying to the school: "Thank you for tolerant guidance and thank you for presenting before me those timeless qualities of wonderment and appreciation — a rich endowment indeed".

Finally, to my successor Britton, I wish the very best of good fortune and, in yielding the helm, I wish him and all who sail with him in the next year — as Mendelssohn suggests in his music — 'A calm sea and a prosperous voyage'!

To you all
Good-bye and good luck!

Departure from the CTS

Although I have closed the previous section of my text with reference to my farewell to the CTS, in this section I intend to retrace my steps back to a period just a few months from the end of the Summer Term, in fact to the time when those of us who were at the end of our school career were contemplating finally leaving school. We fell into three distinct groups: the first consisted of boys who had completed their basic three years of study and, having obtained their Building or Engineering Diploma, were only too eager to be on their way to paid employment; the second consisted of boys who had stayed on for an extra year, or two, to strengthen their qualifications by taking some O.Ls — seven was about the maximum possible; and the third group consisted of boys who had progressed to A.L. — these were the 'elder statesmen' of the CTS. It is a tribute to many of the boys in my first two groups that they went on to distinguish themselves so well in industry, eventually, in several cases, founding their own companies and becoming thereby respected 'captains of industry'. But it is to the third group of boys, to which I belonged, that I will now direct this part of my narrative.

Our school days had been such an integral part of our lives and had continued for so long that I think it is true to say that many of us experienced something of a shock to realise, when the time eventually came, that school days did in fact come to an end! And so it was, in the early Summer of 1959, that I contemplated the prospect of what I may describe as 'life after the CTS'. Now I had to think and plan my life for myself — as did of course all my contemporaries leaving school like myself. The main structure of my immediate future life was already in place, namely, as I have just intimated in the transcript of my School Captain's speech, a course of study at the university — to be more specific the University of Sheffield.

The preparation for those of us intending to go on to further and higher education commenced in the Autumn Term of the year preceding our planned departure — in my case the Autumn of 1958. There was no University Central Council on Admissions (UCCA) in those days — or its successor the University Central Admissions System (UCAS); application to university or college was largely a matter of personal choice and initiative. In the case of boys at the CTS, the first step in the process to gaining entry to a particular institution was to consult with Herbert Wadge. Herbert was quite untiring in his attempt to do his best for his lads; he must have devoted many hours to discussing the future plans of his sixth-formers giving each boy a personal interview. I certainly received the benefit of such an interview with Herbert in which I outlined my intentions to study architecture — which had been formulating in my mind for a number of years. I had set my mind on going to the University of Sheffield. This was a natural choice since Alan Pagan, another CTS Builder to whom I have referred previously, had pioneered the way there in 1957 by gaining a place himself. Since leaving the CTS Alan had dropped in to the prefects' room on a number of occasions to keep in touch with his pals and I had formed the impression that he was enjoying the course. In addition, I had obtained a copy of the Prospectus and was impressed by what it had to say about the Department of Architecture. But Herbert Wadge had other ideas. He was a personal friend of the professor of architecture at the University of Manchester and he drew my attention to the high academic standards that prevailed in this department. Notwithstanding, I had made up my mind to go to the University of Sheffield and eventually Herbert relented, set aside his own views and generously agreed to give my application to study at my home-town university his full support. At this point I will make a digression from reflecting about my personal circumstances to say a few words of a more general nature as to how my generation of sixth-formers prepared for admission to college and university.

To help us to prepare our applications we received guidance in formal letter writing and the creation of a curriculum vitae — or 'CV'. We were advised to list our academic achievements, mention any prizes we had won and to list our extra-curricular interests. I recall stating that I enjoyed 'fell walking', and substantiated this claim with reference to my period at the Outward Bound School at Ullswater. Two or three lads who chanced to catch sight of what I had written — and who had stated on their CV that they liked 'hiking' — surreptitiously changed their text form 'hiking' to 'fell walking' — confirming that imitation is the sincerest form of flattery!

I recall how we were further advised to make some mention of those of our activities or interests that had a direct bearing on our chosen course of study. Most of my immediate contemporaries were intending a career in one of the various branches of engineering and so contrived to work this theme into their letter of application and accompanying CV. In particular I will mention Vice Captain Charlie Prime whom I remember was trying to decided if he should take either a physics

degree, to prepare him for the then pioneering industry of nuclear engineering, or to read for an engineering degree with a bias towards electronics. He eventually opted for the latter and became an expert on guided weapons — thereby consigning himself to a lifetime of secrecy since all his subsequent work in this field was of a classified nature. In my case, as an intending architect, I had to prepare a small portfolio of drawings by way of demonstrating my artistic ability — or at least some inclination in that direction.

I am mindful to recall here a particular circumstance relating to a group of boys who were planning to go to college rather than to university. Let me say first that the late 1950s saw the advent of the so-called Colleges of Advanced Technology — or 'CATs' as they came to be known. Herbert Wadge became an immediate fan of these and their curricular; a few of them had degree-awarding powers, through affiliation with sister universities, and could award what was then a completely new-style degree of Bachelor of Technology — or 'B.Tech.'. Many of the CATs duly transmogrified into the Polytechnics — and have more recently become the 'new universities'. However, concerning life back in 1959 at the CTS, one or two lads led the way with their application to a CAT-style course — and then the flow became a flood!. This prompted Herbert, who could see things getting somewhat out of control, to do a rant one morning in assembly. His theme was 'try to think for yourself' and he likened some lads, who were jumping onto the CAT band wagon, to be "just like so many sheep following one another through a gap in a hedge row". I recall how on another occasion Herbert did an equally impassioned rant against being taken in by high-flown job descriptions. He cited the circumstances of one particular boy who had expressed some interest in a job which was advertised as being a 'Telecommunications Engineer'. When Herbert investigated the matter it transpired the job was in fact little more than erecting telegraph poles! "Use your *gumption* boys!" railed Herbert, making rare use of our Yorkshire dialect, "Don't be so easily led!". He need not have been so concerned; most CTS lads had their heads screwed on and were quite discerning when it came to their choice of careers and college or university courses.

My own application to study architecture at the University of Sheffield required a formal interview which was conducted by Professor John Needham. I took along several of my CTS school books and showed him the work I had done for my Building Diploma. He was quite interested in what I had to show him but asked me if I had any more recent work — of a more artistic kind. I explained that it had not been possible for me to take art at my school and that I had concentrated on maths, applied maths and physics. A long silence followed!, after which he consulted a letter lying on the desk before him. "Your headmaster thinks highly of you", said the Professor, adding, "I think we can offer you a place but you will have to work hard to raise you artistic skills — most students on our course have done more art than you and some have A.L. Art". I will insert here that over the following five years I did indeed have to work hard to raise my artistic skills. But, concerning the interview, all was well and I had secured my place. My letter of acceptance admitted me to the five year Diploma Course in Architecture and, if my A.L. grades were good enough, it stated that I would be enrolled on the degree course. So I returned to the CTS and reported the outcome to Herbert Wadge — remembering to thank him for his reference. Together with my contemporaries, the only thing remaining was to wait for the results. You may remember how, in order to receive these, we had to complete a self-addressed postcard listing the subjects we had taken. When the school was notified of the results, details were completed by the School Office and mailed out to us — sometime in mid August. It was an agonising wait! I will reveal the outcome of my A.L. results in the following section — and will discuss how they involved me in returning to the CTS a year later. For the moment I will briefly describe something else, which has a bearing on my narrative, that was on my mind in the early months of 1959.

One morning my eye caught sight of a poster displayed on the notice board on the main stair which, you may remember, was located immediately opposite the office of Herbert Wadge, in fact just outside the School Office. This notice board was reserved for various official school notices and external communications relevant to school life. The poster that caught my eye was directed at teenage boys who had motor cycles and it urged them to take great care when overtaking another vehicle, especially when at the brow of a hill. Its message was made all the more dramatic by the depiction of a young man accelerating past a motor car — straight into the path of an oncoming vehicle concealed by the brow of the hill! Now all of this is incidental to what I most want to say, namely, that just below this poster was another sponsored by the World University Service — 'WUS' — inviting young men and women to participate in voluntary service in Europe. The aim was to help to construct low-cost homes to help to house the many refugees, displaced by the Second World War, who were still living in camps. The invitation held out the prospect of free travel to Europe and free living accommodation — in a refugee camp! In particular, volunteers were required to work at a camp in Austria located on the outskirts of Linz.

The sight of the WUS poster fired my imagination and I immediately forgot all about the road-safety message that had originally caught my eye. Working in Linz offered the prospect of visiting Vienna — and thereby the chance to visit the birth place and home of so many famous composers. Over the next few weeks I prevailed upon my then close CTS friend with the splendid name Brian Bain Clovis Lister. Brian eventually agreed to come with me and, in due course, we both secured the requisite papers. Herbert Wadge signed my passport photograph and Mr. Nichols wrote me the required character reference.

Having imparted this information I can now take my leave of the CTS. The whole school assembled, in its usual fashion, in the afternoon of the last day of the Summer Term. Herbert Wadge sent those of us, who were about to depart, on our way with many fulsome tributes and I gave my farewell speech and called the school to attention for the last time. I recall how, on leaving the school hall, I chanced to meet Mr. Howell who was standing by the rear entrance near to the main door. I remarked: "I'm sorry I was never much good at sport", to which he smiled and replied, "It's all right — you did your best!". With that I left the CTS main building for the last time in my school career, collected my possessions from my locker and made my way home.

The events which followed, notably my five years of training to become an architect, would quite easily fill another book of reminiscences. I will spare the reader that ordeal and confine myself, in my concluding remarks, to those incidents bearing directly upon my central theme of life and work at the CTS.

Life after the CTS

With school now behind me I could contemplate my immediate future — Vienna beckoned! I duly made my way by boat and train to Linz and worked hard digging out the foundations for the future homes of those refugees then domiciled in various refugee camps near to Linz who were fortunate enough to be re-housed in proper accommodation. I found myself in the company of several other school-leavers and some young people who were already studying at university — notably Oxford and Cambridge. I remember how, on arriving at the camp, attired in my school uniform (!), one of these individuals — a rather superior young woman — condemned my school badge as being 'rather dull'! To my lasting regret, I allowed myself to be intimidated by this remark — even though I had been, in part, responsible for the design — and, the next day, I stealthily unpicked the stitches securing my badge with a kitchen fork and threw my badge away! In retrospect I suppose that was my final symbolic act of severance with my old school. But now, I find myself thinking, how I wish I had that badge as a souvenir of my days at the CTS!

My stay at Linz was not all work and no play; time allowed for a visit to Vienna for me to pay homage to Beethoven, Haydn, Mozart and Schubert either at their places of birth or at the various surviving houses where they lived and worked. Interestingly, on my return to Sheffield, I received a letter from the WUS officials commending me for my work and asking if I would care to return the next year as Head of the Camp — like being a sort of School Captain all over again! I modestly declined. But I did accept the invitation to publicise the work of WUS by writing an article about my experiences, and those of my companions, on the subject of 'Life in a refugee camp'. Extracts from this were later published in *The Star* evening newspaper.

Waiting for me on my return to Sheffield were my A.L. results! I had achieved a distinction for my Engineering and Technical Drawing, a good pass for Physics but only marginal grades for Pure Maths and Applied Maths. The latter were good enough to admit me to the Diploma Course in architecture but not to the Honours Degree. This was a considerable disappointment to me, not least in view of all the hard work that I had undertaken to improve my French in anticipation of studying this subject as an integral part of the degree curriculum. In due course my disappointment receded and was replaced by the exciting prospect of learning all about how to become an architect.

I enrolled for my course of study in architecture in the first week of October 1959. My technical preparation for the course, at the CTS, could not have been better. Architectural Design, I rapidly discovered, required a good understanding of such related subjects as building construction and structural mechanics for which my classes at the CTS provided the ideal introduction. I did find however that my class companions — there were about thirty students in my First Year — were generally much more accomplished than myself in such subjects as painting and colour illustration — which featured substantially in my course. I had to work very hard to develop these skills to the required standard. But these considerations are incidental to what I now have to say; I resolved to improve my A.Ls. and thereby to 'transfer' to the degree course. It would be a monumental undertaking — and, moreover, would lead me back to the CTS!

To read for the degree in architecture the regulations required that I needed good grades in two A.Ls which had to be taken at the same time. I decided on the following plan of action; I would resit my Pure Maths and Applied Maths as a single subject 'Pure and Applied Maths' and, with the new skills I was developing at the university in drawing and painting, I would add a second subject in the form of A.L. Art. The later required passes in three papers, namely. The History of Architecture, Drawing from Life and Painting — altogether nine hours of examinations and six more hours for the maths exams. All this had to be done with scarcely any revision and no preparation — I was too busy with my First Year university studies.

To take Pure and Applied maths I had to obtain the consent of Herbert Wadge; his permission was required since I had to return to the CTS to be enrolled as an 'External Candidate' — I suspect that I made a little piece of CTS history thereby. I paid a visit to see Herbert in the Spring of 1959 to secure the necessary consent. He was slightly baffled by what I was attempting but willingly gave his permission. In addition, I collected a set of all the class textbooks I required from Mr. Thompson — just in case I could find a moment to put in some revision. To take my A.L. Art exams I had to be enrolled at the Mechanics' Institute at Derby — which, I subsequently discovered, was conveniently located near Derby Station adjacent to the railway sidings.

In mid-June of the Summer of 1960, I returned to the CTS to take the two papers in Pure and Applied Maths; I received a few curious stares from boys who were also sitting these exams — doubtless wondering just what their former School Captain was doing in their midst. By the way, we sat the exam in the cloakroom at Cathedral School. My three visits to the Mechanics' Institute at Derby had to be planned like a military operation, given the journey I had to make and the early starting times of the exams. I will recall just one small incident arising from these circumstances. On arriving at the Mechanics' Institute — at the crack of dawn so as to be in good time — I met another candidate who, like myself, was looking for the exam venue. "Are you taking A.L. Art", I asked; "No", he replied, "I'm taking my B.A. Finals of the University of London"! It was then that I realised that the Mechanics' Institute was a regional centre for candidates who were sitting all manner of subjects at different levels.

The Summer Term of 1960 was certainly a very busy period for me with my self-imposed load of two A.L. exams in addition to my full diet of First Year university exams. The sequel to all of this can be quickly told; I passed my two A.Ls and all my university exams, and, on proceeding to my Second Year of architectural studies, was duly admitted to the degree curriculum — for which I then had to enrol for additional classes in Economics and Economic History. But that, as they say, is another story!

In the autumn of 1960 I returned the class maths textbooks that I had borrowed from Mr. Thompson; he

remarked, "Well done", on hearing of the successful outcome of my endeavours. Then, by coincidence, as I was leaving I met Mr. Bee to whom I imparted the same information. "Good", he remarked, with his typical economy of words, following which he disappeared into the Holly Building — never to be seen by me again.

My study of architecture settled into a steady routine of lectures, site visits and practical work, extending for a period of five years — precisely the same length of time that I had spent at the CTS. By way of representing an aspect of this work, I have included amongst my accompanying illustrations, one of my First Year pencil sketches — see Fig. 92. This would subsequently be followed by several hundred other pieces of art work on all manner of architectural subjects. This circumstance prompts me to comment that if any course of study is deserving of John Milton's famous words — *'The life so short, the craft so long to learn'* — it must surely be the study of architecture. But, as I have already intimated, detailed references to this period in my life have no place in this account. I will however highlight a few moments, from the time when I studied architecture, which touch upon my main theme of the life and work at the CTS.

Freshers' Week is the name which most universities and colleges use to describe the week before the start of term in which new students are welcomed and initiated into their new place of learning. In particular, it is a time for finding out about new societies and clubs and deciding which, from the many dozens, to join. I joined three; one was the *Architecture Society*, participation in which was more or less obligatory. We visited buildings — ancient and modern — and attended lectures by eminent architects and designers. The work I had undertaken, years previously for Mr. Edgar Grantham at the CTS, was an admirable preparation for this aspect of my work. The second society I joined was the *University Madrigal Group*. This group, as its name implies, was dedicated to the performance of unaccompanied songs written in different parts, usually four, for combined male and female voices. The group gave recitals at venues in and around Sheffield — including memorable visits to various Derbyshire churches — and further afield to other universities. For my participation in these musical activities, I feel a debt of gratitude to Mr. Hughes for introducing me to part singing — and, may I add, to *Mother Nature* for conferring on me the attributes of a not too bad tenor voice! The third society I joined was the *Music Committee* which was responsible for arranging lunchtime concerts and recitals in the university. I became Treasurer of the society and I will here confess that one year I got the books into such a muddle that the Chairman and Secretary — the latter no less a person than my future wife — had to spend an evening with me to sort things out! My defence is that numbers were never my strong point! I particularly valued my membership of the *Music Committee*; when serving on it I personally met such artists as the guitarist John Williams — who was then only a young man — and, as I have just revealed, I met my wife-to-be Mary. In joining the *Music Committee* I was, once more — to some extent — following in the footsteps of Mr. Hughes who, during his time at the University of Sheffield, had been an active member of this very society. When browsing through the book of minutes I discovered his name amongst the records.

I will turn now to the activities of the University of Sheffield *Rag Day* which will provide a few amusing anecdotes and some fleeting references to the CTS.

Rag Day was, and I believe still is, held by the University of Sheffield on a Saturday early in the First Term of the academic year. It provides a good opportunity for new students to become integrated into the more absurd rituals of university life — such as larking about — and, more seriously, it is a time to think of others and to collect money for worthy causes. An integral part of *Rag Day* — an indispensable part — are the processional *floats* used by the various student societies to promote an awareness of their activities and to generally serve as a focus for good fun and from which to collect the small change tossed by passers-by. In my First Year I was co-opted by the *Architecture Society* to help to design its float. I had by then made friends with some fellow students in the Engineering Department, which, co-incidentally, included a number of former CTS lads — some of them were my exact contemporaries such as David Moran and Geoff Gray. As we student architects progressed with our design, I decided to go and see how the Engineers were getting on with their float. What I saw was quite remarkable! They had constructed a massive cannon, in the shape of a huge phallus — mounted on two large spheres — and inscribed along its sides was the caption — '*Sheffield's Biggest Tool*'! "Typical of Engineers", I thought — although I secretly admired their courage! I believe, in the actual procession, the offending words had to be covered over, in the interests of modesty, leaving the rest of the 'tableau' to the imagination of the observer.

As for myself, I contributed to the design of the Architects' float which was an amazing built-form creation hauled by architecture students dressed as Egyptian slaves — who were 'lashed', as the contrivance proceeded, by one of the department's few women students who was attired in black-mesh stockings — and a few other garments — to make her look distinctly erotic! You could say that our level of invention was only just one notch above that of the Engineers!

The following year I allowed myself to get carried away — *seriously* carried away. Perhaps I was giving expression to some form of repressed tendencies — after being so good and hard working at the CTS!; anyway, this is what happened. I joined a small group of students from the Department of Economics where I was then studying for what was called my 'Outside Subject'. Believe it or not — and I swear this is true — six of us trundled an old iron bedstead through the streets to which was attached a large beer barrel — which we had nicked from a brewery when the foreman was not looking. And, inside the barrel was a lightly clad young woman — and I mean *lightly clad*! But the best is yet to come; amazingly, we hauled our contrivance all the way to Manchester over the Snake Pass! What idiots we were! But we collected a fortune as the young 'nymphet' in our barrel beguiled the passers-by to throw pennies into her barrel! As darkness came on — and it gets very dark in the middle of the night on the Snake Pass! — I thought I would improve the security of our little group by bringing up the rear holding a night watchman's paraffin lamp that I happened to 'find' protecting some road works. In fact it was only one of lots of other such lamps so, in removing one, I had not endangered anyone or anything. But that was not the view taken by a policeman whom we met about half a mile down the road; seeing me with my lamp he called out: "Ere, what are you doin' wi that there lamp!". On hearing the policeman's voice, the young woman in the barrel hid low down to evade his gaze — doubtless for fear of being charged with public indecency! — and I was left to explain my actions! Mr. Plod was not impressed. I should add that at the time I was wearing pyjamas and a bowler hat which, you can imagine, made it difficult for me to be taken seriously. In short, the policeman apprehended my lamp and made off into the dark with it — looking even more comical than myself.

I will add a little more detail to my girl-in-the-barrel tale which almost had a tragic ending. We were all driven back to Sheffield — totally knackered and exhausted — in an old Bedford van. We all piled in the back together with our tins of money and unsold copies of the *Twicker* — the *Rag Day* magazine. The driver, who had followed on behind our bedstead, was as tired as ourselves and — wait for it — he took a bend too fast and drove us off the road into a ravine! I remember the van rolling over and over and then being thrown out onto the grass. The van was a complete 'write off'. I looked about me to see my companions drenched in blood, and, likewise, myself and our unsold copies of the *Twicker*. "God", I remember saying to myself, "I must be dying". But as I stared up at the sky I slowly realised that I felt all right — and further realisation dawned; the 'blood', which was everywhere, was in fact only red paint from a tin we had used to colour the beer barrel to make it look more lurid! We were in fact — quite miraculously — unharmed. However, a woman motorist passing by — and gazing from a distance at our prostrate, pyjama-clad, drenched-in-'blood' forms — went off to phone for help. The result was that a flotilla of police vehicles and an ambulance arrived on the scene — bells ringing like the clappers. Since I was considered by the others to be the least concussed, it was left to me to try to explain — to a *very large* policeman — who we were, why we were dressed as we were, why the young woman was hardly dressed at all and, more importantly, how the Bedford van had come to be lying upturned in a ditch! Finally, he wanted to know why we had been towing a bedstead! All these questions proved very difficult to answer! What I do recall is how, as the policemen clambered down the bank — to what he thought was a scene of carnage — I rose from the ground to greet him — looking for all the world like an Egyptian mummy in a horror film rising from the grave. I then raised my bowler hat in polite salutation and remarked: "Good morning sergeant"! This utterance was so clearly unexpected that it momentarily transfixed the policemen whose facial expression registered nothing short of incredulity. Eventually he had the presence of mind to enquire: "What's going on 'ere then?". I will not elaborate further, other than to add that, several weeks later, we all duly appeared before a Derbyshire magistrate who, being reassured that no serious offence had been committed urged us in appropriate judicial tones: "To transact our youthful enterprises more sensibly in the future". In more ways than one we all had a lucky escape.

Following this experience my last *Rag Day* venture was relatively tame. For this I once more adopted my sartorial bowler-hat-and-pyjamas combination — I should add with a new pair of pyjamas, the old 'blood'-stained ones having been thrown away. Thus attired I spent the best part of a Saturday afternoon in a little deception on the part of Fargate then known as *Cole's Corner*. This, it will be recalled, was the era of the electric trams which still trundled up and down Fargate. I, and a couple of other student friends, conspired to stop these trams by pretending to polish the tramlines! You can well imagine that this was a rather hazardous undertaking! But it was very effective since most of the tram drivers we encountered slowed down — but only after pounding like mad on the bell you may remember which was positioned by the driver's feet. Once slowed down, it was then a simple matter to clamber on board the tram — like pirates boarding a ship, circumvent the protesting Conductor, and finally relieve the bemused passengers of their spare change! Naturally, we had to keep a look-out for the police! During the course of the afternoon we rapidly filled our tins with money. Now this brings me to the interesting bit. No less a place than the main hall at the CTS had been designated as the official location for counting out the money. For this purpose several of our flat-topped dining hall tables had been arranged in the middle of the room and, as we came in from our street-collecting, we emptied out our full tins of coins upon them. I have never seen so much loose change in all my life! To check the process of auditing just how much money had been collected, a number of very accurate weighing machines were used. Once we had counted, say, a pound's worth of pennies — all 240 of them! — these were bagged and weighed in the machine. The scale was so sensitive that if a one-pound bag contained, in error, 239 pennies and one ha'penny, it would alert the official in-charge to the fact that the sum was not correct. Believe it or not, as we counted away in this fashion, we discovered that several of Sheffield's citizens had only donated farthings to our good cause — the miserable buggers!

When my counting was over, I went off to the City Hall to hear one of the Hallé Orchestra's Saturday night *Philharmonic Concerts* — the only problem being that I was still attired in my bowler hat and pyjamas. Since I had a seat reserved in the Organ Gallery, located immediately in front of the conductor, I realised Sir John Barbirolli — the conductor scheduled to take the concert — would take a dim view if he caught sight of a member of the audience attired like a clown. So I proceeded to the CTS toilets, located in the playground, where I removed my pyjamas — which I was wearing over my everyday clothes — stuffed these into the bowler hat — only just — and duly took up my seat on the Organ Gallery. Before the concert started I tried concealing the pyjama-filled bowler hat under my seat, but this was counter-productive since the pyjamas kept spilling out onto the floor! There was nothing for it but for me to clasp my bowler hat tightly on me knee — in full view of the audience! I tried very hard to sit unconcerned as though I was trying to promote a 'bring back the bowler' campaign. I'm sure Sir John caught sight of my hat but it didn't, fortunately, put him off his stride — or should I say his beat!

The events I have recalled were welcome, light-hearted interludes in-between periods of intense hard work — which eventually culminated in 'finals' The outcome of my final university exams provides me with my closing reminiscence bearing directly upon the CTS. I will come straight to the point; I was awarded the degree of Bachelor of Architecture with First Class Honours. Now this circumstance came to the attention of *The Star* newspaper whose Editor, remarkable as it may seem, sent out a reporter to interview me! There is a reason for this; a first class honours degree had not been awarded in architecture for some years so *The Star* decide to run a short piece about me. The text of this is reproduced in Fig. 93. For my endeavours I was also awarded the *Stephen Welsh Prize in Architecture* — see Fig. 94. Naturally I felt proud of my achievements and a few days after getting my result I yielded to an impulse to go and see Herbert Wadge and tell him about them. On arriving at the CTS I found the great man much as I had seen him five years previously, hard at work in his study surrounded by piles of paper. I first of all tactfully helped things along by reminding him who I was and then I told him about my course of study and its successful outcome. He beamed with genuine delight and asked me to go over the details more slowly so that he could take notes. We were getting along fine, indeed, I almost wondered if I was going to be invited to have a cup of tea — or something a little stronger — when there was a knock on the door. "Come in" responded Herbert — his magnificent tones still perfectly preserved — and who should appear but Mr. Thompson — now elevated to the position of Deputy Headmaster. His expression bore a look of some concern but he spared me a friendly glance that broadened into a smile when Herbert informed him of the reason for my visit. But such was Mr. Thompson's anxious state of mind that we had to curtail our conversational exchanges to make way for the message he had come to impart. Turning to Herbert, Mr. Thompson said: "Someone has apparently just shot a pellet from an air pistol from Bow Building which has smashed one of the windows opposite in the City Grammar School!". "Hmm", I thought to myself, "It seems like business as usual at the Central Tech!". On hearing this Herbert leaped from his seat, apologised to me for abruptly curtailing our conversation, and commanded Mr. Thompson to go to the School Office to have the sounding of the 4.10 p.m. bell cancelled — so that he could personally conduct an inspection of the Bow Building.

I have no knowledge as to what Herbert's inspection revealed — but I dread to think what fate may have befallen the culprit if he was indeed discovered. As for the reason for my going to see Herbert Wadge, certain consequential events occurred that I only found out about some weeks later — and then entirely by chance. This is how it came about. My wife Mary was at this time training to be a school teacher — together with several of her graduate contemporaries. One of these friends — a young woman — was, by co-incidence, in employment at the CTS as a trainee teacher; in the early 1960s I believe the CTS was beginning to employ a few women teachers in language-related subjects. One day this friend chanced to meet my wife and recounted how the Headmaster of the Central Technical School — whom she described as being an impressive being by the name of Herbert Wadge! — had just held an even longer morning assembly than usual! My wife was informed that Herbert had taken as his theme the virtues of hard work and the rewards to be obtained thereby; she then added that Mr. Wadge had made specific mention of a former pupil who had just graduated in architecture and — wait for it — as a mark of respect for his achievements the school was to be granted a half-day holiday! "That sounds like my husband Terry", remarked my wife to her friend, and later that evening she told me of these various events. There is yet another little twist in the tale. About a week later I chanced to meet Mr. Hughes who was making his way along Leopold Street — this was in fact one of the very few occasions that I had met one of my former teachers since leaving school. To my greeting of, "How are you", he responded with the remark: "Very well, and thanks to you and your achievements I am now off home for a half-day holiday!".

With that observation, from one sunny period in June 1964, I herewith conclude my series of personal reminiscences drawn from the immediate period when I attended the Central Technical School. I do however have a number of remaining thoughts to share with the reader, concerning the CTS, derived from more recent times.

Homage to the CTS

Over the years, successive generations of former pupils of the Central Technical School have shown their appreciation of, and, indeed, their affection for, their former school by contributing to the activities of the Old Boys' Association. In many ways this is a form of 'homage'. And it is no more palpable than on the occasion of the *President's Dinner* when former pupils — OBAs — meet together, discuss times past, reminisce, hear their President say a few words and listen to the Guest Speaker. And if there is laughter, it is non-malignant pleasantry, or, as Rupert Brooke describes it in the verses that so many of us had to learn, 'Laughter born of gentleness'.

Having just made mention of the Old Boys' Association, this is an appropriate point to cite the earliest surviving documentary record of the OBA. For this I am indebted to Stuart Green who circulated the document in question in his *Newsletter* of 16 October 1995 — the year of Stuart's Presidency of the OBA and, coincidentally, the Golden Jubilee Year of the OBA. The document to which I refer is a letter written by a former teacher of the CTS — Mr. A. McCarthy — recording the inaugural meeting of the OBA. The full text of the letter follows — it is interesting to note what could be secured for the purchase of 1/6d and 2/6d in the distant days of 1946! But, more seriously, note also that the principal subject of the letter concerns the work of the Memorial Committee and its wish to commemorate the former CTS lads who had lost their lives in the then recent war. Here is the text of the letter:

Dear Sir,   17th November, 1946.

OLD BOYS' ASSOCIATION

The members present at the Inaugural Meeting of the Old Boys' Association held in the School on 1st November, 1946, elected a General Committee and a "Memorial Committee".

The next General Meeting of the Association will be held at the School on <u>Friday, 6th December, 1946, at 7.30 p.m.</u> and your attendance is particularly requested.

The General Committee has now made arrangements for a combined Dance and Social to be held at the School on Saturday, 21st December, at 7.30 p.m. Tickets, single, at 1/6d each, will be on sale at the General Meeting.

The annual subscription to the Association has been fixed at 2/6d a year, except for members under the age of 18, for whom the annual subscription will be 1/6d. It is not essential, but it would be convenient if members could arrange to pay their subscriptions at the General Meeting.

The Memorial Committee wishes to draw the attention of all members to the difficulties and delicacy of its task and to ask their co-operation in the collecting and checking of information. It is of the utmost importance that any Memorial Plaque should contain the name of <u>every</u> Old Boy who lost his life as a result of enemy action during the recent war. The Committee earnestly wishes to avoid upsetting bereaved parents and relatives but would be most grateful if they could let the Secretary have the following particulars of any such Old Boys: Name in full, Service (Royal Navy, Army, R.A.F. etc.) or Civilian, date of casualty.

Yours faithfully,
A. McCarthy

Secretary.

The subject of the last paragraph of this letter leads me to comment briefly on the Memorial Plaque. It commemorates the memory of the twenty-four young men — former CTS lads — who lost their lives in the Second World War. The plaque was restored a few years ago by OBA member Colin Degenhart and the unveiling was undertaken by Mrs. Freda Horn whose brother, Robert Holt, is named amongst those listed on the plaque. The following information is contained on the plaque — in the original, the CTS badge is also portrayed:

1939 — 1945
IN PROUD MEMORY

AIREY K.F.	GREENWOOD A.	ROSSINGTON J.C.
ATKIN S.S.	HARDY L.	SYKES P.D.
AUDOIRE B.T.	HOLT R.	TAYLOR H.
BARRON G.	MILLS J.A.	TONKIN H.A.
BLOOR A.W.	MURFITT C.M.	WEBSTER K.
CARTWRIGHT F.	NELSON R.W.	WILKINSON B.F.
CHARLTON B.J.	PEPPER J.S.	WILLIAMS L.J.
FREDLIEB M.	RAWSON W.K.	WRAY C.G.

A second bronze plaque adorns the main entrance to the Firth Building. This is known as the 'Jubilee Plaque' from the fact that it was installed in, and commemorates, the Golden Jubilee Year of the foundation of the Old Boys' Association. About seventy former pupils and teachers were present for the unveiling ceremony which was undertaken by Mr. Ken Westnedge who, as previously remarked, has the distinction of being both a former pupil of the CTS and a teacher — in addition Ken is probably the individual with the longest period of active participation in the affairs of the school and the OBA. The following is the text recorded on the plaque which, on the original, is surmounted by an image of Vulcan — to commemorate The City of Sheffield. Also portrayed is a reproduction of the CTS badge:

THE CITY OF SHEFFIELD
EDUCATION OFFICES
FROM 1933-1964 FIRTH BUILDING WAS USED BY
THE SHEFFIELD CENTRAL TECHNICAL SCHOOL, FORMERLY
THE JUNIOR TECHNICAL SCHOOL. DURING THAT TIME OVER
5,000 BOYS PASSED THROUGH THE SCHOOL. MANY
PROGRESSING TO SUCCESSFUL CAREERS IN THE STEEL,
ENGINEERING AND BUILDING INDUSTRIES OF THE REGION.
THE FIRST HEADMASTER, GWILYN E. THOMAS, WAS
SUCCEEDED IN 1947 BY HERBERT W. WADGE M.B.E.
WHO WAS PROMINENT IN THE DEVELOPMENT OF SECONDARY
TECHNICAL EDUCATION IN THIS COUNTRY. HERBERT WADGE
HAD A PROFOUND LIFE LONG INFLUENCE ON ALL HIS PUPILS.

FLOURISH C.T.S. FOREVER!

THIS PLAQUE HAS BEEN SPONSORED BY
C.T.S. OLD BOYS' ASSOCIATION
GOLDEN JUBILEE YEAR 1996.

Yet a third bronze plaque, bearing a tribute to the affairs of the CTS, is located to the right of the front door of the Education Offices in Leopold Street. This plaque commemorates the founding of Firth College on the site and the later establishment of the Central Technical School. The text of the plaque, which is oval shaped, reads as follows:

> Opened in 1879 as Firth College through the generosity of Mark Firth 1819–1890, an eminent steelmaker and manufacturer. The college was popular for lectures and university extension classes and, alongside the Sheffield Medical School, was the forerunner of the University of Sheffield. From 1905 to 1963 these buildings served as premises for a variety of schools, the last of which was The Central Technical School for boys.

As I have already remarked, over the years former pupils have shown their homage to their former school by joining in the activities of the Old Boys' Association — even if only to receive their regular copy of the *Newsletter*. Some have given more tangible expression of their support for the CTS by taking on the role of office bearers for the OBA. We owe much to this small group of stalwarts to whom it seems appropriate to say — "A hearty thank you Lads"!

One or two former pupils of the CTS have, I know, dedicated certain of their literary works to the memory of their school. My reason for saying this is that I am one such person. Allow me therefore to say a few words here about one aspect of my academic interests and how this has enabled me to pay my own expression of homage to the CTS.

I am particularly interested in the history of the arts and crafts and, in particular, how they were written about in the great pioneering encyclopaedic dictionaries which were published in the seventeenth and eighteenth centuries. I suppose in many ways this interest can be traced directly back to my formative years as a Builder at the CTS. To be more specific, my enthusiasms for these things has its origins primarily in the work I undertook for Mr. Grantham, notably, the short essays I wrote about country houses when I was a member of the Art Club — to which I have made previous reference. I can also trace my interest in trade- and craft-related subjects to the period of my time at the CTS when I, alongside my fellow class members, was required to illustrate the tools of the master craftsman. To cut a long story short, I duly published my own five-volume encyclopaedic dictionary titled *The Encyclopaedic Dictionary in the Eighteenth Century: Architecture, Arts and Crafts*. With these words of explanation out of the way, I can now direct my narrative to how I came to pay my personal expression of homage to the beneficial influences of the Central Technical School. The circumstance is straightforward; I dedicated my volumes as follows:

The Encyclopaedic Dictionary in the Eighteenth Century: Architecture , Arts and Crafts.

Volumes by the Author dedicated to the Central Technical School

---

Volume One

John Harris
Lexicon Technicum
Incorporating works of
Sir Francis Bacon and Sir Henry Wotton

Dedication
To
The Central Technical School Sheffield
1954–1959
In recognition of the formative influence it exerted upon me.

Terence M. Russell

Volume Two

Ephraim Chambers
Cyclopaedia

Dedication
To
The Central Technical School Sheffield
1954–1959
In recognition of the formative influence it exerted upon me.

Terence M. Russell

Volume Three

The Builders' Dictionary

Dedication
To
The Central Technical School Sheffield
1954–1959
In recognition of the formative influence it exerted upon me.
This volume is dedicated to the memory of
John H. Hunter
Fellow of the Institute of Carpenters
Doyen of craftsmen

Terence M. Russell

Volume Four

Samuel Johnson
A
Dictionary
of the
English Language

Dedication
To
The Central Technical School Sheffield
1954–1959
In recognition of the formative influence it exerted upon me.

This volume is dedicated to the memory of
Herbert W. Wadge
MBE MA BSC
Headmaster

Terence M. Russell

I now conclude my series of reminiscences with some remaining observations concerning Herbert W. Wadge.

Herbert W. Wadge M.B.E., M.A., B.Sc.

It is fitting that I should conclude my reflections about the Central Technical School with a section devoted to Herbert W. Wadge who exerted so dominant an influence over the school. I have often wondered if Herbert Wadge consciously moulded himself on the great headmasters of the nineteenth century. In some ways this is a flawed suggestion since Herbert was very much 'his own man' — as the expression goes. He was resolutely independent of mind, fearless, energetic, truculent, tireless in pursuit of an objective and — perhaps above all — a big hearted and emotional man. Herbert Wadge was indeed a very big man — and I am not referring simply to his physical stature. Notwithstanding these resolute qualities, I still incline to the view that there were processes at work, deep down in Herbert's psyche, that inclined him to take as his role models, as I have suggested, the great headmasters from the past. It is worth remembering, in this context, that Herbert's own formative years were spent at Eton College, to which he made occasional reference in morning assembly. But if I had to choose a specific scholar-headmaster upon whom I could well imagine Herbert Wadge might have wanted to model himself it would be Thomas Arnold the famous headmaster of Rugby School. Herbert Wadge certainly had something of Arnold's crusading zeal and 'muscular Christianity'. Those of us who sat through his morning assemblies — or should I say *endured* his morning assemblies — know well of his capacity to speak with great passion and emotion about the things for which he cared. And the things for which he cared were, collectively, his school — our school — the CTS, of which he was manifestly proud.

I can relate a little story which illustrates just how sensitive Herbert was concerning the affairs of his school. I have already indicated that during my time as School Captain there were several occasions when I had to speak with Herbert Wadge about various matters — usually concerning the prefects. On one such occasion I ventured to criticise the CTS curriculum as being excessively inclined to things technical and scientific. I was prompted to pass this — somewhat provocative — remark since, as I have already explained, my personal inclinations were developing more in the direction of the arts. I have to say that my observation was scarcely out of my mouth when Herbert came back at me like the proverbial ton of bricks with the comment: "Here! Take

care what you say! We have much to be proud of in this school!". With that I retreated from the field of battle, as it were, recognising that discretion is indeed the better part of valour! More generally the experience did leave me wondering what it must have been like to have been one of Herbert's colleagues — should they ever have had the misfortune of getting on the wrong side of him!

I have referred to Thomas Arnold and Rugby School which prompts me to call to mind the numerous occasions that I listened to Herbert, in morning assembly, talking about Eton College. In particular I recall Herbert speaking of rising early to go cross-county running — presumably around the famous Playing Fields of Eton — and then to take a cold shower! I found it all difficult to believe since by then — the mid 1950s — Herbert was somewhat slow on his feet; legend held that he suffered from gout but this may have just been schoolboy mischief. (It was certainly my impression that Herbert had attended Eton College as a schoolboy. However, having consulted with the archivist at Eton College, no formal record concerning Herbert W. Wadge has been found in the school archives. Perhaps, therefore, Herbert was more of an admirer of Eton College than an actual pupil?). But, with Eton College in mind, I will now disclose how I, a humble CTS lad, came one day to climb on the roof of Eton College! It happened like this:

About twenty years ago at the University of Edinburgh, where I still work, I held the post of Associate Dean of the Faculty of Social Sciences. One of my responsibilities was to visit schools to advise sixth-formers about the range of university courses available and to guide them concerning admission. One day, out of the blue, I received an invitation from Dr. Eric Anderson, who was then Headmaster of Eton College, to visit his school to have dinner with himself and his House Masters. I accepted the invitation most willingly — even though it meant having to go out to buy a dinner suit. My host was the Vice Provost of the college — a most delightful and amiable gentleman whose responsibilities included looking after Eton's wine cellar! (I suppose the equivalent post at the CTS was that held by Mr. Sam Hedley who was responsible for looking after the school milk!) Dinner was magnificent and I was later allowed to perambulate about the Fellows' Garden which overlooks the River Thames. The next day my host had to depart early for an appointment — leaving me to look after myself until it was time for my own return to Edinburgh. It was then that I noticed, as architects are inclined to do, a staircase leading to the roof. This proved too irresistible to my curiosity; I ascended a creaky flight of steps, encountered a thick oak door, turned a massive iron key and pushed open the door — to be greeted by a blaze of sunshine. After letting my eyes adapt to the bright light a tentatively stepped outside and found myself standing on the lead-coated roof of Eton College!

I can confirm that the view from the vantage point of the roof of Eton College is magnificent! In the distance, Windsor Castle beckons across the greenery and, down below, the Thames winds its leisurely way through the majestic sycamores and plane trees that adorn its banks. The fly fishermen amongst you will know that this is the very stretch of water which was once fished by the seventeenth-century fisherman and writer Izaak Walton — the author of *The Compleat Angler*. His book gives idyllic glimpses of country life long since past away but it also calls to mind pastoral scenes of the very kind still preserved around Eton College on which, at that moment, I feasted my eyes. As I tip-toed amidst the ornate chimney tops, I remember allowing myself a moment of reflection; "What", I asked myself, "would Herbert Wadge think of me now?"!ˑ Then I peered down into the school's inner quadrangle — just a little petrified that the Headmaster Dr. Anderson might catch sight of me! — and I tried to image a youthful Herbert Wadge attired in Eton's distinctive formal dress. At this point my courage failed me, discretion prevailed and I thought it wiser that I should retreat back down the creaky stair and resume the more discreet attitude of a respectable visitor.

My final reflection on what I have just disclosed is that although I may not have ever scaled the dizzy heights of the roof of the Bow Building, like some courageous CTS lads, I can lay claim to have ventured on to the roof of Eton College!

Having just made reference to Herbert Wadge's school days I will compliment this with an observation he once shared with me about his time at the University of London. He was prompted to make his disclosures to me on one of the visits I made to him in his room in my capacity as School Captain. We had been discussing the senior boys' preparation for the forthcoming A.L. exams when Herbert, something to my surprise, allowed himself a moment of personal reflection. He remarked how the Great War had interrupted his own progress to university since, like so many other young men of that generation, he had volunteered for military service. He was in fact too young for active service and therefore joined the fledgling Royal Flying Corps; the reader will find that Len Shipley confirms this in his moving tribute to Herbert Wadge which follows shortly. Herbert then remarked to me how, with the war finally over, he took up his place at London University — more than two years after leaving school. With this, Herbert looked at me — somewhat plaintively — and said: "Do you know, it was so hard for me to return to my studies — trying to keep up with those young chaps straight out of school". At the time (1958), I regarded this as being little more than a passing remark but now, looking back, I am filled with admiration for Herbert's courage in setting aside personal considerations in favour of 'doing his bit' for his country. It is this realisation that makes me feel that the moving words of Rupert Brooke's *The Soldier* — which, as I have explained earlier, he required all the school to learn — meant a great deal to him both as verse and, at a more personal level, as a tribute to the young men of his own generation. With this in mind, I will here pay a tribute, if I may, to Herbert Wadge's youthful resolve in wanting to do his part for his country. To do this I have selected some lines from one of Rupert Brooke's great contemporaries, the war poet Wilfred Owen. Owen died in action just one week before the Armistice was signed. His poem 'Anthem for Doomed Youth', from which I have selected my lines of tribute, movingly embodies the utter despair of the misery and futility of war that came to be felt by the young men of Herbert Wadge's generation:

What passing-bells for those who die as cattle?
Only the monstrous anger of the guns.
Only the stuttering rifle's rapid rattle
Can patter out their hasty orisons.
No mockeries for them; no prayers nor bells,
Nor any voice of mourning save the choirs, —
The shrill, demented choirs of wailing shells;
And bugles calling for them from sad shires.

After these melancholy words it is time now for something in a lighter vein.

I do not recall Herbert Wadge being given any nickname by my contemporaries. Perhaps this is because he was so imposing a figure that he transcended such things. My own name for him at the period of my schooling, was *Herbaceous*; this is a combination of schoolboy word-play and the reality that Herbert seemed, like ubiquitous well-kept borders, to be everywhere. Moreover I don't think Herbert was a particularly funny man — at least from the perception of a schoolboy. Perhaps his gravitas and exposed position of responsibility weighed on him too heavily to allow him to relax his demeanour. Be this as it may Herbert Wadge was no sober sides and there were a few occasions, for example in morning assembly, when he made a conscious effort to be light-hearted. I recall one such morning when he made us laugh by recalling, for some reason, the words of a once-popular sung whose refrain went: "Does the chewing gum lose its flavour on the bedpost overnight?"! I also remember, from the time when Herbert was at the height of his crusading zeal to get as many CTS boys as possible to open a bank account, how he quoted the following lines from a song which was very popular at the time: "You've got to have something in the bank, Frank. You've got to have something to start"! We laughed heartily at that and realised that our Headmaster was not really a god after all but was just like ourselves.

There was one occasion in morning assembly when Herbert had us all convulsed with laughter — but more by accident than design. This is what happened. He had been talking about the inter-war years and the great depression and how this had cast its long shadow over so many lives — including that of my own father who was unemployed for several years. Herbert spoke of the waste of human talent as men stood idly around with no work for them to perform. To reach his punchline he then made reference to the style of pocket watch and chain usually attached to the waistcoat and known as an 'Albert' — derived from Albert the Prince Consort who made this article popular. With all this in place Herbert then uttered the immortal words: "At almost any time of day, on almost any street corner, you could see all the old men with their Albert's sticking out"! I think I can safely say that the spontaneous eruption of uncontrolled laughter which then arose from the whole school had no parallel in the entire annals of the CTS. Herbert, discernibly red-faced, bore his discomfort stoically smiling as if to convey that his words were what he had always intended and carried no hidden double-meaning. It took ages for our mirth to subside.

Herbert Wadge had a number of curious speech idioms which, after hearing so often, we simply took for granted. Perhaps his most curious were '*fud*' for food and '*ten past fo*' for ten past four. In urging us to adopt healthy habits of eating he would urge us to show restraint from consuming too many '*sweetmeats*'; I even once recall him describing such things as '*succulent dainties*'! I also recall Herbert spending an entire morning assembly castigating us for slackness of speech. In particular he lamented the widespread use of 'us books'; "You must be diseased to speak like that", he railed, adding — with a nod in the direction of Holy Scripture: "By your speech shall you be known".

Having returned to the theme of morning assembly, I will call to mind another of Herbert's crusading passions, namely, that every boy in the school should possess a slide-rule — and be familiar with its logarithmic theory and practice. To this end, sometime round about 1955–56, he had one of the technicians make him a large slide-rule — and I mean a large slide rule! One morning, to the school's universal surprise, Herbert marched into assembly proudly bearing a slide-rule which he carried over his shoulder; it must have measured about six feet long! For all the world he looked rather like a window cleaner, but no one dared so much as utter a whisper — even though we were collectively thinking: "What the hell's that?". It soon became apparent as Herbert, before the full gaze of his staff, commenced an impromptu mathematics class. He explained the functioning of the moveable logarithmic scales and how they could be used to facilitate quick numerical calculations, notably, multiplication and division. This was all undertaken with Herbert's typical commitment and bravura. His demonstrations continued over several mornings and culminated in a kind of 'commercial'. He had arranged for us boys to purchase a slide-rule on special terms. You could buy a modest plastic instrument for about eighteen shillings and a more expensive de-luxe instrument made from hardwood — complete with a magnifying lens to help the user read the fine graduated scales. In due course we all had our own slide-rule and learned to complete calculations to three significant figures — or something of the kind.

Chance once conspired that I should meet Herbert outside his room as I was returning the Class Register to its rack; I was then the Form Monitor — I believe that was the title we used — and it was the responsibility of this individual to look after the Class Register when it had been completed. CTS boys may remember that all Class Registers were held in racks on the landing just outside Herbert's room. I had just placed Class 3Ys Register in its place when Herbert emerged from his room and called out: "Boy!", at which I froze on the spot wondering what I had done wrong. In fact I had done nothing wrong, Herbert merely wanted me to go down to his car to collect his briefcase. This was the era of Herbert's green Jaguar which I found parked in its normal place in the school playground. Now, my reason for recounting all this is that, in collecting Herbert's briefcase, I gained an unusual insight into the care he took with his morning preparations. This is what I mean. I had to fiddle for ages with the key to the car door; in fact I took so long I half expected Herbert to come outside to ask me what I was up to. But I eventually opened the door and removed the required briefcase. Secured to it, by means of a paper clip, was a sheet of paper bearing a long list of 'things to do', all carefully annotated in Herbert's neat handwriting. This made me realise just how much effort he expended in planning his day's work; I am sure Herbert was diligent from dawn until dusk with the affairs of his beloved school.

I will now draw these personal reflections about Herbert Wadge to a close. In doing so I will recall those moments in morning assembly when we spoke the Lord's Prayer. Without fail we said these words every day, even when time was limited. Herbert Wadge took his moral obligations seriously, no more so concerning the religious formalities of our collective worship. So here then are the words we said so often together at the start of our working day:

Our Father which art heaven,
Hallowed be thy name.
Thy kingdom come.
Thy will be done, on earth as it is in heaven.
Give us this day our daily bread.
And forgive us our trespasses,
As we forgive those who trespass against us.
And lead us not into temptation;
But deliver us from evil.
For thine is the kingdom, the power and the glory.
For ever and ever.
Amen.

These words provide a fitting introduction to what follows.

On 6 April 1989, the members of the Old Boys' Association were saddened to receive a letter from the then Secretary of the OBA, Mike Ingham, informing us of the following circumstances:

It is with deep regret that I have to inform you of the death, on Thursday 4 April, of Herbert Wadge, at the age of 89.

For the past three years Herbert had been in a nursing home near Barnsley and as a result the funeral will be in Huddersfield which is where his immediate family live. Members of the Association are quite welcome to attend the funeral service which is at 12.00 o'clock on Friday 12th may at the Huddersfield Crematorium.

As Mike's letter implies we were indeed saddened to learn of Herbert's death and many of us resolved to attend his funeral service. In my case it required a great deal of resolve since to arrive at Huddersfield from Edinburgh, at the appointed hour of 12.00 mid-day, required a very early morning departure. I did eventually arrive with — quite literally — just five minutes to spare. I found a large gathering of former CTS lads standing outside the crematorium together with a number of former members of staff. A few moments after my arrival, the funeral cortege appeared bearing Herbert's mortal remains followed by a few members of his family. These included Herbert's younger brother Horace — the family likeness being quite marked. We followed the cortege into the crematorium where we took our seats.

We were welcomed by the officiating clergyman, Reverend Roberts, who passed some general remarks concerning Herbert's contribution to education, in general, and to the life and work of the Central Technical School in particular. But the principal tribute was paid by former teacher Len Shipley. Len spoke simply but most movingly about his former Head Teacher; I think all those who heard Len speak would agree that Herbert could not have received a finer aural tribute to his life and work bearing on the affairs of the CTS.

Some time later, in response to a number of requests from members of the OBA, Len recorded a version of his address. I am most grateful to former OBA Secretary Stuart Green for providing me with a copy of this from which I have made the transcript which follows. It captures well the essence of what was a most moving occasion.

Friday 12 May 1989
Huddersfield Crematorium..
Herbert Willan Wadge M.B.E., M.A., B.Sc.
Former Head of Central Technical School.
Sheffield

A tribute by Len Shipley who was appointed to the staff of the Sheffield Central technical School by Herbert Wadge in February 1948.

As a former member of staff of the Sheffield Central Technical School, I have been asked by Herbert Wadge's family to say a few words this afternoon. Time is very limited, so I cannot hope to emulate the length of his morning assemblies which are legendary.

He was born in Sacriston, County Durham on 26th November 1899. He died in a nursing home near Barnsley on 5th May aged 89. [Note: Len was not in good health when he made his recording and his memory of the date of Herbert's death appears to have let him down — see the extract from Mike Ingham's letter reproduced above.] His M.B.E. was awarded for his service to the National Savings Movement. His honorary M.A. was awarded to him by Sheffield University for his service to technical education.

In 1951, the BBC decided to introduce south-eastern culture to the barbaric north by opening the Holm Moss transmitter and held an exhibition in the School Hall. To coincide, they had delivered a series of lectures on the subject of TV during morning assembly; the phrase describing the operation of the TV cathode-ray tube, 'scan-flashback-scan', passed into CTS mythology.

With the help of Sid Stacey, the Engineering technician, he re-built his touring caravan and constructed a cradle which enabled him to point his chimney stack, giving strict instructions to his wife not to move away from the bottom of the roof ladder!

I must now refer to 'Edi', his wife for almost fifty years. Never in the forefront but always in support — a very gracious lady. This reminds me of a paragraph by the editor of the local paper, many years ago now, referring to a report from the States that there was now a system whereby a driver approaching his home could press a button and the garage doors would open and he could drive straight in. What's new about that said the editor who lived on Darewood Road? One of my neighbours sounds a fanfare on his hooter when about fifty yards away, his wife pops out, opens the garage door and he drives in! High tech? — Central Tech!

It must have been on his last appearance at the Kenwood Old Boys' Association Dinner that my late wife persuaded him to do a couple of circuits of the dance floor.

My final anecdote concerns the last occasion that Les Whyle brought him home from the Royal Hallamshire Hospital in Sheffield. Herbert insisted on replenishing his stock of food on the way home and pushed his trolley round Sainsbury's in his dressing gown and pyjamas.

These apparent trivia are important in illustrating the various sides of Herbert's attitude to life. However, his former teaching career, his work on behalf of technical education, the ATTI — National President in 1954, NUT Executive, the Burnham Committee, and his work for National Savings, pale into insignificance when compared to his devotion to the Sheffield Central Technical school. Many Old Boys have told me that, although not appreciated at the time, they later realised that Herbert had been right and is held by them in great esteem — witness their presence here today.

In 1916 [age 17] he joined the Royal Flying Corps and then transferred into the oldest regiment in the British Army — the Coldstream Guards. Their Regimental Motto, *ne lesacundus* — Second to None, is a standard he maintained to the end of his life. I think it is no exaggeration to say that from 1947 the Sheffield central technical school was his life.

He lived it well!

Having recorded these words, Len then added some further remarks which will be of interest to the reader. This is what Len had to say:

Apart from the Introduction the foregoing is what I intended to say but this had to be amended as I went along in view of what had been said by the Vicar Mr. Roberts whose opening address, incidentally, I thought was superlative and whose prayers were poetry of the highest degree. I tried to give an extemporary talk, so whether I actually said all I planned is not clear in my mind. Since Friday I have had a few requests to let former staff and students know what I said. The above, although not verbatim is the best I can do. I would also add that the fact that about forty Old Boys attended the service at a substantial distance from the centre of Sheffield reflected the great esteem I mentioned in my talk. One Old Boy had left Edinburgh at 05.30 hours in order to attend the service and had then to drive back home.

To conclude, Herbert's brother Horace, also in his eighties, thanked me for my contribution and said: "Old Bert would have enjoyed it"!

I was volunteered into this situation and it worried me considerably but I must thank the Old Boys' Association Committee, Ron Underdown and particularly Mike Ingham for their support. I hope I didn't let anyone down.

I did my best!

Len then added a final passage to his recording as follows:

Since recording the above I have received a letter from Wallace Holland who during the period of Herbert Wadge's Headship of the Central Technical School was the Administrative Director for Secondary Education in Sheffield. I have known him personally, originally through my wife, for over forty years and had written to congratulate him on his eightieth birthday — informing him at the same time of Herbert's death. I have not asked his permission but I am sure he will not mind my quoting the following from his letter:

Your news about Herbert Wadge saddened me. For very many years we exchanged a few words of greetings at Christmas; you know the kind of thing, using the spare space on the Christmas card as a kind of friendly update. And his was so to be depended on that when, five or six years ago, no more card came any more I felt that something must be wrong.

One could not but have a soft spot for him, even with a quiet gentle smile at some of his ways. Although he inherited some difficult problems from his predecessor, even though the latter became an HMI, and his concept of Secondary Technical Education was an attempt to raise the *level* of Junior Technical Education — rather than to think through quite new ideas — he did a good job in not very easy circumstances.

It is sad that the institution which should be his monument has already in his last years been swallowed up in never-ending and sometimes bogus changes which are constantly being inflicted upon education in these days.

Maybe there will still be many who will realise that their successes embrace his memorial.

I recall him with affection.

With these personal tributes for Herbert W. Wadge I now bring my personal reflections of life and work at the Central Technical School to a close. This is not the end of my book but what follows is of a more general nature — though I hope still of interest.

In taking leave of the reader here, I will invoke the spirit of my School Captain's farewell speech made one day — which now seems so long ago — in June 1959:

Good-bye and God bless you all!

Forty years on, growing older and older,
Shorter in wind, as in memory long,
Feeble of foot, and rheumatic of shoulder,
What will it help you that once you were strong?
God gave us bases to guard or beleaguer,
Games to play out, whether earnest or fun;
Fights for the fearless, and goals for the eager,
Twenty, and thirty, and forty years on!

4
A Portfolio of Schoolwork Drawings and Sketches By the Author To illustrate the CTS Curriculum

As has already been explained in the main body of the text, drawings and sketches formed an important aspect of teaching and learning within the curriculum at the Central Technical School. This is understandable given the technical nature of much of the syllabus and the manner in which the trade and craft-related subjects, studied by pupils in Building and Engineering, lend themselves to explanation through illustration. There are other aspects to this which are worthy of mention — so I will make a brief digression here before introducing the drawings and sketches which follow.

All educators know that to draw a picture of something is a good way to learn about it. Such a process requires the pupil to think clearly about the subject under discussion, say when learning about how something is made or how a scientific experiment is undertaken. And so it was at the CTS. Boys were encouraged to illustrate almost every aspect of their work — true to the spirit of the Chinese proverb that 'A picture is worth a thousand words'.

Class instruction invariably commenced by the teacher outlining the broad principles of the subject under consideration. It was the responsibility of the class to listen; in fact most classes were well disciplined and boys generally paid close attention to what the teacher was saying. In the case of craft-based subjects, such as woodwork and metalwork, the teacher usually manually demonstrated a particular technique — invariably with commendable skill. Teachers frequently illustrated the subject under consideration by making reference to their own drawings or diagrams on the blackboard. Some teachers were particular accomplished in this respect. Mr. Hunter, for example, could draw isometric projections of woodwork joints with great skill; similarly, Mr. Thornton took considerable care in the drawing of physics apparatus. And there were several other teachers at the CTS who displayed similar pedagogical competence.

Once a technique had been demonstrated, or an illustration had been drawn on the blackboard, it was the responsibility of the pupil to make notes and sketches which would then form the basis for the ensuing classwork or, more typically, for homework. In this process teachers, of subjects such as history and geography, would also make reference to the class textbook from which an illustration might also be copied or adapted. In the mid 1950s a convention was introduced at the CTS whereby classwork was designated with an 'A', homework was identified with a 'B' and work commenced in class and completed at home was categorised with a 'C' — the purpose of this still remains a mystery.

Most boys at the CTS enjoyed the illustrated part of their schoolwork and sketches and diagrams would often be compared to see how a particular individual had drawn this or that piece of equipment. By this process boys took pride in their work and, as I have remarked previously, a form of friendly rivalry sometimes took place to see who might produce a particularly accomplished sketch. Teachers would often encourage this by upholding a piece of work as an 'exemplar' for the rest of the class to emulate. Initially most boys illustrated their work in pencil perhaps adding colour with crayons or coloured pencils. But finer work could be achieved with a mapping pen and deep black Indian ink and sooner or later many boys 'graduated' to using this medium to illustrate their work.

Drawing as a means of encouraging learning featured particularly in the early years of school life. In the later years as the work became more advanced — often concerned with intellectual concepts and abstract ideas — there was rather less emphasis placed on 'making a drawing' for homework. So, for most CTS boys who still have a collection of school exercise books surviving amongst their collection of school memorabilia, drawings and sketches are to be found predominantly in the work done in their first three years — in effect the work done for the CTS Diploma in either Building or Engineering. This brings me to say a few words of introduction concurring the illustrations which follow.

The subjects selected for illustration follow the order of the topics discussed in the text. Not all of these subjects are illustrated since some subjects either do not lend themselves to illustration or the teacher did not request visual work to be undertaken to augment his particular subject. I will add here in passing a particular word about mathematics for which a considerable number of diagrams and sketches were required. This is particularly true of the work done for A.L. Pure Maths, especially in the fields of co-ordinate geometry and calculus. For these subjects boys were required to sketch intricate graphs and representations of geometrical forms; these were sometimes of considerable complexity — as, for example, when deriving a formula for the volume of a solid object created by revolving intersecting straight lines and curves about an axis. I recall the skill with which our teacher, Mr. Bee, sketched such subjects on the blackboard. A legacy of these diagrams still resides in my surviving maths books — now, I have to confess, quite unfathomable to my mind! Notwithstanding the inherent academic interest this material has, it does not lend itself well to illustration in a work of this kind and so I have decided, with regret, to leave it out.

The next general point I have to make concerns the rigour I have had to exercise in the selection of particular subjects for illustration. The CTS curriculum made extensive reference to drawing and sketching — geometrical exercises, tools, scientific equipment and the like — and a full portrayal of all this work would have swelled the pages of this book beyond its limits. So I have taken a single diagram here and sketch there when half a dozen alternatives competed for selection. Having said that, I will confess to having indulged my own personal enthusiasm for selecting things architectural. This is especially the case concerning the work I undertook for the *Art Club* to which I have made previous reference in the text. More generally I have tried to select examples of work with which former CTS boys will feel an affinity — insofar as they drew similar diagrams and sketches.

My selection has also been to some extent determined by the constraints of technical book production — some images reproduce better than others. There is therefore an emphasis on pen and ink sketches and little reference to pencil work. Colour studies unfortunately could not be included; this has been to the particular detriment of the maps drawn for geography which are here shown in monochrome.

I have taken the opportunity to make brief reference, in my selection of visual images, to two of the more social aspects of life and work at the CTS, namely, the activities of the *Literary and Scientific Society* and the annual *School Athletics Programme.* I trust the names recorded in the pages I have reproduced will stir fond memories for those boys who took part in the activities which these documents represent or alternatively will find pleasure in recalling some of the boys whose names appear in their pages.

To give further interest to the selected subjects I have added small captions. Limitations of space have precluded making extended comments but the reader can refer back to the main text for additional information.

Finally I have taken the liberty, at the close of my selection of illustrations, of including a few images which make reference to the work I did as part of my studies in architecture at the University of Sheffield. This is essentially by way of paying a tribute of recognition of the inestimable value to me of the curriculum of the Central Technical School in paving the way for my future studies. I know this is a sentiment felt by many other former CTS boys who, like me, greatly value the education they received at the CTS and feel no less a debt of gratitude for the manner in which it set them on the path of their chosen career.

School Photograph 1958

The Summer Term came to an end each year at the Central Technical School. Sheffield with the taking of form photographs. These were taken in the playground outside the Bow Building – if the weather permitted! In the event of it raining, the photographs were taken in the School Hall. Similar group photographs were taken of boys who participated in various sports, most notably, cricket, football and swimming. Each year's collection of photographs was added to the school display that was mounted on the walls of the corridors in the Firth Building. Here also were to be seen photographs of the members of the school staff and individual photographs of boys who had distinguished themselves, in one way or another, during the academic year in question. This collection of visual images is now carefully preserved, in photograph albums, and forms a treasured part of the CTS memorabilia of the Old Boys' Association. Most members of the Association also cherish their own school photograph such as the one illustrated here. The author is standing, centre, in the back row. The form Master is Mr. William (Bill) Gregory, known – more affectionately – as 'Pop' Gregory

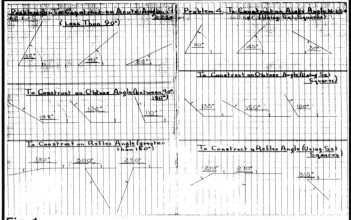

Fig. 1
Geometrical Drawing: The construction of acute and obtuse angles. These studies were homework exercises drawn in 2H pencil with ink titles — the same is true for Figs 2 & 3.

TECHNICAL DRAWING AND WOODWORK

Figs 1–3 are typical geometrical studies undertaken at the CTS as part of classwork and homework for Technical Drawing. Sharp pencil work was required to achieve neat work.

Figs 4 & 5 are typical pen and ink studies completed for the theory part of Woodwork. The tools illustrated were first discussed in class and were then used in practical work. Later boys drew the tools as part of their homework. A form of friendly rivalry ensued to see who could make the most authentic illustrations. Pencil sketches were the norm but to achieve drawings resembling those we saw illustrated in books, Indian ink work was required. This meant drawing the subject first in pencil and then going over it with a mapping pen.

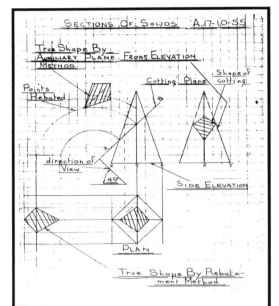

Fig. 2
Geometrical Drawing: Sections of solids created by planes of intersection.

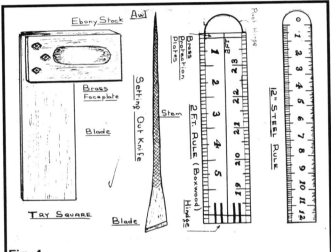

Fig. 4
Woodwork Homework: Tools used for setting out and measuring. These sketches were drawn in Indian ink and received a 'tick', for good work, from Mr. Pilling.

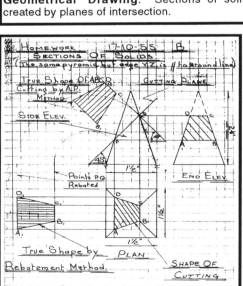

Fig. 3:
Geometrical Drawing: True shape of a pyramid section created by an intersecting plane.

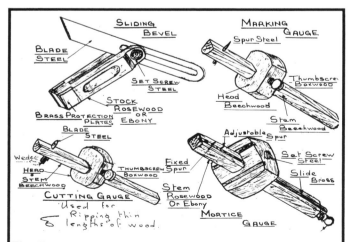

Fig. 5
Woodwork Homework: Various marking gauges are shown with a cutting gauge and a sliding bevel — drawn in Indian ink with ink lettering. This piece of work earned a mark of '10' from Mr. Pilling — see below the text 'Cutting Gauge'.

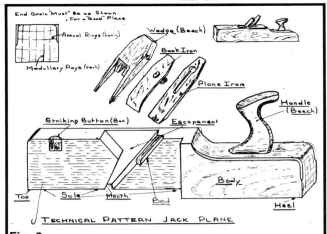

Fig. 6
Woodwork Homework: Cross-sectional view through a technical pattern Jack Plane. This was the beech wood plane used by boys at the CTS for their practical woodwork exercises. It was slightly smaller than the adult version.

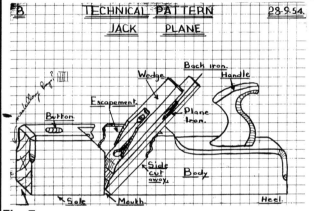

Fig. 7
Woodwork Homework: This drawing is the companion to that shown in Fig. 6. It portrays the same Jack Plane in full pictorial view. Both drawings were done in Class 3Y — one of the two First Year classes for Builders — the other was 3X.

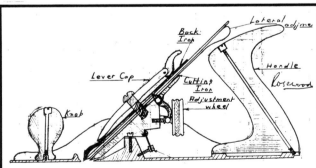

Fig. 11
Woodwork Homework: Cross-sectional view through a metal smoothing plane made by Record Tools Ltd (Hampton's). This plane was bought for me by my father who worked for Hampton's — he was eligible for a 30% discount! Mr. Pilling added 'Rosewood' to my written captions.

WOODWORK AND BUILDING CONSTRUCTION
Figs 6, 7 & 11 are typical illustrations which boys completed as part of Woodwork Theory. Figs 8, 9 & 10 show Building Construction studies which were practised in woodwork classes. These two curricula complimented one another well.

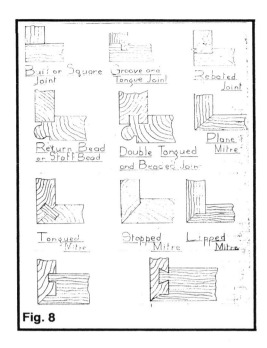

Fig. 8

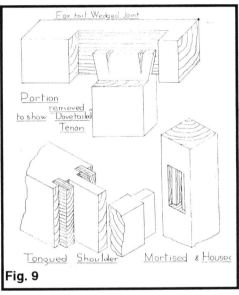

Fig. 9

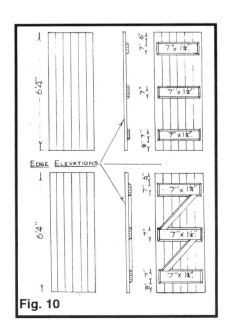

Fig. 10

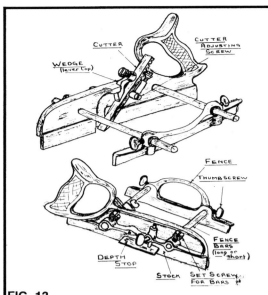

FIG. 13
WOODWORK: Plough Plane
This was the most complex woodwork tool boys at the CTS were required to draw. The use of this plane was strictly monitored to ensure no pieces were lost.

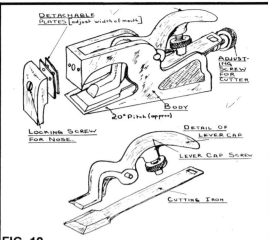

FIG. 12
WOODWORK HOMEWORK
This is an example of an ink drawing of the kind done in Class 6X, and the following year, for O.L. Woodwork. A shoulder plane is illustrated an example of which my father purchased for me — see the caption to Fig. 11.

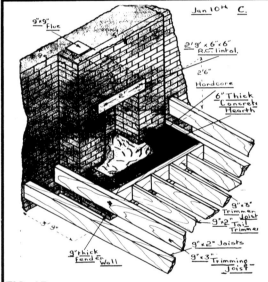

FIG. 15
BUILDING CONSTRUCTION
The trimming of timber joists around a fireplace — typical of the work done by Builders in Class 6X.

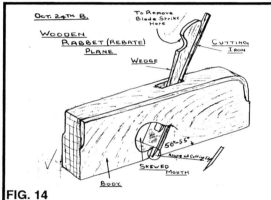

FIG. 14
WOODWORK: REBATE PLANE
The woodwork shop in Bow Building had a magnificent collection of wooden rebate planes of the kind shown in this illustration. There were perhaps as many as thirty or forty planes, each one of which had a unique cutter with which to form a rebate or moulding. Linseed oil kept them in good order.

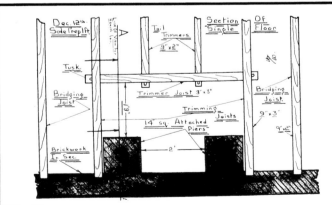

FIG. 16
BUILDING CONSTRUCTION: Plan view of Hearth Construction.

WOODWORK AND BUILDING CONSTRUCTION
Figs 12, 13 and 14 illustrate tools typical of those used in the more advanced woodwork classes at the Central Technical School.

Figs 15, 16 and 17 show Building Construction exercises required in the final year of the Building Diploma.

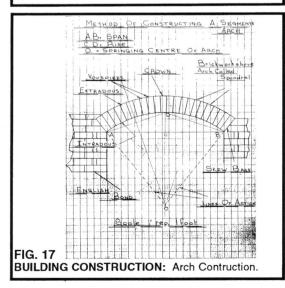

FIG. 17
BUILDING CONSTRUCTION: Arch Contruction.

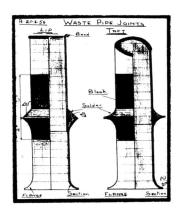

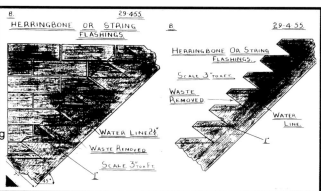

FIG. 18 (left)
PLUMBING
Homework: Spigot and socket connections to a waste pipe.

FIG. 19 (right)
PLUMBING
Homework: Lead flashing as required at a roof-wall junction.

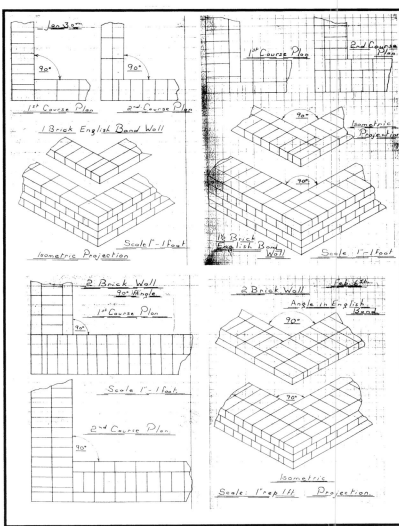

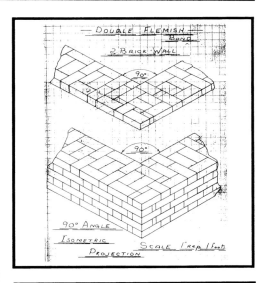

BRICKWORK

FIG. 20 (upper left)
FIG. 21 (lower left)

Four pencil studies are illustrated of English Bond brickwork. This work was started in class (Building Construction) and later completed as homework.

FIG. 22 (above)
Double Flemish Bond brickwork.

These studies show the manner in which the theoretical aspect of Brickwork was taught at the Central Technical School in the form of Building Construction. After the brickwork bonds shown in the diagrams were completed, boys then constructed them in the Brickwork workshop.

FIGS 23, 24 and 25 ART: First Year illustrations drawn at home for Mr. Edgar Grantham's '*Glossary of Architecture*'.

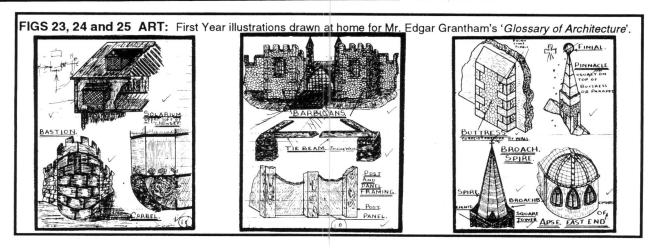

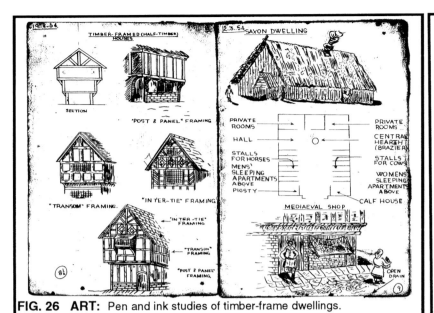

FIG. 26 ART: Pen and ink studies of timber-frame dwellings.

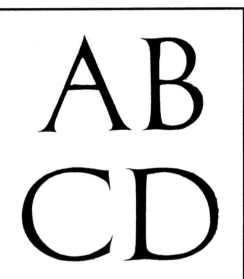

FIG. 29 ART
Block Lettering studies from First Year Art.

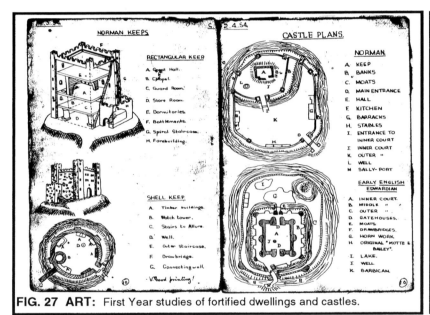

FIG. 27 ART: First Year studies of fortified dwellings and castles.

FIG. 30 ART
Roman Lettering studies for the Art Club.

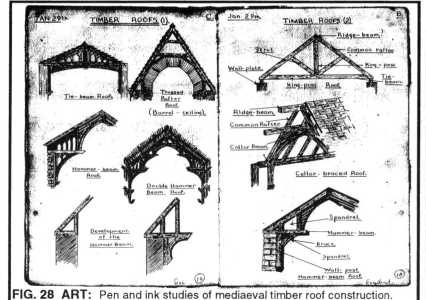

FIG. 28 ART: Pen and ink studies of mediaeval timber roof construction.

ART

FIGs 27, 28 and 29 are reproduced from the Author's large First Year upright 'Drawing Book' which was used for art illustration. The sketches shown form part of a sequence of drawings to accompany Mr. Grantham's lessons on the development of fortified dwellings and castles. The medium is pen and black ink.

Figs 28 and 30 were drawn outside normal class hours as part of the work of the Art Club which was established by the teacher of Art at the Central Technical School, Mr. Edgar Grantham. The Club met each week and a few of us did extra work to develop our interest in art and architecture. The Block Lettering shown in Fig. 29 was *de rigueur* for all art-work classes but the Roman Lettering reproduced in Fig. 30 was much more adventurous — and demanding to set out!

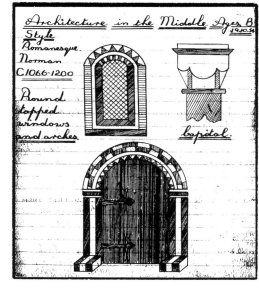

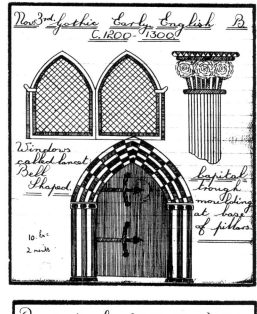

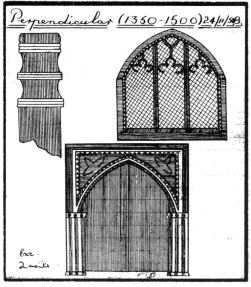

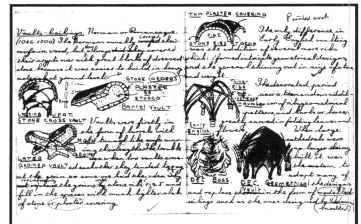

FIG. 31

Art Club Studies: Two pages are reproduced in this illustration from the author's Art Club Sketch Book. Mr. Grantham encouraged members of the Art Club to keep a sketch book and to make notes alongside their sketches. The theme of the sketches shown is 'Vaults'.

THE ART CLUB

Mr. Edgar Grantham founded the Art Club at the Central Technical School in 1955. The Author was a keen member during its short period of existence. As can be seen from the caption accompanying Fig. 31, boys were encouraged to keep a sketch book and to record therein items of visual interest.

One of the Art Club's principal recreational activities was to visit places of special architectural interest — within easy reach of Sheffield. Such visits were made — by motor coach — to Hardwick Hall, Chatsworth House, Nostell Priory and Haddon Hall. Following such visits the members of the Club were encouraged to write an account of their experiences in the form of illustrated essays. Examples of the Author's written work, for these occasions, are to be found in the main text.

FIGs 32–35

These drawings were undertaken as part of the Art curriculum, namely, to illustrate selected terms from 'Glossary of Architecture'. Such work Also overlapped with the more recreational activities of the Art Club.

FIG. 36
History Homework: The study of Norman Britain included making this sketch of a typical Norman castle.

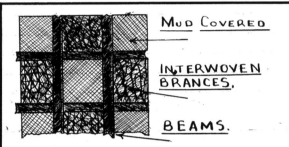

MUD COVERED

INTERWOVEN BRANCES.

BEAMS.

FIG. 38
A sketch of 'wattle and daub' construction taken from an essay on the methods adopted by poor people in the building of their dwellings.

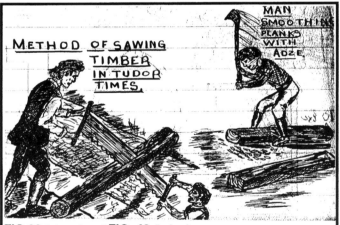

METHOD OF SAWING TIMBER IN TUDOR TIMES.

MAN SMOOTHING PLANKS WITH ADZE.

FIG 39 (above) and FIG. 40 (below)
The study of the dwellings of people who lived and worked on an English Manor was made more interesting by considering how they constructed their houses. The 'pit saw' method of converting wooden planks is shown in the illustration together with a sketch of a man finishing a plank with an adze. Fig. 40 shows the work of the 'harmonious blacksmith'.

A TYPICAL TUDOR HALL

TYPICAL E. PLAN.

LATTICE DEVELOPED LANCET.

FIG. 37
This drawing of a rather grand timber-frame residence was made to accompany a history essay on the subject of 'The manor' — see text.

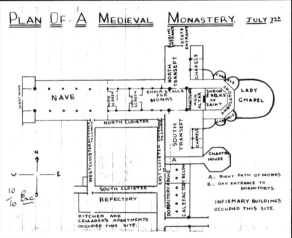

PLAN OF A MEDIEVAL MONASTERY. JULY 7th

FIG. 41
The study of Mediaeval history in Second Year included drawing the plan of a monastery and naming the architectural terms for its various parts. This approach to the study of History combined well with our related work for Art.

HISTORY

The sketches shown in this sequence of illustrations are taken from essays undertaken as part of First and Second Year History. Boys at the Central Technical School were encouraged to illustrate their written work in the manner shown by way of making the subject, in this case History, more interesting.

History lessons followed a regular pattern in which the subject under study was first discussed by the teacher — usually making reference to the class textbook. Then came the hard bit; we had to write an account of what we had understood — making appropriate reference to the relevant facts. The enjoyable bit was to draw a suitable sketch or diagram — although usually for homework.

FIG. 42
As the hand-written title to this illustration indicates, the scene portrayed is a typical street in the Middle Ages. Just discernible in the gloom is a man leading a pig, a 'Friar Tuck' like monk and a shady-looking character resting with his horse. Slops are being thrown from an upper window — in the manner typical of those times.

FIG. 43
Left: Would a man really walk through the streets chained so vulnerably to a wild bear — even in the Middle Ages?
Right: Two gentlemen — clearly of modest means — are shown in contemplative mood as they journey on the high road leading to London.

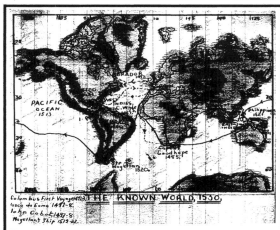

FIG. 45
This map originally accompanied the Author's History essay 'The Elizabethan Seamen' — see the main text. It is typical of the illustrations that CTS boys were encouraged to draw to enhance written work. The map shows the pioneering routes taken by Christopher Columbus, Vasco da Gama, John Cabot and Ferdinand Magellan — names to stir the heart.

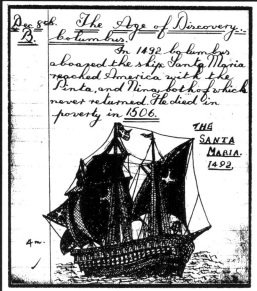

FIG. 44
This ink sketch of the sailing ship 'Santa Maria' accompanied the Author's History essay describing Christopher Columbus's contribution to 'The Age of Discovery' — see the main text.

HISTORY
This page of illustrations continues the historical theme of the preceding sequence of sketches. The drawings shown depict aspects of Second Year study at the CTS concerning the Mediaeval period of English life and the era of the Elizabethan seamen.

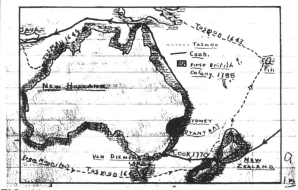

FIG. 46
'The Exploration of Australia' was the title of a History essay from which this map was derived — see the main text. It shows the routes pioneered by Abel Tasman and Captain James Cook.

FIG. 47.
This is a pen and ink sketch of the Guildhall at Thaxted, Essex. It originally accompanied an essay on the Guild System in England. Boys at the CTS made a study of mediaeval trades and crafts and their impact on the economic life of towns and villages under the control of the mercantile guilds.

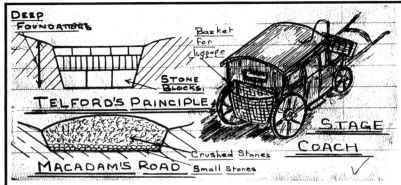

FIG. 48

The sketches shown in this illustration portray aspects of the impact of the industrial revolution on transport and, in particular, of the need for improved roads. This work derives from Third Year.

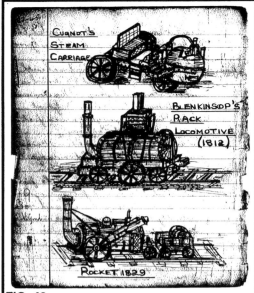

FIG. 49

Our understanding of the era of the industrial revolution was perhaps best captured in the study we made of the advent of the railway system and the 'Age of Steam'.

HISTORY

Figs 48–51 shown here illustrate sketches drawn as part of History homework. The themes represented are various aspects of the Industrial Revolution. Fig. 50 (below-left) depicts pioneering steam ships and Fig. 51 (below-right) shows early forms of mechanically powered road transport. The tramcar illustrated is identical to those used by the Author to travel between home and school!

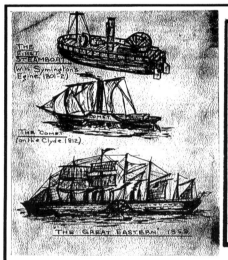

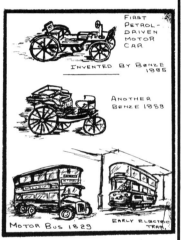

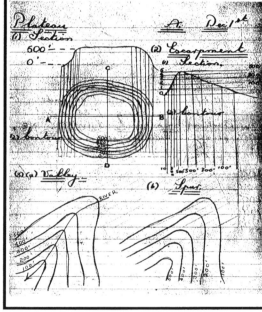

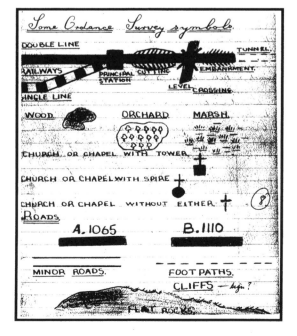

GEOGRAPHY

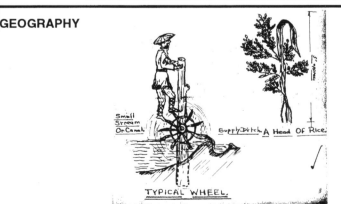

Fig. 52 (above) is an example of First Year diagrams drawn when studying the conventions used by the Ordnance Survey. Fig. 53 (left) is a set of typical studies made of contour representations; these were the first sketches drawn by the Author in pen and ink for schoolwork. Fig. 54 (above-right) shows a Chinaman at work irrigating his field.

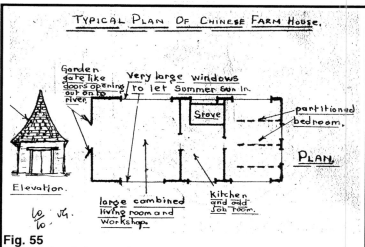

Fig. 55

The study of Geography was made more interesting by making reference to the people of other nations, including their habitations. A Chinese farm dwelling is shown here in this piece of First Year work. Perhaps it is the home of the form-worker shown in Fig. 54.

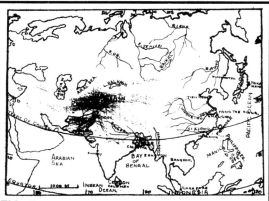

FIG. 56

A Map of Asia. This is one of a series of maps drawn for Second Year Geography. The original sketch was coloured to distinguish the topographical and relief features.

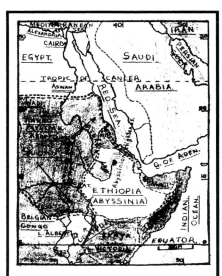

FIG. 57

A section of the Political Map of Africa. This map shows the political boundaries of N. West Africa as they were in the distant days of 1956 when this map was drawn for Geography homework.

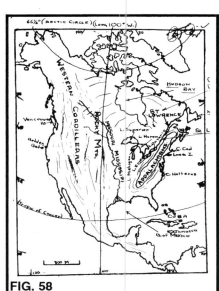

FIG. 58

A Map of North America.
Maps were usually begun in class and were then completed for homework. Enthusiastic boys coloured in their work and added titles in Indian ink.

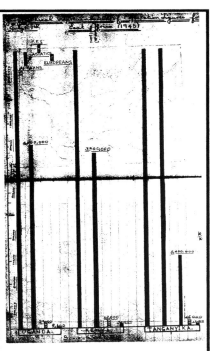

FIG. 60

A histogram of the population of East Africa — as in the post-war period.
As this diagram indicates, school Geography in the 1950s was already beginning to emphasise the problems facing the World due to rapid population expansion.

FIG. 59

A Map of Europe. This map was drawn as part of a study boys in Class 6X made (1956) of the Mediterranean Sea. The work included a visionary project to dam the Mediterranean in order to generate electricity by tidal action — still relevant today.

GEOGRAPHY

The sequence of drawings on this page illustrate typical studies undertaken for Geography classwork and homework at the CTS in the 1950s. The sketches shown accompanied written work done in Second and Third Year (Classes 5X and 6X).

Physical Geography inevitably involved drawing — and colouring — lots of maps and naming the salient features. Geography studies also included learning about the people of other nations — where and how they lived, their habitations etc. Boys also considered such problems as population growth, food supply and schemes for renewable energy — issues which are even more relevant today.

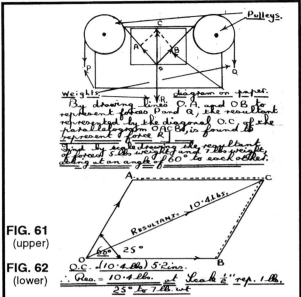

FIG. 61
(upper)

FIG. 62
(lower)

Fig. 61 is a typical illustration reproduced from Mechanics classwork. It shows a simple experiment to establish the resultant of two forces.
Fig. 62 is the resulting parallelogram of forces.

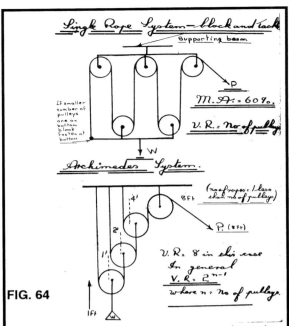

FIG. 64

These diagrams of Pulley Systems were drawn from direct observation of the equipment housed in the Mechanics Laboratory at the Central Technical School.

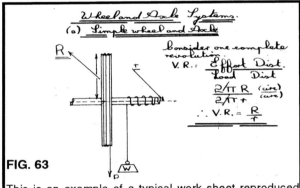

FIG. 63

This is an example of a typical work sheet reproduced from the Author's Mechanics note book.

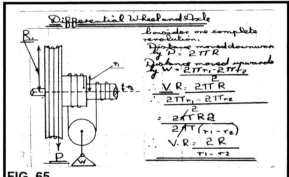

FIG. 65
This diagram further illustrates the apparatus available to boys at the CTS for practical work in Mechanics.

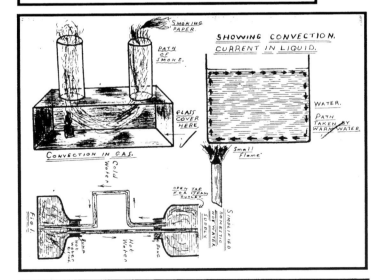

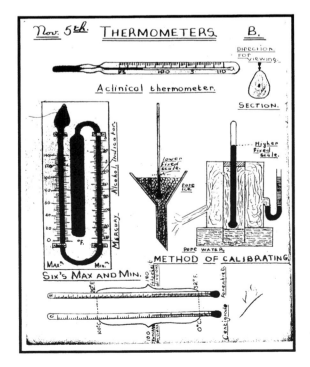

MECHANICS
Figs 61–65 illustrate, in diagrammatic form, some of the equipment use at the CTS to introduce boys to the theory of simple machines.

SCIENCE and PHYSICS
Fig. 66 (above) and Fig. 67 (left) are reproduced from Second Year (Class 5X) note books and illustrate principles of heat convection (Fig. 66) and the calibration of a mercury thermometer (Fig. 67).

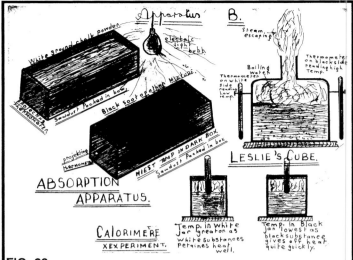

FIG. 68

These studies are reproduced from Second Year (Class 5X) Physics homework. The 'absorption apparatus' was no more than two chalk boxes — used to determine the take up of radiant heat. Leslie's cube was more sophisticated, being a water-filled copper cube to demonstrate the emissivity of a hot surface.

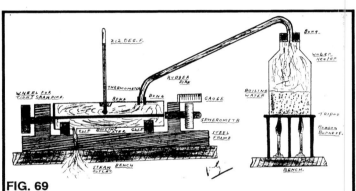

FIG. 69

The determination, by experiment, of the coefficient of linear expansion required the use of the equipment shown in this illustration. This was one of several such laboratory experiments boys undertook in Second Year at the CTS to establish the physical response of materials to rise in temperature.

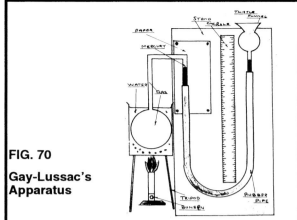

FIG. 70

Gay-Lussac's Apparatus

This equipment was used to demonstrate that the volume of a gas may be altered by a change of pressure as well as by a change of temperature.

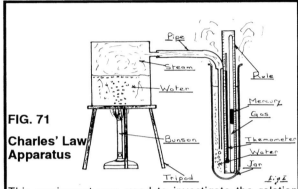

FIG. 71

Charles' Law Apparatus

This equipment was used to investigate the relation between the volume of a gas and its temperature with the pressure kept constant. The similarity between this proposition and that considered in Fig. 70 gave rise to an amusing incident in class — see the main text 'Physics'.

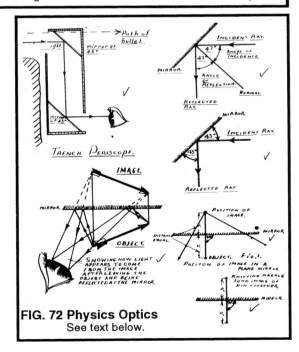

FIG. 72 Physics Optics
See text below.

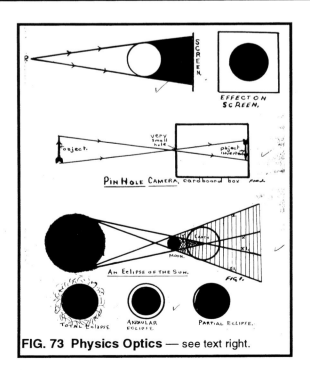

FIG. 73 Physics Optics — see text right.

PHYSICS — HEAT: Figs 68–71 are typical of the sketches boys made for First and Second Year Physics at the CTS.

PHYSICS — OPTICS: Fig. 72 illustrates work done in the study of the Laws of Reflection of light. Fig. 73 is a set of diagrams drawn to illustrate the phenomenon of the solar eclipse.

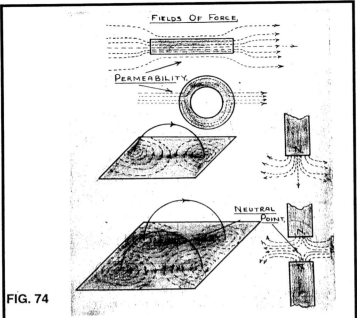

FIG. 74

The study of electro-Magnetism in Second Year was made interesting by performing experiments, as here illustrated, to show that a coil bearing an electrical current generates a magnetic field like that of a typical bar magnet.

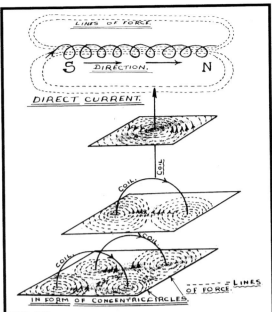

FIG. 75

The diagrams shown here were used to introduce CTS boys to Flemming's 'Left-Hand Rule' and 'Maxwell's Corkscrew Rule' bearing upon the direction of an electrically induced magnetic field.

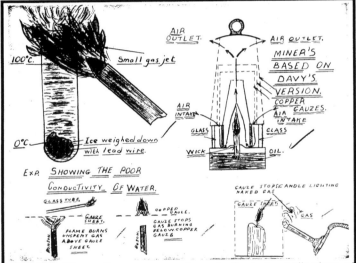

FIG. 76   These diagrams were drawn to illustrate applications of the Bunsen burner and Humphry Davy's miner's safety lamp.

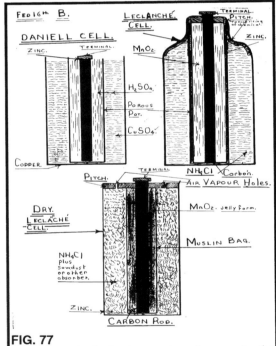

FIG. 77

The 'history' of physics made reference to the electric cells of John Frederic Daniell and Georges Leclanché — the latter commonly associated with the electric doorbell illustrated in Fig. 78.

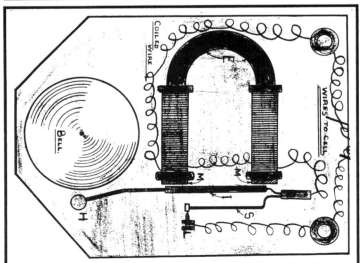

FIG. 78   The study of the practical application of electricity included the electric door bell — a favourite subject of teachers of physics.

PHYSICS

Figs 74 and 75 are diagrams drawn to illustrate how an electrical current creates a magnetic field — made detectable by scattering iron filings on sheets of paper.

Fig. 76 shows further applications of the study of heat — see previous illustrations.

Figs 77 and 78 are diagrams drawn to illustrate practical applications of electricity.

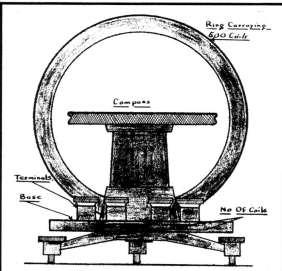

FIG. 79

The side view of a Tangent Galvanometer is illustrated in this diagram. Its name derives from the fact that the strength of the electrical current, passing through its coils, varies as the tangent of the deflection of the needle placed at its centre — see Fig. 80. This apparatus is typical of the more advanced equipment that boys used at the CTS in the study of O.L. and A.L. Physics. The illustration was drawn for Third Year homework.

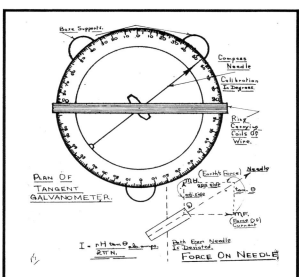

FIG. 80

Plan view of a Tangent Galvanometer. Most boys enjoyed practical work in Physics — especially when using sensitive equipment such as that illustrated in this diagram. Results were recorded in note form and were then written up afterwards together with diagrams as shown in this page of illustrations. In this particular case careful pen and ink work was needed to reproduce the fine calibrated scale around the perimeter of the galvanometer.

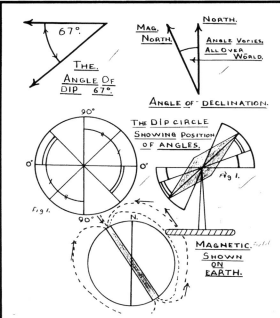

FIG. 81

These illustrations are of studies of the Earth's magnetic field. Measurements of terrestrial magnetism were made with the Inclination Compass or *'Dip Circle'* which boys used to record the angle the magnetic needle made with the horizon — called the angle of inclination or dip.

PHYSICS

The study of natural phenomena in Physics held a particular fascination not least for the interesting and sensitive equipment that was used to measure, for example, small quantities of electricity (Figs 79 and 80) or small magnetic fields (Fig. 81). No less interesting were the optical experiments made with beams of light and polished-glass refracting prisms.

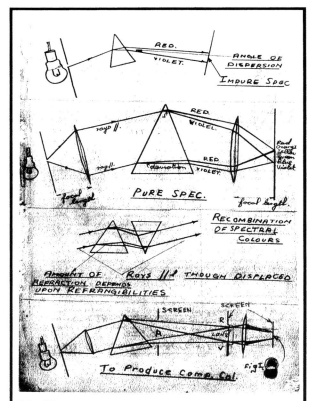

FIG. 82

The study of the behaviour of light passing through a glass prism held a fascination for most boys. In the darkened laboratory a pencil beam of light — as shown above — was traced through a prism to study its dispersive power and to establish the basic laws of refraction. But of greatest fascination were the resulting spectral colours — Red, Orange, Yellow, Green, Blue, Indigo and Violet.

CITY OF SHEFFIELD EDUCATION COMMITTEE

CENTRAL TECHNICAL SCHOOL

DIPLOMA

This is to Certify that

TERENCE MELVIN RUSSELL

after completing the BUILDING Course has obtained a

CLASS I

Diploma, having reached a PASS STANDARD in the following subjects :—

BUILDING DRAWING

with CREDITS in

and DISTINCTIONS in ENGLISH, FRENCH, HISTORY, GEOGRAPHY, MATHEMATICS, SCIENCE, CARPENTRY AND JOINERY, PLUMBING.

S.V.S. Sewell.

Chairman of the Education Committee.

Director of Education.

H.W. Wadge.

Headmaster.

Date 14th MAY, 1958.

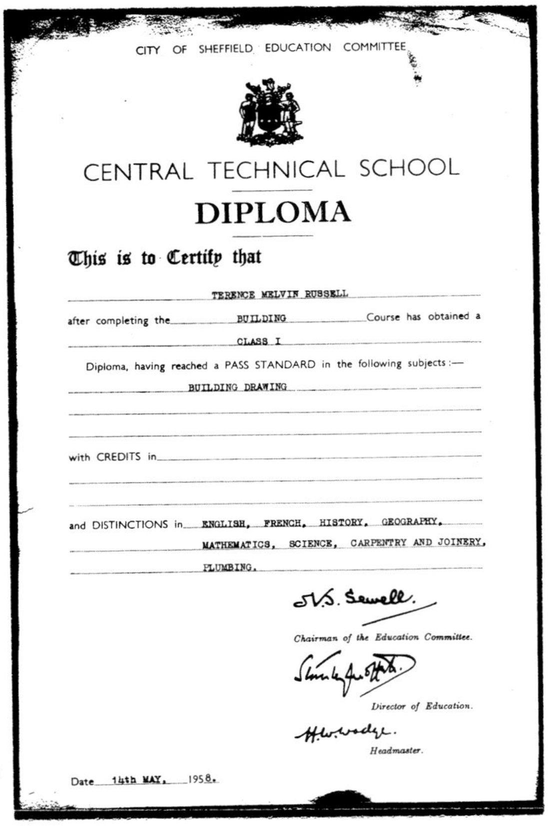

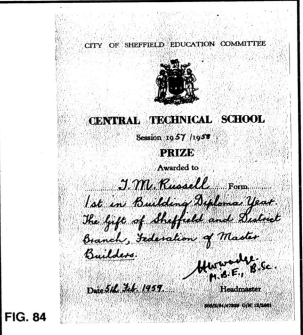

FIG. 83

THE CENTRAL TECHNICAL SCHOOL DIPLOMA

The CTS Diploma was awarded for achievement in either Building or Engineering depending upon the combination of subjects studied. This is a reproduction of the Author's Diploma in Building. All Diplomas bore the signature of the Headmaster, for many years Herbert W. Wadge. As can be seen, the certificate showed the range of subjects studied and the standard achieved with the resulting class of Diploma appearing below the recipient's name.

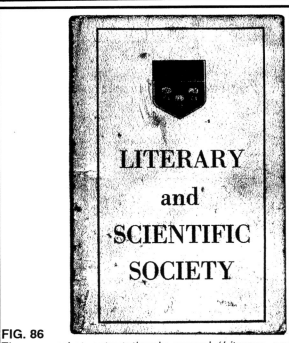

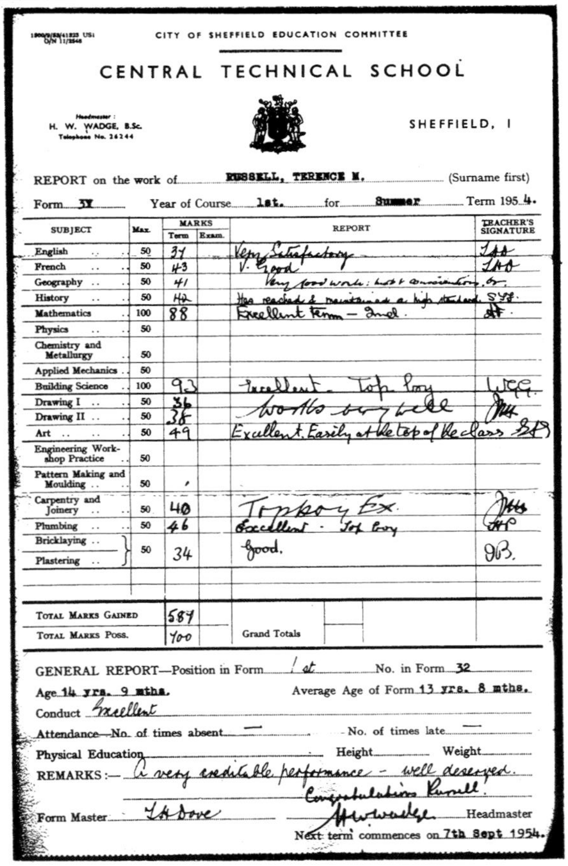

FIG. 86

The somewhat ostentatiously named *'Literary and Scientific Society'* was inaugurated at the CTS in 1958 and flourished for just a few years thereafter, the Author being its first Chairman. Regular meetings were held under its auspices and issues of the day were earnestly debated amongst its ardent and youthful members.

CITY OF SHEFFIELD EDUCATION COMMITTEE

CENTRAL TECHNICAL SCHOOL

Session 1957/1958

PRIZE

Awarded to

T. M. Russell Form

1st in Building Diploma Year.
The Gift of Sheffield and District Branch, Federation of Master Builders.

H.W. Wadge, M.B.E., B.Sc.

Date 5th Feb. 1959. Headmaster

FIG. 84

CENTRAL TECHNICAL SCHOOL PRIZES

Prizes were awarded at the CTS in most subjects and some were sponsored by professional institutions such as the one named in the certificate reproduced above. This is one of the most coveted of all awards, namely, First in the Building Diploma Year. Of interest is the neat handwriting; this was the work of Mrs Wadge wife of the Headmaster Herbert W. Wadge whose signature appears complete with his academic and civic credentials.

CITY OF SHEFFIELD EDUCATION COMMITTEE

CENTRAL TECHNICAL SCHOOL

Headmaster: H. W. WADGE, B.Sc. Telephone No. 26244

SHEFFIELD, 1

REPORT on the work of RUSSELL, TERENCE M. (Surname first)

Form 3Y Year of Course 1st. for Summer Term 1954.

SUBJECT	Max.	MARKS Term	MARKS Exam.	REPORT	TEACHER'S SIGNATURE
English	50	37		Very Satisfactory	
French	50	43		V. Good	
Geography	50	41		Very good work: [illegible]	
History	50	42		Has reached & maintained a high standard.	
Mathematics	100	88		Excellent term – [illegible]	
Physics	50				
Chemistry and Metallurgy	50				
Applied Mechanics	50				
Building Science	100	93		Excellent. Top boy	
Drawing I	50	36		Works very well	
Drawing II	50	38			
Art	50	49		Excellent. Easily at the top of the class	
Engineering Workshop Practice	50				
Pattern Making and Moulding	50				
Carpentry and Joinery	50	40		Top boy Ex.	
Plumbing	50	46		Excellent. Top boy	
Bricklaying / Plastering	50	34		Good.	
TOTAL MARKS GAINED		587		Grand Totals	
TOTAL MARKS POSS.		700			

GENERAL REPORT—Position in Form 1st No. in Form 32

Age 14 yrs. 9 mths. Average Age of Form 13 yrs. 8 mths.

Conduct Excellent

Attendance—No. of times absent — No. of times late —

Physical Education Height Weight

REMARKS :— A very creditable performance – well deserved.
Congratulations Russell.

Form Master T A Dove H.W. Wadge Headmaster

Next term commences on 7th Sept 1954.

FIG. 85

CENTRAL TECHNICAL SCHOOL REPORTS

Boys at the CTS received a Report on their work at the end of each term — signed by subject masters and 'H.W'.

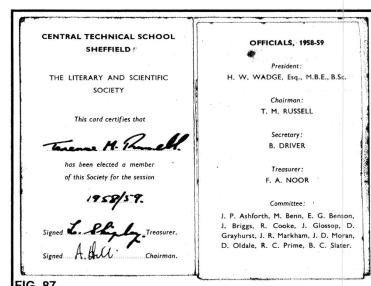

FIG. 87

This is a reproduction of the Author's Membership Card of the *Literary and Scientific Society*. Pupil Committee members are listed to the right.

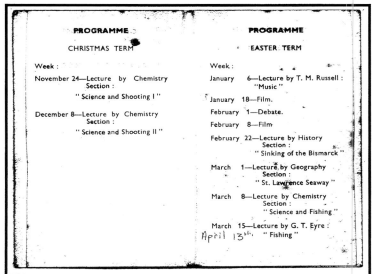

FIG. 88

This illustration lists the inaugural lectures of the newly founded *Literary and Scientific Society*. The Author gave the first lecture of the Easter Term on the subject of '*Music*' — which lasted for over three hours!

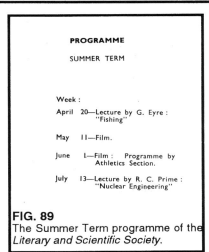

FIG. 89

The Summer Term programme of the *Literary and Scientific Society*.

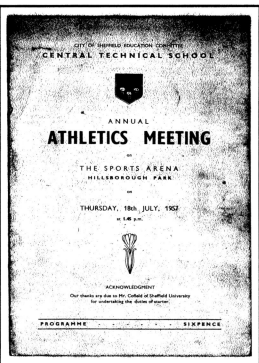

FIG. 90

This is a reproduction of the cover of the Programme for the Annual Athletics Meeting of the CTS in July 1957. The event was conducted very professionally with several teachers acting in various capacities as track officials — see Fig. 91

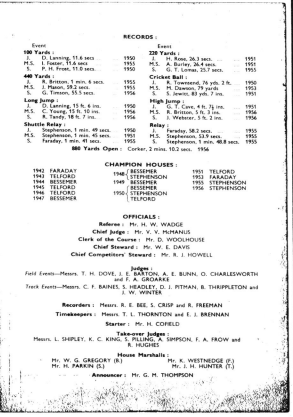

FIG. 91

This page from the Athletics Programme lists the Records held by CTS boys in various events — some of them quite outstanding — and the names of several members of staff and their respective official roles in the games.

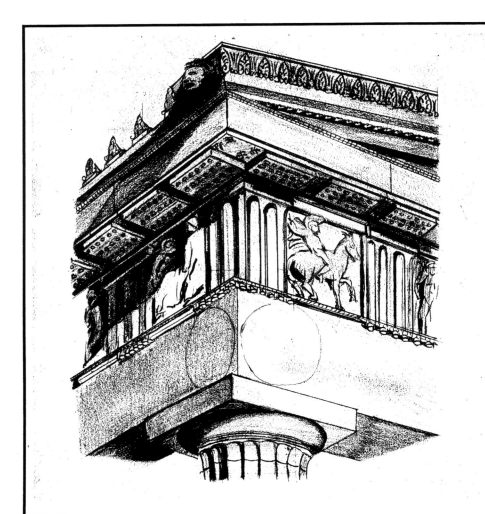

FIG. 92
THE UNIVERSITY OF SHEFFIELD: FIRST YEAR ARCHITECTURE
This reproduction of a pencil sketch is of part of the entablature of the famed Parthenon at Athens. It was drawn by the Author as part of his First Year studies in the Theory of Architecture at the University of Sheffield. The CTS curriculum was a wonderful preparation for undertaking work of this kind — as exemplified in the preceding visual studies.

Man who failed 11-plus gets degree

A 24-YEAR-OLD Sheffield man who failed his 11-pluss has just graduated from Sheffield University with one of the rarest awards — a first-class honours degree in architecture.

Terence Russell, of Glossop Road, Sheffield, took the entrance examination for the Central Technical School two years after failing the 11-plus.

COURSE

He passed, and went on to gain five "A" levels, and then to a five-year architecture course at the University, culminating in his degree and the award of the Professor Stephen Walsh Prize in Architecture.

Now he is doing research into environmental physics with Professor J. K. Page, at the Department of Architecture.

Terence, who has been married a year — his wife teaches music at a city school —will be staying on at the University for one to three years.

FIG. 93
'FAME'
Five — long and arduous — years after the sketch to the left was drawn, the Author duly graduated in Architecture. Word of this reached the Editor of '*The Star*' newspaper whose Reporter produced the above somewhat dramatised piece. For the full story, see the main text under the heading *Herbert W. Wadge*.

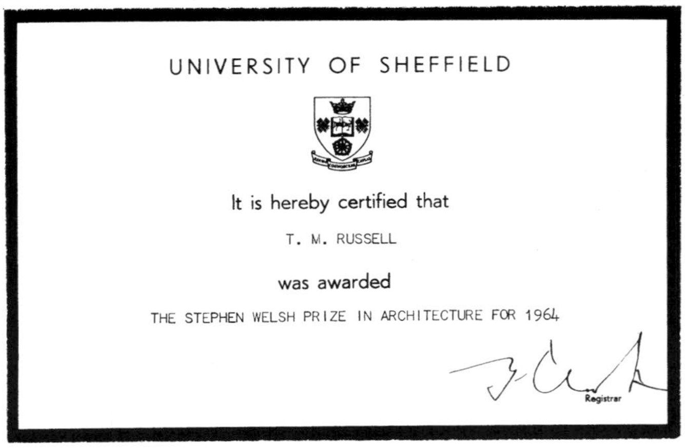

UNIVERSITY OF SHEFFIELD

It is hereby certified that

T. M. RUSSELL

was awarded

THE STEPHEN WELSH PRIZE IN ARCHITECTURE FOR 1964

Registrar

FIG. 94
Stephen Welsh was Professor Emeritus of Architecture at the University of Sheffield. He was of Scottish origin and has the distinction of being the first Scotsman to be awarded the coveted Rome Prize in Architecture. He founded the prize in Architecture bearing his name — to be conferred which was an honour. It was also a valuable award being no less than £50 — a considerable sum in 1964.

5

Admission to the Central Technical School Sheffield A Personal Account

Early Recollections of the CTS

What I have to say in this part of my account is of a more autobiographical nature. For this reason I have extracted the remarks which follow from my principal narrative so that they form, in effect, a free-standing personal account, of how I gained admission to the Central Technical School, Sheffield. Notwithstanding these constraints I trust that what I have to say will be of interest to the reader more widely insofar as my remarks may, I hope, invoke general memories of school life in Sheffield in the immediate post-war years.

My earliest recollections of the CTS predate my actual admission to the school by several years. As a little boy I remember happy days hiking at the weekends in Derbyshire with my parents and my cousin and his family — my maternal aunt and uncle. I was an only child and an only child is a lonely child. So in my early years I turned to my cousin for companionship. This is important and I will introduce my cousin more properly into my narrative in a little while. Suffice it to say here that we grew up together almost as brothers, living in one another's houses and going to the same primary and junior schools.

Our two families would catch the bus on a Sunday, typically, to Fox House or Lodge Moor from Cambridge Lane — just down from Leopold Street where the CTS Firth Building dominates the corner. Perhaps some of you did the same. To my young gaze the edifice looked so grand and imposing — which of course it was and still is. Sometime in the 1950s I actually made a visit to the CTS, again with my cousin, as part of the celebrations for the *International Geophysical Year* — the 'IGY'. This was the time when the explorer Sir Vivian Fuchs made a remarkable polar journey in a caterpillar-tracked vehicle called *The Snowcat*. He recreated Captain Scott's journey of half a century earlier as leader of the British Antarctic Survey. Those of you with a good visual memory may remember that a pen and ink drawing of Sir Vivian appeared on the cover of the *Radio Times* at this time showing him attired in his Antarctic clothing, his resolute gaze staring across the snowy landscape. I remember quite distinctly thinking: "I wish my dad was like that"! (Sorry about that dad.)

Sir Vivian's *Snowcat* was an amazing tank-like machine which was painted mustard-yellow and was on display outside the Midland Station — some of you must remember that? It was placed at the exact location

where, a few years earlier, had stood Reich Marshal Herman Goering's bullet-riddle armoured car. A caption by *The Snowcat* stated that the pressure exerted on the snow by the caterpillar tracks, per unit area, was less than that imposed by a man standing on snow shoes — which I had difficulty comprehending at the time. I wonder, by way of further reflection, if Captain Scott's pioneering caterpillar-tracked machines had been so well designed, would he perhaps have beaten Roald Amundsen to the South Pole? (Elsewhere in my narrative I make a connection — albeit a tenuous one — with myself, the Outward Bound School at Ullswater and the Scott Antarctic Expedition.)

The CTS Firth Building was used to house exhibitions as part of the IGY celebrations and to give the activities an international dimension a radio transmitter was operating in one of the upper rooms. I wandered down the corridors and in and out of various classrooms looking at the different exhibits, maps and wall charts. There were also films to watch. I saw two, one about sheep farming in Northern Ireland and the other on techniques of mining cobalt.

My next personal encounter with the CTS was not to be until several years later when I sat the entrance examination — the circumstances of which I will discuss at the end of this section of my account. For the present I will briefly describe my early education and how it led me to gain admission to the CTS — a long and arduous journey.

"When we were very Young"

Growing up in Sheffield

To establish the context of my admission to the CTS I will first say something of my early life. I will briefly outline my childhood and discuss the schools I attended. In so doing I hope to impart to the reader the nature of my formative years and how certain events from this period shaped and influenced my character. I am speaking here of the first decade of my life, in fact rather more, so there is a fair bit of ground to cover. This is by way of saying that it will take me some little time before I actually reach my principal theme of life and work at the CTS. But in taking time to narrate the events of my early life I hope, far from testing the patience of the reader, I will, through parallel associations, stir fond memories. What I mean to say is that I am aware of how the early lives of many former CTS pupils — and, indeed, those of other readers — are close in kind to my own. I trust therefore that, as I describe certain events in my life, they will stir corresponding thoughts and associations in the minds of other readers about their own lives.

My own particular background was that of a typical Sheffield working-class family. I was brought up amongst like-minded and similarly disposed folk. These formed a close-knit community held together by commonly shared circumstances. The people all about me were hard working, God fearing but not particularly religious, trustworthy, subordinate to authority but proud and independent minded, given to wearing their nice clothes on Sunday and always looking forward to the annual holiday at the seaside especially — in my case — to Blackpool. I have to say that such was the hardship within many families of my acquaintance that they were quite unable to go away for an annual holiday. Verbal exchanges with neighbours were of the kind that is now the stuff of parody and TV sitcom dialogue of the kind: "How are you love?"; "You're not looking too clever!"; "It's a grand day isn't it!"; "They say he were with fancy piece last night!" and so on. It's easy to see where such sea-side entertainers as Albert Moddley derived their end-of-the-pier-show dialogue of the kind: — "Look here. If I a catch your cat peeing on my rhubarb again I'll do for it"! When representatives of the Jehovah's Witness called to our house they would be sent away by my mother with the remark: "Not today thank you"! I was always disappointed by this reaction because I thought our religious visitors might be trying to exchange some household commodity for a goldfish like the rag and bone man who regularly paid us a visit.

We all knew our place in the social order of things. The rent man came once a week and was treated with the utmost respect — likewise the insurance agent. From my mother I learned the importance of having clean underwear for the reason: "You never know what's going to happen to you". Neighbours were always available to help out in times of hardship and would give an indication of their own by a head popped round the kitchen door with the request: "Are you there love? Have you got half a cup of sugar to keep me going until the end of the week"? For grown-ups, the larger themes of birth, life and death were played out to the daily routine of manual work in factories — as portrayed by L. S. Lowry in his representations of north-country industrial life. This calls to mind perhaps the most parodied of all north-country expressions — "There's trouble at mill"! On the two or three occasions however that I actually heard members of my family use this expression it was far from funny. It inevitably signified industrial accidents concerning men and molten steel too horrible to describe. On a lighter and happier note we children played in the secure backyards to the rear of our terrace houses, then, as we grew older, we ventured into the streets and eventually further afield to the parks and woodlands in the neighbourhood.

I was born on 2 October 1939 — at the period of what is typically called the 'outbreak of hostilities'. My earliest memories are, in fact, of the sound of an air-raid siren and of bombs falling. My father was as solid and dependable as his historic-sounding forenames — George Albert. Quite incapable of anger, he was the kindliest of men. He worked for C. & J. Hampton Ltd. for an unbroken period of fifty-three years! His *Long*

Service Certificate now hangs on the wall in my study — a treasured possession. His head was full of fragments of verse some of which he taught me. There were pieces which intrigued me and left me wanting to know more. Here is such an example:

> *Up the airy mountain,*
> *Down the rushy glen.*
> *We dare not go a hunting.*
> *For fear of little men.*

My father also taught me silly things but which made me giggle:

> *Sam, Sam the dirty man,*
> *He washed his face in the frying pan,*
> *He combed his hair with a three-legged chair,*
> *Did Sam, Sam the dirty man.*

And my father whispered things to me which, although I did not fully understand, I realised — from his conspiratorial demeanour — were rather naughty:

> *And the Lord said unto Moses,*
> *All the Jews shall have long noses,*
> *All excepting Aaron,*
> *Who shall have a square 'un'!*

The moments when I learned this doggerel from my father, snuggled up on his lap with his strong workman's arms enveloping me, were truly precious. I learned to read from my father — in a manner of speaking. What I mean is that from his style I learned that 'h' is generally considered to be redundant in Yorkshire — which can be a problem when you actually do want to 'talk proper'. There is something else to add. By all accounts my pre-school proficiency in reading was much admired, prompting neighbours to remark: "He's a bright lad"! But the day came when I started at school — to be described in a moment — when it became all too apparent that I couldn't read a single word! I had simply committed all my little books to memory by listening to them being read to me!

My mother Rose, in contrast to my father, had a feisty demeanour and short temper, qualities which however were combined with a warm and generous nature. Notwithstanding her obvious love for me, in a confiding moment she once disclosed to me how she so-much wanted a daughter that when the nurse presented me to her, following my birth, she just groaned! I think I made up for her disappointment in due course! Like my father she undertook manual work which she disliked intensely because it made her hands all rough and callused. But work gave her companionship and tea-time talk was always about her friends and what had been going on that day at work. I have a photograph of my mother from this time taken at work amidst her circle of companions. She is wearing an overall with a piece of hessian sack cloth for added protection — evidence of the rough nature of her work. Even though we lived under the shadow of the factory where she worked (Tyzack Ltd.) she was invariably late — often because of my own procrastination at breakfast! I learned how to tell the time from my mother. I can still remember sitting on her knee in our kitchen doing the 'o clocks' and the 'quarter pasts'. But it was not in my mother's nature to sit down and read to me so I learned to be resourceful and I occupied myself by making things and endlessly drawing and colouring-in. Sadly not a fragment of my

Terence Russell

Born Oct 1939   Year 1939–1940

Entered Carfield Sept 1944

Left Carfield July 1951

Entered Anns Road Secondary Modern School Sept 1951

Entered Central Technical School January 1954

Carfield Senior School — one had to pass 11+ to go there.
        In 1954? it became Rowlinson Technical School
        at Norton.

childish creations or artistic efforts have survived. However I do have something from this period in my life which not only survives but flourishes. As I will remark in more detail later, I developed a feeling for music through my mother for which I am deeply grateful. I can trace this impulse right back to my formative years — my mother was always whistling and singing.

At the risk of sounding dramatic I owe it to my mother's vigilance that I was not severely scalded and disfigured. It so happens that the circumstances were indeed very dramatic. One evening during an air raid we took refuge in my aunt's Anderson shelter — we did not have an air-raid shelter of our own. The bombs started to fall all about us, inducing my grandfather, who shared the shelter, to wail: "This one's for us. We're done for now"! Such remarks do not inspire confidence! Accordingly my aunt thought everyone should take solace in that great British institution a cup of tea. As she was pouring hot water from a flask a bomb landed so close as to almost fulfil my grandfather's intimations of doom. In fact the bomb in question landed about a hundred yards away from us in Valley Road killing several people. Such was the force of the explosion as to send hot water from the flask cascading in my direction. I was being cradled in my mother's arms at the time and she intuitively swept me out of harm's way taking the full cascade of boiling water onto her right arm. Years afterwards she would narrate these events, as people do, and roll up her sleeve to reveal the almost faded but still blotchy marks scarring her right arm.

My mother and father protected me from the vicissitudes of the war years and lavished upon me the attention typically reserved for an only child — even managing to obtain for me a Hornby train and Meccano set — what more could a little boy want?

As I have remarked, we were a close-knit community separated physically only by backyards. I lived at number 5 Valley Terrace and my grandparents and aunt and uncle lived just round the corner at numbers 25 and 37 Valley Road respectively. At this period — my pre-school years — I spent each morning with my grandmother so that my mother could go out to work. I recall sitting by the fireside watching her drink as essence called 'Camp Coffee' to which she added something called whisky! My grandmother also sipped hot water, telling me that it was good for her bowels. My grandfather was a kindly smiling man who was always impressing upon me the need to be a good boy or, as he put it: "Bill Bailey will get you"! He invariably followed this observation by making a spooky noise. I now realise of course that it was his way of showing his affection for me. But I never did find out who Bill Bailey was!

A childhood friend lived at number 155 Upper Valley Road which for years demarcated the outer geographical boundary of my little world. At the age of about three I learned the need for caution in life in the following way. My dish of rice pudding was too hot and I persuaded my mother to let me place it on the doorstep to cool. When I went back some time later to claim it I discovered that the marauding tom cat next door had scoffed the lot and licked the dish clean!

I will confess here that at the age of three I was a very naughty little boy. I used to take pleasure in going along all the doorsteps of the houses in the immediate vicinity to empty out all the bottles of milk that I found standing out on the doorsteps. To thwart me the milkman had to resort to delivering his milk on the window sills where the bottles were safely out of my reach. I did eventually acquire a social conscience but it took a long time.

I found friendship in the company of my cousin Barrie Bancroft — indeed we grew up together — and, I believe, we exerted a formative influence upon one another. I was six months older than my cousin and quite a bit taller which conferred upon me a feeling of considerable superiority. But I duly got my comeuppance when Barrie, a very bright lad, passed the eleven-plus exam and I did not. I refer to these events elsewhere in my narrative. Although not a CTS lad, Barrie appears in my text from time-to-time in the guise of 'my cousin'.

For all its shortcomings family life provided me with love and security. I can honestly say, along with Edith Piaf — *Non, je ne regrette rien.* My mother's perception however was somewhat different. She struggled valiantly against impossible odds to keep our home as she wanted it. The Meers-brook, from which my district took its name, regularly filled our cellar with several feet of water — to speak of rising damp was an understatement! Much worse, our drains were badly laid and blocked so often that my father had to make a special hole in our boundary wall so that the pools of accumulating waste could be swilled away. When I was aged about ten my mother told me that we had been promised to be re-housed on one of the council estates — she used expressions like 'slum clearance' and 'unfit for habitation'. Sadly that never came about in my mother's lifetime. Moreover from between when I was age ten to fifteen her health deteriorated and during my time at the CTS she succumbed to her illness. These are the facts but I don't want them to sound too melancholy. I had a home, it was warm, there was love, I had my little circle of friends, the sun always seemed to shine and day after day could be spent in play. Ah, but, as the poet says: *They are not long the days of wine and roses* — or, for that matter, ginger beer and conkers.

School eventually beckoned! And it was a challenge! I remember trying to eat my breakfast as slowly as possible in order to delay leaving for school — which only made my mother cross! To make things worse, I always seemed to be surrounded by such confident and vibrant children — perhaps they were just concealing similar feelings to those going on within myself! Modest academic achievement cast a shadow over my early schooling and I was soon relegated to the 'B' stream. My educational route to the CTS was a long and arduous one. Here is how it came about.

Carfield Primary School

The day duly arrived when I was required to attend Carfield Primary School — *Summoned by Bells* in the words of John Betjeman's evocative autobiography. I remember my first day at school very clearly. The weather was, appropriately, dark and threatening and I reluctantly set out clasping my mother's hand dragging my steps as we went. As a consequence, I arrived late to find the classroom already full of children; this conveyed to me the impression they had been there for years — they all looked so established and content. My mother, who was allowed to stay in the classroom for a few minutes, lifted me upon a huge Victorian-style rocking horse repeating, rather unconvincingly, "lovely school"! I was not impressed and when she eventually left the classroom I experienced the first anxious presentiment that my life was changing and that henceforth I would have to be more self-reliant.

I will interrupt my narrative at this point and, by way of general interest, list the members of staff of Carfield Infants School as they were in the immediate post-war years. The information which follows is derived from the *Handbook* of the Sheffield Education Committee for the year 1947. I give the annual salary for each teacher as I have done previously in the case of the members of staff appointed to the Central Technical school.

Helen C. Bingham was appointed Assistant Teacher in 1913 and Head Teacher in November 1924.

(£540)

Mrs Ellen A. E. Anboury was appointed in 1917, left the school in April 1938 and was re-appointed in March 1945. (£420)

Ivy W. Wilson was appointed in August 1922.

(£420)

Winifred M. Blinkhorn was appointed in August 1935.

(£391)

Phyllis Wood was appointed in August 1937.　(£373)

Mary M. Earnshaw was appointed in August 1942.

(£313)

Having introduced these teachers — of whom I have fond memories — I will now return to the theme of my first days at school.

My mother was allowed to accompany me back to school a few days after my first day of schooling as I was required to have a medical examination. This was revealing for the following reason. Until then my knowledge of little girls had been confined to my cousins, from whom I learned caution. I discovered they could scratch and pull your hair. At the medical examination, which took place in the headmistress's room, I had to take off all my clothes — as did two little girls who were also in the room. I still remember that room where we were weighed, had our height recorded and scanned an eye chart on the wall. I then noticed the little girls for the first time. And I realised that whereas I had, what I will call bumpy little bits, my companions appeared to be all nice and smooth! This just goes to prove how observant a little boy can be even at the tender age of five.

In the playground I eventually discovered one of life's great truths, namely, that little girls could in fact be rather nice. Here's how it came about. At the end of break the teacher would come into the playground and ring a large handbell. The idea was you then stood still and — this is the point — took the hand of the nearest girl and walked sedately back into school. Of course, some little girls were to be avoided — but there were some exceptions. It took me an entire year of contrivance to achieve my personal goal — to hold the hand of Miss Judith Fox! Where are you now Judith?

I recall my mother pleading with me to stay at school for my dinner but I stubbornly refused. For some reason I was apprehensive. I was also put off by the smell of food being cooked — the steamy aroma of boiled cabbage is not exactly conducive to the appetite. In point of fact the meals were good and wholesome. Indeed it has often been remarked by dieticians that the

war-time diet of children was nourishing and well balanced. But I refused all this and deprived my mother of obtaining the chance of securing a full-time job which the family so much needed. I therefore had my dinner at home with my mother usually to the accompaniment of *Workers' Playtime* — I can hear the melody in my head now as I write this. To get back to school promptly I had to leave by the time the 12.55 p.m. *Weather Forecast* was being read. If the 1.00 p.m. *News* had started it meant I was late and I had to run like mad. Many is the time though that I heard an immaculate BBC voice say: "Here is the News read by Frank Phillips", or sometimes: "Here is the News read by Alvar LeDell". On very rare occasions you might here: "Here is the News read by Wilfred Pickles"! — this imparted a north-country cadence to what was being reported. Despite spinning out the dinner-time break as long as possible, usually at play with my cousin, I can't remember ever being late for school — not once.

Primary One had a classroom with an open fire which the caretaker maintained from time to time with coke that was stacked in a shed — which served as a shelter when the weather was inclement. I sat near the front of the class close to a large cupboard. Placed on its flat top was a lovely big model of a windmill; how I longed for it to be taken down so that I could turn its sails — alas, it was never to be. On the wall above the cupboard was a picture of the famous *Ten Green Bottles*. They each had a face bearing a look of fear — because they knew they were about to fall. In fact this picture had the effect of making me feel apprehensive. If you are familiar with the painting by Edvard Munch titled *The Scream* you will know what I mean. More congenial to me was a reproduction of the famous painting *The Boyhood of Raleigh* — depicting the young adventurer looking out to sea whilst an old salt tells him a yarn. More perplexing was another art-work reproduction, namely, the equally famous scene titled *When Did You Last See Your Father?* You may recall this depicts a little Cavalier boy. He stands bolt upright on a stool before a table, seated at which is a severe looking Cromwellian officer. In the background his sister is comforted by a woman — possibly her mother. This picture stirred my imagination. Clearly, I worked out in my young mind, the lad was trying to be very brave — so I resolved to be the same when confronting my own tribulations.

The age of innocence was not immediately extinguished the day when I started my primary schooling. Life continued for a few more years in a seemingly endless succession of sunny days and long holidays. Part of the latter I would spend, almost invariably, at Blackpool. Indeed, I have an album crammed with now faded photographs of scenes from holidays spent at this quintessentially working-mans' holiday resort — now the worthy home of Harry Ramsden's grandest fish-and chip shop. It was on one such holiday at Blackpool that my parents encouraged me to have a donkey ride — as devoted parents will. I must have been about three years old and was of a somewhat fearful disposition. Nevertheless, I allowed myself to be put on the back of the animal and all went well for a few paces until the beast tried to make a bid for freedom. It carried me half the length of the beach — chased by the owner and a couple of dozen well-intending holiday makers! To this day I'm not very fond of animals. In passing I will remark that at the tender age I am recalling the phonetic similarity between 'Terence' and 'Terrace' give me some difficulty —

especially when I went to primary school. Let me explain one such instance. To practise our lettering we were required to write our name and address in chalk letters on a slate board. Such was my confusion I clearly recall once writing: 'Terrace Russell, 5 Valley Terence'! I suppose this was an early sign of my being a 'late developer' if you see what I mean.

The classrooms in Carfield Primary School were distributed so that Primary 1 was at one end, near the main entrance, and the classes for the older children were distributed down the corridor. This gave a sense of transition through the school as you moved from one class to the other. In this way I recall progressing from the classes of Miss Anhoury and Miss Earnshaw to that of Miss Wood. Our classes were very large. Some had well over forty pupils of diverse ages and abilities — two members of my class were intellectually impaired and should really have received special care.

There were some mornings when I was very reluctant to go to school. I recall pleading with my mother to be allowed to stay at home. Things became so bad my mother had, on occasions, to accompany me into the classroom. The outcome was that I had to move my desk to the front of the room so that the teacher Miss Wood — a kind young teacher with a lovely golden bracelet — could keep an eye on me. But that just resulted in my feeling conspicuous and only advertised my shortcomings. I found spelling particularly difficult and one day things got so bad that I tore a page out of my spelling book — believing I would not then have to learn the words! As a consequence, I had to take the mutilated book home to show my parents who were then required to replace it. We had to devote a whole Saturday morning 'going into town' to buy the replacement copy — a little book with a blue cover called *Spell Well*.

I remember how, in Primary Three, achievement was rewarded in the form of coloured stars. 'Gold' and 'silver' — cut from shiny paper — were the ultimate symbols for the highest level of reward with other colours — white, green, yellow and red — being reserved for lesser achievements. Our names were recorded, vertically, on a large sheet of paper; the coloured stars, for those so rewarded, were displayed horizontally after their name. Now, this sheet hung on the wall adjacent to where I sat — about two feet from my left elbow. So, as the year progressed, I had a unique opportunity to watch the rows of stars grow in profusion — mostly against the names of other children! But I did get a great many yellow stars for my art work. I was good at that — more details shortly.

I soon realised that school was something you did and that you just had to get on with. Some days were not without a touch of irony. We would often start the day by singing a little song. One such went along the lines: 'Glad to live am I'. Another had the refrain: 'Summer suns are glowing over land and sea, Happy light is flowing bountiful and free'. The reality was that outside, the school was inevitably shrouded in fog and inside, to my young sensibilities, there prevailed an atmosphere of Stygian gloom. You will recall that in Greek mythology the Styx was the principal river of the Underworld across which were ferried the souls of the dead! The comparison is a little extreme but you get the idea.

There were periods of relief from school. These were happy carefree days which we often spent exploring in Meersbrook Park. Sometimes we would venture into the Ruskin Museum, now re-located in the centre of Sheffield. I marvelled at all the lovely drawings and paintings. But best of all was a lovely stuffed peacock in a glass case. We discovered that by jumping up and down you could make its case vibrate and get the bird's head to nod — just as if it had come back to life! Then the keeper would find out what we were up to and would throw us out. Cat Lane Woods was another good place to explore. You could climb trees there, go looking for frog spawn in the upper-reaches of the Meersbrook and generally mess about. Alas, after one such escapade I ended up in the Casualty Ward of the Royal Infirmary as a result of falling from my bike whilst racing a rival. I still have the scar on my right leg as a souvenir of my youthful indiscretion of over fifty years ago. How endlessly long seemed our summer holidays.

I duly progressed from Carfield Primary to Carfield Junior School — the next major step in my journey to the CTS.

Junior School and the Eleven Plus

Carfield Junior School

I enjoyed my four years at Carfield Junior School. They provided me with a sense of security and strengthened my educational foundation. On my return visits to Sheffield I can never resist casting an affectionate glance in the direction of the buildings to recall the days when I walked up the hill to the school from Valley Road with my fiends arguing whether Len Hutton was as good a cricket player as Don Bradman, or what models you could build with a particular *Meccano* set and where you could find good conkers. A number of CTS lads went to this school including David Dickson, David Collins and John Butcher — all my contemporaries and all good friends. My last year at Carfield Junior School was however somewhat overshadowed by the eleven-plus examination, the consequences of which changed my young life forever. But more of that later. For the moment I will linger a little while at Carfield Junior School and say a few words about some of its teachers and the things we did.

Prominently sited at a hilly location at the top of Upper Valley Road we children could see its bell tower from a considerable distance and I can recall hearing the bell ring on a number of occasions. A handbell, rung in the playground, gave the signal that lessons were about to start. Sturdy, stone built and with lofty windows and airy classrooms the school served the Meersbrook catchment area and the immediate environs. I remember the School Hall as being particularly fine. It was there we used to hold our assemblies, have our PT lessons, sing and occasionally dance — it was music and movement to be more precise. And there was a Tuck Shop where you could buy an ice lolly — very welcome on hot days.

Nearby was an Old Peoples' Home where the occupants behaved rather like a hygrometer; on warm days they came out and on cold days they stayed indoors — very sensible. I recall they weren't too pleased if our ball went over the wall into their garden; I know because I was sent to collect it on a few occasions and can remember their remarks! It's a myth that old people are nice and sweet! Well, we all have to grow old don't we!

At Carfield Junior School classes were streamed along the lines of the well established 'A' and 'B' categories with a particular emphasis on streaming in Classes 3A and 3B and Classes 4A and 4B as the eleven plus approached. I was in the B stream throughout my time in the Junior School.

Before proceeding any further with my narrative I will at this point, as I have done before, introduce the teachers of Carfield Junior School as they were in the immediate post-war years:

Ernest W. Chandler trained as a teacher at Chester in the period 1923–25 and was initially appointed to Heeley Bank School. He was appointed to Carfield in August 1925 and Temporary Head Teacher in April 1939. He was appointed to Head Teacher in August 1943.

(£705)

Marvyn A. Atkinson was appointed in November 1944.

(£615)

Frank Lovitt was appointed on August 1927 and, following military service, was re-appointed in October 1945. (£525)

Stanley Vassey was appointed to Anns Road School in August 1928 and to Carfield, following military service, in November 1945. (£525)

James W. Sibley was appointed in November 1945.

(£525)

John McKay was appointed in July 1946. (£437)

Ida Cleathero was appointed in August 1920. (£420)

Bertha Parker was appointed in August 1920. (£420)

Mrs Bessie Bronks was appointed in August 1926 and after leaving was re-appointed in July 1945.

(£404)

Marjorie O. Wing was appointed in August 1927. (£420)

Kathleen D. Lydiard was appointed in August 1930.

(£420)

Marjorie Rubery was appointed in August 1930.

(£420)

Dorothy M. Taylor was appointed in September 1946.

(£270)

As can be seen from the above list, the Headmaster was Mr. Chandler. He was a disciplinarian! He invariably wore a pin-stripe suit complete with a button-hole carnation. His sartorial image was made complete by him wearing a matching shirt, the collars of which were so well starched they actually reflected the light. He had them laundered at the Yun Chinese Laundry which was located on 'Heeley Bottom' (Chesterfield Road) — I know that because Roy Yun, who was a friend of mine, lived there and told me so. (By the way Roy's brother was one of the very first to open a Chinese restaurant in Sheffield.) Mr. Chandler waxed his moustache at the ends into two sharp points which gave his appearance something of a military bearing. (Can I be naughty here and pose the question — "I wonder what it is like to kiss someone with a waxed moustache — especially in the dark"?) Mr. Chandler's somewhat

formal demeanour was further enhanced by the silver-headed cane which he always carried under his arm rather like a field marshal — the sight of which used to give us children the shivers! He was the only teacher to come to school by motor car which he polished beautifully until it shone like a mirror. I recall him saying in assembly: "Please don't touch my car; fingerprints are difficult to remove"! So we treated his car with great respect. It must have been difficult to have been a headmaster in the immediate post-war years with large classes to contend with and the needs of mixed-ability groups to fulfil. Mr. Chandler was an authority on the teaching of spelling, so this topic featured strongly on the curriculum — this was my bad luck because spelling was my worst subject! Mr. Chandler and his staff certainly had their academic high-achievers. Pupils who were successful in the eleven-plus exam had their names inscribed on parchment sheets which were displayed in frames along the full length of the corridor. These were called the *Honours Boards*. Several pupils secured a place at 'King Ted's' which was the supreme eleven-plus achievement. And, as already noted, a few even distinguished themselves by going on — eventually — to the CTS!

My Junior Class 1B teacher was called Miss Escritt — for some reason her name is not listed in the Education Committee Handbook of Teachers from which I have derived my information. With her we started every single day of school by hearing her say: "Now shall we put our thinking caps on!", at which we had to stand and go through the ritual of securing in place the imaginary article of intellectual enhancement. It never did me much good! Miss Escritt lived in lodgings at a rather grand villa in Park Road. I know because one day I carried her briefcase all the way to her door — the effort nearly killed me! I never tried it again. I thought, there must be easier ways of getting into a teacher's good books than this!

Class 2B was taken by Miss Dorothy Taylor. She was very pretty and had a liking for dark-red lipstick which she used to apply in a curvy shape that I now know is called a Cupid's Bow! The reader will discern from this remark the extent to which young Terence was already a keen observer of the applied visual arts! I liked Miss Taylor. She was kind and gentle and had a low soft voice. She once said how nice I could sing! This occurred during a class in which we all had to sing a solo. I sang: *Early one morning, just as the sun was rising*. But the honours for singing in my class went unequivocally to one of my contemporaries called Peter Middleton. Peter had the most angelic boy-soprano voice and could melt the heart with his party piece — an interpretation of *Sorrento*. All the girls were fond of Peter — lucky chap. Here are the names of some of those youthful admirers: Anita Atkins, Carol Barlow, Pauline Page, Christine Wilkinson and Wendy Woolhouse — and that's only those who sat in class in my vicinity!

Peter Middleton was my closest rival in art and could draw birds wonderfully — especially swans swimming in close formation. I will also add here that on Friday afternoons we were allowed to take a book to school of our own choice — whilst the teacher did the register and caught up with other administrative duties. We could also take in something other than a book if we wished which brings me back to Peter. He had a box of colour-tinted glass slides with a special viewer. Such things are common-place now but the impression these back-lit images created, on those of us fortunate to see them, was little short of sensational — we had never seen anything like them before.

In Class 2B we had a fish tank made from a large glass accumulator. In this were a pair of frogs which I observed performed interesting physical exercises, the eventual outcome of which was a lot of frog spawn and then lots of tadpoles! With Miss Taylor we 'did' the *Hanoverians*, the *Plantagenets* and the *Wars of the Roses* — and lots more. I remember these particularly well because I helped to draw some of the wall murals which accompanied our study of these aspects of history. I also remember from this time becoming a fan of Hereward the Wake, the Anglo-Saxon rebel who was the master of the swampy fen country, and — of course — Robin Hood! I was so inspired by the legendary exploits of the latter that I once set out for Nottingham on my bike with the intention of exploring Sherwood Forest — sad to relate, I got no further than Millhouses!

At Carfield Junior School we did our work in exercise books on the back of which was printed a caution. It went as follows: '*DANGER! DANGER! DANGER! When crossing the road — Look right, look left and look right again. A moment's thought may save much suffering*'. I once made a fool of myself by reading out loud the opening words of this caution and pronouncing them as *DANGGER! DANGGER! DANGGER!* I was ribbed mercilessly for my error — a good way to learn. Thereafter I must have read those words over to myself a thousand times — but I still dashed across the road! It was safer to do so in those days. The only vehicles to regularly come down our way were the battery-powered milk float and the coal lorry. Very occasionally a funeral cortege would come to carry away the mortal remains of a neighbour to whom the Creator had made, as it were, an offer they could not refuse.

I could narrate for you many aspects of the Carfield Junior School curriculum — what we did, how and when and what we put in our exercise books. I will refrain from doing so in any detail or else we will never get to my intended objective — the CTS! I will though cite here one particular moment from our classwork because it is of 'historical' interest. One day in Class 3B we were told there would be a *BBC Broadcast for Schools* — an innovation for the period (1949). All became clear a few days later when a loud speaker was wired up in our classroom — with much ceremony. It was obviously an important occasion since Mr. Chandler personally supervised the event. The system was duly switched on and we heard a very BBC voice say: "Good morning children! Are you sitting comfortably"? I felt like replying — "Yes, these wooden desks, which give splinters in your bottom, and their rickety cast-iron frames are lovely"! But the posh voice went on: "Today I am going to tell you about the *Rocky Mountains* and the *Grand Canyon*". Having never been further afield than Blackpool, I had some difficulty in grasping this concept. But the broadcast endeavoured to capture our minds by being funny. Here is what we were told about the size of the Grand Canyon: "Children it is so big that when you go camping, last thing at night you call out — *Wake up!* Then you go to sleep and the next morning the echo comes back — *Wake up!* And so you wake up"! Then we were told about the hot springs and the geysers — which until then, concerning the latter expression, I thought was the name for a couple of old men who lived nearby. The voice said: "The hot springs are so deep children that you can catch fish down at the bottom and then pull them out and, because it is so hot at the top, they come out already cooked"! Well it seemed funny at the time and we laughed, and, as you observe, I remembered it all. Many years later I heard the American singer Burl Ives sing the following lyric which took me straight back to this moment of my childhood:

> *Oh the buzzing of the bees in the cigarette trees*
> *And the soda-water fountains,*
> *Where the lemonade springs*
> *And the bluebird sings,*
> *In the big rock-candy mountain!*

I will direct my attention now to my last two years at Carfield Junior School. For this I need to make brief mention of Miss Kathleen Lydiard who was my teacher for Classes 3B and 4B. Her name is derived from the Greek *Lydia* and denotes a beautiful woman. She was striking in appearance, rather than beautiful, especially when wearing the strong primary colours for which she seemed to have a preference. She regularly appeared before us wearing a shirt-type blouse and skirt secured by a leather belt. More to the point, she was good at drawing and, even more to the point, she took an interest in my own drawing ability and did her best to promote it. This is important to my narrative so I will indulge myself here by recalling a few happy artistic moments from this period in Miss Lydiard's classes (1950–51).

I remember we had a lesson about Cardinal Wolsey and his building of Hampton Court — the favourite residence of Henry VIII. I made a drawing of the palace, using bright red for the brickwork and brown for the sandstone quoins — perhaps the young architect was already stirring inside me. At that moment into the classroom imperiously marched Miss Marjorie Rubery — who taught Class 3A. We called her, rather predictably, Miss Rhubarb! Miss Rubery had a considerable presence. She was a big impressive lady — by which I really mean she had a bosom which seemed to my young gaze to have the proportions of a bay window. Above all, Miss Rubery was friendly and she liked to pop into our classroom to see how we were all getting on — and, I rather suspect, to have a chat with her colleague Miss Lydiard. She was given to walking around the classroom to inspect our work, head inclined to get a better look. She paused at my rendering of Hampton Court and exclaimed "hm" — I knew I had impressed her. She gave me an encouraging nod and asked to me to turn over the pages of my book. I showed her my Roman soldier, completed a few days previously, all attired in protective armour and chain mail. I had coloured this with a mixture of yellow and brown in imitation of bronze. The effect was very striking and earned me some words of praise. Miss Rubery then shared some remarks with Miss Lydiard — glancing in my direction as she did so. I intuitively understood that I was the subject of a favourable comment. It was a moment to savour. Suddenly Miss *Rhubarb* seemed miraculously transformed. I no longer perceived her as being rather bosomy and I realised how much I liked her — an illustration of how flattery will get you everywhere!

Now who can remember the *Festival of Britain* of 1951? I was fortunate enough to be taken by my father to London to see — I should say *experience* — this wonderful event. We went by coach on a work's trip — and stayed at the Russell Hotel! I had smoked salmon for breakfast and left my shoes outside the bedroom door for them to be polished! I wanted to stay there for ever! My most enduring impressions were of the *Skylon* and the *Dome of Discovery* — remember them? Now, one day, back at school, there was a competition to design a poster to celebrate this very festival. I made a colourful composite image of the *Skylon* standing before the *Dome of Discovery* — and won! For a whole week my poster was displayed in the school corridor for all to see!

My last example of enjoying a moment of achievement arising from my drawing skills concerns our class study of the *Great Fire of London* — 1666 and all that. The class made a large frieze of the River Thames showing all the houses blazing and people escaping in barges. I was 'commissioned' — to put it rather grandly — by Miss Lydiard to make a big chalk drawing of Sir Christopher Wren's masterpiece St. Paul's Cathedral amidst all the flames. To do this I had to stand on a stool — thereby making myself rather conspicuous. As I worked away, in walked Mr. Chandler — who was somewhat surprised to see me in my elevated position. He came up to me and paid me lots of compliments. As Mr. Churchill might have said — "This was my finest hour"! Now I wonder who has spotted the problem with my story? The facts are as I have given them. The problem is that St. Paul's Cathedral was *not built* at the time of the Great Fire of London! It was of course conceived as a result of the conflagration — an oversight on Miss Lydiard's part and not noticed either by Mr. Chandler!

My making reference to these little artistic achievements is not gratuitous self-indulgence; they have a bearing, as I have already remarked, on my narrative. It is this. Miss Lydiard and Mr. Chandler decided to put me in for the entrance examination for admission to the Sheffield School of Art. In its day — one should say *era* — this was a very prestigious institution. Just to be selected for consideration for admission was something of an honour — at least it implied you had some creative and artistic ability. But to keep the chronology of events in their rightful place, I need first to say a few remarks about the eleven-plus examination.

The Eleven-Plus Examination

My account is not intended to be a personal treatise on education but I will preface this section with a few remarks of a general nature concerning the post-war educational reforms which had such a profound bearing on the lives of the children of my generation. R. A. Butler — 'RAB'— is justly credited with pioneering the *Education Act* of 1944 which is generally regarded as being one of the major landmarks in the history of education in the UK. The Act dispensed with the pre-war system of 'elementary' education and made provision for a radically new scheme of primary and secondary education. It also raised the school leaving age from fourteen to fifteen years. In passing I will add that, under these arrangements, I came within one year and two terms of leaving school and would have done so had I not been admitted to the CTS. Under the Act secondary education embraced a tripartite division of grammar, modern and technical schools. As we of that generation are well aware, selection was by means of the eleven-plus examination — of which more in a moment.

My Junior School curriculum was typical of the period and placed considerable emphasis upon proficiency in, and an aptitude for, the three R's. Whilst this is perfectly true, my reason for mentioning it is so that I can call to mind, for a bit of fun, how Lewis Carroll described such a formal typical pedagogical regime. He used the following terms: — 'reeling and writhing', 'ambition', 'distraction', 'uglification', 'long derision', 'mystery — ancient and modern', 'drawling' and 'stretching' and 'fainting in coils'! I have explained that I was good at the latter but, sadly, 'drawling' and 'stretching' and 'fainting in coils' were generally relegated to Friday afternoon when the teacher was completing the class register.

At Carfield Junior School before we sat the eleven-plus exam we received some practice to help us to prepare for the actual event. For example, one afternoon a teacher spent about an hour with us slowly reading out lists of words which we were required to write down. At first the words were very simple but they gradually increased in complexity. Towards the end it was obvious that the words were too difficult for us and the teacher stopped his dictation — I should add that he was a 'student' teacher and not one of the regulars. We used to like student teachers because they generally had only limited powers of class control!

Other of our eleven-plus practice tests were conceived around, to use Lewis Caroll's terms, 'ambition', 'distraction', 'uglification' and 'long derision'. I imagine our performance in these tests was not just to give us pupils some practice in exam technique but also to help the school to build up a profile of our intellectual aptitude which could then be combined with our actual performance in the exam and thereby help to establish the next type of school for which we were most suited. Concerning this, I remember how, about two months before taking the eleven-plus exam, my mother and father had to fill in a form placing in rank order the grammar school of my preference. They duly consulted me so I naturally said 'King Edward's'! With hindsight I now see that was somewhat over optimistic!

By way of general interest, I will make a little digression here about the brother of a former CTS lad and say how he got on in the eleven plus — very remarkably. The CTS lad in question was Brian Lister, to be more precise — Brian Bain Clovis Lister. Poor Brian; with all his names he was known as 'BBC' Lister, or — when he tried to conceal some of his names — even worse, BLister! Brian once told me that his elder brother Richard had not simply done well in the eleven-plus exam, he had received a letter from the Education Committee to say that when he took the exam he was the top candidate from amongst all the Sheffield schools! Richard Lister went to Sheffield University at the age of sixteen and had a PhD by the age of twenty two. I recall saying to Brian after he had told me all this: "With such a clever brother, how is it you're so thick?"! Brian saw the point but was not amused. I owe it to Brian to say that after leaving the CTS he went on to train to be a teacher at Loughborough Training College, before it became Loughborough University, and eventually succeeded as a well-respected primary-school head teacher.

The day of my own eleven-plus examination duly dawned. It had snowed heavily during the night — an ill-omen? The snow had halted what little traffic there was making the streets very silent. On arriving at school it was equally quiet since all the other children had been given a day's holiday — as we previously in our turn had enjoyed. The school hall, normally reserved for assembly and 'PT', was now arrayed with rows of portable examination-style desks. Large signs bore the admonition 'SILENCE'. The headmaster Mr. Chandler contributed to the sense of occasion by casting a somewhat stern gaze upon the proceedings — doubtless anxious that all should go to plan. I can still recall where I sat in the hall — about mid-way down and towards the left-hand side of the room. Some instructions were read out to us. We were to attempt the first set of questions in the script book placed on our desk, then to wait for further guidance. Everything seemed so strict and formal. For interest, I will recall some aspects of the papers.

There was an English paper which was set out in various sections. We had to read a passage and then answer questions about it. Then there were a lot of sentences each with a missing word which had to be supplied from words given in brackets. We also had lots of multiple choice questions. I remember one of my blunders. You had to underline a word to rhyme with 'quay'. I didn't know what a 'quay' was so I underlined 'way'! Then we were told to stop. We were given a short break and went out to throw snowballs — that was the best bit of my eleven-plus experience! After the break we had an arithmetic paper. We had to calculate the areas of different shapes; work out the costs of several things, given the unit cost of an individual item; and there were lots of additions, multiplications and divisions. After the exam was over I realised that I had muddled the multiplication and addition symbols and had treated all the sums as additions! But hope springs eternal. "Let's wait and see how you got on", said my mother encouragingly.

The outcome of each candidate's performance in the eleven-plus exam was made known through the post. We were told it was good news to get a big envelope because this was stuffed with information about the recipient's new school and the list of necessary requirements. Conversely it was bad news to get a small envelope which gave a portend of failure. Some weeks after sitting the exam my cousin Barrie, to whom I have referred earlier, came round to our house beaming proudly bearing a large brown envelope. He had passed! As we walked to school, he talked animatedly of the information which he had received concerning his new uniform, the books he was required to purchase, the drawing instruments he needed — and so on. I listened enviously. The postman had not delivered me any such letter. I can still recall the pain I felt which had to be silently endured. I remember thinking, with childish innocence, that perhaps the postman's bag was too full and that my letter would come the next day. How hope can indeed spring eternal and assume such a diversity of forms.

On arriving at school that morning the children discernibly fell into two categories; there were happy and smiling children, contemplating their future at one or other of Sheffield's grammar schools — and eleven-plus entry schools — and there was a second group, which included myself, who looked on with a mixture of envy and disappointment. All but a handful of the children in Class 4A had passed — a remarkable achievement. One boy only in my class, Class 4B, had passed but his was an astonishing achievement. He had won a place at no less an exalted establishment than the King Edward VII School — King Ted's! This lad was

John Corker and I remember how Mr. Chandler came into our class especially to pay him his compliments. I would like to be able to say that we bathed in his reflected glory but the truth is that deep down we each wished we were the lucky one.

The next day my examination result arrived. It was conveyed in the smallest manila envelope available to the Education Committee. Its message was bleak. I had failed the eleven plus and I was informed that it was in my interest to receive my secondary education at Anns Road Secondary Modern School. I received this information with some trepidation because it meant an upheaval in my way of life. Until then, for the last seven years, I had made my way to Carfield School along streets that were familiar. Now I would have to venture forth into the Heeley district — for me relatively unknown territory. But all was not yet lost. I still had hopes of success for another reason.

I have explained that I was good at art and that I was put in for the entrance exam for the Sheffield School of Art. Let me now tell you how I got on.

The Sheffield School of Art

The Sheffield School of Art, or College of Arts and Crafts as it was originally named, was founded as long ago as 1843. The premises were located in Arundel Street and were demolished years ago — something of an architectural tragedy since it was an architecturally distinguished building. Nude models were employed there! My preparations to sit the School of Art entrance exam required me to go and see the headmaster Mr. Chandler. So as required I made my way to his room and knocked on his door — with some apprehension. I found Mr. Chandler seated behind his desk attired, as always, in a splendid suit the vivid stripes of which would have made a tiger envious. He greeted me with a friendly smile and explained that I was required to take with me a set of coloured pencils. Accordingly, he took from his cupboard a brand new box of such pencils and proceeded to sharpen each until it had a point to rival the tips of his waxed moustache. I felt very proud to receive all this personal attention. "Now", he said, "Be sure to return these"! and he handed me the box of pencils. "Thank you Sir", I said rather timidly and clasped the box close to my chest fearful lest the contents should spill out on to the floor. The need for the coloured pencils became apparent to me a few days later.

The time of the School of Art examination was scheduled for 2.00 p.m. — I have reason enough to remember. My mother was unable to accompany me to the School of Art since she had to be at her work — and I lacked the confidence to go to an unknown part of town on my own. An elaborate arrangement was made with a friend whereby I would stand at the bus stop, be greeted with a wave from the bus, get on board, be united with the friend and be taken to the School of Art! How absurd! The plan could never work — and it didn't. I stood at the bus stop for a full hour clutching my box of coloured pencils — searching every passing bus for the anticipated signal. None was forthcoming. The plan had gone wrong. The appointed hour of 2.00 p.m. came and went. Despair. What was I to do? I had set my heart on taking the exam, had told my friends about it and had proudly showed them my box of pencils — individually sharpened by Mr. Chandler! How could I face them and say I had not even taken the exam — revealing thereby that I was not capable of going into town on my own? I returned home to an empty house totally disconsolate. I sat in the kitchen looking at the clock thinking of what the candidates would be doing — and the tears began to flow unchecked. After about an hour there was a knock at the door. My little school pal from next door, Michael Redwood, had been sent to see what was happening — and he bore a message. He uttered what seemed to my young susceptibilities to be doom-laden words: "Mr. Chandler wants to see you"! What courage it required to make the journey back to school! What would I say and what would be Mr. Chandler's reaction? As it transpired, chance intervened; I met Miss Lydiard. All was not lost. By good luck there was to be a second sitting of the exam the very next day — at 9.00 a.m. This time my mother arranged to take an hour off work and we duly set out together on the tram to Arundel Street. I was full of renewed optimism.

We arrived to find about twenty hopeful pupils gathered at the entrance to the School of Art. My mother gave me a friendly hug and I went inside with the other group of boys and girls. The ethos and ambience of the school, and its concern with art, were manifest; pictures adorned the walls and plaster casts, derived from the sculptures of classical antiquity, adorned niches in the corridors. We were ushered into a drawing studio and seated at drawing tables. "Please get your equipment ready" urged the invigilator — a tall man with a beard clothed in an artist's smock. 'Equipment'? I put my box of sharpened pencils on my desk and looked about me to see everyone else emptying their satchels containing tins of crayons, sticks of charcoal and paints and brushes, the very things which I possessed in abundance — at home! I was gripped with the realisation that Mr. Chandler, despite his good intentions, had sent me ill-prepared to demonstrate my artistic abilities.

We were required to draw a scene from still life (not a nude studio-model I should add) and then to create a visual composition based upon a text which was read out to us. It was hopeless. I scratched at my sheet of paper with my limited selection of sharpened pencils whilst all about me the other candidates in the studio applied thick colour to their paper with dextrous skill. I will not elaborate save to comment, by way of anticipating the outcome, that, after all these years, I still feel somewhat resentful that I did not compete with the other candidates on equal terms. If I had, might I have won a place at the Sheffield School of Art? The answer is probably no. I can't blame Mr. Chandler. I am not an artist — just a moderately competent draughtsman. I am proud of the little illustrations which accompany my narrative. But the discerning eye will recognise that they bear testimony more to industry and diligence than to artistic flair. So not being awarded a place at the Sheffield School of Art was probably a fair one in the end. The next day, as required, I returned the box of coloured pencils to Mr. Chandler. I can't recall what he said. Neither does it matter. It's all more than half a century ago.

I owe it to the memory of Mr. Chandler to take leave of him on a more positive note with a little story in his favour. A rather remarkable co-incidence makes this possible. Let me explain. Allow a quarter of a century to pass and imagine I have just concluded looking at the homework of my, then primary-school age, son Thomas — now Dr. Thomas G. Russell B.Sc. Hons Ist Class, M.B., B.Chir. (University of Cambridge). I cast my eye on a little spelling guide of his and remarked: "What a delightful little book!". This remark induced Thomas to

look at me in bleak disbelief that I could apparently be captivated by so dry a pedagogical text. But he dutifully agreed — a delightful example of filial devotion. In point of fact the words in the spelling guide were imaginatively set-out with inventive rules for remembering the intricacies of English spelling. "Let's see who the author is", I said to Thomas. I turned to the title page and stared with a mixture of pleasure and disbelief. I read the name — Ernest W. Chandler!

About two weeks after my brief encounter at The Sheffield School of Art, the Education Committee — for the second time in my young life — sent me a letter confirming that it was in my interest to receive my remaining school education at Anns Road Secondary Modern School. In a moment I will direct my narrative to that period of my life but first I want to take my leave of Carfield Junior School.

I will put on record that I am grateful to Carfield Junior School for blending all the qualities of us children together and for treating us all as equals. More generally, without trying to score any political points, I am grateful for the new social order created by Lord Beveridge and Earl Attlee which did so much for the families and children of my generation.

I find it difficult to be so charitable concerning the eleven-plus examination. I have already acknowledged the vision implicit in Lord Butler's 1944 Education Act which, like the social reforms to which I have just made reference, improved the life-chances of many children. But for those who, like myself, failed the eleven-plus exam it was a different matter. The sense of failure imposed upon us was considerable. We felt relegated and second class. I personally still feel resentful that, for example, my secondary-modern curriculum did not make any provision for the study of modern languages — although it did include basket weaving. I will not elaborate. It is all now in the distant past. It is a source of comfort however to reflect that those of us who did fail the eleven plus now find ourselves in rather exalted company — his Grace the Archbishop of Canterbury and the Deputy Prime Minister both distinguished themselves by failing the eleven plus!

It has to be said that Lord Butler did make some provision in his 1944 educational reforms for those of us who are usually referred to as 'late developers'. I thank him for that and it is to this aspect of my narrative, and how I benefited from being given a 'second chance', that I will now direct my attention.

Secondary School My Admission to the CTS

Anns Road Secondary Modern School

On its hilly site above Heeley, Anns Road Secondary Modern School dominated its surroundings. Today the buildings are all the more prominent now that so many of the nearby houses have been demolished. I used to walk to this school from Valley Road into Albert Road and then ascended a great flight of stone steps that we called the 'forty-nine steps'. In the long summer holiday after leaving Carfield School I consolidated my friendship with other boys I knew who would be going to 'Anns Road', as we called the school, and made a few practice walks there. We were not required to have school uniform at Anns Road Secondary Modern School but my mother, proud of me as always, had kitted me out in a fine pin-striped suit — short trousers at that age. In my lapel I displayed my *Meccano Guild* badge. I had a Number Eight *Meccano* set — how I longed for a set Number Ten!

On arriving at my new school I huddled with the other new boys and girls against the school wall. We all felt rather conspicuous but a teacher was there to take care of us. There was a shed where we could play in poor weather. This was also where coke was stored. At first it could be hazardous to play in the shed because older boys had laid a claim to it — some of us soon picked up courage though and challenged their assumed territorial rights!

Before proceeding any further with my narrative I will at this point, as I have done before, introduce the teachers of Anns Road Secondary Modern School as they were in the 1950s:

Cecil H. Barnard trained as a teacher at Battersea and Chelsea Colleges of Education and was appointed to Lowfield School in August 1920 and later as Headmaster in September 1930. He was appointed Headmaster of Anns Road School in March 1939.

(£1005)

John P. Edlington was appointed in August 1926. (£797)

Lloyd A. Williams was appointed in August 1931. (£725)

Philip M. Cohen was appointed in August 1932. (£797)

Hyman L. Franks was appointed in August 1943.

(£779)

Samuel W. H. Davison was appointed in October 1932.

(£725)

Harold J. Laycock was appointed September 1948.

(£697)

Joseph Cartwright was appointed in December 1948.

(£705)

Cyril G. Hall was appointed in September 1949.

(£640)

Geoffrey Wilson was appointed in September 1954.

(£493)

Eric Smith was appointed in September 1951.

(£725)

Eric J. Vickers was appointed in June 1947.

(£725)

John R. Wright B.Sc. was appointed in September 1954.

(£739)

Gladys I. Cowley was appointed in August 1912. (£675)

Mrs. Gladys Wolfendale was appointed in January 1934.

(£600)

Kathleen M. Tesh was appointed in September 1949.

(£497)

Margaret J. Duxbury was appointed in September 1955.

(£411)

Eric L. Coates was appointed in January 1933. (£725)

Donald J. Page was appointed in August 1931. (£725)

Hilda Howard was appointed in August 1943.

(£601)

At our first assembly we were welcomed to the school by the Head Teacher Mr. Cecil Barnard. He was the kindliest of men with an obvious devotion to children. Physically he was slight but he had a commanding voice and was very audible in assembly. Once more we were streamed into 'As' and 'Bs'; this time I was in the 'A' stream. In my first year at Anns Road School my classroom was located in a small annex. This formed part of an old Sunday-school and had tall, narrow, stained-glass windows. I remember how, as the day progressed, the colour of the light changed as it passed across the pages of my exercise book!

At Anns Road School we soon realised there was discipline, rigour, authority and commitment to high standards. We may have all have failed the eleven plus but we were not treated as second-class citizens. My first year passed with more 'abstraction', 'mystification', 'long derision', 'reeling and writhing' etc. But we now also did woodwork with a teacher called Mr. Scowcroft in a lovely big workshop — for some reason he is not named in the list of teachers I have given above. When boys did woodwork the girls went off to do cookery. I made a stool, with a basket-work top, and a sledge. I take my hat off with respect for my teachers at Anns Road School — there were no fewer than forty-eight pupils in my class! Yet discipline was maintained and we got on with our work in orderly fashion. About half-way through the year a young teacher called Miss Tesh joined the class to help out. She was astonishingly pretty and secured the immediate attention of the boys — not entirely, I must say, for pedagogical reasons!

One day we were told a School Inspector was going to come and would set some special tests. These turned out to be mostly 'IQ' tests — 'brain teasers'. All the class participated in the preliminary tests but two pupils only were selected for more thorough assessments. With hindsight I now appreciate this was some form of follow-up to the eleven plus to give late developers the chance to be considered for transfer to one or other of Sheffield's grammar schools. At this time there was a very bright girl in our class — she was way ahead of the rest of us. How could a girl like that have failed the eleven plus? She duly passed the tests and left Anns Road to go to Abbeydale Grammar School. By happy chance I met this girl a few weeks later on the top of a tram (I mean on the upper 'saloon') — resplendent in her new school uniform. She returned my chivalrous greeting of "Hello" and told me how much she was enjoying her new school. I remember she had an array of about six different pens in her blazer pocket. I was secretly rather relieved she had left our class — because it meant that some of the rest of us then stood a chance of claiming her vacant position as top of the class!

Life and work continued at Anns Road School and we eventually moved up into Senior 2A whose form teacher was Miss Gladys Cowley. She was snowy-white haired, wore gold-rimmed spectacles and always dressed in a bright-red two-piece suit. Estimates of her age ranged as high as a hundred years which was not very considerate of us! I mention this by way of implying that she was a traditionalist — a member of the old school. An aspect of her formal approach to teaching was to instil in us a liking for verse and to commit passages of it to memory. So here, as small tribute to her endeavours, is a fragment from *The Highwayman* which we learned with her:

The moon was a ghostly galleon tossed upon cloudy seas,
The road was a ribbon of moonlight over the purple moor,
And the highway man came riding up to the old inn door.

As will be revealed in due course I have good reason to think kindly of Miss Cowley and her lessons. It was from Miss Cowley that I heard of the CTS for the very first time. One day she asked — of the boys in the class — "Who would like to go to the Central Technical School to learn how to become an engineer"? Three of us responded, myself and two lads by the names of David Dickson and David Collins — they may well be known to some of you. There were no formalities, no practice-sessions tests or anything like that — we were simply given time off from school to go and sit the exam. So a few weeks later I and my two companions set out for the CTS.

We were ushered into the main hall where rows of the ubiquitous examination-style desks were set out. I am speaking of 1953 — which should help to establish this event in the minds of those other CTS Old Boys who also sat this examination. There were papers on: English including comprehension, spelling, word usage and sentence structure; multiplication and division; an arithmetic paper which included questions concerned with the areas of irregularly-shaped objects; and there was a brain-teaser type paper to test our powers of logical reasoning — which was my undoing. A typical question went as follows: "Imagine a line of paving stones bear the letters of the alphabet. Commencing at 'A', proceed five steps, then return three, go forward eight, back five, now forward again ten, back two and finally forward three. What letter does the paving stone bear on which you are now standing?" Confused? So was I. I could see my chances of becoming an engineer receding.

The two Davids, to whom I have referred, passed the examination whilst I received my, by now familiar, Education Committee letter expressing regret at my failure. I duly returned to Anns Road School, resumed my friendships — telling myself "Who wants to be an engineer anyway!" — and applied myself to my basket weaving — I can still remember the names of the three principal weaves, namely *randing*, *wailing* and *pairing*. A whole year passed in this way during which I also learned about technical drawing which I found fascinating with its orthographic projection, isometric projection and all the rest. A boy called Shackleton — 'Shacks' we called him — was the best draughtsman in the class and I used to try to emulate his skills. Shacks was also good at juggling and used to entertain us by tossing three-or-four tennis balls in the air just like a circus performer. Best of all I enjoyed art with a teacher called Mr. Harold Laycock. To some extent he took me under his wing and give me little encouragements — as Miss Lydiard had done some years previously at Carfield Junior School. This prompts me to tell the following story — concerning one of those moments in your young life which you cherish. I had just completed a colourful picture of a troupe of musicians, resplendent in their uniforms and each clasping a shiny instrument, when into the classroom walked the headmaster Mr. Barnard. By chance I was seated at the front of the class and my work caught his eye. He stopped in his progress to Mr. Laycock, stood by my side and said: "Well! Goodness me"! Mr. Laycock came over to us and I enjoyed my two minutes of fame — which actually lasted for two weeks! The reason is this. Outside Mr. Barnard's room was a display area and a notice board where 'good work' was exhibited. This is where my artwork was duly put on display. So all the pupils were able to see my musicians as they went about that part of the school.

Having just elevated myself let me quickly tell you how, just a few weeks later, I was utterly deflated. I should say first that I had made a friendship with a boy called Richardson. It so happens his grandmother had died leaving, amongst her possessions, a stuffed sparrowhawk! To cut a long story short, it was given to me, I took it home, my mother had a fit and it was banished to the garden where its presence promptly scared away all forms of bird life until — utterly defenceless — it finally succumbed to being torn to pieces by a neighbour's cat. (That's all 100% true!) One evening this friend invited me to go round to meet a friend of his who was in his Second Year at the Sheffield School of Art. Having tried to get in there myself, as I have explained, I was naturally keen to meet this lad — deep down I wanted to see if his artwork was as good as mine. Again, to cut a long story short, on meeting this lad he showed me illustrative work and graphic studies which were not just *superior* to anything I could achieve they were orders of magnitude better. I was crushed and humbled. It was a chastening experience. Until then my drawing had been a source of consolation to me. It was months before I recovered my composure and regained a sense of self esteem and respect. The experience, although salutary, helped me put my own limited artistic skills into perspective — no pun intended!

Let me make a brief digression here from Anns Road School for a moment and recall some of the comics we used to read as young boys. Who remembers, from the period about which I am writing, the boys' comics *Wizard* and *Rover*? If you do, then you will also recall the amazing athlete *Wilson of the Wizard* who was eternally youthful and could break all athletic records — with hindsight, I think he must have been taking something the rest of us didn't know about! Then there was the runner Alf Tupper who was also a good athlete; he ran his races on a full tummy of fish and chips provided by a genial fish fryer called Antonio. And do you recall the air ace 'Braddock VC' who featured in the series *I Flew with Braddock*? When superior officers asked his name, he was wont to reply laconically: "Braddock, it rhymes with haddock"! But who will remember *Smith of the Lower Third*? This lad was a public school bounder, always getting into scrapes and confronting authority but somehow also managing to be a ' a dammed good chap'. And who remembers *The*

Eagle and *Dan Dare Pilot of the Future*? Here was true escapism to distant planets to encounter *The Mekon — The Ultimate Development of Intelligence*! He was a little green chap; all head and hardly any arms or legs! But we took it all in and it helped to ameliorate the ordinariness and commonplace of our everyday life.

At this stage in my school life I experienced a rather unique circumstance which I will briefly describe. Carfield School consisted of three sets of buildings, namely, the Primary School, the Junior School and the Senior School. I have briefly discussed the Primary and Junior Schools which I attended. To be admitted to the Senior School — in effect Carfield Secondary Modern School — you had to pass the eleven-plus exam. I have described how those of us who did not do so went to Anns Road School. To my surprise we learned one day from the Head Teacher Mr. Barnard that the entire school was going to be relocated from Anns Road to the premises of Carfield Senior School. This arose from the fact that Carfield Secondary Modern School was re-housed in new buildings at Norton and was re-named Rowlinson School. So, by this curious twist of fate, I returned to my old school of primary- and junior-school days and Anns Road School accordingly assumed the name Carfield Secondary School.

Having failed the entrance exam to the CTS I returned to Anns Road School now re-named and re-located as I have described. Almost a whole academic year passed. By now, in Third Year, the end of my secondary schooling was in sight. I was thirteen and a half — just eighteen months short of the then school-leaving age of fifteen. This time my teacher, Mr. Joseph Cartwright, said one day — again to the boys in the class — "Who would like to go to the Central Technical School to learn how to become a builder?" Better than advanced basket weaving, I mused, and I resolved to sit the entrance examination once more.

Again I set forth for the CTS, one day in the autumn of 1953, in the company of my class mate John Butcher and, from the year below us, Gordon Swan and Gordon Wright. The now familiar rows of examination desks awaited us in the school hall. I remember that I took a seat in the second row from the left at the back — from where I could contemplate all the candidates. I resolved to do my best. The arithmetic and English papers both went well. Then came the 'IQ' reasoning tests; would the lettered paving-stone questions be set, I asked myself? No, in their place was an ingenious group of questions based upon a rather complex geometrical figure. This consisted of a circle, surmounted by a triangle, surmounted by a square — with letters of the alphabet scattered everywhere. For each of the letters — about twenty in all — you had to identify in which combination of the geometrical figures each letter lay — circle only?, circle and triangle?, or all three? This required some thought — but all went well.

Over the next few weeks, never has a postman been so eagerly awaited! But the morning came when a small manila coloured envelope was pushed under the door. Horrors — another failure? No, a false alarm — it was the gas bill! A few days later, on 8 December 1953, a large, reassuringly thick envelope arrived scarcely able to be squeezed under the door (we did not have a letter box) — it bore the postmark of the Education Committee! I snatched it with a mixture of jubilation and apprehension. I was alone, my father having gone off to work in his customary manner just after 6.00 a.m. and my mother an hour later. I could not wait. I opened the letter to read the following — *Dei gratia*!

Examination for Entrance to the Central Technical School Building Department

I have pleasure in informing you that your son has qualified, on the results of the above examination, for admission to the Central Technical School (Building Department) as from January 1954.
The Central Technical School will re-open after the Christmas vacation on Tuesday, 5th January, 1954.

Yours faithfully
STANLEY MOFFAT MA

Director of Education

Together with this letter was a list identifying all the new things that were required; school uniform, boiler suit, woodwork apron, drawing instruments and so on. I took my letter to school and proudly showed it to my form teacher Mr. Cartright. He was very pleased and made the following joke to the rest of the class: "When Russell leaves there'll be no more *rustlings* at the back of the class"! John Butcher, whom it will be remembered I said also took the exam, did not know his result — he had left before the postman called. Mr. Cartright sent him home to find out if his result had in fact arrived. It had indeed and John had also passed — as also had Gordon Swan and Gordon Wright — a remarkable achievement for Anns Road/Carfield School.

Mr. Cartwright sent John Butcher and myself to see the Headmaster Mr. Barnard. He beamed with pleasure, chatted with us for a moment and then suggested we go across to the Junior School to tell Mr. Chandler of our achievement. This we did. Mr. Chandler also beamed with delight and in turn suggested that we should go and tell our former class teacher Miss Lydiard. Accordingly we went along the corridor to find her with Class 4B which we had vacated some three years previously. She told the class of boys and girls of our achievement — who, of course, hadn't a clue what she was talking about. But, all in unison, they went — "Oo"! This made John and I feel, momentarily at any rate, like a pair of geniuses!

I owe much to Anns Road/Carfield School. It helped me in my formative years. I have always regretted not responding to a letter I received, about two years after leaving the school, inviting me to contribute to a leaving gift for Mr. Barnard — *Mr. Barnyard* as we affectionately called him. It's too late to make amends now but I can put on record my appreciation for, and recognition of, all he did to stamp his mark on the ethos of Anns Road/Carfield School.

I remember also the dedicated and hard-working teachers at Anns Road School who, let it be remembered, had to cope with such large classes. For example: in Senior Two, I was in a class of forty-eight pupils (including two Downs' syndrome boys). By way of interest I came sixth with an end-of-term 'score' of 664 from a possible 830; in Senior Three, I was in a class of forty-four pupils and scaled the dizzy heights of 'top-of-the-class' with an end-of-term 'score' of 1032 from a possible of 1300.

I will take my leave of Anns Road/Carfield School with a particular expression of thanks to Mr. Laycock for, as I have remarked, nurturing my artistic abilities. But uppermost in my affections is Miss Cowley — my class teacher in Senior 2A. As a farewell gift she gave me a beautiful penknife with machine-engraved decorations — I have it before me now as I write. On receiving it I had to give her a penny in return — "So that our friendship might not be severed"! I would not part with this penknife for *anything*. It has come to embody — to put it rather grandly — my triumph over adversity. I had journeyed down, at least in part, what the philosopher John Ruskin calls, 'The stony path of learning' — and the portals of the Central Technical School now beckoned before me!

6
" The School in Sheffield with a Playground on the Roof " Transcript of a Live Broadcast BBC Radio Sheffield

The following text is a transcript of a live broadcast originally transmitted by BBC Radio Sheffield titled *The School in Sheffield with a Playground on the Roof.* It describes a 'walkabout' made by Mr. Ronnie (Rowny) Robinson from Radio Sheffield; the following former boys of the Sheffield Central Technical School: Stuart Green, Roger Child, Neil Kitchen and Mike Ingham (Mike); the former member of staff Mr. Len Shipley; the Caretaker of the former CTS premises Mr. Mick Prior (Mick); and a late arrival — a former CTS pupil who is here identified as the 'Mystery Man' (MM).

This text makes a fitting conclusion to the sequence of reminiscences given earlier in this book. The principal participants in the broadcast were all former CTS lads and they each contribute their own thoughts about their school as they explore the Firth and Bow Buildings. They also call to mind some of the things that went on behind the teachers' back — not all of which, as the reader will discover, formed part of the formal CTS curriculum!

Rowny: This is the building in Sheffield that used to have a funny roof.

Stuart: Aye. The Bow Street roof which had a playground on it. And of course I tried to get in touch with Rowny and failed but I wrote in and told him that it used to be a playground, although it was out of bounds to us Central Technical School boys in the 1950s. But from that we got in touch with Rowny and now there's four or five of us down here and we are going to go all round the school and tell Rowny what a wonderful place it was.

Rowny: Now it's important to know that this school isn't a school any more. It hasn't been a school for quite a long time.

Stuart: No. I believe it moved from this site about 1963 although it did go up to Gleedless Valley in 1965 I have been told. But it was formed about 1933 as the Junior Technical School on this site. It became the Central Technical School in the late 1940s and had a wonderful headmaster from 1946 called Herbert W. Wadge M.B.E.

Rowny: He took the hell out of you all and made you the men you are now!

Stuart: Well, he certainly did and so did the masters, but we all succeeded eventually and we all look back at it and have an Old Boys' Association that thrives still. There are people in it who go back to the earliest years

of the 'Tech' in the thirties and we are here now to tell you all about it and all the wonderful characters and the successes that occurred from the great Tech.

Rowny: Are you afraid of going in there because this is going to trample on some memories isn't it?

Stuart: I'm not afraid. I may have an occasional tear in my eye — you never know — but it will be wonderful.

Rowny: This is Rowny on Radio Sheffield. Who else is with us here?

Stuart: Well. Let them introduce themselves.

Roger: OK. I'm Roger Child. I was at this school from 1959 to 1963. There are fond memories for me here. I really enjoyed my time here. This is probably the first time I've been back in thirty years. So it's going to be a real eye-opener for me. I'm not really sure what I'm going to see!

Rowny: Is there anything in particular that you want to check out that is still here Roger?

Roger: Yes. One of the things I remember fondly was up in the Hall. We used to play shove ha'penny on the benches in the Hall. So, I'd really like to look at that and see if they are still there because all the benches used to be marred with little chippings where we used to put our fingers and shove pennies on to the ha'pennies with a comb. It was fascinating.

Rowny: If you find that they are still there what do you think it will do for you in you maturity?

Roger: I think — every time I get with the school and the Old Boys I start to remember and reminisce and feel really comfortable — so I think it will give me some sort of feeling of belonging I guess.

Rowny: BBC Radio Sheffield. We are just round the corner from the back of the City Hall in Sheffield where this lot once saw Buddy Holly — and more of that no doubt before the story's over. But Stuart Green, thanks to him, we are here this morning in the playground as it was. We are introducing ourselves before we set off on a magical mystery tour.

Neil: Hello. I'm Neil Kitchen, currently President of the Old Boys' Association. I was at the school from 1958 to 1962. Again, very fond memories of the place. Like Roger, looking forward to seeing the Balcony where, of course, at lunch we used to watch the world go by — including lots of very nice ladies walking past! *Laughter!*

Rowny: It's coming out now isn't it!

Mike: I'm Mike Ingham. I went to the school between 1960 and 1966 and, unlike the other Old Boys here, I was a superior human being in that I was in the Building stream of the school! *Groans and laughter!*

Rowny: That was better was it? *Laughter!*

Mike: One of the things that really brings tears to my eyes is the fact that the main man in this school when we were here was *the man* Herbert Wadge. We should all realise that we are actually standing on hallowed ground because this spot is where Herbert, as he was affectionately known, used to park his Austin Westminster. *Laughter!*

Mike: That's one of the things that really sticks out in my mind.

Stuart: And his big green Jaguar before that! *Laughter!*

Rowny: So he was all right! Is it true Stuart, before we proceed, that one of your teachers had the nickname *killer*?

Stuart: Oh! That's correct. In fact he is this wonderful gentleman you see here — Len Shipley. He's a wonderful man now but he was called *killer*, that was indeed his nickname! And I am not joking, he lived up to the name absolutely!

Rowny: Mr. Shipley, were your days here happy?

Len: Very! Yes very! I was just thinking a few minutes ago; I met a lot of really great characters here. Just thinking of the staff; I was here for thirteen years from 1948 to 1961 and it was a marvellous staff to work with. Everybody pulled together, socially and everything. We had a marvellous time.

Rowny: Were these lads particularly rough and tough and difficult?

Len: No — not really! *Laughter.* If they were it didn't last long! *Laughter.*

Mike: Not with him around! *Laughter.*

Rowny: We are going to take a journey into the past in the company of Len Shipley who used to teach here at the Central Technical School and used to be the *killer* — although he doesn't look at all dangerous to me! You could knock him over if you wanted! *Laughter.* As we go into the past, I am in the company of Stuart Green and some of the people who were at this school. We've lost Mick Prior. Where's he gone? Never mind! He's the caretaker. He's not a former pupil is he Stuart? We are in your hands.

Stuart: No. Mick knows a lot about the school but he's not a former pupil. For the moment he's gone walkabout!

Rowny: We are going into the first of the buildings. This school was actually in several different buildings?

Stuart: We occupied five different buildings. The main building is the Firth Building which we are entering now. Architecturally and historically it is the most important. It was opened in 1879 by Prince Leopold, being paid for by Mark Firth. Prince Leopold opened it — hence Leopold Street — and it was the forerunner of Sheffield University which in fact was opened twenty-six years later. I understand it may well have opened as a medical school in the beginning.

Rowny: Is it as it was then?

Mike: It looks somewhat different now. The partitioning wasn't there when we were here. This is the entrance to the Hall which we see here.

Rowny: Do you want to go in there?

Mike: Yes! It's quite important.

Rowny: Mick Prior; your our host. Can we go in there?

Mick: Yes! Certainly!

Rowny: We are opening a blue door. Its been painted since they were here in childhood. This is your Hall. What do you think of it? Describe what you can see.

Mike: My first impression walking through the door, for the first time in thirty years, is that it looks a lot smaller. It's full of rubbish now but it does look smaller. When you think that there were 650 kids in here. You know — it's amazing to see that we all got in here.

Rowny: Mike. When were you last in here?

Mike: Oh! 1963.

Rowny: How's it changed?

Mike: Well, obviously it's in poor condition now. It's rather dirty and full of old stored material — rubbish generally. But I remember the Hall particularly looking from the Balcony when I was a more senior boy — a sixth-former — looking down on to the floor of the Hall which was crammed with pupils seated on the floor. My most striking memory of this Hall I think is what was called Formal Dismissal for occasions when we had particularly important visitors. Herbert Wadge introduced this system of the whole school coming to attention as the visitors came in and out, on a word of command from the School Captain.

Rowny: What did the School Captain say?

Mike: He asked the school to stand, then, if I remember correctly, he asked them to stand at ease and then to stand to attention.

Rowny: Were any of you School Captain? General murmurings — No. Do you want sit down now and have a go after all these years? Laughter. I'm Sure we could. That shout of *attention* would get you on your feet!

Mike: Absolutely! Yes! And the whole school would stand stock still while the visitors and staff left. Funnily enough, just before he died I would have thought that was one of the things that Herbert would have really remembered. But he didn't — it had gone from his memory.

Rowny: We walk out of the Hall now. This is ace isn't it?

Stuart: Wonderful Rowny! Wonderful! The other thing about standing to attention is that this is where Late Parade used to take place which was once a week. If the bell had finished ringing you were late — unless you had a good excuse!

Rowny: Were you ever late Neil? *Laughter.*

Neil: Once I recall. *Laughter.* But I've made up for it in later years. *Laughter.*

Stuart: I was on Late Parade quite frequently. *Convulsions of laughter.*

Rowny: Was Joe Cocker ever on Late Parade?

Stuart: I could well believe Joe could have been on Late Parade. Yes indeed.

Rowny: Would this be the same Cocker who became Joe eCocker?

Stuart: Yes indeed! Make no mistake. It is *the same* Joe Cocker.

Rowny: Did you know him very well and sit by him?

Stuart: In fact I didn't know him well. My friend did. He lived at Crookes as did Joe. But Joe was about two years behind me and therefore I didn't know him too well when he was at school. The lad I did know better was Roger Taylor, of course the British tennis player who is still, indeed, the best male British player since Fred Perry.

Rowny: Who else came to through this school?

Stuart: Well, 'Bos' Day — Brian Day — the British breast-stroke champion of about 1958. We think Pete Stringfellow actually went to the school as well.

Rowny: You think he once copped it. What's the story behind that?

Roger: What I have here are some extracts from the prefects' Minutes. If you were a miscreant, as we were called in those days, then you had to attend the Prefects' Parade. The prefects dished out the punishments. And from the Old Boys' Association we have the history of all these. Minutes were taken every week. So I've been ploughing through these for the last couple of nights finding some old ones. One here is dated 1955. This guy Stringfellow was brought by Saville [School Captain] for not wearing a tie. He was given fifty lines. *Laughter.*

Rowny: Is Joe Cocker in the Minutes?

Roger: I've not found Joe Cocker.

Rowny: He couldn't have been a good boy at school! Laughter. Not when he could sing like this:

Joe Cocker

— *What would you do if I sang out of tune?* —

Rowny: BBC Radio Sheffield. And that was an old pupil of the Central Technical School here in Sheffield. He used to sit where we're sitting now in the Hall although there's no mention of him in the Punishment Book! He's Joe Cocker and Stuart Green here and his former pals are upstairs in the Hall. Things used to happen here! The Headmaster used to come out through these doors here didn't he?

Mike: So I'm told. It's a story that has been related by members of staff. We are in the Balcony of the Hall at the moment and Herbert Wadge's Office was at about this level. And what would happen in the morning was this. There are two entrances on to the Balcony and the whole school would be assembled and the staff used to be able to judge, much like a barometer, what sort of a day it was going to be by which of the two entrances Herbert Wadge put his head through before he came down to the floor of the Hall! If it was one side, it was going to be a bad day — he was in a bad mood — and if it was the other side it was going to be a good day!

Rowny: Mr. Shipley, in those days you were the *killer* siting down there with the staff when he came though here?

Len: That's right, and occasionally the Deputy Head McManus would come in for assembly. Depending upon which of them came through the door — let me explain. An older member of staff once told me: "You can always tell. It's like a weather vane! If Wadge comes through its all right! If Mac comes through it's all wrong! *Laughter.*

Rowny: We came up here with these memories to look to see if there are marks on the seats as evidence of the boys playing mischief — abusing their youth! Have we found any evidence?

Roger: I don't think it was an abuse of our youth. We used to spend many a happy hour up here and, if I can play Mike, here's what we used to do.

Rowny: Do you want to do it again for the first time in forty years — it must be? You need a comb. But you don't need combs anymore do you? *Laughter* How the years go by!

Roger: In those days we had pennies and ha'pannies. We couldn't afford all this modern fancy stuff.

Rowny: They're talking pre-decimal these lads!

Stuart: Yes! They were the old-type coins — the big pennies.

Rowny: Nevertheless they're playing again here this morning for the first time in forty years!

Roger: Its *Sheffield Wednesday* against *Sheffield United* of course!

Rowny: And who are you?

Roger: I'm Sheffield Wednesday — definitely!

Mike: I don't want it ever to be said that I'm a Sheffield United supporter! *Laughter*.

Rowny: There're hitting the pennies again what's it like?

Roger: It feels fantastic. It really does. They slide up and down — look. Here we go. Goal! *Laughter*.

Rowny: They use two fingers to make up the goal. Mr. Shipley, if you found them doing that in your old school-teacher days — and you were the *Killer* — what would you do?

Len: I never watched them! I sat down below; I wouldn't dare to catch them up here! *Laughter*.

Rowny: What are you memories Neil? What comes back to you at this moment?

Neil: We used to come up here and eat our sandwiches at lunch time. Also this is where the senior boys used to sit for assembly. The other thing is that we were allowed to play with the existing goals on these seats but we were not allowed to make any more. That did not always happen of course! *Laughter*.

Rowny: Wonderful! There's the dust of more than thirty-five years on here I should think since you were last here. There is a possibility Stuart, isn't there, that you will embarrass yourselves greatly now by singing the school song?

Stuart: Well, I don't think we can actually remember the tune. In fact I don't think we are capable of singing it even if we could! *Laughter*. Certainly we can recite it for you!

Rowny: Come on lads! Who can remember the tune?

Stuart: That would be difficult.

Rowny: You must be very courageous you lot. All the humiliations you went through — like singing this song.

Stuart: I think the words are more appropriate to us in our maturity than when we were sixteen or seventeen years old.

Rowny: You're just going to recite it then? Will you recite it all together. That will gives us all a laugh!

Stuart: Provided we can all see the words. All right. Here we go then:

> *From the Cheviots down to Dover,*
> *From the Wash to Milford Town,*
> *Yea and all the wide world over,*
> *Men are singing thy renown,*
> *Thy renown, O Spartan Mother,*
> *CTS our pride and boast,*
> *Here's good luck to one another*
> *Here's a rousing loyal toast.*
>
> *Chorus — "Flourish CTS for ever!"*

[For the rest of the words of this song, see the main text.]

Stuart: How's that Rowny!

Rowny: *Convulsion of laughter —almost hysterical!* Gives yourselves a round of applause!

Stuart: The original was written by Dr. Dunston, presumably of Dunston's School fame and was adapted by Herbert Wadge.

Rowny: And you'll remember it for ever. A tear in you eye Mr. Shipley there but a slight smile as well?

Len: We always had a good laugh when the lads were singing that. *Laughter*.

Rowny: Because you thought they were ridiculous?

Len: Not quite. But it always caused great amusement amongst the staff. *Laughter*.

Rowny: So we climb over the benches where they used to play artificial football, where they scratched things, put their names and ate their sandwiches. We are at the corridor area where you weren't allowed to wear winkle picklers! They were a problem for you weren't they? This is one of your stories isn't it?

Roger: Yes. Winkle picklers and chisel-toe shoes weren't allowed. Now, after morning assembly, Herbert Wadge would take the inside rail on the stairs every morning and plod up with his eyes down on the steps right against the rail. Now I made the mistake one day of coming in a pair of side-fastening, chisel-toed shoes — and of taking the inside rail coming down! That was fatal! His eyes were down looking at the very thing I didn't want him to see!

Rowny: And are these the steps where he saw them?

Neil: Just about *here*. Yes. And that was the end of that. It was the only time that I was ever summoned to Herbert's office for punishment.

Rowny: Have you worn shoes like that since?

Neil: No! *Laughter*.

Roger: I have here again something out of the old Prefects' Parade related to dress. We were disciplined to wear the right sort of school uniform and be properly dressed. There are three extracts here from back in 1955. Three guys were brought on Parade for matters related to ties. The first one for not wearing a tie — and his excuse was that he had just come out of a workshop. His name was Ellinson of Class 6B. He got a four-hundred word essay for that. Then the next guy up was wearing a string tie and the prefects had a debate to decide whether that was acceptable or not. *Laughter*. They decided it wasn't. *Laughter*. He was Johnson. Then there was a guy called Pagan. He got done for wearing a bow tie! *Convulsions of laughter*.

Stuart: And what about the Teddy Boys?

Roger: Well, let's look. There is another case. Mr. Shipley mentioned Mr. McManus. He gave dictats to the prefects. One of them was: "Any boy caught wearing Teddy Boys' clothes would be given two days grace in which to change into suitable clothing.". If this wasn't done he had to see Mr. Wadge! *Laughter.*

Rowny: Mr. Wadge! His name is everywhere! Where are we going now Stuart?

Stuart: We are walking up to the Bow Building where we will go up to the old school roof where the playground was that was out of bounds to us although I've got something to relate when we get up there regarding our escapades in 1959! *Laughter.*

Rowny: Before we do that, tell us what you did at El Mambo's?

Stuart: The El Mambo coffee bar was at the bottom of the Cambridge Arcade opposite the Palace Union Street and there was also the Teenage Tavern on Pinstone Street. These were very interesting to us boys because Rock and Roll was just getting under way. So we enjoyed going in there to listen to all the music on the Juke boxes. But, of course, Mr. Wadge stepped in and put it on the list of out-of-bounds places which stretched to about fifty locations — such as all the pubs, all the snooker halls and all the shops like Walsh's — etc.! That was a sad moment for me I must say!

Roger: I can remember when Mr. Wadge used to have these sessions in morning assembly when he used to tell us not to go to these places. He didn't call it the El Mambo. He called it the El Grotto so that for anyone who didn't know where it was they wouldn't get to know!

Rowny: We are now going to go up to the roof. We are now standing directly below the building which is marked in front 'Infants' and they had this amazing roof that we heard about on the phone in. Is it true that Buddy Holly came by here?

Stuart: Yes! Buddy Holly appeared in the Sheffield City Hall — I fancy it was in the Autumn of 1958 — it could have been a bit earlier in 1958 and there were, of course, a lot of Buddy Holly fans at this school I can tell you! So we all gathered at the windows in the Holly Street Building, opposite the City Hall, and watched his arrival. It seemed to me that the whole school was present, which belied the subsequent notion that Buddy Holly didn't achieve fame until after he was killed. In fact he was killed on 3 February 1959 in an air crash about three months after we were watching him enter the City Hall.

Rowny: What did he look like? Like the kind of lad you would have at the Central Technical School?

Stuart: He would have been a great pupil. What great music! What music!

Rowny: He was a weedy whereas all you tough lads failed the eleven plus didn't you?

Stuart: Aye! But couldn't he write music — and play it!

Rowny: All right lads! Now we'll find out about the journey to the top — or to the playground on the upside-down school in the middle of Sheffield. And

here we are on the roof! Fearlessly, we have travelled up here! It's a complicated story which has led us up here and we're not at all sure we can get down again! Now Mr. Len Shipley, who taught maths at the Central Technical School until 1961 — and then went to Wollthyop and did various things there, couldn't make this last bit and so we've left him down below weeping amongst his memories in the classrooms! The rest of us have come up on this icy winter's day on to the roof. I am with Neil Kitchen, Roger Child, Mike Ingham and Stuart Green. Stuart's the man whose fault it is that we are up here! We are resolving once and for all what used to happen up here. We are in a playground in the sky.

Stuart: During our time at the Central Technical School nothing should have happened up here because it was strictly out of bounds. But on one particular occasion after we had finished our G.C.E. exams in 1959, this would probably be mid-to-late June, we borrowed — *Laughter* — the key from the house master's drawer, Mr. Sam Hedley, and someone copied it in the machine shop. And the copy managed to undo the door! So, for the last two or three weeks of our school lives we had unlimited access to the school roof!

Rowny: So you made the same journey that we made along those rather scary little corridors and bendy ways and came out where we came out?

Stuart: The same place except that in those days it was a proper full door and there was no difficulty about walking on to the roof. What I do recall very well is that we brought badminton equipment and set up some old blackboards which were up here. We set them up and played badminton to our hearts content. We *borrowed* a couple of crates of milk everyday which Freddie Frow, the master in charge of milk, couldn't understand. And of course one of the boys used to go to him and say: "Why are you frowning Mr. Frow?"! There you go. *Laughter.* So we came up here everyday. But eventually, naturally, we over did it! We started to play five-aside-football with a case ball and a particularly good footballer, reminiscent of Terry Cooper. The lad in question, Sam Housan, couldn't play without full commitment, naturally, and he used to wallop the ball over into West Street amongst the traffic which of course was a potentially dangerous thing to do. So, eventually, Sam Hedley the house master and a posse of prefects found out, came up and pinched about a dozen of us. Luckily most of us were leaving the following week which was very fortunate for us really! He gave us four strokes each but at least didn't take us to Mr. Wadge! If he had done so we would have been in a lot more serious trouble! I would like to mention the people we think were up here at that time.

Rowny: Oh dear! You're going to get them into trouble! Sam Housan certainly.

Stuart: They included Sam Housan certainly. Then there were Geoff Cangley, Stuart Glasby, Geoff Seaton, Malcolm Fleming, Geoff How and the two 'Cs' Cotton and Cowan. Now, whatever these two got into was the 'kiss of death'. *Laughter.* If you were Cotton and Cowan you always got caught — even it was something you didn't do! *Laughter.* So if any of those people are listening — or if there are any other Tech lads — would you like to get in touch with us. We have an Old Boys' Meeting every month on the first Friday in the month except today when it's tonight. And that's at the Tigers' Ground Club House just passed the Dore Moor Inn.

Author's note:
Stuart Glasby, who is mentioned above, has the distinction of being one of the very few CTS lads whose brother also attended the CTS. In Stuart's case, his older brother was Ian Glasby. Both were Engineers. In the CTS Prefects photograph for 1958, Stuart is seated in the front row, second from the right. For more information about these two boys, see the main text.

Rowny: Oh! Very nobby for the Central Tech! *Laughter.*

Stuart: Yes. It's very classy. The intellectuals play crib and dominoes. *Laughter.* But the 'yoboes' like myself prop up the bar and have a good old chin wag! *Laughter.*

Rowny: You yoboes used to play a very funny game of cricket with milk bottles and table tennis didn't you? What's all that about?
Roger: Oh yes. On the last landing down the stairs we used to pinch the one-third pint-bottles of milk and we used to play on two desks. We used to have one of the bottles as the wickets and a ping-pong ball as the cricket ball — on which you could get a phenomenal amount of spin. Somebody actually carved a small cricket bat out of a piece of wood. There would be two teams and depending on where the ball went and which wall it hit you got a different amount of runs. It was a frequent pastime down there! *Laughter.*

Rowny: Ingenious! Let me remind you. We are on the roof of the Bow Street School, as it used to be, of the Central Technical School and we are going to walk towards what used to be Bow Street — and resolve the mystery of that. It's true that Bow Street used not to go where we heard. Who's got the map?

Stuart: I have the map Rowny, no problem. You will notice how West Street is dead straight looking up the road from this corner. As soon as it reaches the corner of Holly Street it deviates slightly to the point where it meets Church Street. Now from where it deviates, only about a hundred yards long, it was once known as Bow Street and hence this is Bow Building.

Rowny: Yes. Just a tiny bit, the section down here by this white building opposite which is now empty.

Stuart: I have a map of 1905 showing the Sheffield centre and it was certainly known as Bow Street at that time.

Rowny: Yes. It's Bow Street School with a playground on top. It's not the only Sheffield school that has a playground on top but it's fairly unusual and it is an extraordinary feeling to come out from the school onto this space here. Mick Prior is the caretaker of these buildings. Mick, you have all the keys. You're a hero — it's nice of you! What do you make of this?

Mick: It's ideal for junior children — as they once were. It's away from the traffic and the older boys and potential hazards.
Rowny: Like losing the ball over the top! Now, I'm rather surprised the parapet wall isn't higher; it's only about four-or-five feet high.

Mick: There was also a fence which has been taken off.

Stuart: As I recall, when we were up here in 1959, there was a wrought iron fence, very low with points on it and facing slightly inwards. Not very high at all, a couple of feet or something like that.

Rowny: We are walking on the ceiling of this school — above the ceiling in fact. We are in the playground that used to be on top of it — the last people, maybe, who will ever play here. There is a scheme for a new building to be put on the top of this and for the whole building to be put to a different use. It used to be the Bow Centre and before that of course it was their school. We have come across here because we are going to get somebody else to cop it aren't we?

Stuart: Look at this!

Roger: What we have found here is proof that someone else other than Stuart and I got up here. Engraved on the wall here are three names and classes. I recognise the classes but not the names. There is an R. Batty who was in A2X and I was in A2X at one time but not the time of this Batty; and a guy called M. R. Goodlad who was in A3. *Laughter.* If he got up here he certainly wasn't! And there's a K. Taylor, or could it be R. Taylor — Roger Taylor?

Author's note:
R. Batty was a Builder. He was a tall boy with prominent ears. He appears in the Class 6X photograph for 1956 — standing in the back row, second from the left. M. R. Goodlad was an Engineer. He appears in the School Prefects photograph for 1957 seated in the front row, third from the left. In the same photograph, seated on the end of this row (right), is Ian Glasby to whom I have referred above as being the brother of Stuart Glasby. K. Taylor was a boy of part Jamaican birth. He studied A.L. Woodwork with me — see the main text for further details.

Stuart: No. It couldn't be Roger Taylor because Roger was never in A3. He stayed on really to play tennis in 6A but never went into A3, as far as I recollect anyway.

Mike: A3 was the snob class. They were the Upper Sixth!

Rowny: You don't think Roger Taylor came up here to practice his tennis? *Laughter.*

Stuart: No. I very much doubt it. He would be away at Western Park. His mum was a good tennis player and I think he did most of his practice at Western Park.

Rowny: It's been a most delightful journey. It's been absolutely wonderful! You've got this big meeting again tonight when you are all hoping to gather together again. What are your residual stories, your last stories before we go and leave the 1950s?

Stuart: I must mention some of the other great guys of the school. There was Jimmy Crawford, the singer in the early 60s, who was called Ron Lindsey and was at the school in the early 50s — and another great swimmer. He was a Yorkshire champion. There was Keith Ellis the Sheffield Wednesday footballer and the headmaster Tony Mooney of Rutlidge Boys Comprehensive School.

Rowny: Now hold it a sec' here because this is going to be the bit that hits the headlines. This is the most interesting connection with what's going on now that you are going to hear.

Stuart: Yes! Tony Mooney is Headmaster of Rutlidge Boys Comprehensive School, Wimbledon, the most famous pupil of which was John Major. Tony Mooney was at the Tech between 1957 and 1963 and Head Boy in 1962–63. He does a lot of writing for the national press and a couple of years ago he wrote an article for the *Independent* headed *My Old Teacher*. The teacher he was writing about was Don Woolhouse who was one of the greatest teachers of this school, an extremely good sportsman, cricketer and a very nice man. Incidentally, Tony Mooney is very proud of the fact that he's the grandson of George Mooney of Sheffield gang wars fame! *Laughter.*

Rowny: I'm not going to say anything about that!

Stuart: I must mention a very successful business man who went to the school, namely, Allan Nuthall. Allan left about 1959, he established his own company very young — age twenty four — and went into display units for frozen foods and that type of thing. He is now the Chairman and Chief Executive of the Nuthall Group of Companies who employ about 350 people and turn over about £20M per year. It's a £5M company and when I was talking to Allan the other day he said he has a yacht which he sailed to Australia last year where it is now parked! It's a damn long way to go and park your yacht! Anyway, I'd like him to know that I'm not doing much this year! *Laughter.* If he wants an *idle* passenger I wouldn't mind! I can't do much, I've got a terrible bad back, but I wouldn't mind being a passenger around Cape Horn on a flat sea! So, if you are listening Allan, bear it in mind! *Laughter.*

Rowny: Wonderful! Now, you've a badge from the school somewhere here — and that is the old school tie that you're wearing there!

Mike: This is the Old Boys' Association tie. The school badge was slightly different.

Rowny: From out of his pocket this man of indeterminate middle age produces a badge as once worn on a blazer when the world was younger! Oh, tears boys tears!

Mike: We all had this badge on our blazer. We had a dark blue blazer with this badge on the breast pocket and a diagonally striped, three-coloured tie, if I remember correctly, with grey trousers. And when we all started we all wore a cap — for the first week or so. If you hung on to it for a week you were doing quite well! The First Years were always referred to as 'fags'. One of the favourite fag-baiting activities of the more senior boys was to take their caps! So you never kept your cap for more than a few days.

Rowny: You naughty boys! *Laughter.* What is that over

there? Is it what I think it is — the old 'dubs' that used to be on top here?

Mick: Yes. That's right. They're the old toilets.

Rowny: Shall we finish our historic broadcast by going and standing up!

Stuart: I think Neil really ought to mention details of the Old Boys' Association.

Rowny: I think he should but first let's go and stand in the dubs. *Laughter.* They're gone now. They disappeared long ago. There's just a kind of heap of tar macadam and some wonky bricks. But at one time, before you're time, children would have stepped across here and up these steps and into what must be the residue of what I think you call the stalls! *Laughter.* You go and stand in one and I'll stand in this one. Stuart, you stand in that one. Wonderful! *Laughter.*

Stuart: We want to take a little care here lads! These might hark back to the cholera epidemic! *Laughter.*

Rowny: They've certainly been here a long time.

Neil: Stuart did just mention the Old Boys' Association. We have a meeting this evening at Sheffield Tigers' Rugby Ground at Dore Moor Inn. We would be very pleased to see some new Old Boys. We start about 7. 30 p.m. normally the first Friday night of every month. We have a dinner coming up at the Kenwood Hall on 26 March at which the Principal Speaker will be Jo Scarborough, the well-known local artist, accompanied by his wife. We would love to see you.

Rowny: It's been brilliant and it's not quite the end of our story today. Stuart, you are laughing away in the sunshine that's just broken through on the roof here in the middle of Sheffield. Tell us why.

Stuart: We've just had a fellah come up here. He's been driving about round town. He hears about Bow Street. He's a Central Tech lad. He got out of his car and he's come up here. *Laughter.*

Rowny: Where were you listening to all this?

MM: I'm on holiday today. I was in my car at Townhead Street and was driving to Chapel Town when I thought I know that voice [Rowny] and I know this other guy's voice [Stuart] and being an ex-Tech lad I thought where are they? You were only five minutes away but I've had to make half an hour's detour to get back here! *Laughter.*

Rowny: Brilliant! Have you had a look round the school?

MM: I saw Len Shipley downstairs.

Rowny: When was the last time you were in this building?

MM: 1960! I was here from 1956 to 1960.

Rowny: Thirty-four years ago. Did you know Joe Cocker when he was here?

MM: No. But I know the Taylor you've been on about. He was Ken Taylor. Not Roger Taylor.

Rowny: The one who left his name on the dubs! *Laughter.* Was it a lousy, brutal school and good 'riddance to bad rubbish'? *Laughter.*

MM: No! It was a great school! The best school I've ever attended!

Rowny: Wonderful! And thank you very much.

Stuart: Thanks to you Rowny and to Radio Sheffield and to Mick Prior for allowing us up on to this roof. I think he's waiting to go for his lunch!

Rowny: Wonderful. Thank you all very much indeed for such a delightful time. This is BBC Radio Sheffield with the Old Boys' Association, the very *young* Old Boys, from the Central Technical School, Sheffield *on the roof* of Bow Street School standing in the loos that were here and will never be used again — at least I hope not! *Laughter.*

7
Postscript

Before taking leave of the reader it is fitting that I should conclude my reminiscences with a few words of general reflection.

I have said in my Introduction that Sheffield has good reason to feel proud of The Central Technical School. I know that this is a sentiment shared by former pupils of the CTS but I trust that the reader who has read this book, and who was not previously familiar with this school, will now also share this opinion.

The founding fathers of the original Sheffield Central Schools (The Sheffield School Board) — with the support of Mark Firth — established a remarkable series of educational establishments. Their vision and philanthropy nurtured elementary and secondary schools, in parallel with Firth College the greater part of which, concerning the physical facilities, would in due course metamorphose into the CTS.

The value and importance to the future lives and careers of the many boys who passed through the CTS is inestimable. This formative influence helped to shape their character and outlook on life and, for the majority, it provided them with an orientation to their eventual career in one of the trades or professions allied to Building and Engineering. Amongst the fraternity of former pupils who meet regularly — in the guise of *The Old Boys' Association* — the enthusiasm, indeed, the *affection* still felt for the CTS, and its former members of staff, is manifestly palpable. Concerning the members of staff, several contributed the greater part of their working lives to the betterment of technical education at the CTS. Their collective skills embraced the practical, the technical, the vocational and the academic. The CTS was pre-eminently 'a place of useful learning'. The staff were unstinting in their tireless devotion to the school and its pupils. They knew their subject backwards, as we say, and many members of staff imparted to their lessons the wisdom they had acquired through several years of experience at their particular trade or profession. This gave an air of authority to their lessons — they knew what they were talking about. And, towering above all like a colossus, dominating everything, shaping educational policy, steadfastly maintaining discipline and inculcating the virtues of morality was the Head Teacher Herbert W. Wadge. Herbert truly permeated the lives of those of us who were fortunate enough to attend the CTS during his period as Head Teacher — one is inclined to say during his *reign* — and the experience was as memorable as it was educationally beneficial. He was a larger than life figure in so many ways being of statuesque physique, possessed of a Stentorian voice and motivated by an indomitable resolve to do his best for his boys. His personal identification with the CTS was absolute and his commitment was no less so. Moreover, he inspired loyalty in his colleagues who worked, as I have already implied, no less hard than he to nurture and inculcate pedagogical precepts allied to technical education.

I have attempted to discuss and illustrate the CTS curriculum, albeit, from the point of view of a Builder. This prompts me to add how admirably suited the CTS pattern of education was to the needs of both intending Builders and Engineers. The syllabus, and its methods of implementation, commendably upheld the founding principles enshrined in the Charter that gave inception to the original Junior Technical Schools. These, the reader may recall — from what I have written previously, included: 'sound preparatory training … practical drawing, measurements and calculations needed in the workshops — the uses of the various tools in the working of wood and metal — [and] the principles of Mechanics, Physics and Chemistry'. The reader may also recall that this Charter recognised, from the outset, the importance of the quality of the members of staff to the system of technical education, viz.: 'In order to ensure that good workshop methods are employed the staff includes men who have had actual workshop experience as well as experience in teaching'. All former pupils of the CTS will know how well these ideals were fulfilled at the Central Technical School, Sheffield. The CTS was, indeed, 'a place of useful learning'.

The social value of the CTS should also be remembered. I have in mind here the particular circumstance whereby the school offered boys who had failed the 11+ examination a second chance to give evidence of their vocational skills and intellectual abilities. This prompts me to pose the question: 'Where would we former CTS lads be now without having had the benefit of a sound education at the CTS?'. But there is another side to my proposition that the CTS had a social value. Let us remember that the school occupied its central location in the very heart of Sheffield for the greater part of half a century. Throughout this entire period the school was under the very gaze of no less than the Director of Education — our next door neighbour — and, moreover, was in full view of the citizens of Sheffield as they passed by along Leopold Street, West Street and Holly Street. I like to think that the sight of so many CTS lads in their neat school uniforms, revealed daily, as it were, to the contemplation of so many Sheffielders, contributed to a collective sense of well-being — even civic pride. Perhaps this is a little fanciful but I have no doubt whatever that such thoughts are consistent with the aspirations that Herbert Wadge had for his school.

The CTS buildings were certainly worthy of their central area location and throughout the period when they functioned as a thriving and active school, they fully reflected the dignity envisaged by the School Board which originally brought them into being. Even today the sturdy grandeur of the Firth Building has the power to evoke a sense of pride overlaid, of course — for many of us, by feelings of nostalgia. But there was more to the CTS than outward show. The facilities were, in their day, second to none. Workshops, drawing offices, laboratories and the more conventional classrooms combined to provide a magnificent suite of accommodation. It has to be conceded that, in the latter era, the school suffered from overcrowding and, more significantly, the lack of readily accessible playing fields was a handicap throughout the entire history of the school.

Most significant, in the functioning of the life of the school, was the assembly hall — the former Firth Hall. This served as a focus for the formal occasions that are at the heart of the daily routine of all schools. In the old Firth Hall generations of boys assembled each day for morning assembly to receive the exhortations of Herbert Wadge! But the school hall was also a place where boys could gather and give expression to collective worship; it was a venue for hymn singing and for practicing the choral singing that was an integral part of Speech Day; and it was a place where the school could meet to enjoy special events such as end-of-term assembly — with its pleasurable associations of school holidays!

I have said elsewhere, but I will repeat it here, that the spirit of the CTS lives on. It lives on through the beneficial influence exerted on its former pupils bearing upon their lives and work. This is a legacy that will endure until the last one of them has ceased to be. Until that time — and let it be far distant — those of us who meet, in the guise of *The Old Boys' Association*, will continue to remember their former school with affection and appreciation.

Index

For the convenience of the reader, this index is arranged under various subject headings that reflect the contents of the book. The illustrations, which accompany the text, are to be found at pp. 133–50. For a detailed list of these, together with the relevant page numbers, see 'Illustrations' p. 7.

Carpentry and Joinery: *see Woodwork*

Chemistry

Departure from the CTS

Diploma of the CTS

English

Mechanics

Members of staff of the CTS

For additional references to members of staff, relating to their subject, see the various subject headings.

Music

Old Boys' Association

Origins and development of the CTS

Outward Bound School, Ullswater

Physical Training

Physics

Plumbing

Pupils of the CTS

Railway Excursions

Religious Instruction
(see Holy Scripture)

Science

School Captain

School House System

School Prefects

Speech Day

Sport and Athletics

Technical Drawing

Wadge, Herbert W

Woodwork